GERMAN LIMITED LIABILITY COMPANY

Wiley Series in
COMMERCIAL LAW

Kaye/Methods of Executing Orders and Judgments in the UK
and Europe
0-471-94029-1 376 Pages

Rajak/European Corporate Insolvency – A Practical Guide
0-471-95239-7 952 Pages

Schoen/The French Stock Exchange:
A Practical Guide for Investors and Advisers
0-471-95550-7 310 Pages

Cooper/Recognition and Enforcement of Cross-Border Insolvency:
A Guide to International Practice
0-471-96310-0 150 Pages

Brown/Corporate Rescue
0-471-95237-0 878 Pages

Volhard & Stengel/German Limited Liability Company
0-471-96581-2 444 Pages

Forthcoming titles

Dine/Eastern European Company Law
0-471-95281-8 400 Pages

GERMAN LIMITED LIABILITY COMPANY

Edited by

Rüdiger Volhard *and* Arndt Stengel

PÜNDER, VOLHARD, WEBER & AXSTER

JOHN WILEY & SONS

Chichester • New York • Weinheim • Brisbane • Singapore • Toronto

Copyright © 1997 Pünder, Volhard, Weber & Axster
Published in 1997 by John Wiley & Sons Ltd,
                Baffins Lane, Chichester,
                West Sussex PO19 1UD, England

                National   01243 779777
                International (+44) 1243 779777
                e-mail (for orders and customer service enquiries):
                cs-books@wiley.co.uk
                Visit our Home Page on http://www.wiley.co.uk or http://www.wiley.com

Other Wiley Editorial Offices

John Wiley & Sons, Inc., 605 Third Avenue,
New York, NY 10158-0012, USA

VCH Verlagsgesellschaft mbH, Pappelallee 3,
D-69469 Weinheim, Germany

Jacaranda Wiley Ltd, 33 Park Road, Milton,
Queensland 4064, Australia

John Wiley & Sons (Asia) Pte Ltd, 2 Clementi Loop #02-01,
Jin Xing Distripark, Singapore 129809

John Wiley & Sons (Canada) Ltd, 22 Worcester Road,
Rexdale, Ontario M9W 1L1, Canada

Library of Congress Cataloging-in-Publication Data

German limited liability company/edited by Rüdiger Volhard and
    Arndt Stengel.
      p.   cm.
      Includes index.
      ISBN 0-471-96581-2 (cloth)
      1. Private companies—Germany.   I. Volhard, Rüdiger, 1931–
  II. Stengel, Arndt, 1963–
  KK2520.G47   1997
  346.43′0668—dc21   96–51961
                                                 CIP

British Library Cataloguing in Publication Data

A catalogue record for this book is available from the British Library

ISBN 0-471-96581–2

Typeset in 10/12pt Baskerville by Footnote Graphics, Warminster, Wilts.
Printed and bound in Great Britain by Bookcraft (Bath) Ltd, Midsomer Norton.

This book is printed on acid-free paper responsibly manufactured from sustainable forestation, for which at least two trees are planted for each one used for paper production.

CONTENTS

The authors are members of PÜNDER, VOLHARD, WEBER & AXSTER, German attorneys-at-law, notaries and tax advisors in Berlin, Düsseldorf, Frankfurt, Leipzig and Munich.

Chapter 21
DISSOLUTION, LIQUIDATION AND CANCELLATION 347
Dr. Rüdiger Volhard

PART VIII APPENDIX

Chapter 22
PRECEDENTS AND INDICES 355
Dr. Rüdiger Volhard and Dr. Arndt Stengel

TABLE OF LEGISLATION

Statutes

PREFACE

The GmbH is the most frequently used legal form in German corporate law. There are approximately 600,000 such companies; each year, around 50,000 new GmbH companies are registered. It can be assumed that about 10 per cent of GmbH companies have foreign shareholders and/or foreign managing directors.

Introduced by the Limited Liability Companies Act of 1892, the GmbH was designed to extend the privilege of limited liability to small and medium-sized enterprises controlled by a small group of shareholders with close personal ties to one another. The major advantage of the GmbH where compared with the various forms of partnership is the limited liability of the owners. In principle, the shareholders are not liable to the creditors for the company's debts, so that their financial risk can effectively be limited to the minimum share capital of DM 50,000. More than half the GmbHs only have the minimum share capital at their disposal.

The establishment and administration of a GmbH is simple, the required minimum capital is low and the statutes can be specifically tailored to the requirements of the shareholders. In comparison with an AG, the GmbH is much more flexible and procedurally less demanding. Generally, transactional costs are lower.

Since shareholders can directly guide and instruct the management of the GmbH, close control over the company can be achieved even with regard to day-to-day matters, making the GmbH particularly useful as the corporate form for a subsidiary or holding company. Therefore, the vast majority of all German subsidiaries of foreign companies are GmbHs.

In the form of a one-man GmbH, the GmbH is often a subsidiary of another legal person (AG or GmbH) or of a foreign enterprise which invests in a German GmbH or makes use of a German GmbH as an intermediate holding company. Many GmbHs assume the personal liability in a GmbH & Co. KG, sometimes with and sometimes without participating in its assets.

The authors attempt to describe the law relating to limited liability companies for foreign investors and their advisors. They thus deal primarily with the company law, tax law and employment law questions which, in their experience, are of particular interest to foreign investors. There are no references to literature to which such a reader would not generally have access. However, references to case-law are useful occasionally for more detailed exploration and as an aid to reasoning.

The editors would like to thank Tillman Rosse, Martin Bouchon and Jane Martens for their valuable assistance. The authors welcome comments and suggestions for improvement, which are requested for the attention of the editors (at Mainzer Landstraße 46, 60325 Frankfurt am Main, Germany, tel: +49 69 7199 01, fax: +49 69 7199 4000).

ABBREVIATIONS

AAV	Work Residence Ordinance
AErlVO	Work Permit Ordinance
AFG	Employment Promotion Act
AG	District Court
AG	stock corporation
AktG	Stock Corporation Act
AnfG	Creditors' Avoidance of Transfer Act
AO	Code of Taxation Procedure
ArbZG	Working Time Act
AÜG	Staff Secondment Act
AufG/EWG	Alien Residence Act - EC
AuslG	Aliens Act
AWG	Foreign Trade (and Payments) Act
BayObLG	State Supreme Court of Bavaria
BAG	Federal Labour Court
BB	Betriebsberater (law journal)
BetrAVG	Company Pension Schemes Act
BetrVG	Employees' Representation Act
BeurkG	Notarial Registration Act
BewG	Tax Valuation Act
BFH	Federal Fiscal Court
BFHE	Federal Fiscal Court Official Case Reports
BGB	Civil Code
BGH	Federal Supreme Court
BGHZ	Federal Supreme Court Official Case Reports (Civil matters)
BImSchG	Federal Emission Control Act
BMF	Federal Minister of Finance
BMJ	Federal Attorney General

BNotO	Federal Rules and Regulations on Notaries
BSG	Federal Social Insurance Court
BStBl	Department of Revenue Gazette
BUrlG	Federal Holiday Entitlement Act
BVerfG	Federal Constitutional Court
BVerfGE	Federal Constitutional Court Official Case Reports
BZRG	Federal Central Register Act
DB	Der Betrieb (law journal)
DM	Deutsche Mark (German currency)
EC	European Community
EGBGB	Introductory Act to the Civil Code
EGV	European Community Treaty
EStDV	Income Tax Regulations
EStG	Income Tax Act
FGG	Ex Parte Jurisdiction Act
GewO	Industrial Code
GewStG	Trade Tax Act
GG	The German Constitution
GmbH	limited liability company
GmbHG	Limited Liability Companies Act
GmbH & Co KG	commercial limited partnership with a GmbH as sole general partner
GmbHR	GmbH-Rundschau (law journal)
GrEStG	Real Property Transfer Tax Act
GrStG	Real Property Tax Act
GSG	Equipment Safety Act
GVG	Judicature Act
GWB	Anti-Cartel Act
Handwo	Handicrafts Code
HGB	Commercial Code
HintO	Court Deposit Regulations
KG	commercial limited partnership
KG	Higher Regional Court of Berlin
KGaA	partnership limited by shares
KO	Bankruptcy Act
KSchG	Unfair Dismissal Act
KStG	Corporate Income Tax Act
KWG	Banking Act

LG	Regional Court
Lösch	Dissolution and Cancellation of Companies and Co-operatives Act
MitbestG	Co-Determination Act
MRRG	Residence Registration Framework Act
NJW	Neue Juristische Wochenschrift (law journal)
NStZ	Neue Zeitschrift für Strafrecht (law journal)
OHG	general commercial partnership
OLG	Higher Regional Court
OWiG	Regulatory Offences Act
RBeratG	Legal Advice Act
RG	Supreme Court of the German Reich
RGZ	Supreme Court of the German Reich Official Case Reports (Civil Matters)
SGB	Social Security Code
StGB	Criminal Code
TVG	Collective Bargaining Agreement Act
UmwG	Business Transformation Act
UmwStG	Transformation Tax Act
UrhG	Copyrights Act
UstDV	Value Added Tax Regulations
UStG	Value Added Tax Act
UWG	Unfair Competition Act
VAG	Insurance Supervision Act
VglO	Composition Code
VStG	Net Worth Tax Act
WM	Wertpapier-Mitteilungen (law journal)
WpHG	Securities Trading Act
ZIP	Zeitschrift für Wirtschaftsrecht (law journal)
ZPO	Code of Civil Procedure
§	section of the cited statute, sections (§§) which are not followed by the abbreviation of a statute refer to the GmbHG – Limited Liability Companies Act.

Part I

FORMATION AND STRUCTURE

Chapter 1

CHOICE OF ENTITY, CHOICE OF LEGAL FORM

Dr. Arndt Stengel

Investors who are either invited to join an existing consortium or acquire a stake in a company wishing to co-operate with them only have a limited "choice of entity". In the absence of such predetermination, the choice of entity is of great importance due to the tax and organisational consequences.

1. Possible structures for doing business in Germany

1.1 The foreign corporation in legal transactions

Every foreign corporation is recognised within Germany if – which is assumed as a general rule of experience – it has its genuine registered administrative office in the country in which it was founded.[1]

1.2 Branch

Foreign investors can either establish a branch office[2] of the corporation in their home country or incorporate a German subsidiary. A branch office is sometimes preferable for tax purposes, but registration is complicated. Investors can also do business directly from abroad, i.e. without setting up a permanent establishment in Germany. Branches are often found in highly regulated industries, such as banking. However, most investors prefer an incorporated subsidiary over a branch.

---

[1] OLG Hamm DB 95, 137.
[2] *Post*, p. 20.

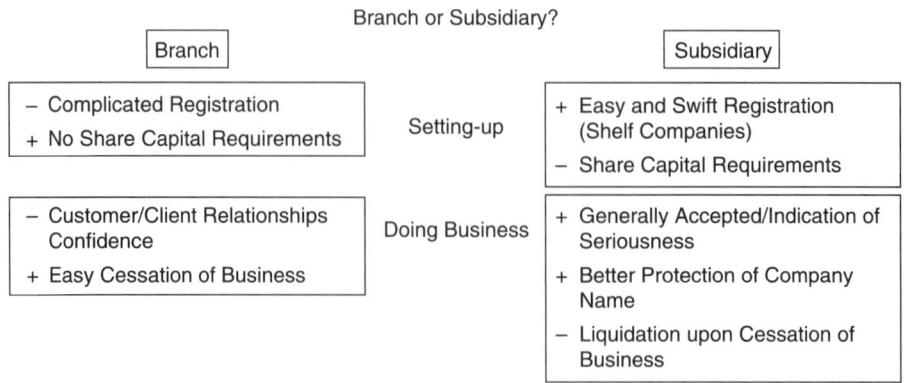

1.3 Subsidiary

The subsidiary is the generally accepted way of doing business. It gives third parties confidence in the investor's intentions to continue business in Germany. As regards taxes, an incorporated subsidiary also allows an unrestricted loss carry-forward, so that there is no risk of future profits not being used to compensate for initial losses.

1.4 Joint venture

The foreign company can act together with a company within Germany in the form of a joint venture, either directly or through a German subsidiary. Legally, the joint venture is a civil law partnership and is described in that context.

2. Forms of companies and partnerships

In Germany, the decision whether to establish a corporation (and which) or a partnership is not so easily taken as in most Common Law countries. The system of organized entities in Germany, i.e. legal persons and non-incorporated groups, is rather confusing, but the following can be viewed as the principal structures:

- limited liability company: GmbH;
- stock corporation (Plc): AG;
- limited partnership: KG (with its three sub-species GmbH & Co. KG, Einheits-KG and Publikums-KG);
- civil law partnership: Gesellschaft bürgerlichen Rechts;
- in some cases also the silent partnership: stille Gesellschaft.

2.1 Legal persons

Stock corporation (Aktiengesellschaft – AG)

The establishment and organisation of a stock corporation (AG) involves numerous formalities. The articles of association of the AG must comply with the mandatory rules of organization laid down in the Stock Corporation Act (Aktiengesetz – AktG). For instance, the law requires a third corporate organ between the general meeting of the shareholders (Hauptversammlung) and the board of directors (Vorstand), namely the supervisory board (Aufsichtsrat). The shareholders' influence on the board of directors is only exerted by their power to elect the members of the supervisory board who, in turn, elect the members of the board of directors. The directors alone are responsible for the management of the company. A shareholder interfering with this right is liable for damages.

The strict body of rules governing an AG makes this type of company ideally suited for a large number of shareholders. The AG is the only type of German company which can have its shares quoted on a stock exchange and can issue debentures and convertible bonds which may be publicly traded (apart from the rare partnerships limited by shares, KGaA).[3]

Any enterprise, domestic or foreign, which acquires more than five per cent of the shares of an AG must notify the corporation of this in writing.[4]

Further notification is required if the enterprise acquires a majority of the shares or votes.[5]

In addition, duties of notification exist within the framework of the preparation of a group balance sheet[6] (20 per cent threshold) and for companies quoted on the stock exchange – with thresholds starting at five per cent – in accordance with the Securities Trading Act (Wertpapierhandelsgesetz – WpHG).[7]

Although the Stock Corporation Act was amended in 1994 in order to deregulate the law governing the AG, to make this legal form attractive for smaller, privately-held businesses, the general position is still that the main

---

[3] *Post*, p. 7.

[4] § 21 para. 1 Stock Corporation Act (AktG).

[5] § 21 para. 2 AktG. As yet, however, there is no obligation to tender for the remaining outstanding shares once a certain percentage of shares has been acquired. Nevertheless, there is a Takeover Code (Übernahmekodex) of the Börsensachverständigenkommission (stockmarket expert commission) at the Federal Ministry of Finance, which contains recommendations for the parties participating in voluntary public takeover bids. It only applies to those enterprises quoted on the stock exchange which have recognised it. It is intended to specially mark these enterprises on the stock exchange list.

[6] § 313 para. 2 no. 4 Commercial Code (HGB).

[7] WpHG of 26.7.1994, BGBl. I 1749. The Act is an expression of the endeavours to strengthen the international competitive ability and attractiveness of Germany as a financial centre in view of the future free movement of capital in Europe (and increasingly worldwide). This, for instance, includes the institutionalized supervision of trading in securities by a state authority, the Federal Supervisory Office for Securities Trading (Bundesaufsichtsamt für den Wertpapierhandel) in Frankfurt am Main, duties of notification incumbent on financial services companies participating in stock exchange trading concerning stock exchange transactions undertaken, duties of publication incumbent on issuers concerning all circumstances relevant to the share price, and the criminal law pursuit of insider dealing.

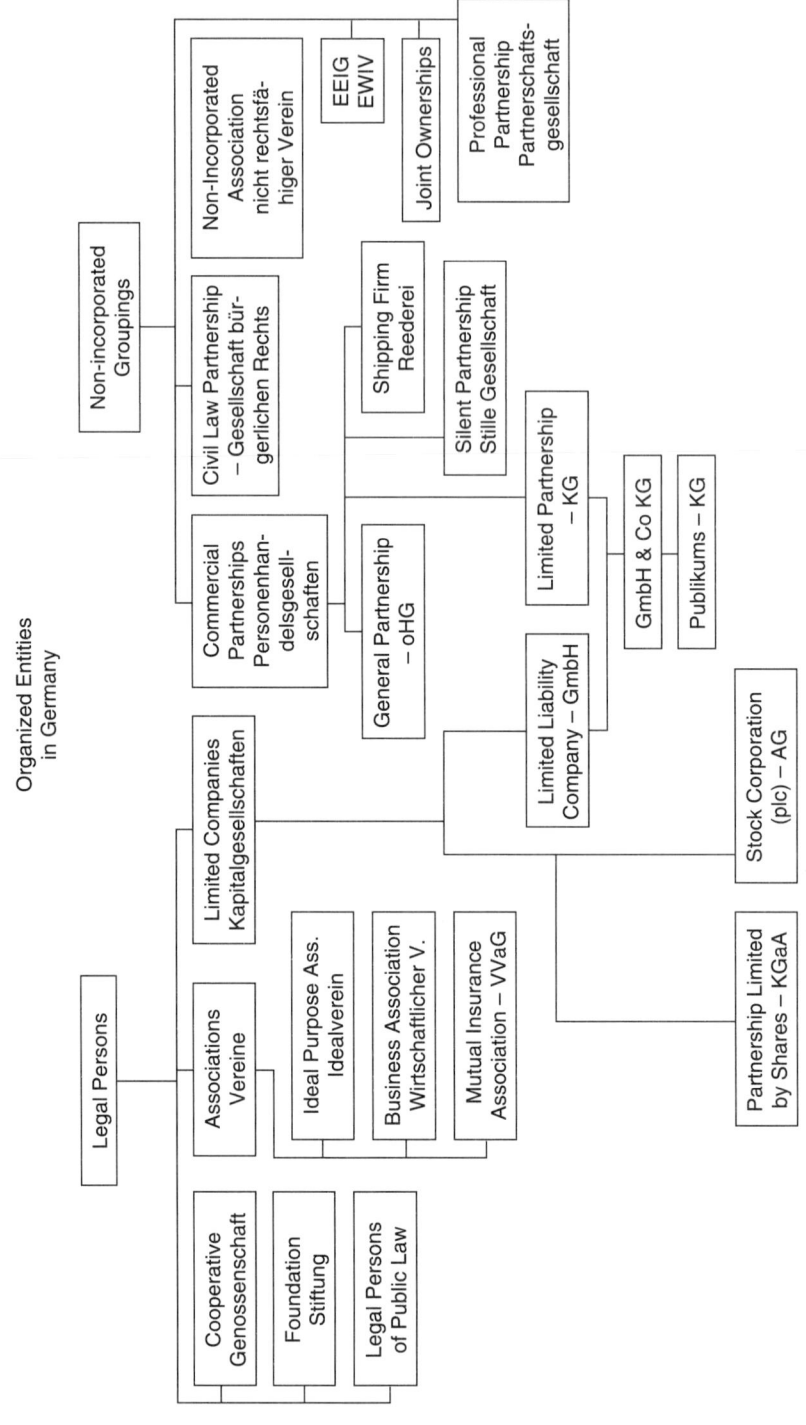

motivation for establishing a company as an AG is the intention that it will even-tually go public. However, due to the recent facilitation of the transformation of businesses in Germany,[8] establishing a business as a different form of entity in no way prohibits having it transformed into an AG at a later stage if going public is desired.

Partnership limited by shares (Kommanditgesellschaft auf Aktien – KGaA)

The Kommanditgesellschaft auf Aktien (KGaA) is a not particularly widespread (but recently increasingly fashionable) special form, in which there is at least one general partner participating in the company – alongside the limited liability shareholders holding the nominal authorized capital divided into shares – who is personally liable for the obligations of the company with all his assets.[9]

The relationship of the personally liable partners amongst one another and to the limited liability shareholders in the partnership limited by shares, and to third parties, is governed by the law on commercial partnerships,[10] as is the power of management and representation. For the remainder, the law governing the AG is mostly applicable.[11]

The KGaA also has a mandatory supervisory board; however, it does not decide on the appointment and dismissal of personally liable partners, does not lay down standing rules and regulations for the management and usually cannot make transactions dependent on its consent. In practical terms, the supervisory board of a KGaA only has rights of information and examination.[12]

The restricted rights of the limited liability shareholders in the partnership limited by shares conform to the strong position of the managing partners who are personally fully liable for the obligations of the company. This liability can be restricted to the assets of a legal person if, for example, a GmbH can assume the position of the personally liable partner, as in the case of the GmbH & Co. KG, though this has not yet been decisively clarified.[13] The management of the KGaA then lies with the managing directors of the GmbH.

Limited liability company (Gesellschaft mit beschränkter Haftung – GmbH)

The possibility of restricting the liability to the assets of the company with a low minimum capital (DM 50,000) makes the GmbH attractive. It is always used when a legal person is needed which can be easily managed. Only one per cent of the legal persons with a commercial business purpose which are founded in the private sector are not GmbHs.

Among the special features of the law governing the GmbH (laid down in the Limited Liability Companies Act – GmbHG) which are important for the choice of entity are firstly, the vast possibilities of customizing the articles of association

---

[8] *Post*, chapter 18.
[9] § 278 para. 1 AktG.
[10] §§ 278 para. 2 AktG, 161 *et seq.* HGB.
[11] § 278 para. 3 AktG; special features are set out in §§ 279 *et seq.* AktG.
[12] §§ 90, 111 para. 2 AktG.
[13] OLG Hamburg NJW 69, 1030.

to the needs of the enterprise and, secondly, the right of the shareholders' meeting to give the managing directors not only guidelines of management, but specific instructions regarding any particular business on which the shareholders wish to exert influence.

2.2 Partnerships

Civil law partnership (Gesellschaft bürgerlichen Rechts)

General

Most investors outside the real estate market never become aware of the civil law partnership (Gesellschaft bürgerlichen Rechts). The partnership is the most basic form known to German partnership law. Every group of more than one person joining to pursue a common purpose outside one of the legal forms specified under company and partnership law is regarded as a civil law partnership. There are no requirements as to registration or form. The civil law partnership does not need to have either assets or a specific organization. Civil law partnerships are subject to rules laid down in the German Civil Code (BGB).[14] There are only a few mandatory provisions, for example on duration and liquidation.

The civil law partnership presupposes a partnership agreement, which can also be concluded formlessly and even by apparent conduct. By law, all partners only have joint powers of management and representation, and the profits are distributed *per capita* according to optional statutory law. This is usually regulated otherwise.

The civil law partnership is not a legal person, but rather a community of partners. The assets of the partnership thus do not belong to the partnership but rather to the partners to be held as joint property.[15] All partners are jointly and severally liable for the obligations of the partnership. However, this liability can be restricted to the extent that the power of representation of the partners is contractually regulated in a way that the partners are not committed above and beyond the assets of the civil law partnership.

In particular, the civil law partnership is suitable for non-commercial real estate transactions and for joint ventures of all kinds.[16]

Joint venture

Owing to the broad definition of a civil law partnership, two or more parties joining together in order to pursue the purpose of a joint venture form a civil law partnership, irrespective of the fact that they might wish to do business through a joint venture company. The civil law partnership is a "sub-partnership" (Innengesellschaft) if it is not designated to be active vis-à-vis third parties but only exists for the internal purposes of the joint venture parties.

---

[14] §§ 705 *et seq.* BGB.
[15] "Gesamthandseigentum".
[16] Apart from associations of craftsmen and self-employed persons (doctors, architects, attorneys).

A joint venture can be structured as an equity joint venture, where two or more parties agree to collaborate according to a joint venture agreement in a joint venture company which is formed or acquired at the same time or at a later date. The opposite is the contractual joint venture, where the parties agree on collaboration without the intention of developing the business through a common entity.

It appears that a closer collaboration requires one, or sometimes more, joint venture companies, as the separate structure allows a clear identification of the common business which is necessary for joint control and profit sharing.

This is different, however, where the purpose of the joint venture is confined to a "mutual most-favoured treatment" and ancillary activities (such as mutual support of marketing, exchange of staff), which sometimes is the aim of strategic alliances linking the activities of partners coming from different countries.

A third form is the asymmetric joint venture, where the parties acquire minority stakes in each other's subsidiaries which are active in the relevant market segments.

The joint venture contract serves as a basic agreement and should include all important aspects relating to the co-operation of the partners. The joint venture contract creates a civil law partnership amongst the joint venture parties with the purpose of operating the joint venture business.[17]

As regards the relationship of the joint venture agreement to the articles of association of the joint venture company, the joint venture agreement is clearly only a contractual obligation as to how the parties should act, whilst the articles of association may lay down rules, the breach of which renders the offending acts void.

The joint venture agreement can be treated as confidential, but the articles of association are open to public inspection. It is thus sometimes difficult to decide whether clear enforceability or confidentiality should prevail.

There are no requirements as to form or registration for the joint venture agreement. If it includes the obligation to set up a GmbH, however, the agreement must be notarially recorded.

General commercial partnership (Offene Handelsgesellschaft – OHG)
The OHG differs from the civil law partnership in that the purpose of the company is the operation of a fully commercial trade[18] under a joint business name, and that every partner is under an obligation to manage and represent the company by law. In the case of the OHG too, the personal liability of each partner is not restricted in relation to the creditors of the company.[19]

The OHG is registered in the Commercial Register together with the names of all partners.

---

[17] § 705 BGB.
[18] § 1 HGB.
[19] § 105 para. 1 HGB.

Structure of the Joint Venture

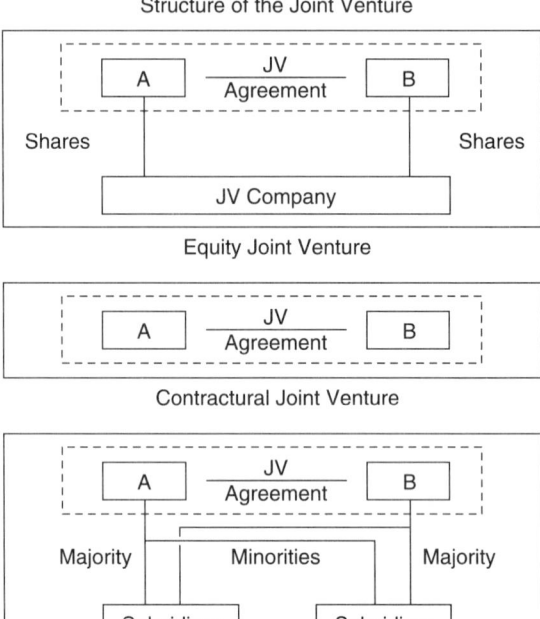

Equity Joint Venture

Contractural Joint Venture

Asymmetric Joint Venture

Commercial limited partnership (Kommanditgesellschaft – KG, GmbH & Co. KG)

A limited partnership (Kommanditgesellschaft) differs from an OHG in that in the case of at least one partner, liability is limited to the amount of a certain capital investment (limited partner – Kommanditist), whilst at least one other partner is liable to an unlimited extent (general partner). The commercial limited partnership is not a legal person but can nonetheless acquire assets, incur liabilities, sue and be sued under its business name. The commercial limited partnership is registered in the Commercial Register together with the names of all partners and the liability investment of the limited partner.

A legal person can also be a personally liable partner. The legal form of the GmbH & Co. KG is widespread. It unites the advantages of the personal partnership with the advantage of limited liability, because the only personally liable partner, the GmbH, is only liable with the assets of the company. However, this must be expressed in the business name, which must contain an addendum identifying the limitation of liability.[20] In addition, the business name of the KG must contain the business name of the general partner,[21] but must distinguish itself from the latter if both are located in the same place.[22]

In some respects, the GmbH & Co. KG is treated like a limited company. In

---

[20] § 19 para. 5 HGB.
[21] § 19 para. 2 HGB.
[22] § 30 HGB.

particular, the employees of the KG are attributed to the general partner GmbH,[23] from which the necessity of forming a supervisory board may arise. Moreover, sufficient ground for bankruptcy proceedings is constituted not only by illiquidity – as in the case of partnerships – but also by overindebtedness, as in the case of limited companies.[24]

GmbH as general partner without equity participation

It is above all advisable for tax reasons not to have the GmbH participate in the capital of the KG.

The expenses incurred for the management would then have to be reimbursed to it, and a remuneration for the liability risk assumed would have to be agreed in advance, because an undisclosed distribution of profits could otherwise be assumed (e.g. five per cent of the equity capital).[25]

Equal participation in GmbH and KG

Frequently, the shareholders of the GmbH are also the limited partners, which is ensured by corresponding "interlocking provisions" in both the articles of association of the GmbH and the partnership agreement of the KG. In this case, the partnership agreement must also be notarially recorded, because it contains the obligation to transfer shares in the GmbH under certain circumstances.

Unitary partnership (Einheitsgesellschaft)

In the case of the GmbH & Co. KG, the limited partners or third parties (e.g. their managing directors), or the KG, can be owner of all the shares in the GmbH. In the last-mentioned instance, a so-called unitary partnership (Einheitsgesellschaft) comes into existence.[26]

As the KG is represented by the GmbH, and the GmbH in turn by its managing directors, the latter would have to exercise the rights of the KG as shareholder of the GmbH in the general meeting of the shareholders. This is neither desired nor is it always legally possible (e.g. not for resolutions concerning the appointment, removal and discharge of the managing directors).[27] Thus, the limited partners must be authorized to safeguard the shareholders' rights of the KG together with the GmbH. If the company (the GmbH or the KG) has a supervisory board, then the exercise of voting rights can also be transferred to it.

Investors' commercial limited partnership (Publikums-KG)

The commercial partnership has another advantage, which is of an organizational nature: the partnership agreement can restrict the rights of the limited

---

[23] § 4 para. 1 Co-Determination Act (MitbestG).
[24] §§ 130a, 130b, 177a HGB. As far as information about the partnership on its stationery is concerned, the GmbH & Co. KG is treated like the GmbH (§§ 125a, 177a HGB); *post*, p. 40.
[25] BFH BB 77, 346.
[26] Its advantage lies in the contractual provision of security for equal participation of the partners in both partnerships, the implementation of which is complicated by reason of §§ 5, 15, becomes unnecessary. The proper raising of the share capital (and also the capital contributed by the limited partners) must be guaranteed, which is why the GmbH shares must be fully paid up.
[27] § 46 No. 5.

partners to influence the management (i.e. the general partners) to certain basic decisions similar to the shareholders' rights in a corporate structure. The GmbH as general partner, itself managed by its managing directors, can then run the business independently without much interference by the limited partners and without holding a financial interest in the partnership's equity.

This structure is often implemented in the so-called "Publikums-KG" (investors' commercial limited partnership), which is used by companies or individuals initiating an investment (who are often the shareholders of the general partner GmbH). By way of a private placement, in most cases through banks or independent agencies, the partnership interests are sold to private investors. Investors tend to look for tax advantages rather than good prospects for return on investment.

Since this market for private placement is not regulated, there are many dubious initiators, although such investment funds – if properly structured and organized – can yield a high return after tax for the investor.

Silent partnership (stille Gesellschaft)

The silent partnership is primarily financial participation in the commercial enterprise of another.[28] It is a commercial partnership which is not registered and is not visible to third parties (so-called sub-partnership). The corporation or individual running a business agrees with the silent partner that the latter pays to the partnership a certain amount as a partnership interest and receives in return a share of its profits (and losses, if participation in the losses was not contractually excluded).[29] Contributions in kind or the contribution of labour by the silent partner are also conceivable.

Normally, a silent partner has no rights to influence the business. Rather, its relationship to the business is of a merely financial nature. However, the parties can agree to grant the silent partner additional rights. If the silent partner's position is strengthened in a way similar to the position of a limited partner in a commercial limited partnership, the silent partnership is called atypical (atypische stille Gesellschaft). In this case, the silent partner is in the same tax position as a limited partner, but remains unseen, and the general structure of the business remains intact (i.e. it does not change into a partnership).

3. Objects which may be pursued by the company

Any conceivable lawful purpose may be pursued in the legal form of a GmbH. In particular, the GmbH can operate any type of business. The same applies to subsidiaries of foreign enterprises, because they – unlike branches – are not in

---

[28] §§ 230 *et seq.* HGB; post, IX.1.3.1.
[29] §§ 239 *et seq.* HGB.

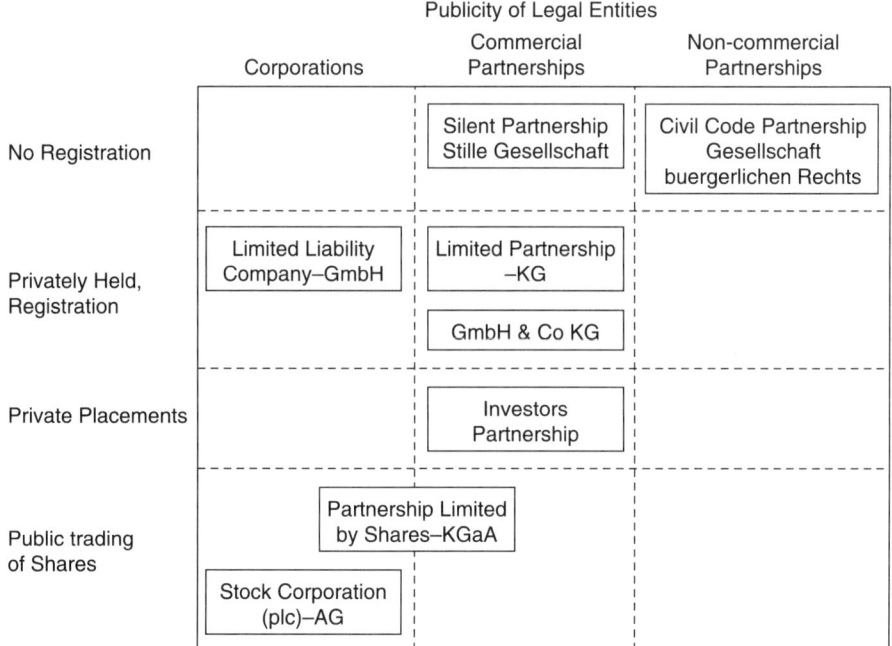

Publicity of Legal Entities

	Corporations	Commercial Partnerships	Non-commercial Partnerships
No Registration		Silent Partnership Stille Gesellschaft	Civil Code Partnership Gesellschaft buergerlichen Rechts
Privately Held, Registration	Limited Liability Company–GmbH	Limited Partnership –KG / GmbH & Co KG	
Private Placements		Investors Partnership	
Public trading of Shares	Stock Corporation (plc)–AG	Partnership Limited by Shares–KGaA	

principle subject to the law relating to foreigners, but are classified as a German entity.

The freedom to specify an aim is, however, subject to certain restrictions.

In the first place, bank transactions must be mentioned. The individual bank transactions are enumerated in the Banking Act,[30] and include deposit business, discount business, dealing in securities, safe-deposit services, investment business, guarantee business and credit transfer business, as well as the incurrence of obligations to acquire debts under a loan before they fall due. Whilst they can in principle be pursued in the form of a GmbH, however, they require a licence from the Federal Banking Supervisory Office in Berlin.[31] The licence shall be enclosed with the application for registration in the Commercial Register, as no registration can be made without it.[32]

The same applies to capital investment companies.[33] Capital investment companies are all enterprises whose sphere of business is directed at investing money lodged with it in its own name for joint account of the depositors in accordance with the principle of the diversification of risks in securities or real property separately from its own assets, and to issue share certificates concerning the rights of depositors.

---

[30] § 1 para. 1 Banking Act (KWG).
[31] § 32 Banking Act (KWG).
[32] § 43 KWG.
[33] §§ 1 para. 3, 2 para. 1 Capital Investment Companies Act (KAGG).

By contrast, private building and loan associations, mortgage banks, ship mortgage banks and a certain form of risk-capital investment company enjoying tax concessions cannot be operated as a GmbH.

Similarly, insurance business is also for the most part removed from the GmbH sphere: the licence to operate an insurance business may only be issued to enterprises in the form of an AG or a mutual insurance association.[34] Thus, companies with limited liability only have a supplementary function in the insurance sphere, such as, for example, marketing companies.

In addition, there are branches of industry or trade such as pharmacists and the operation of the auctioneering trade, in relation to which legal persons – and therefore also the GmbH – are excluded.

The licensing requirement of a business which can be conducted as a GmbH does not make the purpose of the company impermissible. However, the lack of a licence may constitute an obstacle to registration.[35] If statutory provisions make the licence for a commercial enterprise dependent on personal qualities or qualifications, then this – for example the registration of a GmbH in the Register of Craftsmen[36] – is the equivalent of an official licence.[37]

The operation of a GmbH as a holding company is permissible without restriction. In practice, this is in particular widespread in groups of affiliated companies: in many cases, they are structured in such a way that a GmbH (a so-called intermediate holding company) is interposed between the company heading the group (parent company) and the enterprise within the group. It holds the interest in the enterprise within the group and runs that enterprise, whilst the parent company restricts itself to holding and managing the GmbH shares.

The so-called joint venture company is based on a joint venture agreement[38] by means of which the participating companies undertake to carry out a joint project. A GmbH is often chosen as a joint venture company by reason of its flexibility and the influence of the shareholders on the business activities.

The GmbH is also especially suitable for the success of foreign investments in German real property.

4. Tax aspects of the choice of legal form for the foreign investor

Whilst the choice of legal form should not primarily be made for tax reasons, the tax structure of the investment plays a decisive role for the foreign investor.

---

[34] § 7 para. 1 Insurance Supervision Act (VAG).
[35] § 8 para. 1 no. 6.
[36] §§ 1, 7 para. 4 Handicrafts Code (HandwO).
[37] *Post*, p. 276 on the commercial enterprises requiring a licence which may be operated as a GmbH. BGHZ 102, 209, 211 *et seq.*
[38] *Ante*, p. 8.

The formation of the following alternative commercial forms of business organizations in Germany may be taken into consideration by foreign investors:

- a corporation (GmbH or AG);
- a partnership (KG or GmbH & Co. KG, in most cases);
- a permanent establishment within the country; or
- the conduct of direct transactions from abroad.

These forms are different in respect of book-keeping obligations, the basis for tax assessment, the taxation of the profits generated by activities within Germany, and the possibilities of loss compensation.

4.1 Book-keeping obligations

German tax law provides for book-keeping obligations, in particular for corporations and partnerships situated within the country. Permanent establishments of foreign investors – which are not legally independent entities – are only subject to book-keeping obligations if the branch has been registered in the Commercial Register,[39] or if certain turnover, profit or business assets thresholds are exceeded.[40] There is no book-keeping obligation in the case of direct transactions.

4.2 Tax assessment basis

Since companies and partnerships are legally independent, there is no need to delimit assets and profits as in the case of a permanent establishment (e.g. branch). However for tax purposes, unreasonable transfer pricing agreements between the German entity and the shareholders will be adjusted on the basis of the market price (arm's length principle). In partnerships, payments which the partners receive in return for services to the partnership (e.g. remuneration for the activities of a managing partner) do not reduce the business income within the country. In a corporation, debt financing by shareholders' loans is only possible to a restricted extent.[41]

The permanent establishment and its foreign head office form one legal and economic unit. The allocation of profits or assets between the head office and the permanent establishment, which causes difficulties in practice, is undertaken either by the so-called direct method, i.e. on the basis of book-keeping at the permanent establishment, or in accordance with the indirect method, i.e. by a proportional allocation of the expenditure and earnings of the head office to the permanent establishment.

In the case of direct transactions, the outcome resulting from international business relationships will be allocated to the foreign enterprise.

---

[39] § 13c HGB.
[40] § 141 Code of Taxation Procedure (AO).
[41] § 8a Corporate Income Tax Act (KStG); *post*, p. 129.

4.3 Taxation of profits

The profits generated by the activities within Germany may be subject to taxation both within the country and abroad. The description which follows is restricted to the individual income[42] or corporate income tax[43] consequences of activities within Germany which are relevant for the comparison of legal form.

A German corporation is subject to corporate income tax on all its profits, irrespective of whether they result from sources within or outside Germany. Retained profits of the company are subject to a corporate income tax rate of 45 per cent. Distributed profits are taxed at a corporate income tax rate of 30 per cent and are in addition subject to capital yield tax[44] withheld at a rate of 25 per cent of the cash dividend. However, if a tax treaty is applicable, the capital yield tax rate usually only amounts to between five per cent and 15 per cent. In the case of EU parent companies, this may result in a full exemption from capital yield tax.

Taxation within Germany of the profits of permanent establishments and of partnerships is only insignificantly different. If the parent company or the partner is a foreign company, then only profits from sources within Germany are subject to corporate income tax at a rate of 42 per cent (limited tax liability). If the partner is an individual, then the profits are subject to income tax at a maximum tax rate for business income of 47 per cent.[45]

Generally, in the case of direct transactions, the profits are not subject to German taxation. However, in the case of certain cross-border transactions, for example the leasing of movable property, the transfer of licences or artistic, sporting or similar presentations, a capital yield tax is withheld at a rate of 25 per cent.[46]

The letting of real property in Germany without the formation of a permanent establishment is subject to income tax at a maximum rate of 53 per cent (if the lessor is an individual) or a corporate income tax rate of 42 per cent (if the lessor is a foreign company). If the lessor is a company, the capital gains derived from the sale of the real estate are also subject to taxation in Germany.

4.4 Possibilities of loss compensation

Losses of a German corporation can only be compensated by a loss carryback or a loss carryforward. A loss compensation with other profits of a foreign investor is usually excluded.

In the case of permanent establishments and partnerships, a distinction must be drawn: if no tax treaty applies, then the profits of the partnership or permanent establishment situated within Germany will be included in the tax assessment basis of the partner or head office, in so far as loss compensation restrictions

---

[42] "Einkommensteuer".
[43] "Körperschaftsteuer".
[44] "Kapitalertragsteuer".
[45] § 32c Income Tax Act (EStG).
[46] § 50a EStG.

under the law of the foreign home country do not apply. If, by contrast, a tax treaty is applicable, then losses of the partnership/permanent establishment usually may not be compensated with profits of the foreign investor if the tax treaty provides for tax exemption in the country of the head office/partner in relation to profits generated at the permanent establishment.

Proceeds generated by direct transactions are included directly in the investor's (home country) tax assessment bases.

4.5 Consequences of the choice of legal form

The decision in favour of a specific form of a foreign investment cannot be taken independently of the circumstances of the individual case. In particular, the decision must take into consideration the specific regulations of the taxation system in the home country, for example, the way in which the bases of assessment are determined, tax rates and measures for the avoidance of double taxation.

General tax recommendations on the choice of legal form can thus at best be recommendations as to tendencies. The following applies to the comparison of corporations, partnerships, permanent establishments and direct transactions:

If, by reason of a tax treaty, international inter-company dividend exemption[47] applies, then the legal form of a corporation is usually more advantageous than that of a partnership/permanent establishment. In the case of distribution payments, a corporation is subject to corporate income tax at a rate of only 30 per cent, instead of the 42 per cent corporate income tax or the maximum 47 per cent income tax of the foreign head office or partner. This corporate income tax advantage is not cancelled out by the disadvantage of the deduction of capital yield tax withheld if the applicable tax treaty restricts the rate of capital yield tax (as is usually the case) to up to 15 per cent.[48]

The legal form of a corporation is also usually the best alternative from the tax point of view if the credit-method[49] has to be applied according to the applicable tax treaty.[50] It is unlikely that all German tax deductible from tax payable can be in fact credited in the home country of the shareholder. However, the credit method has the effect of an exemption of dividends from tax in the home country of the shareholder.

Direct business transactions may, in particular, be advantageous in comparison with the investment through a corporation or partnership/permanent establishment if the German earnings are countered by business expenditure in Germany.

The assessment of the advantages of the individual commercial alternatives cannot ignore the taxation of a periodic business transaction. This is all the

---

[47] "Internationales Schachtelprivileg". Dividends paid by a German subsidiary to its foreign parent company are exempted in the state of the parent company if certain conditions are met.
[48] Art. 10 para. 2 OECD-Model Tax Treaty.
[49] "Anrechnungsmethode".
[50] E.g. Art. 23 para. 1b of the US-German Tax Treaty.

more significant if a restructuring or a termination of the investment within the country is intended in the foreseeable future. The structuring of the investments of private individuals within the country should, in particular, also take into consideration any inheritance tax consequences which, by reason of the special features of the inheritance tax assessment of GmbH shares, would place the investment in the legal form of a GmbH at a disadvantage when compared with a partnership or permanent establishment.

Chapter 2

FORMATION OF THE GMBH

Dr. Rüdiger Volhard

The formation of a GmbH requires the drafting of a notarial deed,[51] in which the founders (or the single founder)[52] give the declarations of formation, undertake the obligation to pay in the share capital[53] and lay down the articles of association.[54] Furthermore, the founders must appoint the managing directors,[55] which can (but usually does not) take place outside the deed. The managing directors so appointed bear the duty of submitting an application for the registration of the GmbH in the Commercial Register at the local court for the GmbH's registered place of business.[56] The GmbH only comes into being as such upon registration.[57]

1. The articles of association

Very little is prescribed by statute for the minimum content of the articles of association: they must contain the business name and the registered place of business, the purpose ("object of the company") and the amount of the share capital, together with the contribution to the share capital to be paid by each shareholder.[58] In practice, it is usual, and indeed recommended, to include a whole series of regulations which alter the optional statutory law, or are not prescribed by statutory law but are valid only if they are included in the articles of association.[59]

---

[51] *Post*, p. 26.
[52] *Post*, p. 24.
[53] *Post*, p. 22.
[54] *Post*, p. 19.
[55] *Post*, p. 35.
[56] *Post*, p. 33.
[57] *Post*, p. 37.
[58] § 3.
[59] § 3 para. 2. Regulations not mentioned here which belong to the optional content of the articles of association are discussed further in chapter 3, also in connection with the subject-matter they regulate.

1.1 Business name

The business name of the GmbH is the name under which it acts in commercial life ("conducts its business").[60]

The name must either describe the company's purpose or contain the name(s) of one or more of the shareholders. A combination of a description of the company's purpose and of the shareholders' name(s) is also possible. In addition to these elements, a combination of letters, such as an abbreviation of the shareholders' names, may be used. The company may also use fancy names or its trademark in its firm name, provided that the name still allows the objects of the company to be recognized.

The name of a shareholder is often included; in the case of foreign enterprises, this is frequently the name of the parent company, if necessary with the addition " . . . (Deutschland)". The business name or parts of it can be in a foreign language, as long as they can be understood and at least one shareholder comes from the relevant sphere of the language.

In any event, the expression "mit beschränkter Haftung" or the abbreviation mbH must be included in the name.[61]

Limitations on the choice of the name of a GmbH are contained in various statutes, and must be considered before a name is chosen. In particular, there must be a clear distinction between the business name and all other business names which already exist in the same place and which have already been entered in the Commercial Register.[62] The business name must not only be compared with all other GmbHs, but also with the business names of other legal persons, personal partnerships and individual traders. The addition of the legal form (e.g. GmbH) alone is not sufficient for the distinction.

1.2 Registered office

Any place within the Federal Republic may be chosen at will for the registered office, but the place must have a connection with the GmbH; if this is not so, the choice is null and void as an abuse, and registration shall be refused. It is not necessary for the management to be present, or the administration to be conducted, at the registered office of the GmbH.

Principal place of business
The GmbH always has its principal place of business at the registered office.[63]

Branch
The GmbH may have branch offices[64] in which business is conducted in a place spatially separate from the principle place of business, under the direction of a

---

[60] § 17 para. 1 HGB.
[61] § 4 para. 2; BGHZ 62, 230; OLG Frankfurt BB 74, 434.
[62] § 30 para. 1 HGB.
[63] § 13h HGB.
[64] "Zweigniederlassungen"; §§ 13 to 13c HGB.

branch manager who is authorized to act independently. The branch is not an independent legal personality: it thus has no separate statutory representative (managing director) and no assets of its own. The representative power of procurators (authorized signatories holding full commercial power of representation)[65] and authorized agents[66] can be restricted to the business of the branch if the branch has its own business name, e.g. through the addition of " . . . GmbH Zweigniederlassung X".[67] Such full commercial powers of representation are only registered in the Commercial Register of the branch establishment, which shows the restriction.[68]

It is also permissible for limited companies with their registered office abroad to establish branches inside the country.[69]

Transfer abroad of principal place of business

German law provides that the law of the company (*lex societatis*) is the law of the state in which the company has its actual administrative office. The registered office as stipulated in the articles of association is not decisive.[70]

The decisive factor is the place where the management is carried out and where the representative organs appointed to manage the company are situated, i.e. the place where the fundamental decisions of the management are actually implemented in day-to-day acts of management.[71]

The law of the place where the registered office is situated decides on the existence of a legal person, i.e. at first concerning its existence, but also on the commencement and scope of the legal capacity in general.[72]

A GmbH formed under German law with its actual administrative office abroad is not considered as having been validly founded from a German point of view, because it does not fulfil the formation preconditions of the state where the registered office is situated which are necessary to obtain legal capacity.[73]

1.3 Object of the enterprise

The object of the enterprise is the material sphere in which the GmbH intends to conduct its business activities.[74]

---

[65] "Prokuristen"; *post*, p. 174.
[66] "Handlungsbevollmächtigte"; *post*, p. 175.
[67] § 50 para. 3 HGB.
[68] BGHZ 104, 61.
[69] §§ 13e, 13g HGB.
[70] BGHZ 53, 181, 183; 78, 318, 334.
[71] BGHZ 97, 269.
[72] BGHZ 128, 44.
[73] BGHZ 53, 181, 184; 97, 269, 272. The situation is otherwise if, even given the registered office theory, international private law refers to the law of a third country, or refers back to German law, OLG Frankfurt, NJW 90, 2204. Thus, if a GmbH which has been validly formed under German law has its administrative office in a state which follows the foundation theory, then there is a referral back to German law, which is assumed by German law under the terms of Art. 4 Introductory Act to the German Civil Code (EGBGB). The company shall also be treated as having legal capacity under the registered office theory.
[74] If the GmbH is intended to assume the personal liability in a KG, then not only this but also the line of business pursued by the KG must be stated.

The object of the enterprise must make the central focus of the GmbH's business activities sufficiently clear for the participating economic groups.

In addition, by describing the object to a sufficiently concrete extent, the shareholders also protect themselves within the internal relationship from unauthorised instances of exceeding the powers of representation of the managing directors, which are unrestricted in relation to third parties.[75] A managing director whose acts exceed the object of the company acts in breach of his duties. However, the object of business activities does not restrict the power of representation. German law is not familiar with a doctrine of *ultra vires* in the case of legal persons.

1.4 Amount of the share capital

The share capital is the capital "guaranteed" (promised) by the shareholders to the creditors of the GmbH. Creditors must be able to rely on the amount specified in the articles of association having been available to the GmbH, at least at the outset. The minimum capital is DM 50,000.[76] The Limited Liability Companies Act attempts to ensure the full raising[77] and maintenance of the share capital.[78] In order to remove the share capital from the shareholders' grasp,[79] it is posted in the balance sheet as a separate item of the liabilities.[80]

A distinction must be made between share capital[81] and equity.[82] Equity includes the "subscribed capital" (= share capital), capital reserves,[83] namely a premium obtained upon the issue of shares (Agio) and additional payments into the equity capital made by the shareholders, as well as reserves formed out of profits.[84] Whilst the equity capital of the GmbH varies, the amount of share capital laid down in the articles of association can only be changed by an alteration of the articles of association.[85]

Registration in the Commercial Register is only effected once the entire share capital has been taken up (subscribed) by the shareholders. In contrast to the Common Law system, there are thus no unissued shares. The shareholders must raise the capital if new shares are to be created.

1.5 Capital contributions to be paid in

The capital contributions are specified in Deutschmarks. They may differ in

---

[75] *Post*, p. 139 and p. 160.
[76] § 5 para. 1.
[77] *Post*, p. 34.
[78] *Post*, p. 122.
[79] § 30.
[80] § 42 para. 1.
[81] "Stammkapital".
[82] "Eigenkapital".
[83] "Kapitalrücklagen".
[84] "Gewinnrücklagen"; § 272 HGB.
[85] *Post*, p. chapter 8.

amount, but the figure must be divisible by 100.[86] The minimum nominal amount is DM 500.[87]

The individual capital contributions assumed, i.e. the shares, must be stated as fixed amounts in the articles of association.[88] This also applies to contributions in kind.

The statement of the shareholders and the capital contributions assumed by them can only be dropped from the articles of association at a later stage after full payment in. However, in the case of contributions in kind, the specified information must remain for at least five years after the registration in the Commercial Register.

At the time of foundation, no shareholder may assume more than one original capital contribution, i.e. one share. Shares in the company acquired at a later date remain independent[89] in order to secure any recourse against the legal predecessor who may not have paid in his capital contribution.[90] Shares in the company have no fixed face value (such as DM 1) but are dependent on the capital contribution. For instance, if the company is established by one single shareholder and has a share capital of DM 50,000, there is only one share of DM 50,000.

Cash contributions

Unless otherwise agreed and officially announced, capital contributions assumed shall be paid in cash. In each case, a quarter of the value shall be paid in, at least a total of DM 25,000, before the GmbH is registered.[91] The shareholders decide on the calling-in of the remaining capital contributions; the debt then falls due with the managing directors' request for payment in.[92]

Contributions in kind

If it is intended that a capital contribution should not be paid in in cash but rather by the transfer of other items of property (goods, rights), the subject-matter of the contribution in kind and the amount of the original capital contribution to which the contribution in kind relates shall be stated in the articles of association.[93] Contributions in kind must be transferred to the GmbH[94] before the application for registration.[95]

---

[86] § 5 para. 3.
[87] § 5 para. 1.
[88] § 3 para. 1 no. 4.
[89] § 15 para. 2; Until a possible amalgamation; *post*, p. 96.
[90] BGHZ 42, 91.
[91] *Post*, p. 34.
[92] By law, the remaining capital contributions must be paid if the shares in the company are united in the hands of one shareholder, or the company alongside him, within three years after the registration of the GmbH, unless the shareholder furnishes security for the remaining capital contributions or transfers a part of the shares in the company to a third party; § 19 para. 4.
[93] § 5 para. 4.
[94] § 7 para. 3.
[95] *Post*, p. 34 and p. 108.

Special features of the foundation of a one-man GmbH

At the time of formation, the company does not need more than one share-holder. He may at the same time be the managing director. The formation is governed by the general provisions, with several special features: the founder must separate the capital contribution from his other assets and must create the managing directors' exclusive power of disposition over it. Cash contributions must also be fully paid up, unless the founder furnishes security therefor.[96]

1.6 Special shareholder rights

If shareholders are intended to have special rights, such as, for example, rights of participation in the profits or voting rights differing from the participation quota, or the right to be appointed managing director, commitments to take up shares or subscription rights, rights of pre-emption or of purchase in relation to shares in the business, etc., they must be specified in the articles of association.

If this is not the case, they are not associated with the membership, but rather exist merely under the law of obligations, and are not automatically transferred together with the interest in the company held by the entitled shareholder. They also do not place an obligation on the purchaser of a share belonging to a shareholder who bears the obligation. In addition, they are at the disposal of the majority, whereas if they were included in the articles of association, they may only be adversely affected with the consent of the entitled shareholder. Conversely, an increase in the obligations to make payment requires the consent of the shareholder affected.[97]

1.7 Duties to perform additional services and liability to make further contributions

Further obligations of the shareholders as such to the GmbH, which are assumed alongside the duty to pay capital contributions, must be included in the articles of association. The same applies to the obligation to make further contributions,[98] i.e. to pay funds to the company over and above the amount of the capital contributions if a resolution to make a call is passed. This is intended to enable the shareholders to make flexible adjustments of the capital requirement without complicated increases in share capital.[99] However, little use is made of this in practice, because the shareholders have an even simpler and equally flexible possibility of making adjustments according to the capital requirement through shareholders' loans.[100]

---

[96] § 7 para. 2.
[97] § 53 para. 2.
[98] §§ 26 *et seq.*
[99] *Post,* p. 117.
[100] *Post,* p. 300.

1.8 Supervisory board and advisory council

The articles of association can provide for a third organ between the shareholders' meeting and the management. Its composition and powers can be regulated at will in the articles of association. In the case of companies with many employees, a supervisory board is compulsory.[101]

1.9 Concluding provisions

Certain general provisions may be found in the final sections of the articles of association.

Place of jurisdiction clause

In the absence of any provisions to the contrary, actions against the GmbH shall be lodged at the place where it has its registered office,[102] whilst actions against the shareholders shall be lodged at their place of residence.[103] The agreement of a place of jurisdiction for the latter cases in the articles of association (usually the place of the company's registered office) is only binding for shareholders who are business people.[104]

Arbitration clause

Often, disputes amongst the shareholders themselves or between the shareholders and the company are intended to be settled outside the ordinary courts and decided by an arbitration tribunal, which is mostly formed on an *ad hoc* basis.

The decision on the challenge of shareholders' resolutions[105] and on the declaration of nullity of the GmbH[106] cannot be transferred to an arbitration tribunal.[107]

The arbitration tribunal may, however, decide on claims to the declaration of a shareholders' resolution as valid, claims to expulsion from the company, to the provision of information, to the dissolution of the GmbH and concerning all reciprocal obligatory claims of the shareholders.

Severance clause

It is usual to include a clause which clarifies that the invalidity of individual provisions does not affect the validity of the remainder of the articles of association, and that a gap arising as a result of this or for any other reason will be filled out with a valid provision which, in a permissible way, comes as close as possible to what was intended.

---

[101] *Post*, p. 197.
[102] § 17 Code of Civil Procedure (ZPO).
[103] § 13 ZPO.
[104] § 38 para. 1 ZPO. This restriction does not apply to parties without a general place of jurisdiction within the country, OLG Koblenz ZIP 92, 1234; BGHZ 123, 347.
[105] *Post*, p. 273.
[106] § 75 para. 2.
[107] Reform of the law is intended on this point.

Formation expenses

Formation expenses[108] are all expenditure to be paid to shareholders or other persons as compensation or reward for the foundation or its preparation. Formation expenses also include the costs of foundation, namely notarial and court fees arising from the foundation of the company, the application to have it registered, registration and announcement, but also any costs for obtaining a necessary licence.

If the GmbH is intended to bear the costs of formation, this must be specified in the articles of association;[109] if it is not yet possible to specify an exact figure, then an estimate must be given in the articles of association.[110] Otherwise, the founders shall bear the foundation expenses or shall be reimbursed by the company.

2. The pre-incorporation association

A pre-incorporation association exists prior to the formation[111] of the GmbH by the notarially recorded conclusion of the articles of association,[112] if the shareholders have agreed that they intend to found a GmbH.[113]

If it already commences business activities and general commercial business is conducted, the pre-incorporation association[114] is classified as a general commercial partnership;[115] if not, it is a civil law partnership.

If the pre-incorporation association already has assets, then they must be transferred individually to the pre-incorporation company[116] after the formation of the GmbH, or to the GmbH after it has been registered.[117]

The shareholders are personally liable for obligations entered into at the pre-incorporation stage; unless it is otherwise agreed, they are jointly and severally liable to an unlimited extent. This liability does not extinguish upon the registration of the GmbH.

3. Notarial recording

The articles of association must be notarially recorded,[118] otherwise they are null and void.[119]

---

[108] §§ 26 para. 2, 37 para. 4 no. 2 AktG.
[109] OLG Hamm GmbHR 84, 155; OLG Düsseldorf GmbHR 87, 59 and GmbHR 91, 20.
[110] BGHZ 107, 1.
[111] "Establishment", § 1.
[112] § 2 para. 1.
[113] This agreement, the pre-incorporation contract, is not binding on the participants, unless – exceptionally – it is notarially recorded, BGH DB 88, 223.
[114] "Vorgründungsgesellschaft".
[115] §§ 1, 105 HGB.
[116] *Post*, p. 31.
[117] BGHZ 91, 148; BGH NJW 92, 2698 *et seq.*
[118] § 2.
[119] § 125 BGB.

The form of the notarial recording is prescribed in §§ 6 et seq. of the Notarial Registration Act (BeurkG). The notary takes down a notarial protocol which specifies the parties and their declarations,[120] which is read out loud to the participants in the presence of the notary (usually by him), is approved by them and is personally signed by them and the notary.[121] The articles of association are usually not included in the foundation protocol, but rather attached to it as an appendix, which must likewise be read out loud. The deed does not have to be in German if the notary has a good command of the foreign language chosen. If one participant does not have a good command of German, the deed can be drawn up in German if – instead of being read out loud in German – it is translated by the notary or an interpreter called in to assist. The participant can require that a written translation be executed and submitted to him for perusal.[122] Foreign participants often choose to be represented at the notarial recording by authorized representatives with a good command of German.

Along with the declaration that a GmbH is being founded, the deed must contain the compulsory declarations which must be included in the content of the articles of association,[123] if the articles of association are attached as an appendix, but in any case the obligation to assume the capital contributions to the share capital. In addition, it must contain the appointment of the managing director(s), unless this is done in a declaration in writing, which is, however, unusual.

Immediately after the conclusion of the act of foundation, the registration and the list of shareholders[124] shall be signed if the managing directors are present. The notary shall take this opportunity to instruct the parties on the preconditions for the declaration of suitability to be given by the managing directors.[125]

3.1 German notary's office

The notarial recording[126] is the recording by a German notary. Depending on the geographical region in question, he may exclusively be a notary (so-called pure notary)[127] or may at the same time be an attorney-at-law (so-called lawyer-notary).[128] Those who are purely notaries can be independently self-employed, or civil servants.

Every notary fulfils state tasks and exercises sovereign powers for this. Alongside his recording activities, he acts in an impartial advisory capacity within the

---

[120] § 9 para. 1 BeurkG.
[121] § 13 BeurkG.
[122] § 16 BeurkG.
[123] § 3.
[124] *Post*, p. 33
[125] *Post*, p. 35.
[126] § 2 para. 1.
[127] E.g. in Cologne, Düsseldorf, Hamburg, Leipzig and Munich.
[128] §§ 3 para. 1,2 Federal Rules and Regulations for Notaries (BNotO); e.g. in Berlin, Frankfurt, Hannover and Stuttgart.

framework of the precautionary administration of justice in the structuring of legal relationships. The notary receives fees from the parties which are laid down by statute; they are determined by the value, type and subject-matter of the individual transaction.[129]

The notary is personally liable for compensation for culpable breaches of his official duties,[130] but only in a subsidiary way in the case of notarial recordings where he is merely guilty of negligence (a breach of the necessary duty of care). If there is another party liable to pay compensation (e.g. a lawyer who advised him at the notarial recording), then the party who has suffered damage must first attempt to recover compensation from him.

Alongside the parties, anyone who is a direct participant and whose interests are affected by the concrete legal transaction and who has thus been in contact with the notary (so-called contact person) is also considered as being entitled to bring an action. Likewise, third parties who do not participate in the official action but who are directly affected by it in law are also entitled persons.[131]

3.2 Execution and authentication in a foreign country

The German notary must charge the statutory fees. As these are dependent on the value of the subject-matter, the (cheaper) notarial recording abroad, namely in nearby Switzerland, is often taken into consideration in instances involving large sums. It is disputed whether the prescribed form of recording is satisfied in such a case.

The form is observed if it either corresponds to the law to be applied to the legal relationship formed on the basis of its subject-matter ("law of the transaction", "legal system governing the transaction"), or the law of the state in which the legal transaction is conducted (the proper legal form at the place where the transaction is entered into). A precondition for this is that the law of the relevant state recognises a corporate form comparable to that of the GmbH.[132]

By contrast, it is sometimes assumed that legal transactions affecting the constitution of the GmbH, i.e. in particular the formation of the GmbH and alterations to the articles of association (but not the assignment of interests in the company),[133] are only effective as far as form is concerned if they comply with the prescribed form of the law of the transaction, i.e. of the Limited Liability Companies Act. If it is equivalent to German law, the notarial recording by a foreign notary is also sufficient. The recording is viewed as equivalent if, according to his legal education and position in legal life, the foreign authenticator exercises a function corresponding to the activities of a German notary, and if

---

[129] §§ 140 *et seq.* Regulation on *Ex-parte Costs (KostO)*.
[130] § 19 BNotO. The BNotO, the BeurkG and the pertaining implementation ordinances are the decisive provisions for the content of the official duties, together with the service regulations for notaries, which are uniform in the Federal States.
[131] BGH WM 59, 1436.
[132] Art. 11 para. 1 EGBGB; BayObLG NJW 78, 500; OLG Frankfurt DB 81, 1456; OLG Düsseldorf WM 89, 643; order to refer the case to another court: OLG Stuttgart NJW 81, 1176.
[133] BGHZ 105, 324; left open in BGH ZIP 94, 18855.

rules corresponding to those for the creation of deeds under German notarial recording law apply.[134]

3.3 Attestation in a foreign country

Public attestation is prescribed for certain legal transactions (e.g. the power of attorney for formation,[135] applications for registration in the Commercial Register,[136] declarations of assumption within the framework of an increase in share capital).[137]

The content itself is not certified, but rather the provision of the declaration by its signature, which must be executed in the presence of the notary[138] or recognised before him.[139] The German notary cannot act abroad as the bearer of an office, and thus cannot certify any signatures there.

Foreign notaries
Foreign notaries may carry out valid attestations of signature. As far as such attestation is concerned, criteria of equivalence with regard to the legal education of the notary such as in the case of notarial recording[140] are irrelevant.[141] By contrast, it is doubtful whether the cautionary instruction[142] on the suitability as managing director[143] can be given by a foreign notary.[144]

The attestation certificate of a foreign notary is a foreign public deed, the authenticity of which will only be assumed by German courts after it has been "legalized",[145] i.e. after the confirmation of the authenticity of the deed by the consulate of the state in which the deed is intended to be used. In the case of deeds which are intended to be used in Germany, this would be the German consulate in the state in which the deed was created.

However, there are numerous regulations in international conventions[146] in accordance with which legalization is not required but rather a so-called "apostille"

---

[134] BGHZ 80, 78; a different view was taken by reason of the German notary's duty to conduct an examination and to instruct, OLG Hamm NJW 74, 1057; OLG Karlsruhe RIW 79, 567; OLG Hamburg NJW-RR 93, 1317 (for the general meeting of an AG). Other transactions requiring notarial form, in particular the conveyance of land, are only valid if they were recorded before a German notary.

[135] § 2 para. 2.

[136] § 12 HGB.

[137] § 55 para. 1.

[138] The signature of a business name or that of a personal name for deposit at the court (§ 8 para. 5; *post*, p. 36) must be executed in the notary's presence; § 41 BeurkG.

[139] § 40 BeurkG.

[140] *Ante*, p. 28.

[141] However, in exceptional cases the recognition of foreign attestation certificates may be doubtful if the foreign law prescribes wholly different forms of attestation, such as, for example, the attestation provided for under Brazilian law on the basis of similarity with a sample signature deposited with the notary at an earlier point in time.

[142] § 8 para. 3 GmbHG.

[143] *Post*, p. 35.

[144] LG Ulm GmbHR 88, 195.

[145] § 438 para. 2 ZPO

[146] Especially in the Hague Convention of 05.10.1961 on the Legalisation of Foreign Documents.

Form Requirements

Notarial Deed	Notarial Attestation of Signature	Agreement in Writing	Special Form
– formation of company – transfer of shares in a <u>GmbH</u> (not AG shares or partnership interests) – transformation of business – transfer of title in real estate and related business – pledges, liens, mortgages on GmbH shares and real estate – agreement to dispose of one's entire assets – other	i.a. applications to the commercial registries and other registries	– promissory notes – guarantees – consumer credit agreements – other	– transfer of title in certain IP rights – wills – other

(additional attestation by a foreign authority) is sufficient, or both are unnecessary. The apostille certifies that the notary who executed the attestation is actually a notary appointed to do this under the foreign law in question.[147]

It should be taken into consideration that the registry court can require the certified translation of every written document drafted in a foreign language, including attestation certificates.[148]

Consulates

German consular officials are authorized to take down minutes or issue certificates concerning facts and procedures which they have undertaken in the exercise of their office; in particular, they may attest signatures.[149] However, German consular officials are in principle only competent to assist German citizens. A series of international consular agreements determines that foreign consuls may certify deeds, and that such deeds are equivalent to public deeds created inside the country.

3.4 Powers of attorney

Representation is permissible for all legal acts, with the exception of assurances to be given with various applications for registration. Notarial recording of the power of attorney is not prescribed for any individual case. The grant of a power of attorney (and the confirmation of the power of attorney and the declaration of the permission) only requires notarial attestation in the following instances:

---

[147] A list of foreign authorities who grant the apostille is contained in the Appendix.
[148] §§ 184 Judicature Act (GVG), §§ 8, 9 German Ex Parte Jurisdiction Act (FGG), § 50 Notarial Registration Act (BeurkG). See OLG Cologne, WM 88, 1749.
[149] § 10 para. 1 no. 2 of the Consular Act – Konsulargesetz.

- for the conclusion of the articles of association (here the notarially attested power of attorney is a precondition of validity[150] but the notarially certified subsequent approval is also sufficient;[151]
- for applications for registration in the Commercial Register;[152]
- for the subscription of shares in connection with an increase in share capital.

3.5 Implementing power of attorney

It is expedient that foreign participants grant a far-reaching implementing power of attorney in the foundation protocol in favour of members of the notary's staff, in case alterations (e.g. the business name, object of the enterprise) are necessary for the registration.

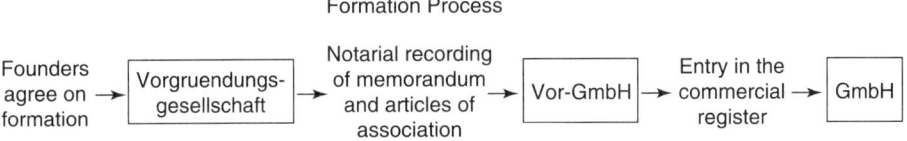

Formation Process

4. The pre-incorporation company (Vor-GmbH)

A pre-incorporation company (Vor-GmbH) exists in the case where the GmbH has been formed by the notarially recorded conclusion of the articles of association[153] but does not yet exist as a GmbH "as such" because it is not yet registered,[154] and where the founders are following the registration procedure.

For the most part, GmbH law already applies to the pre-incorporation company. In contrast to the pre-incorporation association, the pre-incorporation company formed with the foundation of the GmbH is an organization subject to special law which is comprised of the provisions on formation laid down by statute or in the articles of association, and the law of the GmbH having legal capacity, in so far as it does not presuppose registration.[155]

4.1 Representation of the Vor-GmbH

The Vor-GmbH can be committed by those acting for it who are in possession of a power of attorney, irrespective of whether they acted for the Vor-GmbH, the GmbH in formation or the GmbH without any addition,[156] unless the validity of the

---

[150] § 2 para. 2.
[151] § 177 BGB.
[152] § 12 para. 2 HGB.
[153] § 2 para. 1.
[154] § 11 para. 1.
[155] BGHZ 20, 281; established case-law.
[156] BGHZ 62, 216, 221; 64, 11, 14, 91, 148, 152.

transaction has been made expressly dependent on the registration of the GmbH. It is not sufficient to use the business name of the GmbH without any addition. The usual addition is "iGr", being abbreviation for "in the process of formation".

As the statutory representatives of the company, the managing directors in principle have the organ-related power of representation for the GmbH, which cannot be restricted.[157] This statutory power of representation is created upon the registration of the GmbH. It is disputed whether this power already exists for the Vor-GmbH. As the Vor-GmbH can also only act through organs, the managing directors are in any case entitled to perform all acts which are necessary to ensure that the GmbH is registered. After the notarial recording of the articles of association, the founders can agree that the GmbH shall commence business even before registration.

4.2 Liability

Vor-GmbH
The pre-incorporation company is liable for obligations entered into on the basis of legal transactions if it is validly represented. It is liable for culpable conduct on the part of its organs.[158]

Shareholders
It is still unclear to what extent, and to whom, the shareholders of the Vor-GmbH are liable. According to the case-law of the Federal Supreme Court, the shareholders are liable to the company (internal liability). The liability is limited to the amount of the capital contribution.[159] In a recent judgment,[160] the Federal Supreme Court adheres to the concept of internal liability but extends it to all losses of the company prior to registration. Without limitation to the capital contribution, the shareholders are liable *pro rata*, according to the percentage of the share capital they hold. As far as liability cannot be enforced against one of the shareholders, the others become liable for that part as well, again on a *pro rata* basis.[161] The further development of case-law remains to be seen.

Liability of persons acting before completion of incorporation
Any person who, after formation[162] acts "in the name of the company" prior to the registration of the GmbH, is personally liable,[163] irrespective of whether he acted in the name of the Vor-GmbH or the future GmbH.[164]

---

[157] §§ 35 para. 1, 37 para. 2; *post*, p. 139.
[158] Analogous application of § 31 BGB.
[159] BGHZ 65, 378, 382; 72, 45, 48; 80, 129, 144; 80, 182, 184. Direct liability towards the creditors of the company (external liability) is supported by BSG GmbHR 86, 228; OLG Frankfurt GmbHR 94, 708; OLG Saarbrücken GmbHR 92, 307; BAG ZIP 1892.
[160] BGH WM 96, 581.
[161] § 24.
[162] Notarial creation, BGH GmbHR 85, 214.
[163] § 11 para. 2.
[164] BGHZ 62, 221; 64, 11, 14; 91, 148, 152.

For the most part, the liability only affects managing directors and founding shareholders who act like managing directors. In particular, it is important if the registration of the GmbH does not take place, because it expires upon registration in so far as it relates to obligations which were validly created for the Vor-GmbH and which pass to the GmbH formed upon registration by way of universal succession.[165]

4.3 Liability for deficit balance

When it comes into being, the GmbH must be equipped with its share capital as the indispensible basis of liability.

The founders may already have used up the liability assets before registration. In such a case, they must equalize the deficit balance in existence at the time of registration.[166] The deficit balance is the amount by which the assets of the GmbH fall short of the sum of the share capital and the genuine liabilities. Thus, the shareholders are liable for the difference between the company's assets at the time of registration and the obligations, including the share capital, or between the net equity and the nominal amount of the share capital.

The claim is treated as a claim to the payment of missing cash contributions. For this reason, it is the GmbH which is entitled to it. The GmbH's creditors can only call the shareholders to account if the registration has failed. On the other hand, the liability for the deficit balance, like the claim to capital contributions which have not yet been paid in, does not expire upon the registration of the company.

5. Application for registration and registration in the Commercial Register

5.1 Application for registration

All procedures which require registration in the Commercial Register[167] must be notified. This application for registration must be made by the managing directors, not by the shareholders. All managing directors must apply for the registration of the formation of the GmbH,[168] otherwise the number of managing directors authorized to represent the company shall be sufficient.[169]

Managing directors may have themselves represented for the application

---

[165] *Post*, p. 38.
[166] BGHZ 80, 129, 136.
[167] *Post*, p. 271.
[168] § 7 para. 1. The same applies in the case of increases and reductions in the share capital; § 78.
[169] *Post*, p. 137.

for registration[170] but not for the assurances to be given[171] and not for the signature.[172]

The applications for registration require notarial attestation.[173] In the case of applications for registration by a person holding a power of attorney, the power of attorney must be attested.[174]

Declarations on the raising of capital

Formation by contributions in cash

In the application for registration, the managing directors must give the assurance that the payments of the original capital contributions have been made,[175] and are permanently placed at their disposal.[176] Thus, a quarter of the nominal amount of every original capital contribution must be paid up, amounting to a total of at least DM 25,000. If the application for registration has been signed at the time of incorporation[177] it must not be filed before the notary has received confirmation that the contributions were made.

The assurance must also encompass the extent to which the start-up capital has been encumbered by previous charges from obligations. If, as a result of transactions of the Vor-GmbH, the assets at the time of registration no longer cover the share capital, the registration shall be refused regardless of the liability for the deficit balance.[178] Some registry courts, therefore, require the assurance that the assets do cover the share capital at the time of application for registration.[179]

The transfer payment on to an account of the Vor-GmbH satisfies the requirement of payment in for disposal at will; an account expressly specified as a "managing directors' account" is not necessary.

The assurance may not be given by a representative.

The managing directors are liable under criminal law for incorrect declarations,[180] and under civil law for damages.[181] Liability to pay damages exists not only in relation to the company but also in relation to shareholders and third parties who have suffered damage as a result of their reliance on the correctness of the information.

Formation by contributions in kind

Contributions in kind must be paid over to the company (the Vor-GmbH)[182] before the application for registration in such a way that they are permanently

---

[170] OLG Cologne NJW 87, 135; this is, however, disputed; for the other view BayObLG NJW 87, 137.
[171] *Post,* pp. 34–35.
[172] *Post,* p. 36.
[173] § 12 para. 1 HGB.
[174] § 12 para. 2 HGB. *Post,* p. 271 for the examination of the application for registration by the court.
[175] § 7 para. 2.
[176] § 8 para. 2.
[177] *Ante,* p. 26.
[178] *Ante,* p. 33. BayObLG BB, 91, 2391 and BB 92, 1160.
[179] Proof at OLG Frankfurt WM 92, 1317.
[180] § 82 para. 1 nos. 1 and 4.
[181] § 9a.
[182] *Ante,* p. 31.

placed at the disposal of the managing directors.[183] The assurance must be given in the application for registration that this has taken place.[184]

Representation of the company

Specifications of representation

The shareholders must appoint managing directors[185] who represent the company. At the time of formation, this normally takes place in the minutes of the foundation meeting. If only one managing director is appointed, then he is the sole legal representative of the company. If several managing directors are appointed, they are authorized to represent the company jointly; statute provides that all managing directors must then act jointly.[186] Normally, the articles of association specify that, where there are several managing directors, each of them is entitled to represent the company together with one other managing director (or procurator, who is an authorized representative holding full commercial powers of representation, "Prokurist"), and empowers the shareholders to grant one managing director individual powers of representation.[187]

In addition, any exemption of a managing director from the prohibition on self-dealing shall be notified for registration.[188]

Declarations on suitability as managing director

Any person who has bindingly and non-appealably been convicted of a bankruptcy offence (bankruptcy, breach of accounting duty, fraudulent preference of a creditor, unlawful preference of a debtor)[189] may not be the managing director of a GmbH before the expiry of five years after the judgment has become binding and non-appealable.[190]

In addition, any person who has been prohibited from exercising a profession or an occupation, or carrying on a trade or a branch of a trade, by a court judgment or an enforceable decision of an administrative authority, may not act as managing director in a GmbH whose object corresponds – either as a whole or in part – to the subject-matter of the prohibition, for the period for which the prohibition takes effect. The period during which an offender is held in a public institution by virtue of official order shall not be included in the calculation

---

[183] § 7 para. 3.
[184] § 8 para. 2.
[185] § 16 no. 5.
[186] § 35 para. 2.
[187] In the application for registration, the power of representation must not only be notified in the abstract, thus as joint or individual representative authority in accordance with the law and the articles of association, but also concretely, i.e. for the actual managing directors announced (§ 8 para. 4). In the case of joint powers of representation, the following formulation is necessary: "The managing directors X, Y and Z each represent the company together with another managing director or with a procurator (an authorized signatory with full commercial powers of representation)". If a managing director has an individual power of representation, irrespective of the number of managing directors present, this shall be expressed in the following way: "X shall represent the company alone".
[188] § 181 BGB; *post*, p. 141.
[189] §§ 283-283d Criminal Code (StGB).
[190] § 6 para. 2.

of the period. The managing director of a GmbH is obliged, without any restriction, to furnish the Commercial Register with information as to the existence of circumstances of the nature specified, which stand in the way of his appointment as managing director.[191]

Signature

The managing directors shall sign their signatures "for safekeeping by the court".[192] This old-fashioned provision is intended to enable those participating in transactions to compare the handwritten signature in business life with the deposited signature and thus to verify its authenticity and binding validity for the company.

The signature below the application for registration is also sufficient for "signature".[193] A managing director may not be represented for the purposes of signature. The signature must be notarially attested.[194]

Appendices

Articles of association

The articles of association shall be included with the application for registration.[195]

List of the shareholders

In addition, a list of the shareholders – signed by the parties making the application for registration – must be included with the application. Their names, first names, status and place of residence must be evident from this list, together with the amount of the original capital contributions assumed by each of them.[196]

Legitimation of the parties making the application for registration

If the managing directors are not appointed in the articles of association or in the minutes of the foundation meeting, the shareholders' resolution on their appointment must be included.[197]

Signature sheet

The signature of the managing directors does not have to be executed in the application for registration, and will not normally take place in the case of the appointment of procurators, but rather on a separate signature sheet. This shall then be included with the application for registration.

---

[191] In the application to the Commercial Register for the registration of his appointment, the person appointed as managing director must give the assurance that there are no circumstances which stand in the way of his appointment as managing director and that he has been instructed on his unrestricted duty to furnish information to the court (Commercial Register); § 8 para. 3. The notary gives such instruction under the terms of § 53 para. 2 Federal Central Register Act (BZRG).
[192] § 8 para. 5.
[193] However, it must then be attested as the execution of the signature and as the signature in itself.
[194] § 12 para. 1 HGB.
[195] § 8 para. 1 no. 1.
[196] § 8 para. 1 no. 3.
[197] § 8 para. 1 no. 2.

Documents relating to contributions in kind

Contracts which form the basis of the ascertainment of contributions in kind or which were concluded with regard to their implementation, i.e. relating to their transfer to the Vor-GmbH, shall be included, together with the agreement on setting off the transfer against the duty to pay in contributions.

In addition, the report on formation on the basis of contributions in kind which must be prepared[198] shall also be included. In the report, the founding shareholders must set out the major considerations supporting the appropriateness of the valuation of contributions in kind.[199] All circumstances which enable the registry court judge to make a proper assessment of the appropriateness and intrinsic value of the contribution must be specified. This may include purchase contracts, invoices, proofs of manufacturing costs, information concerning the prevailing market and stock exchange prices, and in the case of real property the documents of the municipal committee of experts, or earlier purchase prices for the same or comparable items. The valuation of interests in enterprises, industrial property rights and the like usually requires the opinion of an expert.

Where an enterprise or significant parts of an enterprise are brought in, then in addition the net annual profit of the last two years prior to the application for registration – the annual surplus or deficit[200] – but at least the results to date, shall be submitted, in so far as this is possible. In practice, it is usual to submit a contribution balance sheet which has been attested by a tax advisor or chartered accountant.

Official licences

If the object of the enterprise requires an official licence,[201] then the licence deed shall be included.[202]

Powers of attorney

If the articles of association were signed by representatives,[203] then a certified copy of these notarially attested powers of attorney shall be included.[204] If the application for registration is signed by representatives of the managing directors, the notarially attested powers of attorney shall be enclosed with it.

5.2 Effect of registration in the Commercial Register

The GmbH "as such" comes into being upon its registration in the Commercial Register.[205]

---

[198] §§ 5 para. 4, 8 para. 1 no. 5.
[199] § 5 para. 4.
[200] §§ 266, 275 para. 2 no. 20 or para. 3 no. 19 HGB
[201] *Post*, p. 276.
[202] § 8 para. 1 no. 6. This also applies to the proof of registration in the Register of Craftsmen, BGHZ 102, 209.
[203] § 2 para. 2.
[204] § 8 para. 1 no. 1.
[205] It is considered the universal successor of the Vor-GmbH, BGH NJW 82, 932.

Duty to make capital contributions

Irrespective of the time of registration, the duty to make capital contributions continues to exist until the original capital contribution assumed has been paid up and is placed at the disposal of the managing directors.[206]

The value of the contributions in kind must correspond to the original capital contributions which were assumed in return for them; if this is not the case, an additional cash payment shall be made.[207]

The shareholders are only personally liable over and above the capital contributions paid in if the share capital was impaired prior to registration.[208] If the payment of the shortfall in the contribution cannot be collected from a shareholder and also cannot be covered by the sale of his share, the remaining shareholders have to raise the deficit in proportion to their shares.[209]

From the time of registration onwards, only the GmbH itself is liable in relation to third parties to the extent of its own assets.[210] If registration does not take place, then the founding shareholders are liable for obligations entered into by the appointed managing directors in the name of the GmbH on the basis of the permission granted to them.[211]

Liability of person acting prior to incorporation

The liability of persons acting for the GmbH prior to its registration[212] expires upon the registration of the GmbH in the Commercial Register if the GmbH is then available as debtor.[213] This is not the case if the persons who acted did not have a power of attorney or if they exceeded their power of representation.

5.3 Bogus formation of a company

False information supplied to the registry court for the purposes of registration[214] is punishable as bogus formation of a company.[215] False information is also considered as having been given if paid up capital has already been impaired at the time the assurance is given, without material assets of equal value having been obtained in return.

5.4 Formation and purchase of an off-the-shelf company

As a result of the occasionally lengthy duration of the formation procedure – periods of six to eight weeks are usual – the purchase of so-called "storage" or

---

[206] § 19.
[207] § 9.
[208] *Ante*, p. 33.
[209] § 24. Also *post*, p. 105, and p. 109 on undisclosed contributions in kind.
[210] § 13 para. 2. *Post*, p. 115 for exceptional cases of piercing the corporate veil.
[211] *Ante*, p. 32; KG WM 94, 1288.
[212] *Ante*, p. 32.
[213] BGHZ 69, 95; established case-law.
[214] § 9a.
[215] § 82 para. 1.

"shelf" companies has become established in practice. This concerns the new economic establishment of an enterprise in the legal guise of a GmbH which already exists but is not commercially active.[216]

A notary to whom an investor turns for the formation will, if he has experience in dealing with foreign clients, usually have a shelf company at his disposal in cases of urgency whose stated object of the enterprise is "the management of its own assets". The investor purchases the GmbH by the acquisition of the fully paid up shares in the company.[217] The assumption of commercial activities must then be preceded by a corresponding alteration of the articles of association, by means of which the object and the business name are adapted to the new purposes.

The advantage of using a shelf GmbH is primarily that the company already exists as a GmbH, and can thus commence trading at once without the risk of liability of persons acting before the completion of incorporation[218] and of liability for a deficit balance.[219]

6. Conduct of the company in business dealings

6.1 Use of the business name

The GmbH is not only entitled but rather obliged to use the business name in commerce. By reason of the principle of establishing the genuineness of the business name, it shall be used in the form in which it is registered in the Commercial Register.[220] The use of an abbreviated form of the business name instead of the full business name is in principle not permitted.[221]

In particular, where transactions of the parties with legal consequences are concerned, this applies to the information on letter paper,[222] price lists, business papers, telephone book entries, etc. A breach constitutes a regulatory offence which carries the threat of a fine.[223] If the GmbH has another business name which is different from the business name entered in the Commercial Register, the registry court shall ensure that the GmbH desists from using the business name by fixing an administrative fine.[224]

However, there are two exceptions to this principle. The additional reference to the company ("GmbH") may be abbreviated, even if it is written out in full in

---

[216] BGHZ 117, 323.
[217] *Post*, chapter 6.
[218] *Ante*, p. 32.
[219] *Ante*, p. 33.
[220] BGH NJW 91, 2023, 2024; LG Düsseldorf DB 81, 686.
[221] BGHZ 30, 288, 292; OLG Düsseldorf DB 70, 923.
[222] *Post*, p. 40.
[223] § 146 Business Regulation Act (GewO).
[224] § 37 para. 1 HGB.

the registered business name.[225] In the identification of the enterprise or of products of the enterprise (in contrast to its owner, the GmbH), contractions of the business name, trademarks and the like may be used as the so-called trade name if they do not operate as a complete business name.[226]

6.2 Information in the letterhead

Certain information must be included in the business letters of a GmbH.[227] For the purposes of this section, business letters include telexes and telecopies, but do not include postcards or telegrams, which are not considered to be correspondence in the ordinary course of business. All business letters which are directed to a specific addressee must state the following:

- the legal form of the company, that is "Gesellschaft mit beschränkter Haftung" or the abbreviation thereof, GmbH;

- the legal registered office of the GmbH, e.g. Frankfurt am Main;

- the court at which the GmbH is registered and the company's number in the court's Commercial Register, e.g. Amtsgericht Frankfurt HRB 1234 (District Court of Frankfurt, Commercial Register No. 1234);

- the surnames and at least one of the first names (written in full) of all the managing directors of the GmbH;

- if the GmbH has formed a supervisory board, the name of the chairman, provided a chairman has been appointed.[228]

This information is not required in communications or reports which are sent or issued in connection with an existing business relationship and where it is customary to use pre-printed forms, completed only with special data required for each individual case.[229] Examples of these pre-printed forms would be delivery notes and invoices. An existing business relationship will be presumed if the parties have already exchanged business letters on several previous occasions, which stated the information required. Order forms are not covered by the abovementioned exemption, even though they may be pre-printed forms.[230]

The information prescribed does not have to be included in advertising brochures and notices which are sent out to a general section of the public rather than a specific business customer or client.

---

[225] BGHZ 62, 230.
[226] BGH NJW 91, 2023, OLG Stuttgart BB 91, 993; OLG Düsseldorf DB 70, 923.
[227] § 35 a.
[228] If a GmbH makes statements as regards its share capital in its letterhead (a provision hardly ever used), then it must also state the aggregate amount of outstanding contributions to be paid in cash.
[229] § 35a para. 2.
[230] § 35a para. 3.

Managing directors or liquidators who contravene these provisions will be fined by the court at which the GmbH is registered.

7. The "faulty company"

Articles of association may be null and void for material or formal reasons.[231] If the Vor-GmbH[232] has entered into business or even been registered, then such defects in the past are insignificant. The GmbH will be treated as having been validly founded. The dissolution of the company as a result of rescission or termination is only justified if the defect continues to exist. These principles developed for the so-called faulty company accord due weight to the fact that the company "called into being" ought not – in the interests of trade – to be handled as null and void, but also that the shareholders cannot "reverse" their payments, or can only do so with difficulty.

After the registration of the GmbH, the company can only be declared null and void in response to a nullity action brought by a shareholder, managing director or member of the supervisory board if there are especially serious defects.[233] Apart from this, the three remaining possibilities are termination, resignation or dissolution.[234]

8. Shareholders' agreements outside the articles of association

The shareholders may also regulate their relations with one another and with the company in various ways under the law of obligations.[235] Such agreements may be regulations on the appropriation or distribution of profits, on the appointment and dismissal of directors (or members of the supervisory board), the establishment of financing duties, loss-bearing duties, and liabilities to make further contributions or pay subsidies, voting trusts, duties of tender, rights of pre-emption and the like.

Such agreements are not part of the articles of association, even if they relate to points which could be regulated in the articles. They are only binding on the parties to the contract, and they only bind legal successors if they have been contractually assumed by them.

---

[231] E.g. by reason of an immoral purpose or of taking advantage in an immoral way, § 138 BGB, or if a founder has challenged his declarations by reason of mistake, fraudulent misrepresentation or threat, §§ 119 et seq. BGB, or because the articles were not properly and completed recorded by a notary, § 2 para. 1.

[232] *Ante*, p. 31.

[233] They are listed in § 75.

[234] § 60.

[235] *Ante*, p. 24.

9. Ostensible parts of the articles of association[236]

Certain agreements between the shareholders under the law of obligations which could also validly be agreed outside the articles of association are often included in them, e.g. restraints of competition, appointment of managing directors, perhaps with remuneration (profit-orientated bonuses) and pension regulations. Such regulations are ostensible in so far as they do not belong to the articles of association in the material sense. The alteration of them does not constitute the alteration of the articles of association, no specific form is necessary for their validity unless otherwise specified, and a shareholders' resolution with a simple majority is all that is required.[237]

10. Contravening the articles of association

10.1 Overriding the articles of association[238]

If the shareholders deviate from the articles of association by a resolution, without having formally altered them and without intending to do so in the long-term, e.g. the appointment of organs or appropriation of the profits contrary to the articles, then this is termed as "overriding the articles of association".

In so far as such resolutions do not operate for the future ("resolutions for action"), they are voidable as being contrary to the articles of association,[239] if not all shareholders agree, including the shareholders who did not participate in the adoption of the resolution. The voidability falls away if the resolution satisfies the formal requirements for a change in the articles of association, having been passed with the majority required for a change in the articles and having been registered.

Resolutions which override the articles of association and which take effect for the future are null and void if they were not adopted and registered in the form of a change to the articles of association.[240]

10.2 Violation of the articles of association[241]

Transactions which are not in keeping with the articles of association are classified as violations of the articles. Owing to the unrestricted nature of the powers

---

[236] "Unechte Satzungsbestandteile".
[237] BGHZ 18, 205; 38, 161.
[238] "Satzungsdurchbrechung"; BGH NJW 93, 2246.
[239] *Post*, p. 75.
[240] *Post*, p. 75.
[241] "Satzungsverletzung".

of representation vested in the managing directors,[242] such transactions are usually valid in relation to third parties, although they constitute a breach of the membership rights of those shareholders who do not consent and can result in a liability for damages.

11. Alterations to the articles of association

In order to be valid, every alteration to the articles of association must have been decided in a shareholders' resolution[243] with a majority of at least three quarters of the votes cast,[244] which must be notarially recorded[245] and must be registered by the managing directors in the Commercial Register,[246] as a result of which it then acquires validity.[247]

The most important cases of alterations to the articles of association are changes in the business name, the registered office, the share capital, the power of representation,[248] or the introduction of restrictions on the disposal of shares in the company, or their withdrawal.

---

[242] *Post*, p. 139.
[243] § 53 para. 1; *post*, 69.
[244] *Post*, p. 69.
[245] § 53 para. 2.
[246] § 54 para. 1.
[247] § 54 para. 4.
[248] E.g. the exemption from the prohibition of self-dealing (§ 181 BGB) or the authorisation therefor.

Chapter 3

SPECIAL REGULATIONS IN THE ARTICLES OF ASSOCIATION

Dr. Rüdiger Volhard

1. Shareholders' resolution[249]

The shareholders adopt their resolutions by voting in shareholders' meetings under the preconditions set forth in the articles of association (or otherwise only with the written consent of all shareholders);[250] this can also be done without convening a meeting (in writing, by telephone, by telefax or by electronic data transfer).

1.1 Convening the shareholders' meeting[251]

The Act contains little concerning the convention[252] and conduct[253] of shareholders' meetings. A shareholders' meeting is only compulsory if it is evident from the balance sheet that half the share capital has been lost[254] or if "it appears necessary in the interests of the company"[255] or if a minority (at least 10 per cent of the share capital) so requires.[256] Otherwise, resolutions may also be passed if a request is made for votes to be cast in writing. It is recommended to stipulate a longer period of notice for the meeting than is provided for by statute.[257]

1.2 Chairmanship of the meeting

Furthermore, regulation of the chairmanship of the meeting and the keeping of minutes is also appropriate (e.g. the chairman of the supervisory board, if

---

[249] "Gesellschafterbeschluß".
[250] § 48 para. 2.
[251] "Gesellschafterversammlung".
[252] §§ 49 to 51.
[253] § 48.
[254] § 49 para. 3.
[255] § 49 para. 2.
[256] *Post*, p. 154.
[257] One week under the terms of § 51 para. 1.

there is a supervisory board, or the oldest shareholder in terms of age, or the shareholder with the largest capital share or the person elected before the agenda is embarked upon (in the last-mentioned case, it would have to be regulated who chairs this election), because differences of opinion amongst the shareholders could otherwise give rise to several chairmen with contradictory statements as to whether a resolution has been adopted and a corresponding number of sets of minutes.

1.3 Entitlement to participate

It is also expedient to include a regulation concerning entitlement to participate: is the shareholder allowed to be represented by anyone or only by co-shareholders? Shall he be entitled to appear with an advisor?

A shareholder is permitted to have himself represented, even if there is no regulation concerning this in the articles of association. The right of participation is not strictly personal, nor is the right to vote,[258] yet the shareholder cannot simply participate in the meeting together with his advisor, unless he wishes to participate himself and must necessarily be accompanied by an advisor in order to compensate for a considerable specialist disadvantage when compared with the other shareholders. A regulation in the articles of association is thus advisable.

1.4 Quorum

The Act does not contain any prescriptions as to the need for a quorum. In order to avoid chance results, it is recommended that the ability to adopt a resolution should be made dependent on the presence of a minimum proportion of the share capital (e.g. 75 per cent). This quorum does not have to be reached in a further meeting which is called by reason of the lack of a quorum in the first.

1.5 Minutes

The Act only provides for notarial recording for alterations to the articles of association and for minutes to be taken in the case of resolutions of the one-man company.[259] There are no other requirements of form for shareholders' resolutions which do not alter the articles of association.

It is normally specified in the articles that all resolutions of the shareholders' meeting must be taken down in minutes to be signed by the chairman and the keeper of the minutes chosen by him, which shall be sent to all shareholders without delay.

---

[258] § 47 para. 1.
[259] §§ 53 para. 2, 48 para. 3.

1.6 Adoption of resolutions outside the shareholders' meeting

Resolutions may be passed outside the shareholders' meetings.[260] Generally, the articles of association make express provision for the possibility of formless resolutions (by telephone, telegraph or fax). Under the terms of the Act, such resolutions are only permissible if all shareholders consent to either the proposal for the resolution or the type of voting. It is usually regulated in the articles that it is sufficient if all shareholders participate in the voting and no shareholder objects to the type of voting.

1.7 Assertion of faults in resolutions

The Limited Liability Companies Act does not regulate how shareholders can defend themselves against faulty resolutions of the shareholders' meeting. The legal concepts of stock corporation law are applied to a far-reaching extent.[261]

The period of one month from the passing of the resolution onwards is only valid as a guiding principle for the time-limit within which to lodge an action for rescission.[262] It is a minimum time-limit, but may on the other hand only be exceeded for imperative reasons.[263] The best solution is to avoid any uncertainty by specifying the time-limit (e.g. two months) in the articles of association.

2. Restrictions on the disposal of shares in the company

Shares in the company may be freely sold and are (compulsorily) inheritable.[264]

2.1 Consent requirements

It is usual to make the disposal of shares (e.g. assignment or encumbrance) dependent on the consent of the company.[265] It shall be declared by the managing director once the shareholders have decided on it with a simple majority. The shareholders decide at their own discretion. Refusal to give consent does not require justification, but it may not be arbitrary.

Assignment without consent is provisionally invalid.[266] It becomes valid if the consent is subsequently granted, and invalid if the consent is refused. The assigning shareholder is entitled to participate in the voting on the resolution

---

[260] § 48 para. 2.
[261] *Post*, p. 74 and p. 272; BGH WM 92, 17.
[262] § 246 para. 1 AktG.
[263] BGHZ 101, 113, 117.
[264] § 15 para. 1.
[265] § 15 para. 5.
[266] § 177 BGB.

concerning the consent because the matter does not concern a legal transaction with the company;[267] he is also obliged to do so because the assignment carried out in the knowledge of the requirement of consent results in the subsidiary duty in relation to the assignee to bring about this consent.[268]

If a share is held in trust for a third party, the shareholders have a claim to information concerning his identity if the transferability is restricted.[269]

2.2 Rights of pre-emption[270]

Rights of pre-emption in favour of the other shareholders in proportion to their shareholdings are common. The right of pre-emption entitles the remaining shareholders to require the assignment of the share in the company (proportionally) to them as soon as the shareholder wishing to sell has concluded a contract of sale with a third party concerning this.[271] Upon exercising of the right of pre-emption, a contract with the party exercising it comes into being under the same conditions as in the contract concluded, unless – as is often the case – the purchase price has been laid down in the articles of association (so-called "limited" right of pre-emption).

The shareholder wishing to sell finds himself in an awkward situation if the other shareholders neither consent to the assignment to the third party (to which he has no claim in principle), nor exercise their right of pre-emption. It can be agreed that:

- the shareholders' consent to the assignment is considered as having been given if they do not exercise their right of pre-emption, or
- the shareholder is entitled to resign from the company in return for a settlement if the shareholders neither consent nor exercise their right of pre-emption.

Certain restrictions of the rights of heirs are also widespread.[272]

2.3 Duties to tender[273]

It is often agreed that a shareholder who intends to sell his share shall first offer it for sale to the other shareholders. It is advisable to then allow him to sell his share at will if the other shareholders do not make use of the right of purchase. If necessary, they can be granted a right of pre-emption: however, this is usually only the case if the shareholder sells at a price lower than that at which he offered his share to the other shareholders.

---

[267] § 47 para. 4.
[268] BGHZ 48, 163, 166 *et seq.*
[269] § 15 para. 5.
[270] "Vorkaufsrechte".
[271] §§ 504 *et seq.* BGB.
[272] *Post*, p. 101.
[273] "Andienungspflichten".

3. Management[274] and representation[275]

The managing directors are the statutory representatives (organs) of the GmbH.[276] In accordance with the Act, the principle of collective representation[277] applies if nothing else is provided for; thus, all managing directors must act jointly. If a different regulation is intended to apply, it must be laid down in the articles of association, at least in the form of authorizing the shareholders to grant individual powers of representation.

The articles of association usually specify that where there are several managing directors, two of them are authorized to represent the company together, or one managing director may do so together with a procurator. However, they can also specify that the managing directors or individual managing directors shall have powers of sole representation or that the shareholders may grant the power of sole representation to the managing directors.

If the articles of association provide for joint representation, then if only one managing director is present, he may not henceforth represent the GmbH alone,[278] but rather a further managing director must be appointed by the shareholders. If necessary an emergency director has to be appointed by the court of the GmbH's registered office at the application of a shareholder, of a managing director or a creditor.[279]

Accordingly, it is recommended that the regulation on joint agency should be supplemented by the provision that, if only one managing director is appointed, he may represent the GmbH alone.

4. Restraint of competition and duty of confidentiality

4.1 Restraint of competition[280]

During membership of the company

The law does not provide for a general restraint of competition on the shareholders, not even in the period of membership of the company. Such a restraint on competition can be, and usually is, founded in the articles of association.

However, even in the absence of a regulation in the articles, restraint of competition in an individual case may also arise from the duty of loyalty under company law[281] if a shareholder is managing director, or can achieve his objectives

---

[274] "Geschäftsführung".
[275] "Vertretung".
[276] *Post*, p. 139.
[277] § 35 para. 2.
[278] OLG Hamburg GmbHR 88, 67.
[279] Analogy to § 29 BGB.
[280] "Wettbewerbsverbot".
[281] *Post*, p. 61. BGH WM 78, 15; BGHZ 91, 1; not for sole shareholders who are not subject to a duty of loyalty, BGHZ 119, 257; BFH ZIP 95, 1890.

in the company by reason of a majority shareholding or special rights.[282] An express regulation should be included in the articles of association.

In addition, a close personal tie in a so-called "personal" GmbH, i.e. if the number of shareholders is small and emphasis is placed on the personal active participation of the shareholders, can give rise to a restraint of competition out of the duty of loyalty.

Every restraint of competition is restricted by public morals[283] and the prohibition on cartels.[284] Restraint of competition is only permissible if it does not noticeably influence market conditions. The agreement of such restraint of competition is at least unobjectionable from the point of view of cartel law[285] if it serves the continued existence and the maintenance of the enterprise and prevents its being undermined "from the inside".[286]

After retirement from the company

A subsequent restraint of competition must be regulated in the articles of association or in an individual contract.[287] Restraint of competition resulting from the duty of loyalty can only exist for the period after retirement from the GmbH in special exceptional cases.[288]

The agreement of restraint of competition for the period after retirement from the GmbH in relation to both the GmbH and the purchaser of a share, which is limited in time and which is, if necessary, limited geographically and as to content, is permissible if it serves the justified interest of the enterprise or the purchaser, and if – with reference to place, time and the object of the exercise of a profession – it does not unreasonably impede the economic activities of the shareholder.

The permissibility of such an agreement shall be measured against the requirement of public morals[289] and against the prohibition in principle of contracts imposing a restraint of competition.[290] Legal transactions which breach public morals are null and void.[291] A breach of public morals is considered as given where a contract is concluded which restricts the economic freedom of movement of the other partner to such an extent that he loses his free self-determination. Contracts which influence the market conditions for the trade in goods or commercial services by imposing a restraint of competition are likewise invalid.[292] The decision whether a restraint of competition is permissible in accordance with these principles is in particular taken in view of its purpose,

---

[282] BGHZ 89, 162, 166; on the permissibility of the contractual agreement, BGH WM 88, 1357.
[283] § 138 BGB.
[284] § 1 GWB.
[285] § 1 Anti-Cartel Act (GWB).
[286] BGHZ 68, 6; 70, 331; 104, 246.
[287] BGH DB 90, 2588, 2589.
[288] OLG Düsseldorf BB 89, 1576.
[289] § 138 BGB.
[290] § 1 GWB.
[291] § 138 BGB.
[292] § 1 GWB.

its extent in terms of geographical area, subject-matter and duration, and the justified interests of the company and the shareholders.[293]

It should be taken into consideration that the economic value of the restraint of competition is usually taken into consideration in the settlement[294] which a departing shareholder receives.[295]

The restraint of competition should be worded as narrowly and as precisely as possible in accordance with the circumstances of the individual case. Periods of longer than two years should not be agreed, because the relationship between the departing shareholder and the company's clients has usually disappeared within this period to such an extent that no significant losses arise from competing activities.[296]

The prohibition[297] does not apply to restraints of competition which specify the duties of the parties in a transaction which is neutral from a cartel law point of view, e.g. in the case of break-up of the business and the departure of the shareholder from the GmbH.[298]

If the restraint of competition exceeds the permissible duration, it will be reduced by the court to the permissible length. If it goes beyond the permissible extent in terms of content, it is and remains invalid.[299]

4.2 Duty of confidentiality[300]

Confidentiality duties only refer to secrets of the company, namely business or trade secrets. The law places their disclosure under criminal sanction.[301] However, the provision only applies to the disclosure of secrets by managing directors, members of the supervisory board and liquidators.

As far as shareholders are concerned, a duty of confidentiality may arise out of the duty of loyalty owed under company law. In order to have a sound basis, it is usual to regulate in the articles of association that every shareholder is obliged to maintain secrecy in relation to third parties concerning confidential matters which come to his knowledge in his capacity as shareholder within the framework of his activities for the GmbH, in particular concerning the balance sheets and the discussions and resolutions of the shareholders, and to maintain this secrecy even after he has left the company. An exception to this is usually made for the submission of balance sheets of the GmbH to banks and the notification to lawyers, chartered accountants auditors and tax advisors, who are under a professional duty of confidentiality, if and to the extent to which this is necessary for the safeguarding of the shareholder's own justified interests.

---

[293] BGH WM 86, 1282 (shareholder-director); BGH DB 90, 2588.
[294] § 61, *post*, p. 347.
[295] BGH WM 86, 1282.
[296] BGH DB 90, 213.
[297] § 1 GWB.
[298] BGH BB 94, 44.
[299] BGH GRUR 79, 657.
[300] "Verschwiegenheitspflicht".
[301] § 85.

5. Appropriation of profits[302]

The shareholders decide on the appropriation of profits.[303] Consequently, the simple majority decides whether, and to what extent, profits shall be distributed.[304] Each shareholder has a right to have a resolution passed on the appropriation of profits but – unless this is regulated in the articles of association – he has no right to a distribution of profits, nor to a specific amount thereof. If the majority decides not to distribute profits but rather to plough back profits into reserves, the minority can only object to this if there has been a misuse of the voting power of the majority (a breach of the duty of loyalty).

It may thus be advisable to specify principles for the distribution of profits in the articles of association.

6. Retirement[305]

6.1 Resignation[306]

The life of the GmbH is indefinite unless the articles of association regulate otherwise. A termination of the articles of association is not possible unless provision is made for this in the articles themselves. However, every shareholder may resign from the company if he does not wish to remain in the GmbH,[307] with the result that his interest shall be withdrawn or assigned, at the company's choice.[308]

It is usual to agree in the articles of association that each shareholder can resign from the company with a reasonable period of notice. However, this right is presented as a right of retirement: the termination does not result in the dissolution of the GmbH but rather the retirement of the member terminating the relationship.

6.2 Expulsion[309]

A shareholder can be expelled from the GmbH even in the absence of a regulation concerning this in the articles of association. The Act only specifies failure to pay in the original capital contribution and additional payments as reasons for expulsion.[310] However, the right of expulsion for cause (= if it is unreason-

---

[302] "Gewinnverwendung".
[303] §§ 29, 46 no. 1.
[304] § 47 para. 1.
[305] "Ausscheiden".
[306] "Austritt".
[307] BGH ZIP 92, 237.
[308] The statutory protection of capital must be observed, § 30. If, in accordance therewith, the purchase or the withdrawal are not possible, dissolution is the only remaining answer, § 61; *post*, p. 347.
[309] "Ausschließung".
[310] §§ 21, 28 para. 1.

able to expect the remaining shareholders to continue the GmbH with him) is recognised even without the need for a regulation in the articles of association.

Nevertheless, it is expedient and usual to make provision in the articles of association for the exclusion of a shareholder and the withdrawal of his share for important reasons associated with him personally[311] (e.g. where a share in the company is mortgaged or a shareholder becomes insolvent). The GmbH can then bring an action for expulsion on the basis of a shareholders' resolution with a three quarters majority.[312] The party to be excluded may not participate in the voting on this resolution. The exclusion comes into effect as soon as the judgment becomes legally binding. The judgment must also specify the settlement to be paid. Disposal of the share in the company held by the expelled party must be secured through withdrawal or assignment.

6.3 Withdrawal and compulsory assignment[313]

A shareholder can also be expelled by the compulsory withdrawal of his share in the company. The withdrawal is only permissible if provision was already made for it in the articles of association at the time the membership was acquired[314] or was subsequently included in the articles of association with the consent of all owners of shares who might be affected. The resolution on withdrawal leads to the destruction of the share in the company and thus of the owner's right of membership.[315]

Withdrawal can have the following effect on the share capital and the remaining shares:

- the share capital remains unchanged and is higher than the nominal capital of the remaining shares;
- the withdrawal can be linked to a reduction of the share capital,[316] which shall be notarially recorded and for the registration of which an application must be made;[317]
- the nominal amounts of the remaining shares in the company are increased; or
- new shares are issued to replace the shares in the company which have been withdrawn.

Instead of withdrawal, the articles of association may also make provision that, under the same preconditions, the shareholders' meeting may resolve that the party affected shall be obliged to assign his share to co-shareholders or to third parties; furthermore, the articles of association can empower the company or

---

[311] BGHZ 16, 317, 322 *et seq.*; 80, 346, 351 *et seq.*
[312] BGHZ 9, 157, 177.
[313] "Einziehung".
[314] § 34 para. 2.
[315] BGH NJW 83, 2880; GmbHR 91, 362; OLG Karlsruhe GmbHR 85, 362.
[316] § 58.
[317] *Post*, p. 122.

the shareholders' meeting to effect the assignment itself or themselves, exempting it or them from the prohibition on self-dealing.[318]

7. Credit balance in case of partition[319]

7.1 Statutory right to a settlement

According to the statutory regulation concerning settlements,[320] a shareholder who is leaving the company "shall be paid what he would receive upon partition if the company were to be dissolved at the time of his retirement". Although this wording would suggest the assumption of fictitious liquidation values,[321] the statutory claim is quantified by the actual value of the living enterprise; in principle, this corresponds to the price which would be obtained if the enterprise were sold as a whole. The statutory settlement is thus based on the full value of the enterprise, including the value of the business as a going concern (goodwill) and the hidden reserves.[322]

Settlement at the current market value is, however, disadvantageous to the liquidity of the company in view of the outflow of capital, and can even threaten its continued existence. It often raises difficult questions of valuation which ususally necessitate the production of an (expensive) expert opinion. The interest in the party leaving the company in obtaining the highest possible settlement is thus weighed up against the interest of the company in a moderate settlement which is ascertained easily. It is thus recommended that the claim to a settlement and its amount be regulated in the articles of association.

7.2 Settlement clauses[323] in the articles of association

Within the framework of the freedom of contract under company law, the shareholders can in principle structure the regulation of the settlement according to their needs.[324]

However, the settlement cannot be restricted or excluded at will. Thus, clauses which lead to a settlement claim which falls considerably below the current market value of the interest cause difficulties. A disproportion which exists from the outset between the statutory settlement value and the claim laid down in the regulations[325] must be distinguished from a disproportion between the two values which only arises at a later stage.[326]

---

[318] BGH WM 83, 956.
[319] "Auseinandersetzungsguthaben".
[320] § 738 BGB for the Civil Code partnership, which applies to the GmbH by analogy.
[321] *Post*, p. 101.
[322] BGHZ 9, 168; 16, 322; 65, 24; 116, 359, 370 *et seq.*, 375.
[323] "Abfindungsklauseln".
[324] BGHZ 116, 359, 368.
[325] *Post*, p. 55.
[326] *Post*, p. 55.

Considerable divergences from the outset

Upon review by the courts, a disproportion from the outset will be assumed if the settlement provided for in the articles of association lags behind the statutory settlement to an unreasonable extent "arbitrarily and lacking any objective justification", in particular if such a far-reaching restriction of the settlement is not necessary for the continued existence of the GmbH. For this reason, the interests of the retiring party and of the company itself are weighed up; concrete information, such as the duration of membership of the retiring party, his part in building up the company, etc., shall be taken into consideration here. However, the establishment of borderlines in detail gives rise to difficulties.[327]

If a gross disproportion exists between the actual value and the settlement value of the share, the clause contravenes public morals and is thus null and void.[328] A settlement amounting to the current market value of the share shall take the place of the settlement for which provision was made.

The relevant shareholder can assert an initial nullity of settlement clauses at any time, e.g. by the so-called proceedings for annulment,[329] which can be lodged against the company. However, the nullity is cured if more than three years have passed since the registration of the articles of association, or changes thereto, in the Commercial Register.[330]

Disproportion arising subsequently

If a disproportion only arises in the course of economic developments, the clause is valid but will be corrected by the court, because the shareholder is entitled to a "reasonable" settlement. The yardstick for the settlement and the amount of the settlement shall then be determined afresh by way of the so-called supplementary contractual interpretation of the articles of association in view of the changed situation as regards assets and earnings, in accordance with the principles of good faith,[331] taking into consideration the concrete circumstances. In this context, the basis of the assessment which was agreed by the shareholders at the conclusion of the contract constitutes an important point of reference: thus, where a book value clause has been agreed,[332] for example, the court must give appropriate consideration to the interest of the company in the continued existence of the enterprise expressed therein, and must specify an amount lying between the book value and the current market value.[333]

7.3 Individual types of clause

The danger of having to pay a much higher settlement close to the current market value by reason of an invalid settlement clause, or one which has been modified

---

[327] BGHZ 116, 359, 375 *et seq.*
[328] § 138 BGB.
[329] By analogy with § 241 no. 4 AktG.
[330] § 242 para. 2 AktG by analogy.
[331] §§ 157, 242 BGB.
[332] *Post*, p. 56.
[333] BGHZ 126, 226, 242 *et seq.*

by supplementary interpretation of the contract, can only be countered by establishing the most precise possible clause which at the same time takes into consideration the dynamic development of the situation as regards assets and earnings of the company.[334]

Book value clauses[335]

The agreement of a settlement at the book value of the interest in the company is very widespread. This is taken to mean a settlement by means of which the shareholder is excluded from the silent reserves and the goodwill, but that along with his fixed original capital contribution on the capital account and any credit balance on a private or loan account, he shall be entitled to a proportion of the profits for the current business year, and to all items shown in the commercial balance sheet or the tax balance sheet with a reserve character, in accordance with his participation quota.[336]

Book value clauses are, in principle, permissible but risky in view of their complete disconnection with the capitalized income value of the enterprise. In order to be safe, it is thus recommended that a percentage of the capitalized income value is laid down as the minimum settlement. Alternatively, the articles can provide that all silent reserves (or all those which accrued during the membership of the GmbH) are disclosed in an apportioning balance sheet at the relevant date of retirement (or on the nearest relevant date), but goodwill remains out of count.

However, book value clauses can also lead to a settlement amount which lies above the proportional value of the enterprise, either because the enterprise has no income, or because certain risks and strains on the GmbH's business cannot be recognized from the balance sheet, such as missing or unendowed pension reserves or the periodic adjustment of company life annuities to provide for old age or infirmity. If a negative trade interest has arisen as a result of losses, the retiring shareholder does not participate in it.

If a book value settlement is decided upon, then a so-called saving clause should be included in the articles of association, which provides that in the case where the settlement regulation is not applied, the will of the shareholders determines the payment of a permissible (minimum) settlement, but at most x per cent (e.g. 50 per cent) of the proportional capitalized income value.[337]

Capitalized income value clause[338]

Settlement clauses which are orientated towards the capitalized income value present no difficulties, as they follow the statutory model of the valuation of an

---

[334] *Post*, p. 96 on the methods of assessing shares in the GmbH.
[335] "Buchwertklauseln".
[336] Also *post*, p. 97. BGH GmbHR 79, 104; 85, 192.
[337] Example: "If the settlement provided for in the articles of association contradicts compulsory law and is thus not decisive, a new permissible settlement shall be agreed which comes closest to it, but which amounts to a maximum of 50 per cent of the capitalized income value".
[338] "Ertragswertklausel".

interest.[339] In particular, it is recommended that the bases of computation for the future income and the capitalization interest rate should be laid down. A settlement which lies a certain percentage below the proportional capitalized income value established in this way usually accords sufficient weight to the aim of securing the continued existence of the enterprise.

Material value clauses and net worth tax value clauses

A lower settlement than one in accordance with the capitalized income value mostly results from basing the settlement on the material value of the enterprise. This is not determined by the purchase price but rather in accordance with the costs which would be incurred in replacing (the economic assets of) the enterprise, not taking into consideration the goodwill or trade interest of the company. Material value clauses are in principle unobjectionable.

So-called net worth tax value clauses assess the settlement in accordance with the most recently established net worth tax value of the share in the company. It is based on an estimate carried out at intervals of three years which combines the capitalized income value method and the material value method (one third capitalized income value, two thirds material value – the so-called "Stuttgart Procedure"). These clauses, too, are usually unobjectionable.[340]

---

[339] *Ante,* p. 54 and *post,* p. 98.
[340] *Post,* p. 98 and p. 100 on the valuation methods and their disadvantages.

Part II

SHAREHOLDERS AND SHARES

Chapter 4

SHAREHOLDERS

Dr. Rüdiger Volhard

1. Duties of the shareholder

1.1 Duty to pay capital contribution

Every shareholder is under an obligation to pay in the capital contribution he has assumed, either at the time of formation or upon an increase in share capital.[1]

1.2 Duty to perform additional services

Other obligations of the shareholders apart from those of payment in to the equity capital of the GmbH must also be included in the articles of association in order to be valid. Such duties are rare. They may affect all shareholders or only individual shareholders. They often constitute the counterpart to special shareholders' rights (such as for example rights of pre-emption or purchase).[2]

Restraint of competition[3] or shareholders' rights and duties of supply and subscription, or payments of money such as, for example, a premium (surcharge) upon the assumption of original capital contributions, also constitute additional obligations.[4]

1.3 Duty of loyalty[5]

The duty of loyalty is of central importance for the determination of the (rights and) duties of the shareholders, both in relation to the GmbH and in relation

---

[1] *Ante*, p. 22. The same applies if the articles of association place the shareholders under an obligation to make further payments in to the equity capital of the GmbH (additional contributions), § 26.
[2] *Ante*, p. 48.
[3] *Ante*, p. 49.
[4] Their subsequent establishment requires the consent of all shareholders who are affected; § 53 para. 3.
[5] "Treuepflicht".

to one another. In particular, it influences the rights of the majority in relation to the minority[6] but also applies in reverse.[7]

The duty of loyalty imposes an obligation to actively promote the company. The shareholder must participate in all measures which are necessary to preserve what has been created; even a positive duty to vote may result from this.[8] Conversely, there is also a duty of loyalty on the part of the company in relation to the shareholders,[9] the breach of which can trigger claims to compensation.

Duties of forbearance and of allegiance are founded by the duty of loyalty, in particular the prohibition on damaging the company in one's own interests. However, a sole shareholder has no duty of loyalty to the company, in so far as the interests of the creditors are not affected.[10] Furthermore, the duty of loyalty is the foundation for the duties in the GmbH group, such as the liability of the dominant enterprise in a *de facto* group.[11]

For the shareholder who exercises decisive influence, restraint of competition follows from the duty of loyalty.[12]

2. Shareholder rights

2.1 Right to a proportion of the profits (and liquidation proceeds)

The shareholders have a claim to the net income for the year plus any profit carried forward, minus any loss brought forward,[13] in proportion to their participation in the share capital,[14] in so far as the articles of association do not regulate this otherwise.

A claim to payment against the GmbH only arises by virtue of a resolution on the appropriation of profits passed by the shareholders' meeting.

The shareholders shall pass a resolution on the appropriation of the profits shown in the adopted annual statements.[15] In the annual statements, the net income for the year can be retained (as a whole or in part), either by being ploughed back into reserves formed out of profits,[16] or if the decision is taken to carry such income forward.[17] In this case, a resolution only remains to be

---

[6] Minority protection, post V.4. BGHZ 14, 25; BGHZ 65, 15, 18 et seq. (group charges); 76, 352, 357 (dissolution); 98, 276 *et seq.* (increase in share capital); 101, 113, 1 (immoral withdrawal); BGH WM 78, 15 (prohibition on damaging the corporate enterprise by the reckless pursuit of one's own interests, even if there is no prohibition on competition); BGHZ 103, 184.

[7] BGH AG 95, 368.

[8] BGH WM 86, 1348; 87, 133 (on the general commercial partnership).

[9] BGH WM 91, 99.

[10] BGHZ 89, 162, 166.

[11] *Post*, p. 262 and p. 263.

[12] BGH BB 92, 2384.

[13] § 29 para. 1.

[14] § 29 para. 3.

[15] § 46 no. 1.

[16] §§ 266 para. 3, 272 para. 3 HGB.

[17] § 266 para. 3 A. IV. HGB.

passed on the annual profit:[18] if no annual profit remains to be distributed, a resolution on the distribution of profits becomes unnecessary.

If the articles of asssociation do not stipulate the appropriation of the profits,[19] the majority shall then decide whether distributions shall be made, and if so, the amounts to be paid out.

2.2 Voting right[20]

The right to vote is the shareholder's most important right to participate in the management. Every shareholder is entitled to the right to vote, in so far as it is not excluded in the articles of association, which is possible. Such an exclusion is also permissible (other than in the AG) if the relevant shareholder is not granted preference upon the distribution of profits.

The voting power is determined in accordance with the participation in the share capital; usually, one vote is granted for every DM 100 of a share. The creation of multiple voting rights is permissible, as is the restriction of the voting right to a maximum number.[21]

2.3 Right to information and right of inspection[22]

Every shareholder has a claim to information concerning matters of the GmbH.[23] The right to information is vested in the individual shareholder, whether or not he has voting rights.

The managing directors have to provide information upon request. The shareholder must clarify his need for information, and must give his reasons for the request for it, thereby demonstrating why he needs the specified information.

The shareholder's right to information is very extensive. In particular, he has the right to all information which relates to his interest in the control, profits and assets of the GmbH. This includes information on planning, research and development in connection with the GmbH. It would also include information on the organisation, the personnel, the pension scheme and the tax affairs of the GmbH. Information can also be obtained on the risks relating to contracts, loans or guarantees. The right to information can extend to requiring information on associated companies, be they subsidiary or controlling companies.

The right of inspection includes not only the right to inspect books and accounts, but also the right to examine technical computer records, such as, for example, software and microfilm.

The information or the access for inspection must be given without unreasonable delay. It can be given orally or in writing, or in whatever form is considered

---

[18] § 268 para. 1.
[19] *Ante*, p. 52.
[20] "Stimmrecht".
[21] *Post*, p. 70 and p. 71 on prohibitions on voting and duties of voting.
[22] "Auskunfts- und Einsichtsrecht".
[23] § 51a.

appropriate. However, it may only be given orally (other than in a shareholders' meeting) if the shareholder demanding the information agrees. Reasonable technical assistance must be given to a shareholder inspecting the GmbH's accounts and records if requested.

The shareholder is under a duty of confidentiality with regard to the information obtained.[24] The managing directors may refuse to furnish such information and to permit such inspection if it is to be feared that the shareholder will use such information or inspection for purposes that do not to refer the company's objectives, and will inflict a disadvantage on the GmbH or an associated enterprise.[25] Such refusal requires a resolution of the shareholders. If the managing directors intend to refuse information, they must call an extraordinary shareholders' meeting or obtain a written resolution of all the shareholders. The shareholder requesting the information is not permitted to vote on this matter.

The managing directors can refuse to give information, even without a shareholders' resolution, if there is a prohibition (with or without penalties) against releasing such information, e.g. the information is protected by the Data Protection Act,[26] or because it simply does not have the information and it would be unreasonable to obtain it either on legal or practical grounds. The information may also be governed by a secrecy agreement with a third party. The directors may likewise consider the request for the information to be unreasonable because of the disproportionate effort required to obtain it.

A shareholder who has been refused information for which a request was made or has been refused a right of inspection is entitled to apply to the court.[27]

2.4 Rights of action

Apart from the shareholders' right of action against resolutions which are contrary to the articles of association or which are illegal,[28] each shareholder also has the right to pursue claims to which he is entitled against the GmbH with court assistance.

It is unclear whether the shareholder can also assert claims of the GmbH against co-shareholders, against managing directors or against third parties if the managing directors forbear from doing so. In particular, it is disputed whether every shareholder can pursue claims arising out of breaches of duty on the part of the managing director by an action for payment to the GmbH ("*actio pro socio*"), or whether a shareholders' resolution is necessary for this. At all events, the case-law permits actions of the shareholders irrespective of a resolution of the shareholders' meeting in the case where, in a GmbH with two

---

[24] *Ante*, p. 51.
[25] § 51a para. 2.
[26] "Bundesdatenschutzgesetz".
[27] § 51b GmbHG in conjunction with § 132 AktG; *post*, p. 336 on the shareholder's rights in case of bankruptcy.
[28] *Post*, p. 74 and p. 272.

shareholders, claims of the GmbH against the other shareholders are concerned,[29] or if, as a result of the balance of power within the GmbH, it cannot be expected that the management will assert a claim for compensation, and it would thus be unreasonable to expect the shareholder affected to pursue such an indirect route in first forcing the company to assert the claim to compensation.[30]

2.5 Special rights[31] of shareholders

A shareholder may only assert special rights which are not intended to be placed at the disposal of the majority if such rights are recorded in the articles of association.[32]

Otherwise, they can be adversely affected or removed by a resolution of the shareholders with a simple majority.[33] If an alteration of the articles of association is necessary for this, then the consent of the party affected is also necessary, as long as the core area of the membership is not affected, which cannot be encroached upon even with the consent of the shareholder.[34]

3. Possible shareholders

Any individual, legal person or partnership can become a shareholder of the GmbH, irrespective whether it is German or foreign. Officers of the GmbH can be shareholders.

---

[29] BGHZ 65, 15, 21.
[30] BGH WM 82, 928; BGH NJW 90. 2627; OLG Düsseldorf ZIP 94, 619.
[31] "Sonderrechte".
[32] Such as, for example, multiple voting rights, the right to management or to the appointment of members of the management or the supervisory board, in particular claims to payment or supervisory powers.
[33] § 47.
[34] *Post*, p. 73.

Chapter 5

RESOLUTIONS OF THE SHAREHOLDERS

Dr. Rüdiger Volhard

A distinction must be made between the individual rights of the shareholders and the rights of the shareholders' meeting as a collective organ of the company. If no provision is made for an advisory council or a supervisory board,[35] then the shareholders' meeting and the managing directors are the only organs of the company. The shareholders' meeting, as a meeting of the members and owners of the GmbH, is the more important organ, taking precedence over the managing directors.

1. General

The shareholders' meeting is responsible for all matters of the GmbH which are not conferred on the managing directors or the optional supervisory board by the articles of association, or which are incumbent upon the compulsory supervisory board in accordance with statute,[36] or in so far as individual shareholders or shareholders-directors[37] are not granted special rights in accordance with the articles of association.[38] By law, the following are in particular subject to the determination of the shareholders:

- adoption of the annual statements[39] and the appropriation of profits;[40]
- the appointment and dismissal of the managing directors, their supervision and the formal approval of their activities;[41]

---

[35] *Post*, chapter 12.
[36] *Ante*, p. 25.
[37] I.e. Shareholders being managing directors.
[38] *Ante*, p. 19.
[39] "Feststellung des Jahresabschlusses".
[40] "Gewinnverwendung"; § 46 no. 1.
[41] § 46 nos. 5 and 6.

- the decision on the appointment of procurators (Prokuristen) and author-ized agents[42] (they are appointed and dismissed by the managing directors);
- the selection of an auditor;[43]
- the assertion of claims for compensation of the GmbH against the manag-ing directors and the legal representation in court of the GmbH as against them;[44]

and the shareholders are in addition, naturally, also responsible for all "basic resolutions", such as for:

- the alteration of the articles of association,[45] in particular for increases or reductions in capital;[46]
- the consent to transformations;[47]
- the consent to intercompany agreements;[48] and
- the passing of resolutions on the dissolution of the GmbH.[49]

The articles of association may reserve further tasks to the shareholders, and can in particular specify that their consent is a requirement for certain manage-ment measures. Usually this is only significant for the internal relationship[50] by reason of the unlimited nature of the representative authority.[51] Within the framework created by statute, by the articles of association[52] and possibly the barriers resulting from the service agreements, the shareholders can issue instructions to the managing directors. In complying with such instructions, the managing directors can at the most be liable to the company's creditors but not to the shareholders.[53]

By contrast with the shareholders of an AG, the shareholders' meeting can take decisions on all management matters and can issue instructions to the managing directors. However, the articles of association must leave the manag-ing directors a "basic stock of their own substantive decisions in questions of business management". The duties placed upon managing directors with regard to the maintenance of capital,[54] the Commercial Register and the public interest cannot be taken away from them. These duties include, i.e. the require-ment to keep accounts, the duty to prepare annual statements and the obligation to file a bankruptcy petition.

---

[42] § 46 no. 7, § 35 para. 1.
[43] § 318 para. 1 HGB.
[44] § 46 no. 8.
[45] § 53.
[46] §§ 55, 56 and 58.
[47] *Post*, chapter 18.
[48] *Post*, p. 259.
[49] § 60.
[50] § 37.
[51] *Post*, p. 139 and p. 160.
[52] § 45.
[53] § 43 para. 3.
[54] § 43 para. 3.

2. Adoption of resolutions

Resolutions are adopted by the casting of votes which is a declaration of intent requiring receipt. It becomes effective, and thus irrevocable, once the relevant votes are cast in the meeting, or otherwise upon receipt.[55]

2.1 Quorum

A meeting of the shareholders which has been properly called[56] can pass resolutions on all matters, irrespective of the number of shareholders present, provided that the resolutions were notified at least three days in advance together with the announcement of the meeting, by means of registered letter.[57]

However, further preconditions for a quorum are usually laid down in the articles of association, such as a minimum proportion of the represented share capital and longer notice periods for the calling of meetings.[58]

2.2 Majority requirements

The majority necessary for the adoption of a resolution is dependent on its subject-matter. In general, a simple majority of the votes cast is decisive in all matters concerning the GmbH.[59] The articles of association can stipulate a larger majority.

Any person not present does not count. Representation is permitted but requires a written power of attorney.[60] The articles of association can provide for a restriction stipulating that representation is only permissible by other shareholders or by persons who are placed under a professional duty of confidentiality.

Fundamental resolutions, in particular alterations to the articles of association, require a qualified majority (three quarters of the votes cast). In addition, they must be notarially recorded.[61]

The consent of all shareholders, including that of those who do not take part in the adoption of the resolution, is necessary for the alteration of the purpose of the company, and the consent of every shareholder affected is necessary for encroachment upon or revocation of special rights.[62] Moreover, such consent shall be necessary for all resolutions which constitute a serious infringement on membership rights and thus also adversely affect the value of the shares.[63]

---

[55] § 130 BGB.
[56] §§ 49-51.
[57] § 51.
[58] *Ante*, p. 45 and p. 46.
[59] § 47 para. 1.
[60] § 47 para. 3.
[61] § 53 para. 2. However, the dissloution order is only subject to this requirement if the dissolution takes place at a time at which, in accordance with the articles of association, the GmbH could not be terminated.
[62] § 35 BGB; similarly § 53 para. 3.

2.3 Power of attorney for voting rights

The right to vote can in principle also be exercised by an authorized proxy. However, it is often stipulated in the articles of association that only co-shareholders or relatives of a shareholder may be granted such authorization, and that authorized proxies must prove their identify with a written power of attorney.

As the right to vote cannot be separated from the business interest, the grant of an irrevocable power of attorney for the right to vote, with a waiver of the right to vote by the grantor of the power of attorney, will be viewed as impermissible. By contrast, an irrevocable power of attorney which does not involve displacement is permissible. The shareholder can frustrate the acts of his proxy by appearing and voting in the shareholders' meeting. If a "spin-off of voting rights" is nevertheless required, this can be achieved indirectly through the articles of association permitting the creation of shares without voting rights, and those with multiple voting rights.

2.4 Prohibitions on voting (exclusion of the right to vote)

In order to keep resolutions free of special influences which may result from the individual shareholders' own interests, there are statutory prohibitions on voting in the case of resolutions by means of which a shareholders's activities as managing director are to be formally approved, or by which he is to be exempted from an obligation to the GmbH, or which relate to a legal transaction or a legal dispute with him.[64] No one shall be the judge of his own cause. In addition, shareholders with conflicting interests may not participate.[65]

A distinction is drawn between legal transactions in which the shareholder acts quasi as "a third party" in relation to the GmbH ("individual legal transactions") and those in which the shareholder asserts his membership rights ("special legal transactions"). Where the latter so-called "company-internal" transactions are concerned, the prohibition on voting does not generally apply.[66]

It does not apply, i.e. to the appointment of members of organs. Thus, the shareholder may also vote on his own appointment and dismissal as a managing director,[67] and on his dismissal or the termination of his contract of employment. This does not apply if dismissal or termination are for cause.[68] He may not vote in a vote to expel him from the company, but can vote on the adoption

---

[63] *Post*, p. 72.
[64] § 47 para. 4.
[65] BGHZ 80, 69.
[66] BGH DB 74, 621; DB 77, 342.
[67] BGHZ 18, 205, 210; 51, 209, 216.
[68] BGHZ 34, 371; NJW 69, 1483; NJW 87, 1889. For the exclusion of the right to vote in the case of dismissal, the mere assertion of cause is sufficient, unless the GmbH consists of two shareholders holding equal interests, BGHZ 86, 177, 181 *et seq.*

of a resolution on the withdrawal of a share or the termination of membership as long as the articles of association do not provide otherwise (as is often the case), and on consent to the assignment of his share.[69]

Votes cast contrary to a prohibition are null and void. If they were relevant for the result of the voting, then the resolution shall be declared null and void in response to an action for a declaratory judgment. As for the rest, the consequences are controversial.[70]

2.5 Voting duties

The right to vote is a shareholder's right. Generally, it is left up to him whether he exercises the right and for what purpose, as long as he is not obliged to vote in a certain way[71] on the basis of the articles of association,[72] or by reason of a voting trust agreement. By the application of law, a duty to vote will only be assumed under very narrow preconditions and as an exceptional case.[73]

In particular at times of financial crisis, the question is raised as to whether shareholders are under an obligation to participate in an increase in capital. In principle, the obligation of the shareholder in a GmbH is restricted to his duty to pay in his original capital contribution. Apart from exceptions in the foundation and establishment phase, he is not personally liable for the debts of the GmbH.[74] Additional contributions must only be paid if the articles of association so stipulate.[75] Every increase in the duties to make payment requires the consent of all participating shareholders.[76]

The shareholder may have to consent to the capital measure as such by reason of the duty of loyalty in order not to "prevent a sensible restructuring of the company which is desired by the majority – including a reduction of equity capital forming a part of the capital reconstruction concept – for reasons of self-interest".[77]

Nevertheless, he is not obliged to make further capital contributions by a resolution to increase the share capital. At his discretion, he can commit himself to this if he is permitted to assume an original capital contribution of the increased capital and also actually takes over this share.[78]

---

[69] BGJU 9, 157; 48, 163, 167.
[70] *Post*, p. 272 for the possibilities of legal remedies.
[71] *Post*, p. 72.
[72] E.g. in the case of rights of *nominatio* held by other shareholders.
[73] BGHZ 44, 40, 41 (increase of the remuneration for activities paid to a shareholder as managing director of a general commercial partnership); BGHZ 64, 253, 258 (exclusion of a shareholder from a limited partnership (KG)); BGH WM 85, 195 (duty of consent in the publicly held limited partnership, with further references); BGH NJW 85, 974 (consent to a moratorium).
[74] § 13 para. 2.
[75] §§ 26 *et seq.*
[76] § 53 para. 3.
[77] BGHZ 129, 136.
[78] § 55.

2.6 Form of the minutes of the shareholders' meeting

The minutes of the shareholders' meeting must only be notarially recorded in the case of an alteration to the articles of association.[79] Other resolutions must only be recorded in writing if they must be submitted to the Commercial Register.

3. Voting agreements[80]

The shareholders can validly place themselves under an obligation (e.g. by a pooling agreement) only to cast their votes in agreement with other shareholders (with consent after a ballot among the partners). The fulfilment of such duties is enforceable.[81] It is disputed whether such a voting agreement can be validly entered into in relation to third parties (such as lenders, beneficiaries to a fiduciary agreement, usufructuaries).

The breach of a contractual obligation gives rise to a duty to pay compensation, but the casting of the vote is only invalid and the resolution thus voidable, if all shareholders have committed themselves reciprocally in this way.[82]

4. Protection of the minority

In principle, the simple majority of the votes cast is decisive.[83] A qualified majority, or the consent of all shareholders, is only required by law in important matters.

This protection of the minority has been extended or supplemented by the following regulations, in accordance with which – apart from the purpose of the articles of association, compulsory law and good public morals – barriers to the controlling authority of the will of the majority above all emerge from the principle of equal treatment and the duties of loyalty (to the GmbH and the minority shareholders).

4.1 Equal treatment

Given the same preconditions, all shareholders have a claim to equal treatment.[84] No one may arbitrarily suffer a disadvantage without his consent. Thus, differ-

---

[79] § 53 para. 2.

[80] "Stimmbindungsverträge".

[81] For example, by a claim to the provision of a declaration of intent which is considered as having been furnished once the judgment becomes binding and non-appealable in law (§ 894 ZPO; BGHZ 48, 163; BayObLG BB 86, 484; OLG Koblenz, NJW 86, 1692.

[82] Likewise, if provision is made for the duty in the articles of association; BGH NJW 83, 1910; 87, 1890; established case-law.

[83] BGHZ 48, 163, 167.

[84] This is expressly regulated for the public limited company by § 53a AktG. As far as the GmbH is concerned, a series of individual provisions are based on this principle: §§ 19 para. 1, 24, 26 paras 2 and 3, 31 para. 3, 47 para. 2, 72.

entiations which are not objective are forbidden. Likewise, it is usually prohibited to take into consideration personal relationships outside the company.

In particular, the right to equally subscribe to shares in the event of increases in capital results from the duty of equal treatment. In accordance therewith, every shareholder has a claim to assume a new share in accordance with his participation quota upon an increase in equity capital. The exclusion of this subscription right, for example in order to be able to take on new shareholders or to enable a subscriber to pay in contributions in kind which the old shareholders cannot, is an encroachment on the membership and shall only be permissible against the will of the shareholders affected if it is necessary in the interests of the GmbH, and is proper and is proportional (i.e. cannot be replaced by a less drastic measure).[85]

This situation may arise if the GmbH needs economic assets which it cannot buy but can only obtain through contributions in kind, or if the co-operation with another enterprise or the inclusion of a new (majority) shareholder for the purpose of capital reconstruction shall be made possible through the exclusion of the subscription rights.

4.2 Core area of membership[86]

The so-called core area of the membership within the control of the majority includes the right to convene meetings,[87] the right to information,[88] the right to retire from the company for cause,[89] the right to bring an action for rescission or proceedings for annulment[90] and the right to participate in meetings of the shareholders. Encroachments on this core area will be viewed as null and void, even if the shareholder consents to them; a provision in the articles of association with such contents would likewise be null and void.

"Basic membership rights"[91] are distinguished from the core area rights described above. Such basic membership rights are disposable with the consent of the party affected. However, this consent is only required for direct encroachments, e.g. on voting rights, profit shares, settlement, and also through the introduction of withdrawal, creation of added difficulties in the event of sale or inheritance, or restriction of the settlement. Such resolutions are provisionally invalid without the consent of the shareholder affected.

Mere indirect encroachments (e.g. the alteration of the profit share, which results from an increase or decrease in capital) do not fall within the control of the majority. The legality of the resolutions passed by the majority can be reviewed in this instance through an action for rescission.

---

[85] For a stock corporation: BGHZ 71, 40; 83, 319.
[86] "Kernbereich der Mitgliedschaft".
[87] § 50.
[88] § 51a.
[89] *Ante*, p. 52.
[90] *Post*, p. 272.
[91] "Grundmitgliedschaftsrechte".

4.3 Protection from takeover

In practice, shares in a GmbH cannot be sold at will. The articles of association normally provide that the assignment requires the consent of the company (represented by the managing directors) or the shareholders' meeting in order to be valid (so-called restriction of transferability).[92] In addition, the minority shareholders can protect themselves from takeovers if they require the inclusion in the articles of association of relevant rules upon the creation or purchase of shares:

- the articles of association may provide that shares can only be transferred with the consent of all shareholders;
- alternatively, it is possible to take the decision with a (simple or qualified) majority, but to exclude the vendor shareholder from the voting on the consent to the sale by means of the articles of association;[93]
- the introduction of a maximum voting right in accordance with the articles of association can (at least initially) make the acquisition of a share less attractive, because the purchaser cannot (immediately) achieve his objectives or it is at any rate made more difficult to achieve the majority necessary for the consent to the sale;
- restraint of competition in the articles of association can at least stand in the way of the participation of a competitor.

The consent of all shareholders of the dependent GmbH is necessary for the conclusion of company-transfer agreements.[94]

4.4 Protection from other abuse of voting rights

By contrast, the minority is not protected from the majority seeking to achieve its objectives within the the boundaries set within the duty of loyalty[95] and the barriers specified above. Thus, for example, the dissolution of the GmbH can be resolved, against the will of the minority, with a three quarters majority. This does not require any further justification. As long as the majority does not thereby seek a special advantage, the minority is obliged to accept it.[96]

5. Defects in resolutions

The Limited Liability Companies Act does not regulate how shareholders can defend themselves against faulty resolutions. The basic ideas of company law governing stock corporations are applied and a distinction is made between invalidity, nullity and voidability.[97]

---

[92] "Vinkulierung".
[93] Otherwise, he may also vote, BGHZ 48, 163, 167; BGHZ 80, 69.
[94] This view is challenged, however; *post* p. 257.
[95] *Ante,* p. 61.
[96] BGHZ 76, 352 (on the GmbH); 103, 184 (on the AG).
[97] BGHZ 51, 9, 210; *post* p. 42 on the procedural side.

5.1 Invalidity

Resolutions which can still become valid through the consent of the shareholders are provisionally invalid. The invalidity can be asserted by a general action for a declaratory judgment.[98]

5.2 Nullity

Resolutions are null and void, i.e. invalid in relation to all persons, if they are based on particularly grave breaches of the law.[99] These constitute formal breaches (faults in the calling of a meeting, failure to observe the prescribed notarial form) or defects as to content (breaches of provisions which exclusively or predominantly protect creditors, or other provisions in the public interest, in particular such as provisions for the protection of capital).[100]

The nullity can be asserted at any time, but also by an action for a declaratory judgment of nullity which has no time-limit.[101] Shareholders, managing directors and individual members of the supervisory board all have a right of action. The action must be brought against the GmbH.

The defect in notarial recording is cured by the registration of the resolution in the Commercial Register.[102] In the case of other faults, cure only takes effect three years after the registration.[103]

It is doubtful whether the nullity can be cured by the grant of consent to the resolution by the shareholder who is affected by the defect.[104]

5.3 Voidability

All other defects in a shareholders' resolution only lead to their voidability by the assertion of an action for avoidance, which is restricted by a time-limit.[105] If an action for avoidance is not brought, or if it is rejected in a legally binding, non-appealable way, then the resolution is fully valid. If the action for avoidance is successful, the court declares it to be null and void by judgment.[106]

---

[98] § 256 Code of Civil Procedure (ZPO); there are no special features under company law for this.
[99] They are listed in § 241 AktG, which is applicable by analogy.
[100] §§ 30 et seq. Nullity will also be assumed in the case of measures "giving rise to a situation", such as instances of breaking the articles of association with permanent effect (alteration of the articles of association or their formalites, in particular without registration). Ante, p. 000; BGHZ 123, 15.
[101] By analogy with § 249 AktG.
[102] § 242 para. 1 AktG.
[103] § 242 para. 2 AktG; BGHZ 80, 212, 216 et seq.; BGH ZIP 95, 1983.
[104] § 242 para. 2 AktG argues in favour of this since 1994; prior to this, case-law and literature in part took the opposite standpoint.
[105] Post, p. 273.
[106] Post, p. 273. BGH NJW 88, 1844; OLG Hamburg GmbHR 85, 1. On the grounds for an action for avoidance, see p. 155. The avoidance of the resolution is to be distinguished from the avoidance of the voting. The latter follows the rules for the avoidance of declarations of intent (§§ 119 et seq. BGB). The addressees of the notice of avoidance are the other shareholders. Even if the successful avoidance brings down the majority necessary for the resolution, the resolution is not null and void by reason of this; this defect can only be asserted by an action for avoidance: OLG Munich WM 84, 260.

An action for a declaratory judgment on the result of the resolution is permissible in place of the action for avoidance if the parties disagree on the content of the resolution.[107]

---

[107] This shall also apply if there is dispute as to whether a vote was cast in breach of loyalty and is thus null and void: OLG Hamburg GmbHR 92, 43.

Chapter 6

SHARES IN LEGAL RELATIONS

Dr. Rüdiger Volhard and Dr. Arndt Stengel

The share in the company[108] refers to the shareholder's right of participation in the GmbH. It encompasses the entirety of the shareholders' membership rights and duties associated with the assumption of the original capital contribution. The nominal value of the original capital contribution assumed – not that which was actually paid – reveals the proportion of a shareholder's participation in relation to the shares held by the co-shareholders. The share confers on its owner a legal position similar to ownership in relation to the GmbH and its assets.

Shares in a GmbH can pass by means of universal succession (for example through succession on death or transformation), or by means of individual succession on the basis of a legal transaction under the law of obligations.

The share is not physically represented (for example in an instrument) but rather constitutes an "invisible" right to the value of the company's assets. In contrast to stock, it does not constitute a fund for financing purposes suitable for the public capital market.

1. Purchase and sale of shares in the company

In principle, shares in the company may be transferred freely.[109]

1.1 Distinction between transactions under the law of obligations and transactions *in rem*

The legal transfer of shares comprises two separate legal acts which are independent of each other, namely the agreement under the law of obligations and

---

[108] "Geschäftsanteil"; § 14.
[109] § 15 para. 1; *ante* p. 47 on the possible restrictions.

the conveyance *in rem.* This distinction is based on a fundamental principle of German civil law, the so-called principle of abstraction. In accordance therewith, the whole procedure leading to the change of legal ownership in an item to be transferred (chattel, real estate, right or claim) is split into two sets of acts which are independent of one another in the legal sense:

- the commitment under the law of obligations to transfer the subject-matter of the agreement (in particular purchase,[110] exchange,[111] or gift[112]). This agreement does not yet change the position of the shareholder, but rather merely gives rise to the obligation on the part of the vendor to transfer the share to the purchaser. This obligation is fulfilled by the conclusion of a further agreement,

- the transfer transaction *in rem*, which is the "assignment" of the share.[113]

In most cases, both steps are incorporated into one document, but this is not necessarily the case. The (obligationary) purchase agreement and the transfer agreement (*in rem*) follow separate rules under German law.

1.2 Corporate acquisitions

German law offers a number of possible legal structures for mergers[114] and acquisitions, as well as combinations thereof. The structure of an M & A transaction, in particular with respect to cross-border transactions, is usually tax motivated. Not only corporate issues but also the ultimate financing of the acquisition, including additional working capital having to be provided to the target after the acquisition, must be considered, amongst other things to ensure compliance with the thin capitalization rules.[115] The legal procedure can be structured as an asset deal or a share deal.

Purchase by singular succession (asset deal)
The enterprise of the so-called target company is transferred in its entirety to the purchaser by the individual transfer of all material and immaterial business assets, i.e. real estate, chattel, rights, know-how, goodwill, etc.

Two-echelon transaction
Legally, a distinction must be made between the obligationary contract of sale[116] and the various individual transfers *in rem* (singular succession), which are determined in accordance with the rules which apply for the individual business

---

[110] § 433 BGB.
[111] § 515 BGB.
[112] § 516 BGB:
[113] §§ 398, 413 BGB. A future share can also be transferred. The transfer becomes valid with the subsequent registration of the GmbH or of the increase in capital in the Commercial Register; BGHZ 21, 242, 245; BGH WM 94, 2286.
[114] *Post,* chapter 18.
[115] Debt/equity ratios; *post,* p. 131.
[116] § 433 BGB.

assets (claims and bearer instruments by assignment, movable property by agreement and handover, real estate by a change of registration in the Land Register on the basis of notarial agreement, etc.). Each asset (and liability) has to be clearly defined in the purchase and transfer agreement (including its appendices).

The necessity of the individual transfers can make an asset deal complex and expensive. Some legal positions cannot be transferred at all. As a rule, public law licences and permits cannot be transferred; the purchaser has to make a fresh application for them to be issued.

Since the vendor will not automatically be released from his liabilities by transferring them to the purchaser, the consent of each individual creditor is required for the vendor to be effectively replaced by the purchaser as the new debtor. Moreover, if a company has been stripped of all its valuable assets by way of an asset transaction, it must always be carefully verified whether the sale of assets may be considered as a redistribution of the company's share capital: this may lead to personal liability on the part of its shareholders or partners.

If the assets have not been specified with sufficient precision, but rather only vaguely described as the entire business of the company, the purchase agreement is only valid if it is notarially recorded. While an asset deal generally does not need notarial recording (apart from cases in which GmbH shares – as assets of the entity – or real estate are involved), such notarial recording is necessary for the purchase agreement if there is any doubt as to accurate specification, and the entire assets of the vendor are sold.[117] In addition, a subsequent transfer of the assets by way of separate agreement would nevertheless need the assets to be specified individually.

Statutory assumption of liabilities

In general, the purchaser will only be liable for those obligations of the acquired business which he expressly assumes. However, there is automatic assumption of liability by the purchaser of assets of the acquired company by operation of law in the following cases:

Civil law

If all or almost all (approximately 85 per cent or more) the assets of a company or individual are acquired, creditors of the target company are protected by way of an automatic assumption of liability by the purchaser. The liability is restricted to the value of the assets transferred.[118]

Tax law

The purchaser of a business is liable for certain business-related tax debts of the vendor. This liability only arises if the business operations are continued. For

---

[117] § 311 BGB.

[118] The relevant provision of the German Civil Code, § 419 BGB, ceases to have effect by the end of 1998, but remains applicable until then.

this tax liability, it is irrelevant whether the legal owner of the material assets of the business operates the business himself or through a third party on the basis of, for example, a lease agreement.

Joint and several liability is imposed on the old and the new owners for tax debts which have their sole basis and origin in the acquired business operation. This, in particular, concerns commercial earnings tax and turnover tax.[119] With-holding tax on salaries and wages, and corporate income tax, are not affected by this assumption of liability.

The purchaser is liable only for tax debts which accrued within the last full calendar year prior to the transfer of the business. As a result, the purchaser incurs a maximum liability period of two years if the transfer takes place at the end of a given year. Again, the purchaser's liability is limited to the assets transferred.

Commercial law

In every case of acquisition of a business where the purchaser continues the use of the company name, he assumes joint and several liability for all debts of the vendor originating from the vendor's business operations.[120] If the company name is not continued, no liability arises under this provision. The practical rel-evance of this assumption of liability is thus restricted. Furthermore, the parties can agree that no such transfer of liability shall occur, which agreement is valid vis-à-vis third parties if it has been registered in the Commercial Register and has been made public, or if creditors of the company have been informed accordingly.

Employment law

The Civil Code secures the continuance of the individual employment relation-ships with the company in the event of the transfer of the business. If a business or part of a business is transferred to a new owner, the purchaser assumes all rights and obligations under the employment contracts at the time of the trans-fer.[121] The vendor and purchaser are jointly and severally liable. Liability extends only to those employees attributable to the part of the business sold. Liability covers arrears in the payment of wages, outstanding bonus payments and fringe benefits, arrears of pension payments as well as contributions to pension schemes and rights to future pension benefits acquired prior to the transfer of the business. Withholding tax and social security contributions payable by the employer are not covered.

Purchase through the acquisition of a company (share deal)

In contrast to the situation in an asset deal, the enterprise passes to the pur-chaser in a share deal through the sale of (usually all) shares, which the vendor

---

[119] *Post*, chapter 14.
[120] § 25 HGB.
[121] *Post*, p. 195.

holds in a company, to the purchaser. Whilst in the case of an asset deal, the legal entity of the enterprise remains with the vendor, in a share deal the legal entity is transferred to the purchaser. A share transaction is in general much simpler and involves less documentation than an asset transaction, since no individual transfer of title to the company's assets is necessary, but only a clear definition of the shares to be sold and assigned.

The sale and the transfer of shares in a GmbH (both steps, if in separate documents) have to be notarially recorded in order to be valid. This also applies in any situation in which the sale or assignment of GmbH shares is part of an overall, inseparable transaction, in which case the entire transaction needs to be notarially recorded. If shares in a GmbH are sold parallel to partnership interests in a GmbH & Co. KG[122] of which the GmbH is the general partner, therefore, the transfer of the partnership interests usually has to be notarially recorded as well.

1.3 Warranties

The warranties for defects in the shares are governed primarily by the contract on which the transaction is based, as in the case of defects in the GmbH or its enterprise. However, even where there is no detailed regulation in the contract of sale itself, the German law of sale supplies a number of legal remedies for such cases. In an international comparison, it is considered as purchaser-friendly, so that it may well be to the purchaser's advantage to waive guarantee regulations in the contract of sale.

The German law of sale distinguishes between the purchase of a right and the purchase of a material thing (chattel or real estate) or an aggregate of things. The purchase of shares in a GmbH is in principle the purchase of a right. The vendor is liable – irrespective of fault – for the continued existence of the right or for its usual or agreed quality (so-called verity), but not for its economic value (financial reliability).[123]

However, the general view is that in the case of the purchase of one or more shares which constitutes a corporate acquisition when considered from an economic point of view,[124] the rules governing warranty for defects of an aggregate of material things are authoritative, since the quality of the enterprise is concerned.[125]

Warranty for defects of material things is fundamentally different from the warranty for defects of rights: whilst the vendor of a right does not have to furnish a warranty for the quality of the enterprise represented by the shares, the vendor of a material thing is liable, because he is responsible for the present condition of the material thing or the aggregate of things. The warranty for the lack of the so-called warranted qualities is important here: the vendor is under

---

[122] *Ante*, p. 10.
[123] BGHZ 65, 250; OLG Naumburg GmbHR 95, 378, 379.
[124] *Ante*, p. 78.
[125] RGZ 120, 283, 287; 150, 397, 400, 402; BGHZ 65, 246, 248, 250.

an obligation to pay compensation – irrespective of fault – if, at the time the contract was concluded, he gave rise to the impression that he intends to warrant for the existence of particular qualities of the object of sale which were of significant importance for the decision to purchase, and for all the consequences of their absence.[126]

The minium percentage of shareholdings according to which the rules on the warranty for defects in material things apply has not yet been conclusively clarified. However, this ought to be the case where the acquisition of the qualified majority of 75 per cent of the shares necessary for an alteration of the articles of association is concerned, because this opens up comprehensive entrepreneurial structuring possibilities for the purchaser.[127]

If there is no room for warranty for defects in rights or in material things, the vendor may nevertheless be placed under an obligation to pay compensation for breach of pre-contractual duties (so-called *culpa in contrahendo*), e.g. in the preparation of faulty balance sheets. In contrast to the statutory guarantee regulations, the claim to compensation presupposes fault (negligence is sufficient) which must be proven by the purchaser.[128]

1.4 Merger control

The purchase of an enterprise may, as an "amalgamation" of the participating enterprises, be subject to merger control. Indeed, even the purchase of a minority participation in the capital or the voting rights may be sufficient to realize facts and circumstances which are relevant under cartel law. This also applies to real property transactions.

A distinction must be drawn between German and European merger control.

German law
Scope of application
German cartel law as laid down in the Anti-Cartel Act (Gesetz gegen Wettbewerbsbeschränkungen – GWB) applies to every restriction on competition which has a noticeable effect within the country, in accordance with the internationally recognised *lex causae*. This also encompasses mergers executed abroad which affect the German market.[129] According to directives issued by the

---

[126] The BGH imposes strict requirements on the concept of defects and qualities: in accordance therewith, an enterprise is defective if its usefulness as a whole is not given, i.e. its economic base is shaken; BGH NJW 70, 556; WM 70, 819, 821. Information concerning the turnover, the earnings and the earning power of the company, and the amount of its existing liabilities, are not warranted qualities; BGH WM 77, 712; 79, 102; 88, 1700.

[127] The borderline here is heavily disputed; OLG Naumburg GmbHR 95, 378, 379 with reference to BGH NJW 80, 2408, excludes the application of the liability for defects in material things below the 75 per cent threshold.

[128] BGH NJW 90, 1658, 1659; 80, 2408, 2409; WM 88, 1700; OLG Hamburg ZIP 94, 944, 945.

[129] § 98 para. 2 GWB.

Federal Cartel Office,[130] such repercussions on the German market are to be reckoned with if:

- both participants (or enterprises associated with them) were active in the German market prior to the relevant action; or
- the sphere of activity of one of the participants precedes or comes after the sphere of activity of the other, and there is the likelihood that the enterprise within the country will obtain goods from its foreign business partner.

To the extent to which European law is applicable, there remains no room for German cartel law.

Merger
By law, a merger as defined in cartel law[131] is given:

- in the event of the purchase of all or a significant part of the assets of the target enterprise;[132] or
- in the event of the purchase of at least 25 per cent of the shares (or a corresponding participation in share capital) or the voting rights in another enterprise; or
- in the event of the acquisition of an additional stake if it results in a 50 per cent shareholding or a majority.

The same applies to the formation of a joint venture,[133] which is already considered as having materialized under German cartel law if at least two enterprises each hold a stake of 25 per cent in a third enterprise. The provisions on merger control are applicable if the activities of the joint venture will have an effect on the German market. Such effects may, in particular, be expected if there is the possibility that the foreign business partner might have established itself on the German market if the transaction had not been carried out.

Post-merger notification
If the participating enterprises, and enterprises associated with them, have achieved joint proceeds from turnover of at least DM 500 million in the last business year preceding the merger, the Federal Cartel Office shall be notified of this acquisition subsequently. Mergers which have been completed and which only have to be notfied after the merger are dissolved with the issue of a negative injunction.

Pre-merger notification
If the worldwide turnover of one company reaches DM 2 billion or the turnover of two companies involved reaches DM 1 billion each, the parties must notify the Federal Cartel Office prior to the merger.

---

[130] "Bundeskartellamt"; post, p. 280.
[131] On mergers in the company law sense, see chapter 18.
[132] § 23 para. 2 no. 1 GWB.
[133] Ante, p. 4.

The Federal Cartel Office examines in advance whether the merger gives rise to a dominant position in the market or strengthens such a position. In this case, it must, in principle, prohibit the merger. The enterprises affected may lodge an objection to such a decision at the Berlin Court of Appeal or can apply for a permit of the Federal Minister of the Economy.

Transactions which must be notified cannot be carried out prior to the grant of consent by the Federal Cartel Office; legal transactions which breach the prohibition are, in principle, invalid. The implementation of a corporate acquisition which breaches a prohibition is considered as a regulatory offence and is punished with considerable fines.

European merger control

The European merger control is primarily governed by the European Merger Control Regulation of 21 December 1989 (EMCR),[134] if the merger gives the purchaser a certain influence on the target enterprise[135] and is of Community-wide importance.[136] German cartel law is, in principle, not applicable if these criteria exist. A corporate acquisition as defined in the EMCR is assumed if:

- two or more hitherto independent enterprises merge; or
- one enterprise acquires direct or indirect control of another enterprise through the purchase of interests in that enterprise, assets or by contract;

The merger acquires Community-wide importance if:

- the worldwide overall turnover of all participating enterprises amounts to more than 5 billion Ecu; and[137]
- the Community-wide overall turnover of at least two participating enterprises amounts in each case to more than 250 million Ecu;[138] and
- a participating enterprise obtains less than two thirds of its EU turnover in one and the same member state.

In contrast to the German law, the EMCR provides exclusively for preventative control in the form of a duty of notification to the EU Commission. Until the investigation procedure is concluded, the execution of the merger is prohibited, according to the EMCR or the decision of the Commission.[139] The investigation ends with the decision of the Commission on the compatibility of the merger with the Single Market. If the merger gives rise to a dominant position in the market, or strengthens such a position, the Commission will declare it to be incompatible with the Single Market. The enterprises participating in the

---

[134] Regulation no. 4064/89 Abl. L 257/14 of 21.09.1990.
[135] Art. 3 para. 1 in conjunction with para. 3 EMCR.
[136] Art. 1 para. 2 EMCR.
[137] The Commission intends to introduce a proposed measure to reduce the turnover threshold to two billion Ecu.
[138] See Art. 1 EMCR for details.
[139] Art. 7 paras. 1, 2 EMCR.

project may lodge a claim against the decision with the European Court of first instance.[140]

1.5 Tax law and acquisitions

Share deal

In the case of a share deal, the enterprise of the target company passes to the purchaser by the sale of (usually all) shares of the vendor. For tax purposes, it is necessary to distinguish between the acquisition of shares in a corporation and interests in a partnership.

In corporations

If a corporation is acquired, its tax balance sheet remains unaffected. The acquisition of shares in the company does not result in an immediate step up of the assets of the target company, i.e. the hidden reserves of the company are not realized. The company can only continue to claim deductions for depreciation based on the existing book values. The acquired hidden reserves, which amount to the difference between the costs of the acquisition and the book values of the company, can thus not be asserted at the level of the acquiring company in order to reduce the tax burden. This is because the investment in the companies shares does not qualify as a depreciable asset. The purchaser of the shares can only assert the costs of the acquisition of the shares upon a later sale or – if the shares are held in the business assets of the purchaser – by claiming an extraordinary depreciation of the shares to the lower fair market value.[141]

As far as the vendor is concerned, the capital gain resulting from the sale of the shares in the company is not subject to income tax in relation to an interest of up to 25 per cent, if the interest forms part of the private assets of the vendor; in the case of a sale of a so-called substantial participation (a participation of over 25 per cent) out of private assets, the profit from the sale is subject to taxation at only half the average tax rate, as long as it does not exceed DM 30 million.

If the GmbH owns real property and if 100 per cent of the GmbH shares are acquired, the share deal triggers real property transfer tax.[142]

In partnerships

Legally, the acquisition of interests in a partnership is qualified as a share deal. For tax purposes however, the acquisition is treated as a partial purchase of the material and intangible assets of the partnership. At partnership level, the share deal will lead to a dissolution of the hidden reserves through the increase of the

---

[140] Art. 173, para. 4, 168a para. 1 EEC Treaty.
[141] The fair market value ("Teilwert") is the amount which the purchaser of the whole enterprise would fix for the relevant individual business asset from a going-concern point of view: § 6 para. 1 no. 1 EStG.
[142] § 1 para. 3 Real Property Transfer Tax Act – GrEStG.

book values in the tax balance sheet of the partnership. The purchaser can reduce his tax burden by depreciating the acquired hidden reserves in a supplementary tax balance sheet.

If the vendor is an individual, the capital gain from the sale is taxed at a preferential rate of half the average tax rate.[143] The capital gain from the sale of the interest is exempted from trade tax on income.

The sale of an interest in a partnership which owns real property will usually trigger real property transfer tax if an essential proportion of the interest in the partnership is acquired. A proportion of more than 95 per cent is assumed to be an essential proportion.

Asset deal

In an asset deal, the business operation of the target company passes to the purchaser in its entirety by means of the individual transfer of all material and intangible assets. A distinction must be made between the acquisition of the assets from a corporation and the acquisition of the assets from a partnership.

In corporations

In contrast to the share deal, the acquisition of the business operation of a corporation is subject to corporate income tax and to trade tax on income at the level of the vendor corporation. The purchaser capitalises the assets in his balance sheet at their acquisition cost. The acquisition costs can thus be depreciated for tax purposes at the level of the purchaser (i.e. the acquiring company).

In partnerships

The acquisition of the assets of a partnership does not differ from a share deal as far as taxation of income is concerned. The purchaser can depreciate the total acquisition costs which reduces his tax burden. The partners – in so far as they are individuals – are taxed on the capital gains from the sale of their interests at only half the average tax rate. They are exempt from trade tax on income.

Real property transfer tax

If real estate is purchased in an asset deal, real property transfer tax will be triggered.

Combination of share deal and asset deal (combination model)

In comparison with an asset deal, the purchase of shares in corporations (share deal) has the disadvantage that there is no realization of the hidden reserves of the company purchased. Therefore, the company can only depreciate its assets on the basis of the residual book values, which are usually below the shareholder's costs of acquisition. By contrast, the asset deal has the disadvantage that the sale of the business is subject to corporate income tax and trade tax on income to the full extent at the level of the vendor company. The so-called

---

[143] §§ 16, 34 EStG.

combination model combines the respective advantages of the share deal and the asset deal.

With the combination model, the purchaser (a corporation, partnership or permanent establishment) acquires the shares in the target corporation (share deal). Thereafter, the target sells its assets to the purchaser (so-called internal asset deal) and distributes the profits resulting from the sale to the purchaser. To the extent to which the distributed profits from the sale of the assets have been subject to corporate income tax, the purchaser will be entitled to a tax credit on his individual income or corporate income tax liability. This tax credit increases the profit distribution and corresponds with the corporate income tax paid by the target for the profits arising from the sale of its assets.

The shares of the purchaser in the target company are reduced in value by the distribution of profits. The purchaser can thus claim an extraordinary depreciation to the lower fair market value of the shares of the company purchased, by reason of the distribution.[144] The extraordinary depreciation ultimately neutralises the income from the profit distribution at the level of the shareholder for individual income or corporate income tax purposes, because the reduction in value of the shares corresponds to the amount of the profits distributed.

Trade tax on income, however, is not reduced by the extraordinary depreciation by reason of the distribution.[145]

The transformation of investments which cannot be depreciated into assets which are depreciable (step-up) can therefore be realized with the combination model. There is no additional corporate income tax burden because the purchaser's tax credit on the distributed profit corresponds with the corporate income tax paid by the target and the purchaser's extraordinary depreciation neutralises the income from the profit distribution. It is a disadvantage of the combination model that the target has to pay trade tax on income. In addition, the combination model can trigger double real property transfer tax, if the target company holds real property and all shares in the target company are purchased.

Transformation model

The disadvantages of the combination model can be avoided by the so-called transformation model: the purchaser buys the shares in the target corporation so that they form part of his business assets, or he buys a substantial participation, i.e. a participation of more than 25 per cent.[146] Subsequently, the target will be transformed into a partnership by changing its legal form. From a tax point of view, this change in legal form is regarded as a transfer of assets from the target corporation to the target partnership. However, this transfer can take place at book value, so that no transfer profit arises at the level of the target corporation.

---

[144] "Ausschüttungsbedingte Teilwertabschreibung".
[145] § 8 no. 10 GewStG.
[146] § 17 EStG.

For the purposes of determining the acquisition profit of the target partnership, the shares in the target corporation are considered as having been contributed to the target partnership's business assets at their acquisition cost or at book value.[147]

Thus, by assuming the assets of the target corporation, the partnership incurs a takeover loss amounting to the difference between the book value of the assets and the book value or acquisition costs of the shares. This takeover loss is first of all reduced by the creditable corporate income tax of the transferred company. Thereafter, it will be set off by an increase in the book value of the transferred assets up to the fair market value, thus creating additional potential for depreciation.

Example:

The persons operating a business enterprise, A and B, acquire the shares of X-GmbH. The balance sheet of the company provides the following picture:

Assets		Liabilities	
Assets	1,500	Subscribed capital	400
	————	Reserves (EK 45)[148]	1,100
	1,500		1,500

Acquisition costs of the shares in the company: 3,500.

The purchasers transform the company into a partnership through a change in legal form[149] and continue the book values.

At the level of the partnership taking over the company, the following takeover loss results:

Book value of the transferred assets	1,500
– Book value of the shares in the company (acquisition costs)	– 3,500
= Takeover loss (first stage)	– 2,000
+ Corporate income tax credit balance	
$= \dfrac{1,100 \times 45}{55} =$	+ 900
= Remaining amount Takeover loss (second stage)	– 1,100

The takeover loss (second stage) amounting to 1,100 shall be allocated to the transferred assets.[150] The following hidden reserves are meant to exist:

• Assets	600
• Goodwill	500
Total	1,100

After the transformation, the balance sheet of the partnership will thus be comprised in this way:

---

[147] § 5 paras. 2, 3 UmwStG.
[148] "EK 45" means equity which was subject to corporate income tax at a rate of 45 per cent.
[149] *Post*, chapter 18; §§ 190 *et seq.* Business Transformation Act (UmwG).
[150] § 4 para. 4 Transformation Tax Act (UmwStG).

Assets		Liabilities	
Assets	2,100	Equity capital	2,600
Goodwill	500		_____
	2,600		2,600

The corporate income tax credit of 900 will be credited against the partners' (A's and B's) individual income tax or corporate income tax burden. This gives rise to positive liquidity effects.

In the example, the increase in the book values leads to the creation of additional potential for depreciation of 1,100.

Trade tax on income does not arise either at the level of the transferring company (because there is no transfer profit) or at the level of the partnership. It is contested whether the change in legal form triggers real estate transfer tax.

If necessary, the partnership can be transformed back into a corporation. However, the transformation back into a GmbH without a compelling reason is viewed by the tax authorities as an abuse of the law if it takes place within a shorter period than seven years.

The transformation model is also suitable for non-residents, in order to ensure the most tax-efficient structuring of the acquisition of shares in a GmbH. A precondition is that the shares in the GmbH must have been acquired through a corporation, partnership or permanent establishment located within the country.

1.6 Proof of the status as a shareholder

As shares in a company are not notarially recorded, it is not possible to acquire absolutely reliable information about the ownership of shares in a company.

The shareholders of the GmbH are not registered in the Commercial Register.[151] The publicity of the membership is ensured by a list of shareholders which is included in the Commercial Register files, which must be updated annually[152] and which is open to inspection by everyone.[153] However, the assignment of a share in the company must only be registered with the company.[154] It is not necessary to adjust the Commercial Register files, so the position with regard to the shareholders may have changed since the submission of the list of shareholders.

Any party acquiring a share in a business can make the acquisition dependent on representations as to the history of the share. Yet even the submission of an uninterrupted chain of notarially recorded declarations of assignment does not provide absolute security as to whether a person is the owner of a share in the

---

[151] § 10.
[152] §§ 8 para. 1 no. 3, 40.
[153] § 9 para. 1 HGB.
[154] § 16.

GmbH. It is conceivable that one of the assignors may have assigned his share twice. The second "assignment" is worthless in such a situation, because the assignor is no longer the owner of the right, and a purchase of shares in the company in good faith is excluded.

2. Questions of form regarding the sale of shares

2.1 Executory agreement

The contractual obligation to transfer a GmbH share must be notarially recorded in order to be valid.[155] Otherwise, it is null and void.[156] However, the defect in form is cured by the notarial recording of the assignment.[157] The separate notarial recording of offer and acceptance is permissible.[158]

The fact that only one party binds itself (as is the case with an offer) has no influence on the compulsory legal form. The legal transaction also needs notarial recording if it is not directly aimed at the transfer or the purchase of ownership, but rather where the obligation is still dependent on a condition (option). If the creation of the contract depends on the decision of the purchaser to buy, the requirement of form follows from the fact that the vendor is under an obligation to transfer if the right of option is exercised. By contrast, the exercise of the option is not regarded as requiring special form.

A pre-contractual agreement which gives rise to a commitment to conclude a contract requires notarial recording. So does every agreement in accordance with the content of which one party is – within the framework of reasonable economic action – "left with no option" but to conclude the contract for the transfer of the interest.[159]

2.2 Assignment[160]

The assignment of an interest in a GmbH must also be notarially recorded in order to be valid. Otherwise, it is null and void.[161]

---

[155] § 15 para. 4.
[156] § 125 BGB.
[157] § 15 para. 4; *post*, p. 90 and p. 91.
[158] § 128 BGB.
[159] Such indirect compulsion can also result from serious disadvantages which are agreed for the case in which the contract is not concluded. For this reason, an agent's agreement must be notarially recorded, even if it does not give rise to the obligation to conclude a contract, if the principal is intended to be obliged to pay a remuneration (commission, but the name is irrelevant), even if the contract is not ultimately concluded. Such disadvantages are only harmless if they do not go beyond the obligation to pay (reasonable) reimbursement of expenditure (including remuneration for work). Likewise, a "contractual penalty" promise in the case where there is no conclusion of a contract must be notarially recorded in order to be valid, irrespective of the fact that claims can arise from *culpa in contrahendo* even without observing this form.
[160] "Abtretung".
[161] § 125 BGB.

2.3 Curing defects of form

If the transaction giving rise to an obligation has been simply concluded in writing or orally, without observance of notarial form, it becomes valid with the assignment of the share.[162] However, this cure only takes place if the assignment is valid, and, in particular, if the notarial form has been observed.[163]

The validity of the assignment only depends on the preconditions for the assignment of shares set out in the articles of association being fulfilled, and on the assignment of the share having been completely recorded by a notary. For the question of completeness, the transaction giving rise to an obligation remains out of count.[164]

However, the effect of the cure is restricted to the nullity which arises as a result of defects of form. Material defects in the obligationary contract are not cured, even by assignment which is valid as far as form is concerned.

3. Rights in shares

3.1 Sub-participation[165]

Definition

Sub-participation is a "silent" participation (invisible from the outside) in a share.[166] The person holding a sub-participation in a GmbH share does not acquire a joint holding in the share, but rather only acquires claims under the law of obligations arising out of the sub-participation contract. The person holding a sub-participation only participates in the profits which accrue to the share in which he holds a sub-participation, but not in the company.[167]

An open sub-participation can also be formed with the consent of the shareholders, which grants the sub-participants direct rights (and duties of loyalty) in the company. If the duties contained in the sub-participation contradict those in the articles of association, the latter take precedence, because the articles of association form the basis of the sub-participation.

If there is no contractual regulation of participation in the profits, the rules governing silent partnerships shall be applied by analogy,[168] so contractual

---

[162] § 15 para. 4.
[163] BGH GmbHR 89, 194, 195.
[164] BGH GmbHR 93, 106. However, it is necessary for the cure that the parties still be in agreement about the obligationary transaction at the time the assignment is notarially recorded; BGH ZIP 94, 1687, 1688 et seq. A consequence of the cure is that the entire content of the obligationary agreement becomes valid, including its ancillary agreements; BGH NJW-RR 87, 807; BGH GmbHR 93, 106.
[165] "Unterbeteiligung".
[166] *Ante*, p. 12.
[167] In so far as nothing else is agreed, the sub-participation is governed partly by the provisions for the civil law partnership, and partly by those on the silent partnership; BGH BB 94, 1597 on the differentiation from the trusteeship.
[168] § 231 para. 1 HGB.

regulation is recommended. The reasonableness of the share held by the sub-participant is a precondition of its recognition for tax purposes; the established case-law on the silent partnership can be called upon to judge the reasonableness. The duration may be freely agreed; if no regulation is specified, the sub-participation is considered as having been concluded for an indefinite period, and can be ended by both parties through termination.[169]

Once the share in the company is transferred to a third party or the shareholding ends by other reason, the aim of the sub-participation can no longer be achieved.[170] The sub-participation is dissolved by this and the proceeds shall be distributed between the participants.

Typical and atypical sub-participation

As in the case of the silent partnership, a distinction is made with the sub-participation between the typical and the atypical form. If the typical sub-participation comes to an end, the sub-participant receives a settlement at book value; in the case of an atypical sub-participation, he receives a settlement of the "true" value, i.e. also taking into consideration silent reserves. In any event, the settlement may be freely agreed. An atypical sub-participation is given where the sub-participant is treated as if he were co-owner of the principal share (with rights of co-determination).

3.2 Trust[171]

Definition

Any person who is a shareholder in his own name but for the account of another, the grantor of the trust,[172] is a trustee.[173] The trustee is the shareholder, but the trust agreement gives rise to duties owed to the grantor of the trust under the law of obligations, which must be observed in exercising the shareholders' rights.

Trust is usually based on an agency relationship.[174] Trust in civil law is not comparable to the Common Law concept. It is a ficudiary agreement between the trustee and the grantor. The rule of privity of contract applies in that in principle, there is no effect in relation to third parties. "Trust", according to German law, is part of the law of contracts.

Form of founding a trust

If the trustee becomes a shareholder at the time the GmbH is founded, then the trust agreement does not require special form; the obligation to act in accordance with the instructions of the grantor of the trust as far as the share

---

[169] BGHZ 50, 320.
[170] § 726 BGB.
[171] "Treuhand".
[172] "Treugeber".
[173] "Treuhänder".
[174] §§ 662 *et seq.* BGB.

assumed is concerned, and to hand it over to the grantor (transfer the interest to him) if necessary, arises by statute,[175] and no notarially recorded contract is necessary for this.[176]

If the trustee only acquires the share later, either from the grantor of the trust or from a third party, the trust agreement requires notarial recording[177] because in it the trustee undertakes to transfer the share in accordance with the instructions of the grantor.

Trust for personal benefit and trust for the benefit of another

A distinction is made between trust for personal benefit and trust for the benefit of another. Trust for personal benefit mostly serves as security for a loan given to the grantor of the trust, like liens or the transfer of ownership by way of security. It entitles the trustee to draw the emoluments from the share (trust for use) and is thus similar to a usufruct.[178] From the point of view of the creditor, a pledge[179] is often preferable to a trust, because it does not burden him with obligations out of the shareholder relationship.[180] The trust for the benefit of another serves a purpose of the grantor of the trust, mostly the purpose of not having to disclose his position as a shareholder in relation to third parties. In this case, it is a pure administrative trust; within the internal relationship, the grantor of the trust is entitled to the emoluments.

Relationship to the company

The trustee is entitled to the right to vote as the shareholder, but in relation to the grantor of the trust he may not exercise it without consideration for the grantor. The claims of the grantor of the trust under the law of obligations are normally secured in legal terms.[181]

If the trust is agreed on an undisclosed basis, because the grantor of the trust does not wish to appear openly as a shareholder by reason of other legal relations, or does not wish to reveal himself to the other co-shareholders as a party holding a share, then conflicts may arise between his interests and the interests of the other shareholders. The duties of the trustee as shareholder must take precedence. Otherwise, the danger arises that the interest may be withdrawn for breach of shareholders' obligations, or that the trustee may be excluded as shareholder for cause.[182] This must be borne in mind in the drafting of the trust agreement.

---

[175] § 667 BGB.
[176] § 15 para. 4.; OLG Frankfurt GmbHR 92, 368.
[177] § 15 para. 4.
[178] *Post*, p. 94.
[179] *Post*, p. 94.
[180] Namely liability for original capital contributions, §§ 19, 22, 24.
[181] E.g. by granting a power of attorney and anticipatory assignment with the authorization of the grantor of the trust for its acceptance, with the exemption from § 181 BGB (see p. 141). In particular, the trustee is empowered to exercise the shareholder rights, which is permissible as a revocable power of attorney (BGH DB 76, 2295, 2297), and transfers to the grantor of the trust his claims to profit shares, credit balance in case of partition and liquidation proceeds.
[182] P. 52.

As far as liability for original capital contributions, and prohibitions on voting, are concerned, the grantor of the trust, as the economic owner, is treated as a shareholder.[183]

3.3 Usufruct[184]

The usufruct of a share in a GmbH is an encumbrance *in rem* which entitles the usufructuary to "possession and enjoyment".[185] It must be distinguished on the one hand from the sub-participation as a mere contract under the law of obligations,[186] and on the other hand from the trust, in which the owner of the share is the trustee.[187] The creator of a usufruct remains a shareholder and thus owner of the membership rights, which cannot be split up.

The usufruct is created in accordance with the provisions which apply to the transfer of the share,[188] i.e. by a notarially recorded contract.[189] If the articles of association make provision for further preconditions for the assignment,[190] these must also be observed.

It is disputed whether the legal transfer of the voting right to the usufructuary is permissible. The predominant view is that the voting right remains with the shareholder as a right which is inseparable from the membership.[191]

The usufructuary has a claim to possession and enjoyment (emoluments), in particular to the payment of the proportion in the profits falling to the share in the GmbH which is encumbered, but also to a proportion of the liquidation proceeds and other claims to compensation of the shareholder.[192]

3.4 Liens

Pledge[193]
The pledging of a share follows the rules laid down for the transfer of shares,[194] i.e. it requires notarial recording.[195]

---

[183] This is expressly the case for liability at the formation stage, § 9a para. 4 and for contributions by the shareholders which replace capital, § 32a para. 3; BGH NJW 60, 285; BGH WM 77, 73, 75; OLG Hamburg DB 84, 1515.
[184] "Nießbrauch".
[185] §§ 1030, 1068, 1085 BGB.
[186] *Ante*, p. 91.
[187] *Ante*, p. 92.
[188] § 1069 para. 1. BGB.
[189] § 15 para. 3.
[190] § 15 para. 5.
[191] OLG Koblenz NJW 92, 2163, 2165, with further references. An invalid transfer of the voting right to the usufructuary can be reinterpreted as a revocable power of attorney to exercise the voting right. It is recommended that, by way of precaution, an express irrevocable authorization of the usufructuary should be created.
[192] §§ 1068, 1030 BGB.
[193] "Pfandrecht".
[194] § 1274 BGB.
[195] § 15 para. 3.

In so far as the articles of association provide that the transfer of shares is not permissible or requires consent,[196] this also applies to the pledging thereof. The consent to the pledge which is granted once is at the same considered to be consent to sale within the framework of the enforcement of the lien.[197]

The pledgor remains shareholder, retaining all rights and duties attaching to membership. In particular, he remains entitled to the administrative rights, such as the right to vote. He is not restricted in their exercise by the pledge, even in relation to the lienholder.

On the basis of the pledge, the lienholder may obtain satisfaction out of the encumbered share. This is usually effected on the basis of an enforceable title through execution, but the enforcement of the lien can also be agreed without title by means of public auction.[198]

Upon the assignment of the claim secured by the pledge, the pledge in the share passes to the new creditor;[199] upon assignment of the share, the pledge passes to the new shareholder by operation of law.

Levy of execution[200]

On the basis of an enforceable title (judgment, court settlement, enforceable deed), a creditor can levy execution upon the share of his debtor.[201] He can also seize individual rights, such as the claim to profits. As a result of the levy of execution, the shareholder can no longer dispose of his share to the disadvantage of his creditor. However, he remains a shareholder and as such retains the rights of co-determination (in particular the right to vote). The share is encumbered with a lien of execution similar to a pledge.

The levy of execution becomes valid upon the service of the transfer order to the company. Thereafter, the company may make distributions to the creditor with releasing effect.[202]

Satisfaction is obtained by public auction or sale by private sale of the shares on the basis of a court order.[203] However, the articles of association usually provide that a seized share can be withdrawn or must be transferred.[204] The execution lien then continues in (encumbers) the claim to a settlement.[205]

If the creditor has levied execution upon the shareholder's claim to the profits, it will usually be transferred to the creditor for withdrawal at the same time,[206] who can then require information from the GmbH on the state of the existing claim, and can require payment once it falls due.[207]

---

[196] § 15 para. 5.
[197] A part of a share can also be pledged with the consent of the company (§ 17 para. 1).
[198] § 1277 BGB.
[199] § 1250 para. 1 BGB.
[200] "Pfändung".
[201] §§ 857, 829 ZPO.
[202] §§ 836 para. 2 ZPO.
[203] §§ 857, 821, 844 ZPO.
[204] Ante, p. 52.
[205] BGH BB 72, 10.
[206] § 835 ZPO.
[207] § 840 ZPO.

4. Partition and amalgamation of shares in the company

Each share maintains its independence in the way in which it is assumed at the time of formation of the GmbH (or at the time of the relevant increase in the share capital),[208] subject to its partition or the amalgamation of several shares.

4.1 Partition[209]

A share may only be partitioned for the purpose of selling a partial share or for the purpose of dividing an inherited share; this may also only be done if the articles of association do not rule out partition.[210] Partition requires the consent of the company,[211] which must be declared in writing by the managing directors on the basis of a shareholders' resolution, and must specify the identity of the purchaser and the relevant nominal value of the new shares which result.[212] The nominal amount of each new share must be at least DM 500 and must be divisible by 100.[213]

4.2 Amalgamation[214]

Fully paid up shares vested with the same rights may be amalgamated or subdivided afresh by means of a resolution with the consent of the shareholder affected.[215]

5. Valuation of shareholding

5.1 General

The value of a share is of decisive importance when it is purchased, but also in other cases such as, for example, in assessing the settlement due to a shareholder when he leaves the company or if he is expelled from the company for cause.[216] It is also important for the assessment of the money paid upon withdrawal of shares,[217] in the fulfilment of duties to take over a share or for the transformation where shareholders leave the company.[218]

---

[208] § 15 para. 2.
[209] "Teilung"
[210] § 17 para. 4.
[211] § 17 para. 1.
[212] § 17 para. 2.
[213] § 17 para. 6.
[214] "Zusammenlegung".
[215] E.g. four shares of DM 1,000, DM 19,000, DM 15,000 and DM 15,000 respectively may be amalgamated into a share of DM 50,000 or subdivided afresh into two shares of DM 24,500 and DM 25,500.
[216] *Ante*, p. 54.
[217] § 34.
[218] *Post*, chapter 18.

The Limited Liability Companies Act contains no rules for the valuation. It is governed by the aim pursued in the given case (purchase, compensation). Thus, various valuation methods have been developed, which sometimes result in valuations which are widely divergent from one another.

In principle, the value of a share corresponds to the amount which a third party would pay as the purchaser of the share. It is derived from the price which would be obtained from the sale of the enterprise as a whole.[219] Given that every purchaser looks at the expected income in assessing the purchase price, the value is predominantly determined by the income value appraisal method,[220] or less frequently by the material value method.[221] However, the articles of association can, and often do, prescribe a different valuation.[222]

5.2 Book value

According to the commercial balance sheet[223]

The commercial balance sheet says little about the value of an enterprise, as the balance sheet items often lie below the current market value at the relevant computation date. On the one hand, they are limited by historical values (cost of acquisition or manufacture)[224] and are influenced by the effects of building silent reserves.[225] On the other hand, the balance sheet does not show general enterprise risks; the book value usually differs considerably from the "real" value. However, the commercial balance sheet is important if the (proportional) book value is decisive for the settlement which shareholders are to receive.[226]

The book value of the share is based on the stake in the share capital, the capital reserves and profit reserves of the company and a possible profit and loss carry-forward. The silent reserves, the goodwill, economic assets not entered on the assets side of the balance sheet and pending transactions are thus not taken into consideration.

According to the tax balance sheet[227]

In principle, the same applies to valuation in accordance with the tax balance sheet, because the commercial balance sheet is decisive for the preparation of the tax balance sheet.[228] However, the tax balance sheet is considered as more reliable, because the fair market value for tax purposes, i.e. the amount which the purchaser of the whole enterprise would fix for the relevant individual asset

---

[219] BGHZ 116, 359, 370; BGH NJW 85, 192.
[220] *Post*, p. 98.
[221] *Post*, p. 98.
[222] *Ante*, p. 54.
[223] "Handelsbilanz".
[994] § 253 para. 1 HGB.
[225] §§ 249 para. 2, 253 paras. 4 and 5, 254, 279, 280 HGB.
[226] *Ante*, p. 56.
[227] "Steuerbilanz".
[228] § 5 para. 1 Income Tax Act (EStG); so-called principle of relevance.

within the framework of the overall purchase price,[229] may constitute a minimum threshold value.

On the other hand, assets can sometimes be drastically undervalued by special depreciation allowances which are permissible for the realization of extra-fiscal objectives (economic policy, structural policy or regional economic policy objectives).

5.3 Material value[230]

The decisive factor for the material value is the value of the assets of the enterprise, i.e. the assets and operating assets in existence at the relevant computation date. Contrary to the case of the book value, the silent reserves and the economic assets not entered on the assets side of the balance sheet are also taken into consideration, but not the goodwill.

The value is determined by what it would cost to build up an undertaking with the same productive efficiency at the relevant computation date. Thus, the assets and liabilities must be brought into the calculation at the replacement prices on the relevant computation date (so-called reproduction value).

Thus, neither the investments in know how and goodwill, which are often decisive for the enterprise, nor the (future) earnings find expression in the material value. The material value is usually too high in the case of enterprises whose earnings are weak, and too low where enterprises with high earnings are concerned. However, it may be used as an auxiliary or controlling value.

5.4 Capitalized income value[231]

If the articles of association do not provide otherwise, the current market value of the interest is almost uniformly understood as the capitalized income value.[232]

The basic concept behind the calculation of the capitalized income value is the determination of the value of the enterprise according to the cash value of the future success. The future success includes all net payments out to the investor from the enterprise, such as dividends, undisclosed distributions of profits, profits from sale and liquidation distributions.

An indicator of success is the surplus of earnings over expenditure (so called earnings surplus). The difficulty lies in predicting the future earnings: they must include not only recognisable positive and negative aspects of the development of the enterprise, but also the general economic development to be expected.

Lump sum method
Traditionally, the prediction is guided by the results of the enterprise in past years, the average value of which is projected into the future (so-called lump

---

[229] § 6 para. 1 no. 2 EStG.
[230] "Substanzwert".
[231] "Ertragswert".
[232] BGH NJW 92, 892, 894.

sum method). The estimated future earnings are then capitalized by the means of financial mathematics. In accordance therewith, the future results are discounted with the aid of a capitalization rate of interest, based on the assumption that the enterprise will have an indefinite life.

$$\text{Capitalized income value} = \frac{\text{Average result} \times 100}{\text{capitalization rate of interest}}$$

The capitalization rate of interest serves to determine the present value of future results (cash value) related to the relevant computation date and thus discounted to the present. The higher the rate of interest, the lower the capitalized income value.

The basis for the determination of the capitalization rate of interest is the assumption that the long-term credit market investment of the amount received for the interest must correspond to the income to be expected on the basis of the capitalized income value of the enterprise. In accordance therewith, the expected income is viewed as interest paid on the capital employed, and it is examined whether capital would obtain the same income if it were invested in fixed interest-bearing securities in the public sector in the forecast period. Usually, this interest amounts to 7.5 to 8.0 per cent in Germany.

As an enterprise can usually compensate for constant inflation with price increases, a discount for inflation is usually undertaken on this rate of interest, which normally amounts to 0.5 to 2.5 percentage points.

On the other hand, an excess charge may be necessary if the enterprise is exposed to special risks in the future which do not exist if an alternative investment in the capital market is chosen. This excess charge usually amounts to 0.5 to 2.0 percentage points.

Analytical method

As the past results are not necessarily typical for the future, then – in particular in the case of larger enterprises – the estimate of the future success is not based on results achieved in the past. Instead, each individual profit and loss position, and every expense item, is examined separately and estimated for the future. In this way, estimated profit and loss accounts are prepared, out of which the annual income is derived. As the accuracy of these predictions decreases with the temporal distance of the periods from the time of ascertainment, the future is divided into planning phases:

- *Phase 1*: the most immediate future, which can be planned in detail, with individual plan estimates (1-3 years);
- *Phase 2*: Trend expectations and derivations from the plans of Phase 1 (e.g. further five years);
- *Phase 3*: only rough estimates which are usually made on the basis of the final value in Phase 2.

This division is only an example. In practice, often only two phases can be distinguished. The capitalization takes place in accordance with the lump sum method, although it should be borne in mind that each phase must be calculated separately, which presupposes a different computation formula.[233]

5.5 Net worth tax value ("Stuttgart Procedure")

The net worth tax value is the value decisive for tax purposes.[234] It is determined in accordance with the so-called "Stuttgart Procedure"[235] and is primarily composed two thirds out of the material value and one third out of the capitalized income value. The material value here is determined on the basis of the taxable value of the business assets.

The inclusion of the capitalized income value takes into consideration possible excess profits or profit shortfalls; it thus serves a correcting function. However, the Stuttgart Procedure can be unsuitable for finding an objective value, because the tax balance sheet values usually lie far behind the actual value of the assets.

5.6 Other valuation methods

DCF method (discounted cash-flow)
The calculation of the capitalized income value is similar to the so-called DCF method developed in the USA. Under both methods of calculation, future payments are discounted in relation to the relevant computation date, but with the difference that the capitalized income value is based on future earnings and expenditure, whereas the DCF procedure is based on future payments in and payments out. The capitalized income value procedure discounts occurrences which affect net income (credit balances), whilst the DCF procedure discounts cash flows. The difference becomes clear in allowable tax depreciations and provisions. Both reduce the earnings of the undertaking as items of expenditure, but do not influence the liquidity: in relation to the allowable tax depreciations, the liquidity has already flowed in the year in which the economic asset was purchased; provisions only affect liquidity once the reason for their formation actually occurs.

Thus, the DCF method provides a more accurate assessment of the value of the enterprise than the capitalized income value method: the usefulness decisive for the value of the enterprise is expressed in the future excess arising out of the payment flow between the enterprise and third parties, in particular to the extent to which it is placed at the disposal of the owner of the enterprise (e.g. the central management of a group). However, by reason of the widely different

---

[233] For details of the capitalized income value method, see the opinion HFA 2/1983 of the German Institute of Chartered Accountants, WPG 83, 468 *et seq.*
[234] §§ 9, 11 Tax Valuation Act (BewG); *post*, p. 243.
[235] Net Worth Tax Official Guidelines, Sec. 3 to 16 and 73.

circumstances in the USA (tax system, accounting principles, financing patterns) it cannot be adopted in Germany without being modified.

Mean value method

The mean value method combines the capitalized income value and the material value methods with one another. It is based on the consideration that the valuation of a high-earning enterprise solely according to its earnings leads to very high results, but leaves the threat of competition and any losses in income which may result therefrom out of consideration. Therefore, the value of the enterprise should be determined out of the future-orientated, uncertain capitalized income value and the rather conservative material value.[236]

Liquidation value

The liquidation value is the sum of the prices which would be obtained in the event of an immediate sale of the enterprise's assets (so-called individual sale prices). After the deduction of the debts and the liquidation costs, the net liquidation value is obtained. In principle, the liquidation value may only be laid down if the enterprise is actually liquidated.[237] In cases in which the capitalized income value procedure is laid down, it represents the lower limit of the value.

6. Inheritance of shares

Upon the death of a shareholder, the share passes to the heir or heirs, who can only exercise the rights attaching to the share jointly.[238] The inheritability cannot be excluded or restricted. However, provisions may be included in the articles of association which ensure that the share passes to certain persons. The heirs may only partition the share in real terms without the consent of the company if the articles of association expressly permit this.[239]

The articles of association can provide that the GmbH may, or indeed must, withdraw the share upon death. The withdrawal must take place within a reasonable period after the death.[240]

The articles of association can also determine that the heir is under an obligation to assign the share included in the estate to the company, other shareholders or third parties.[241] The assignment must be notarially recorded.[242] The additional consent of the shareholders is not required, even if the articles of association otherwise provide for this.[243]

---

[236] In comparison to the Stuttgart Procedure, the material value is determined according to the commercial value of the assets.

[237] BGH MDR 1986, 919, 920.

[238] § 18.

[239] § 17 para. 3.

[240] For the preconditions of the withdrawal, see *ante*, p. 53; BGH BB 1977, 563; OLG Munich ZIP 1984, 1349.

[241] BGHZ 92, 386, 390.

[242] § 15 para. 3.

[243] *Ante*, p. 47; BGHZ 92, 386, 392.

It can also be specified that the share can be withdrawn if the heirs refuse to fulfil their obligation to assign. The articles of association can also make provision for the implementation of a procedure for the forfeiture of shares,[244] i.e. the exclusion of a shareholder who is not entitled to succession.

Finally, it may be provided that the content of the share alters upon death, e.g. certain special rights or duties, do not pass to the successor.

7. Co-ownership of the share

The share may be held by several persons. The most important cases are the civil law partnership,[245] the community of heirs (joint heirs) and the community of part-owners, which arises because several persons acquire an original capital contribution jointly for co-ownership either upon the formation or assignment.

The co-owners are not each shareholders by themselves, but are treated as one owner. They must thus exercise the rights conferred on them by the share jointly.[246] They are jointly and severally liable for the payments to be made for the share.[247] Conversely, legal acts of the company which the company must undertake in relation to the owner of the share are valid if they are only undertaken in respect of one of the persons jointly entitled, unless the persons jointly entitled have appointed a joint representative and have notified this to the company.[248] Furthermore, in the case of a community of heirs (joint heirs), the legal acts of the company must be made in relation to all the heirs during the first month after the death of the shareholder.[249]

---

[244] *Post*, p. 107.
[245] *Ante*, p. 8.
[246] § 18 para. 1.
[247] § 18 para. 2.
[248] § 16 para. 1.
[249] § 18 para. 3.

Part III

CORPORATE FINANCE AND CAPITALISATION

Chapter 7

EQUITY POSITION

Dr. Rüdiger Volhard

1. Contributions in cash and in kind

The Limited Liability Companies Act permits both contributions in cash and in kind.[1] Both forms of capitalization are equally appreciated. However, in the interests of ensuring that capital is raised properly, the Act requires that the original capital contributions be paid as they were assumed.

1.1 Contributions in cash

As far as formation is concerned,[2] contributions in cash must be paid in and placed at the ultimate disposal of the managing director.[3] It must be stated that payment is intended to be made for the capital contribution owed.[4]

Payment on to a company account or managing director's account
The transfer to an account is considered as a "cash" payment. The payment is made by credit note. The account holder does not necessarily have to be the GmbH, but the managing directors must be able to dispose of the amount credited. The payment on to a trust account or notarial trust account also releases the debtor's liability to pay his capital contribution. The debtor of a capital contribution cannot set off a counter-claim against the GmbH against his liability to pay.[5] This claim could only be paid as a contribution in kind.[6]

---

[1] § 5.
[2] *Ante*, p. 23.
[3] § 8 para.2.
[4] Subsequent information to this effect is not sufficient, if the amount is no longer at the disposal of the GmbH: OLG Hamburg GmbHR 94, 468.
[5] § 19 para. 2.
[6] § 5 para. 4.

Disposal at will[7]

The capital contribution paid must be finally placed at the disposal of the managing directors.[8] The decisive factor is that the debtor of the capital contribution should no longer have access to the money. Thus, a bank which is itself a debtor of a capital contribution is not released from its obligation by payment on to an account of the GmbH held by it.

If the capital contribution is credited to an account with a debit balance, the capacity for disposal at will is only given if the managing directors may nevertheless dispose of the amount freely, such as, for example, by reason of a line of credit which has not yet been exhausted.[9]

Pre-payment

The obligation to pay the contribution in cash is created with the declaration of assumption given at the time of formation. A further, express declaration is not required, other than is the case with an increase of capital.[10] Rather, the articles of association contain the declaration of membership, which gives rise to the obligation of each founder to pay the original capital contribution assumed therein.

The early payment of the contribution to the pre-incorporation company[11] does not relieve the contributor from his obligation to pay in his original capital contribution if the purpose to which it shall be put is not stated, and the amount paid in is no longer at the disposal of the management when the GmbH is registered in the Commercial Register.[12]

Late payment

A payment made by the shareholder (without consideration) into the equity capital of the company, which is not directly connected with the formation (or an increase in capital), only repays the capital contribution debt remaining unsettled if the shareholder makes the payment with this stipulation.

Disposition by the company of claims to capital contributions (in particular set-off)

The assignment (and also the levy of execution) of claims to original capital contributions is not permissible[13] unless the company receives full consideration in return.[14]

In contrast to the prohibition on set-off by the shareholders,[15] the set-off by the GmbH of the claim to the capital contribution against the counter-claim of

---

[7] "Freie Verfügung".
[8] § 8 para. 2.
[9] BGHZ 96, 231, 241; 113, 335; NJW 91, 226.
[10] *Post*, p. 119.
[11] *Ante*, p. 26.
[12] BGH ZIP 92, 1303.
[13] Except if the company has gone into liquidation, BGH WM 92, 1273.
[14] BGHZ 53, 17; WM 85, 730.
[15] § 19 para. 2.

the shareholder is permissible in principle, but is subject to restrictions: set-off is only permissible against the claim to the remainder of the capital contribution; the minimum capital contribution (in each case one quarter of the original capital share)[16] must be paid in cash, because it is intended to provide the GmbH with a minimum level of liquidity.

The counter-claim of the shareholder may not originate from the formation phase of the company, i.e. before the liability to make the original capital contribution arose. Such claims may only be paid in as contributions in kind.[17] Likewise, the counter-claim may not have its origins in the transfer of assets, as the party assuming a capital contribution in cash cannot be released from this obligation by contributing assets.[18]

Finally, the counter-claim must also be due, uncontested ("liquid") and above all have full economic value. Full value is only given if the company is in a position to make safe payment of all the debts of the company which are due, which for example is excluded if it is overindebted or only solvent to a limited extent. A claim for repayment of a shareholders' loan which is made as a set-off and which fulfils the function of capital replacement[19] is not considered as having full economic value.[20]

Set-off – which can be declared by one party – must be distinguished from mutual settlement, by means of which both parties agree on the set-off of two opposite claims. Mutual settlement mainly acquires practical importance if one or both claims are not yet due, because this is not necessary, contrary to the situation regarding set-off, which requires that the claim declared by the party wishing to off-set it must have fallen due. However, mutual settlement is only valid under the same strict preconditions as set-off, so there are restrictions: whilst the claim to the remainder of the capital contribution does not have to have fallen due, the counter-claim here must also be due, liquid and have full economic value, so that capital flows into the GmbH. Settlement can thus only serve to avoid payments moving back and forth.

Expulsion and contingent liability

If a shareholder fails to fulfil his duty to pay a capital contribution, then the company can attempt to enforce the claim to payment through litigation, or can initiate an expulsion procedure (forfeiture/withdrawal of shares).[21] After the expiry of the time-limit for payment set for him, a shareholder's share and any part-payments he has already made are declared to have been forfeited.

---

[16] § 7 para. 2.
[17] BGHZ 113, 335, 341.
[18] § 19 para. 5; *post* p. 109 on circumvention in the form of "undisclosed contributions in kind".
[19] §§ 32a, 32b; *post*, p. 318.
[20] A set-off by the GmbH may be permitted by way of deviation from these restrictions if the claim to the capital contribution is seriously threatened, such as if the shareholder becomes insolvent or the claim to the contribution cannot be realised for factual reasons, but also if the GmbH would be harmed by failure to declare the set-off, because – in order to fulfil its obligation to the shareholder – the company would have to spend more than it would receive in return, BGHZ 15, 57 *et seq.*
[21] § 21.

Liability for the amount of the original capital contribution which the expelled shareholder failed to pay attaches in the first place to his legal predecessor, who can acquire the share in return for payment of the outstanding amount.[22] If there is no legal predecessor on hand or if payment cannot be obtained from him, then compulsory sale of the share may be attempted.[23] If no purchaser can be found or if the sale does not lead to the full payment of the outstanding amount, then the former shareholder continues to be liable for the amount of the arrears despite his exclusion.[24]

If the original capital contribution cannot be covered in this way, then the co-shareholders must pay in the deficit in proportion to their shares. Amounts which cannot be obtained from the individual shareholders shall be distributed amongst the remaining shareholders in proportion to their shares.[25]

1.2 Contributions in kind

The Act classifies two different procedures as "contributions in kind",[26] namely the contribution in kind in the narrower sense, in which assets shall be transferred instead of a cash contribution, and the related acquisitions in kind, by means of which the duty to make the capital contribution is fulfilled by settlement with the remuneration for the takeover of assets, which could also be transferred from a third party. The party making the contribution in kind in the narrower sense receives a share in return for it, whilst the party to an acquisition in kind receives a claim of remuneration for the subject-matter.[27] Where the contribution in kind in the narrower sense is concerned, the contributor does not have to pay in the contribution in cash. As consideration of the acquisition in kind, the company owes the contributor a remuneration, which will be set off against the capital contribution he owes. The following is valid for both procedures.

Every contribution in kind must be specified as such in the articles of association.[28] Only then is its payment (if it has full economic value) suitable by way of settlement for the capital contribution debt.

The contribution in kind does not pass to the company automatically once it has been laid down in the articles of association. The shareholder only fulfils his duty if he makes the payment (transaction to perform a contract). The ownership of movable items of property must be transferred.[29] Claims must be assigned.[30] If the transaction to perform the contract must be notarially recorded, such as in the case of transferring ownership in real property,[31] then

---

[22] § 22.
[23] § 23.
[24] § 21 para. 3.
[25] § 24.
[26] § 5.
[27] See § 27 para.1. AktG by the way of comparison.
[28] § 5 para. 4.
[29] §§ 929 *et seq.* BGB.
[30] §§ 398 *et seq.* BGB.
[31] §§ 837, 925 *et seq.* BGB.

for reasons of cost it should be included in the minutes of the foundation meeting of the articles of association.

The intrinsic value must be examined preventatively. The relevant time for the valuation is the receipt of the notification by the Commercial Register. In the case of an overvaluation of the contribution in kind, the party making payment must pay in a contribution in cash amounting to the difference between the stated and the actual value.[32] If the overvaluation is noted by the court, registration will be refused until the deficit has been paid in.[33]

In addition, the shareholders are liable to pay compensation, and the managing directors of the GmbH are likewise liable for damages if they are aware of the overvaluation.[34] The overvaluation is a criminal offence[35] in the case of willful conduct.

If a contribution in kind was made, although it was not agreed, it is irrelevant whether the contribution in kind has instrinsic value. Even if it has the full value of the contribution owed, contribution in kind which was not agreed as such does not release the contributor from his duty to pay in his capital contribution in each.

Undisclosed contributions in kind[36]

If no express agreement has been reached on a contribution in kind, money must be deposited at the disposal of the managing directors. If the latter are intended to use the money from the party who assumed the obligation to purchase items of property or to pay for such items acquired from him, then in reality a contribution in kind ("veiled" or "undisclosed") is made. The contributor could have or ought to have brought the economic asset purchased by the company with the deposited amount into the company himself (as a contribution in kind).[37] The undisclosed contribution in kind does not release the party assuming the contribution from his duty to make the capital contribution;[38] he remains liable for the duty to pay a contribution in cash arising out of the declaration of assumption.

By contrast, it is harmless if the participants already know what the company intends to do with the money before the payment of the contribution in cash. So-called agreements as to use between the contributor and the company are thus harmless if they merely serve to achieve specific purposes of the company and there is no intention to pay back to the shareholders the funds put into the company.[39]

---

[32] § 9 para. 1.
[33] § 9c.
[34] § 9a, possibly also §§ 826, 823 para. 2 BGB in conjunction with § 266 StGB.
[35] § 82 para. 1.
[36] "Verschleierte Sacheinlagen" or "verdeckte Sacheinlagen".
[37] It is irrelevant whether the redemption amount is settled against the amount to be paid in, if the company uses a cash payment (already made) for redemption in accordance with an agreement reached, or whether it first of all repays the loan claim and then pays the cash contribution debt of the creditor, BGHZ 110, 40, 60 *et seq.*
[38] § 19 para. 5.
[39] BGH BB 92, 1806, 1808, with reference to WM 90, 1820, 1821 (on "disposal at will"); LG Koblenz WM 91, 1507.

"Payments back and forth" with a close material and temporal link are considered as an indication of undisclosed contributions in kind. The sequence in which they are made is unimportant.

Consequences of undisclosed contributions in kind

In spite of the payment of the contribution in kind (which may well have intrinsic value), the contributor remains under an obligation to pay the contribution in cash, in particular in the case of insolvency. He can require the repayment of the contribution in kind as an unjust enrichment,[40] as the desired effect was not achieved. However, where the GmbH is bankrupt, this claim is only an unpriviliged receivable in bankruptcy. In the worst case, the contributor pays twice.

A creditor of the company who has occasioned the distraint and transfer of the claim to the capital contribution on the basis of a title for execution[41] can call the contributor to account for the payment of the cash contribution.

Thus, where funds are intended to be used to the advantage of the contributor, the contribution in kind route should always be followed. Case-law tends towards assessing the economic repercussions of transactions between the company and shareholders for the proper raising and maintenance of capital from the point of view of protection of the creditors.

Curing undisclosed contributions in kind

Prior to the registration of the GmbH, the contribution in cash can still be replaced by a contribution in kind by means of an alteration of the articles of association. It was for a long time a matter of contention whether this was still possible after the registration: this has now been recognised by the Federal Supreme Court.[42]

However, publicity and registry control must remain guaranteed through the observance of the provisions for the formation of a company on the basis of non-cash contributions and the provisions governing intrinsic value at the time of the alteration. For this, the Federal Supreme Court[43] requires the following: a report on the alteration of the cash contribution to a contribution in kind, which shall be signed by all managing directors and the shareholders affected by the alteration; the submission of a balance sheet attested by a chartered accountant for the purpose of proving the intrinsic value of the claim to be brought in;[44] possibly the contract on the contribution (or the passing) of the claim; and the assurance of the managing directors that the claim brought in has intrinsic value and has been transferred (or passed) to the company.

If the examination of the court reveals that the value of the contribution in

---

[40] § 812 BGB.
[41] §§ 829, 835 ZPO.
[42] BGH ZIP 96, 668.
[43] BGH ZIP 96, 668, 673.
[44] *Ante*, p. 37.

kind at the time the notification thereof was received[45] does not cover the original capital contribution assumed, registration shall be refused.[46]

2. Maintenance of capital and limited liability

2.1 Return of capital contributions[47]

The amount of the nominal capital declares a "liability fund" which, in the interests of the creditors, may not be touched, but which must rather be covered by the GmbH's assets before assets of the company can be distributed to the shareholders. For this purpose, the nominal capital is entered as a debit item[48] in the balance sheet,[49] irrespective of whether it has been paid in or not.

Deficit balance[50]
The return of capital contributions to the shareholders is only permissible after a reduction in capital,[51] or the withdrawal of shares[52] or the purchase of fully paid up shares by the GmbH out of the assets which go above and beyond the amount of the share capital.[53] The Act[54] prohibits the payment out of assets which are required for the maintenance of the share capital, i.e. of distributions which, if made, would lead to, or aggravate, a deficit balance.[55]

In the case of the GmbH,[56] the distribution to the shareholders of the assets not needed to cover the amount of the share capital is not, in principle, prohibited. However, there is a tendency to protect assets, which is item-related: the managing director may not give away company assets (e.g. machinery, claims, patents) to shareholders, even if the share capital is not attacked, if there is a strong likelihood that the economic collapse of the GmbH would result.

The basis for the assessment of a "deficit balance" is the last annual balance sheet of the GmbH, which shall be projected forward to the time of the payment out. The dominant view is that silent reserves may only be disclosed in the course of this process to the extent to which this would be permissible in the

---

[45] § 9.
[46] § 9c.
[47] "Einlagenrückgewähr".
[48] § 266 para. 3 A I HGB.
[49] § 42 para. 1.
[50] "Unterbilanz".
[51] § 58.
[52] § 34.
[53] § 33.
[54] § 30.
[55] The provision is also applicable by analogy if the nominal capital has already been eaten away, and payments can only be made out of borrowed funds, i.e. at the cost of the company's creditors (BGHZ 76, 335, established case-law).

annual statements and is actually carried out in practice in the next annual statements.[57]

It is contentious whether the management must prepare an interim financial statement on which the assessment of the capacity to make payments out shall be based. If it does not do so, it is not exculpated if it makes distributions against the law.[58]

Protection of the share capital also applies to "normal" transactions with the shareholders. Thus, the payment of salary to shareholder directors, and a management bonus which is independent of profits, constitutes a contravention against the law[59] if the share capital has to be impaired for this purpose, unless the claim to remuneration is reasonable, taking into consideration the economic position of the company.[60]

Managing directors, procurators or persons holding general powers of attorney may not be granted credit out of the assets necessary to maintain the share capital.[61] The grant of security is also encompassed by this.

Transactions whose implementation constitutes a breach of the Act[62] are valid, but the company can refuse fulfilment in so far or as long as such fulfilment is not possible without a breach of the Act being committed.[63] In any case, prohibited instances of performance must be reimbursed to the company.[64] The recipient has the choice of whether he returns what he received or keeps the asset and pays the necessary amount of the difference. Likewise, repayment of (and the payment of interest on) shareholders' loans[65] at the cost of the assets necessary to maintain the share capital is impermissible, and places an obligation on the recipient to reimbursement.[66] If the recipient is not able to make reimbursement, the remaining shareholders are liable for the satisfaction of the company's creditors in proportion to their shares.[67]

Collateral of the GmbH for shareholder obligations

Furthermore, the nominal capital is also protected from the use of the company's assets as security for the liabilities of a shareholder. If a shareholder pays his capital contribution or the purchase price for shares with borrowed funds, he should use his assets as security, i.e. must pledge his shares. Assets of the company may at most be used as security if the claim under a right of recourse, to which the company is entitled in the case of the realization of the security

---

[56] Other than in §§ 58 *et seq.* AktG.

[57] BGHZ 81, 252, 216; ZIP 82, 563, 566.

[58] I.e. in contravention of § 30 para. 1.

[59] § 30 para. 1.

[60] BGH BB 92, 1583.

[61] § 43a.

[62] § 30.

[63] BGH NJW 88, 139, 140; *post*, p. 155 on the relevant duty of the managing director.

[64] § 31 para. 1. Where the recipient acted in good faith in trusting that there were sufficient company assets, this is only so if it is necessary for the satisfaction of creditors; BGHZ 81, 365.

[65] *Post*, p. 134.

[66] § 31.

[67] § 31 para. 3.

against the relevant shareholder, has intrinsic value,[68] and the company receives appropriate consideration for the grant of the security (commission or bank guarantee fee).

The executory agreement and the disposition are null and void,[69] if the parties expressly decide on a payment out to be borne by the share capital,[70] or otherwise knowingly and collusively contravene the law.[71]

Where secured transactions are concerned, it is disputed whether a "payment out" is already constituted by their creation. This is important for the time at which a deficit balance is ascertained.

Given that security is in principle to be entered "below" the balance,[72] the creation of a security is viewed as neutral from a balance sheet point of view. This explains why the creation itself does not yet lead to a deficit balance. If it can already be foreseen, however, that the security will be called upon and the claim under a right of recourse against the shareholder will not have intrinsic value, a reserve fund for the imminent calling to account must be entered on the liabilities side of the balance sheet. This position is not balanced by a claim to recourse against the shareholder since this cannot be entered on the assets side of the balance sheet. The creation of security in spite of an imminent calling to account and the lack of possibilities for recourse thus constitutes a breach of the prohibition to pay back the share contributions.

Undisclosed relocation of assets[73]

In company law, an undisclosed relocation of assets[74] refers to a reduction in assets of the company caused by the corporate relationship or prevention of an increase in the assets of the company, which has an effect on the level of the income and is not connected with an open distribution.[75]

This definition does not require funds to be diverted to the beneficiary, nor an outflow away from the company; it is also unimportant whether the participants subjectively desired an undisclosed distribution of profits, or were aware of it. Shareholders and persons close to them may be beneficiaries.[76]

"Caused by the corporate relationship" covers everything which a prudent and conscientious business manager would not have permitted in relation to someone who was not a shareholder or a person close to the shareholder in the concrete case. In the transactions in goods and services between the company and the shareholders/persons close to them, it is thus decisive whether the

---

[68] Otherwise, there is not only a breach of § 30 but also a criminal breach of trust, § 266 StGB; *post*, p. 168.

[69] *Ante*, p. 77 as regards the difference.

[70] § 134 BGB.

[71] BGH GmbHR 53, 58 following on from RGZ 113, 241, 244.

[72] § 251 HGB.

[73] "Verdeckte Vermögensverlagerung".

[74] In tax law: an undisclosed distribution of profits, § 8 para. 2 Corporate Income Tax Act (KStG); *post*, p. 224.

[75] BFH BStBl II 89, 475; 89, 631; 90, 237.

[76] BFH BStBl II 85, 635.

payment or performance, or the consideration, are reasonable in the individual case when compared with third parties. Particular requirements apply in the relationship between the GmbH and the dominant shareholder. Here, there may be an undisclosed distribution of profits in spite of an exchange of services under reasonable conditions if the agreements are not concluded clearly, unambiguously and completely (especially with regard to the remuneration) in advance, are valid in civil law and have actually been carried out.[77] A shareholder is considered as dominant if he controls the majority of votes for general resolutions of the GmbH.[78]

Under company law, an undisclosed relocation of assets[79] which touches the share capital is always impermissible, regardless of whether anything is "undisclosed". The company has a claim for restitution, which the managing directors must assert.[80] By contrast, undisclosed relocations of assets are not always prohibited under company law if the share capital remains untouched, the principle of equal treatment is observed, and it is covered by a resolution of the shareholders' meeting.

It is also permissible to distribute assets which are not required to cover the share capital (including through the dissolution of silent reserves) to the shareholders if the principle of equal treatment is observed, or if they are in agreement therewith.[81] On the other hand, relocation of assets – if they are prohibited – can constitute a criminal breach of trust.[82]

Undisclosed distributions of profits, in particular, appear in the form of an excessive salary for the shareholder-director (or a salary to be paid with retroactive effect), sales to shareholders which are too cheap (or purchases which are too expensive), unreasonable rents or leasehold rents, the grant of loans with a rate of interest which is too low, etc.

"Own shares"[83]

The GmbH may only acquire its own shares under certain restrictions. Firstly, the contribution for the share in question – including any amount arising out of deficit balance liability[84] – must have been fully paid up.[85] Secondly, the pur-

---

[77] However, if an occupation is carried out by a shareholder for his own account, this is not sufficient to be attributed to the company simply because it also falls within the company's stated object. In addition, an undisclosed distribution of profits by reason of a breach of restraint of competition committed by the shareholder-director presupposes that he takes advantage of information or business opportunities of the company, for the handover of which a third party would have paid a fee; BFH DStR 95, 1873.

[78] BFH BStBl II, 78, 659; indirect dominance is sufficient. *Post*, p. 225 with regard to tax repercussions.

[79] § 30.

[80] § 43.

[81] BGH WM 84, 136; WM 85, 1266.

[82] § 266 StGB; BGHSt 3, 32; 30, 127; BGH NStZ 82, 465; 84, 118. The company is protected, which is why the sole shareholder-director can be held punishable for a breach of trust: BGHSt 30. 127; BGH NStZ 82, 465.

[83] "Eigene Geschäftsanteile".

[84] *Ante*, p. 33.

[85] § 33 para. 1.

chase must be made out of the assets which exist in addition to the amount of the share capital, and the company must be in a position to form reserves in its next annual statements under the terms of § 272 para. 4 HGB out of statutory funds or funds determined freely by the articles of association (profits, profits brought forward, free reserves).[86] The reserves must correspond to the amount of the value of the "own shares" to be entered in the assets side of the balance sheet.[87] They may only be dissolved if the "own shares" are sold, withdrawn or written off as allowable tax deductions.

Other than in the case of withdrawal,[88] or the forfeiture of shares,[89] the share continues to exist after the purchase. However, the voting right attaching to the "own shares" cannot be exercised. The company does not receive the share of the profit to which it would be entitled, but this is rather distributed amongst the other shareholders in proportion to their holdings.

A further sale of the shares by the company is permissible. The managing directors will always be required to obtain a shareholders' resolution prior to the transfer, unless the articles of association do not contain a special regulation in this respect.

2.2 Piercing the corporate veil[90]

The direct calling to account of shareholders by the company's creditors (so-called piercing the corporate veil, or enforcement of liability against the shareholder) is connected with the securing of capital. The term "piercing the corporate veil" refers to circumstances under which the principle of the limited liability[91] is broken through, and the shareholders become liable with their personal assets.

At least where shareholders with a dominant influence are concerned, reliance on the statutory principle of separation of company and shareholders constitutes a breach of good faith in the following cases:

- in the case of so-called asset or sphere intermixture: this is given where private or company assets are mixed as a general rule (and not just in an individual case), e.g. by faulty or veiled accounting;[92]

- if the separation of GmbH and shareholders in the organizational sphere is no longer recognisable, such as because of the use of similar business names. The sole shareholder-director is, for example, liable for pre-contractual fault if his own economic interests are concerned,[93] or tortiously for compensation if he systematically converts the bank credit of

---

[86] § 33 para. 2.
[87] § 272 para. 4 HGB.
[88] *Ante*, p. 53.
[89] *Ante*, p. 107.
[90] "Durchgriff".
[91] § 13 para. 2.
[92] BGHZ 124, 282.
[93] BGH WM 88, 781; BGH WM 84, 475.

the company into comercial credit, e.g. satisfies the bank from the proceeds of goods which have been sold on, but leaves the purchase price for these goods unpaid;

- if the exemption of the shareholders from liability is deliberately used to the disadvantage of the company's creditors, which is, in particular, the case if the GmbH alone must bear the risks of the business activities, but has no chance to reap profits;

- possibly also by reason of unambiguous, considerable under-capitalization. Here, however, the company is entitled to claims, not the company's creditors.[94] The BGH has not yet affirmed this in the case of mere undercapitalization[95] but has often assumed shareholder liability under the (sometimes subjective) preconditions of "deliberate immoral damage" under the law of torts.

In addition, a creditor of the company can levy execution upon claims for restitution of the GmbH[96] and have them transferred to him for withdrawal,[97] even when the preconditions for piercing the veil are not given, and may thus gain access to the shareholder's assets.

2.3 Liability in a qualified *de facto* group

Group liability is not a case of piercing the corporate veil.[98] This concept, which is peculiar to German law, gives rise to a responsibility on the part of the controlling shareholder for the dependent company.

The rules on liability developed in the case-law in a (simple) *de facto* group give rise to a claim of the GmbH to compensation against the majority shareholder if he is responsible for damaging measures; in a qualified *de facto* group, claims to loss compensation also arise. A risk of liability only arises if the majority shareholder acts in breach of his duty; this is a precondition of the qualified *de facto* group. The shareholder must have recklessly harmed the interests of the dependent company in a way going above and beyond certain concrete individual interventions which can be compensated.[99] There is no group liability where compensation for the damage in an individual case is possible.

---

[94] Undercapitalization is construed by some authors as a tortious offence (which gives rise to direct claims from creditors), namely the illegal acquiescence in damage to third parties by the participation of the undercapitalized company in business transactions (liability out of § 823 para. 2 BGB in conjunction with protective statutes in favour of third parties, e.g. § 826 BGB; "social shifting of risk").

[95] BGHZ 68, 312; BGH NJW 77, 1683, 1686.

[96] § 30, undisclosed distribution of profits.

[97] §§ 829, 835 ZPO.

[98] *Post*, chapter 15.

[99] BGHZ 122, 123; *post*, p. 264.

Chapter 8

CHANGES IN SHARE CAPITAL

Dr. Rüdiger Volhard

All changes in share capital are changes to the articles of association and therefore, like all changes to the articles of association, require a three quarters majority of the votes cast and notarial recording. The articles of association can also specify other requirements.[100] The resolution does not require the presence of all shareholders before the notary. Representation is permissible. All changes in share capital – like all changes to the articles of association[101] – must be notified to the Commercial Register[102] and only come into effect upon registration.[103] All managing directors have a duty of notification;[104] they owe this duty to the GmbH.

1. Increase in share capital[105]

1.1 Cash increase in share capital[106]

Adoption of the resolution
The shareholders decide on the increase in share capital[107] with a three quarters majority of the votes cast.[108] The increase in share capital on which a resolution has been adopted comes into effect upon its implementation. This involves:

- the assumption of the capital contributions for the increased capital;
- the payment of the minimum capital contributions;[109]

---

[100] § 53 para. 2.
[101] § 54 para. 1.
[102] §§ 57 para. 1, 58 para. 1 no. 3, p. 120.
[103] § 54 para. 3.
[104] § 78.
[105] "Kapitalerhöhung".
[106] "Barkapitalerhöhung".
[107] § 53 para. 1.
[108] § 53 para. 2.
[109] *Post*, p. 119.

- the application for registration and registration of the increase in share capital in the Commercial Register.

Normally, the share capital is increased by a specific amount,[110] and in return for the issue of new shares. Instead of forming new shares, the nominal amounts of the existing fully paid up shares can be increased.[111]

The new shares must at least be issued at par (at their nominal value). The resolution may provide for an additional charge (premium). This is done where new shareholders are admitted in order to balance out the proportion of the silent reserves attributable to the existing shareholders. The admission of new shareholders or an alteration to the participation quotas with no premium or with a premium which is too low generally does not constitute an undisclosed distribution of profits of the company.[112]

At present, it is not advisable to carry out a cash increase in share capital by the use of dividends as capital contributions for the increased share capital. If:

- the company is in a crisis;[113] or

- the repayment into the company was agreed with the shareholders prior to the distribution of the profits; or

- the distribution is unusually high, in order to facilitate a significant increase in share capital in this way,

then this course of action presents problems from the point of view of the proper raising of capital. Otherwise, the procedure should appear as a cash increase in share capital which is unobjectionable. However, the courts have already viewed the procedure as an undisclosed increase of capital in kind,[114] and required that the dividend claims be brought in as contributions in kind.[115]

Subscription rights

If the statutory subscription right of the shareholder,[116] which is unwritten but nevertheless approved by the case-law, is not excluded, no permission must be given for particular persons to assume shares. In this case, all shareholders are entitled to assume new shares in proportion to their existing participation in the share capital. The right to subscription can be excluded by shareholders'

---

[110] The increase by a maximum amount is also permissible, although very rare: the share capital is then increased by the amount for which new capital contributions have been assumed.

[111] Other than is the case with a stock corporation (§ 182 para. 4 AktG), the full payment in is not a precondition for the increase in share capital. However, by reason of the liability for outstanding capital contributions, a shareholder objecting to the increase in share capital is entitled to resign from the company, LG Mönchengladbach NJW-RR 86, 837.

[112] *Ante*, p. 113; BFH BStBl II, 75, 230. However, if a shareholder receiving favourable treatment at the same time participates in a company participating in the company increasing its share capital, an undisclosed distribution of profit to him comes into question here, BFH BStBl III 67, 626.

[113] *Post*, p. 315.

[114] *Ante*, p. 108.

[115] BGHZ 113, 335; OLG Cologne WM 90, 1385; OLG Cologne BB 94, 1374.

resolution. If those who shall be permitted to assume new shares are already shareholders, they have no right of vote in that resolution.

Declaration of assumption

The assumption shall be declared by the party/parties entitled to assume. This can be included in the minutes with the resolution on the increase in share capital or[117] by a separate written declaration with notarial attestation of signature.[118] Representation on the basis of a notarially attested power of attorney is permissible.[119]

The assumption must be accepted by the company. The "permission" for the assumption in the resolution can be viewed as an anticipated acceptance of their declarations of assumption; at any rate, the acceptance lies in the notification that an increase in share capital has been carried out.[120]

A shareholder-director who has assumed a share out of the increase in share capital requires exemption from the prohibition of self-dealing in order to accept his declaration of assumption (and for the application for registration).

Payment of the capital contribution

The capital contribution for the new share from the increase in share capital should only be paid after the adoption of the resolution and the declaration of assumption. Otherwise, there is the danger that it does not release the party assuming the capital contribution from his obligation to pay.[121]

By comparison, the courts of second instance affirm the settling effect of pre-payments in relation to increases in share capital which have not yet been resolved and assumed,[122] if there is a close temporal connection between the pre-payment and the subsequent increase in share capital, if the purpose of the pre-payment is already clear at the time at which it was made and is verifiable by third parties as being a pre-payment for the imminent increase in share capital, and the pre-payments are disclosed as such in the resolution on the increase in share capital and in the application for registration of the increase in share capital to the Commercial Register.

---

[116] P. 72.
[117] Which may be cheaper where large amounts are concerned.
[118] § 55 para. 1.
[119] § 2 para. 2 by analogy; § 167 para. 2 BGB is not applicable, OLG Neustadt GmbHR 52, 58.
[120] BGHZ 49, 121.
[121] BGH WM 95, 156. It is not clarified whether this also applies in urgent cases of restructuring, if the advance payment in is necessary to manage the crisis and takes place with a close temporal connection with an immediately imminent step to increase share capital which was initiated with all appropriate acceleration; OLG Stuttgart ZIP 94, 1532. According to BGH WM 94, 791, the repayment of a loan claim with funds from the capital contribution coming from the increase in share capital is only permissible if the loan claim is liquid and due, and has full economic value (as stated in BGHZ 90, 370), and the principles governing undisclosed contributions in kind do not intervene (*ante*, p. 109).
[122] OLG Düsseldorf ZIP 81, 847, 855 *et seq.*; WM 981, 960, 963 *et seq.*; in principle, also OLG Hamm ZIP 86, 1321 *et seq.*; GmbHR 91, 198, 199; for the opposite opinion, LG Düsseldorf ZIP 86, 1251, 1253.

Application for notification and registration

Once it has been resolved, the increase in share capital shall be notified for registration after the increased capital is covered by declarations of assumption, and the minimum capital contributions (in each case a quarter of the nominal amount, together with a possible premium)[123] have been paid in and are at the final disposal at will of the managing directors.[124] All managing directors[125] are under a duty to apply for registration and shall give assurances of this.[126] False declarations in connection with increases in share capital are punishable under criminal law.[127]

The declarations and a list of those assuming contributions shall be enclosed with the application for registration.[128]

1.2 Increase out of corporate funds[129]

The capital may be increased without the supply of new funds on the basis of a balance sheet by the transformation of reserves into share capital. In the course of this, new shares may be issued or the nominal amounts of the old shares may be increased; a combination is also permissible.[130] This has the advantage for the company – but the disadvantage for the shareholders – that company assets which to date were capable of being distributed, are subject to rules governing non-repayable share capital.[131]

The preconditions for this transformation are:

- in the last annual statements,[132] the capital reserves and reserves formed out of profits, which are intended to be transformed into share capital, are specified as such, or the amount which is to be transformed into share capital has been specified as a payment into these reserves in the last resolution on the appropriation of profits;[133]

- no loss (or loss carryforward) is shown in the balance sheet;[134] and

- the last annual statements have been adopted and a resolution has been passed on the appropriation of profits.

---

[123] If, in the case of a one-man company, only one shareholder assumes the increased share capital, the capital contribution must be paid in full or security must be provided for the remainder, as in the case of formation, §§ 56a, 7 para. 2.

[124] *Ante,* p. 34; § 57 paras. 1, 2.

[125] § 78.

[126] § 57 para. 2.

[127] § 82 para. 1.

[128] § 57 para. 3, nos. 1, 2.

[129] "Kapitalerhöhung aus Gesellschaftsmitteln".

[130] § 57h.

[131] §§ 30, 31; *ante,* p. 62.

[132] The statements for the last business year which expired before the resolution was passed, § 57c para. 2, or if the resolution was based on a different balance sheet which satisfies the requirements of § 57f, also in this.

[133] § 57d para. 1.

[134] § 57d para. 2.

The balance sheet date may precede the application for registration of the resolution by a maximum of eight months.[135] The same rules which apply to increases in share capital in return for capital contributions are valid here too for issues of form, majority requirements,[136] subscription rights[137] and applications for registration.[138]

In addition, the following is necessary:[139]

- the submission of the balance sheet forming the basis of the transformation with the confirmation of the auditors (if necessary, the last attested annual balance sheet); and

- the assurance of all managing directors that, according to their knowledge, there has been no reduction of the assets between the balance sheet date of the balance sheet taken as the basis and the date on which the application for registration is made, which would have stood in the way of the increase in share capital if it had been resolved on the day the application for registration was made.

1.3 Increase of share capital in kind[140]

If the share capital is increased in return for contributions in kind, then the subject-matter of the contribution in kind and the amount of the original capital contribution to which it relates must be laid down in the resolution.[141] Chattels, real estate, rights and claims are all considered to be contributions in kind.

The contributions in kind must have been paid in before the application for registration, i.e. their subject-matter must have been transferred to the GmbH.[142] An assurance to this effect[143] has to be given upon application for registration, for which the same regulations apply as govern cash increases in share capital.[144] The application for registration shall be accompanied by the contracts which form the basis of the determinations,[145] or which were concluded for their execution.[146] Neither proof of the intrinsic value nor a report on the increase of capital in kind corresponding to the report on the formation of the company on the basis of non-cash contributions at the time of that formation[147] is prescribed by statute. Nonetheless, the registry courts mostly require a report on the increase of capital in kind, as they must investigate the intrinsic value

---

[135] §§ 57e para. 1, 57f para. 1.
[136] § 57c para. 1.
[137] § 57j.
[138] § 57c para. 4.
[139] § 57i para. 1.
[140] "Sachkapitalerhöhung".
[141] § 56 para. 1.
[142] §§ 57 para. 2, 7 para. 3.
[143] § 8 para. 2.
[144] § 57.
[145] § 56.
[146] § 57 para. 3 no.3.
[147] § 5 para. 4.

and can request documents for this purpose. If an overvaluation is established, the registration of the increase in share capital must be refused.[148]

If claims or shares are assigned, this can take place in the record; in this case, a separate implementing agreement may be dispensed with. As far as other items are concerned, the implementing contracts shall be submitted (e.g. the transfer of ownership of items of property). Only if contributions in kind as such are laid down in the resolution on the increase in share capital does their payment effect release from the duty to pay in the capital contribution assumed.[149]

If the managing directors are intended to purchase items with the funds paid in as cash contributions by the person assuming a capital contribution, or to pay for those items acquired from him, or to repay an existing claim of the person assuming a capital contribution against the company, an "undisclosed contribution in kind" exists.[150] The capital contribution is then considered as not having been paid; the shareholders continue to be liable.[151]

2. Reduction in share capital[152]

The shareholders can also decide on a reduction in the share capital.[153] It too is a change in the articles of association and thus requires a three quarters majority of the votes cast.[154] Once resolved, the reduction in share capital becomes valid upon its registration in the Commercial Register. This presupposes that:

- the resolution on the reduction in share capital has been announced three times in the newspapers authorized to publish company announcements, together with a request that the company's creditors should contact the company;[155]
- one year has passed since the last announcement;[156] and
- the creditors who have contacted the company have been satisfied or given security for the claims asserted.[157]

The share capital is usually reduced by a fixed amount. However, it may also be reduced by a maximum amount if it is specified at the same time how the final amount shall be determined, such as in accordance with the outcome of withdrawal (forfeiture) proceedings or in accordance with the anticipated deficit balance in the annual statements which have still to be drawn up.

---

[148] §§ 57a, 9c.
[149] § 19 para. 5.
[150] *Ante*, p. 108.
[151] §§ 19, 24.
[152] "Kapitalherabsetzung".
[153] § 53 para. 1.
[154] § 53 para. 2.
[155] § 58 para. 1 no. 1.
[156] § 58 para. 1 no. 3.
[157] § 58 para. 1 no. 2.

The share capital may at most only be reduced down to the amount of the minimum share capital (DM 50.000). The nominal amounts of the shares must only be adjusted in the resolution on the reduction in share capital if they are not affected in equal measure by the reduction. However, each remaining share must amount to at least DM 500 and must be divisible by 100 if the reduction is effected in order to pay back capital contributions or to release shareholders from obligations to pay capital contributions.[158]

The purpose of the reduction shall always be stated in the resolution.[159] The intention may be to rectify a deficit balance, to provide a settlement for shareholders resigning from the company or to release obligations to pay in capital contributions or to pay back capital contributions.

3. "Capital write down"[160]

The reduction of the share capital which takes place at the same time as an increase in share capital is termed a capital write down. The capital write down means that the shareholders realize the (sometimes partial) loss of the equity capital paid in and either pay in further capital contributions themselves or with other contributors who become shareholders by assuming the shares resulting from the increase in share capital.

Such a capital write down often becomes necessary if the company is in crisis, in order to avoid insolvency by the supply of new funds.[161]

---

[158] § 58 para. 2 in conjunction with § 5 paras. 1 and 3.
[159] By analogy with § 222 para. 3 AktG; BayObLG GmbHR 79, 11.
[160] "Kapitalschnitt".
[161] *Post*, p. 328.

Chapter 9
DEBT POSITION

Dr. Rüdiger Volhard

Until now, the focal point of these considerations has been the financing of the GmbH with own capital and reserves giving rise to liability (equity). However, the shareholders are in principle also free to undertake the financing of the enterprise through the supply of loans (so-called debt capital) and thus to secure the financing flexibility often required. The procurement of additional financing funds can above all become necessary:

- for the implementation of investments;
- to cover losses; and
- for the repayment of other liabilities.

The loan funds may be made available by third parties or by the shareholders themselves. The loan may be in money or in kind.

1. The distinction between equity and debt

Although equity and debt ultimately serve the same purpose, both financing methods are qualitatively different. This is above all evident in situations posing a financial threat: losses affect equity in the first place and only affect debt after that; in the case where the enterprise becomes insolvent, the equity as liable assets is lost, whilst the debt is "only" depreciated.

1.1 Equity

Equity is characterized by the following features:

- the lenders of the capital are, in principle, the shareholders;

- the lenders of the capital cannot terminate the relationship freely;
- an assertion is excluded in the winding-up of the company.

Equity consists of:

- the paid up share capital;
- the capital reserves;
- the unappropriated profits brought forward;
- the silent reserves.

1.2 Debt capital

All capital which is not equity capital is debt capital. The main forms of debt capital are:

Bank loans
Bank loans constitute the most important form of debt financing. However, in view of the often relatively low level of equity financing, banks frequently make the grant of loans dependent on the provision of security not only by the company but also by the shareholders (mortgages, suretyship), which cancels out the advantage of the liability being limited to the assets of the GmbH.[162] In addition, the grant of security by the shareholders harbours the risk that it will be treated as equity in a financial crisis.[163]

Shareholder loans[164]
The shareholders are not obliged to provide the company with funds or loans going above and beyond the capital contributions assumed. If no other third party can be found to furnish a loan, the shareholders often attempt to finance the company with loans. Then such loans are treated as equity capital.[165]

Financing by participation
In practice, considerable importance attaches to financing by third parties with none of the voting rights which would be associated with participation in the share capital, and sometimes also without the remuneration for the provision of capital being dependent on annual profit or loss of the GmbH. These are hybrid forms of financing which display elements of both debt and equity.

Silent partnership
The legal form of the silent partnership[166] is used in various ways to raise capital. It can serve purposes similar to a sub-participation,[167] in which the

---

[162] § 13.
[163] *Post,* p. 322.
[164] "Gesellschafterdarlehen".
[165] *Post,* p. 316.
[166] *Ante,* p. 12.
[167] *Ante,* p. 91.

participating party participates in one or more shares rather than in the commercial enterprise.

Silent partnerships entered into by capital investment companies or investment and venture capital companies have now developed into their own special form of enterprise (so-called GmbH & Still). These investors take advantage of the restriction on liability without having to sacrifice the advantages regarding the taxation of earnings which are enjoyed by a personal partnership.[168]

In particular, the transformation of reserves by reinvesting them as a silent participation is particularly important in practice: reserves of the GmbH are distributed as dividends and are then put back into the GmbH in the form of silent interests as debt. The obligation to plough profits back into the company can either be laid down in the articles of association (as a duty to perform additional services or pay further contributions) or outside the articles of association by means of special contract in favour of the company.

In comparison with an increase in share capital, this procedure has the advantage under company law that there is no need for notarial recording, and that the funds placed at the company's disposal can be withdrawn more easily; there is also a tax advantage in the far smaller burden of distributed profits when compared with accumulated profits.[169]

The silent partnership is a sub-partnership without company assets, in which the silent partner participates with a capital contribution in return for participation in the profits. The true, "typical" silent partnership enables a lender of capital to take part in the profit and (if not otherwise agreed) in the loss of the financed commercial enterprise, without making him a joint owner of a business enterprise. In this way, the encumbrance of the GmbH with interest liabilities independent of profits can be avoided. In contrast with this, the false, "atypical" silent partner is, tax-wise, treated like a joint owner of the business enterprise.

Typical silent partnership

The true, "typical" silent partnership is the participation of the silent partner in the commercial enterprise of the "owner", in this case the GmbH, in return for a participation in the profits.[170] The owner is the sole owner of the business assets, both in rem and under the law of obligations.[171]

The capital contribution can be either a cash contribution or a contribution in kind. The contractual parties are free in the valuation of the capital contributions. This constitutes a major advantage of the silent participation over the (more complicated) increase in share capital in kind.[172] In addition, the capital contribution can be paid back at the end of the contractual relationship, with-

---

[168] *Post*, p. 221.
[169] *Post*, p. 230.
[170] §§ 230 *et seq.* HGB.
[171] If the formation of joint assets, so-called "joint property", takes place, the result is a commercial partnership or civil law partnership, BGH NJW 53, 818.
[172] *Ante*, p. 108.

out a formal reduction in share capital (for the purpose of the repayment of capital contributions) having to be resolved.[173]

The level of the participation in the profits may, in principle, be agreed at will. However, a disproportionately high rate of interest on the capital contribution will not be recognised from a tax point of view if the silent partner himself is a shareholder of the GmbH. Generally, tax recognition requires terms under which independent third parties would have furnished the silent contribution.[174] Where the silent partner is at the same time shareholder-director of the owner (GmbH & typical silent partner), the relationship is characterised by the lack of a difference of interest such as exists between third parties. In these cases the "reasonableness" of the distribution of profits will be examined to see whether it constitutes an undisclosed distribution of profits.[175]

The "reasonable" share of the profits paid to the silent partner – having first taken into consideration special payment contributions – is mainly determined by the proportion of his capital contribution, to be specified at nominal value, in relation to the total value of the enterprise of the GmbH. An annual minimum interest rate can be agreed with the silent partner, which does not constitute participation in the profits. However, only the participation in the losses can be contractually excluded, not the participation in the profits.

If the silent participation is granted by way of gift, which comes into consideration in the case of intentional undervaluation or overvaluation, or if the silent partner undertakes to bring in a piece of real property, a GmbH share or a fractional part of his assets, notarial recording is compulsory.[176]

Atypical silent partnership

The false, "atypical" silent partnership is also a sub-partnership without company assets, but the atypical silent partner is also treated from the point of view of the law of contract and for tax purposes as if he had a partnership interest in the business of the GmbH. This can be accompanied by powers of management or other rights of co-determination on the part of the silent partner.[177]

It is decisive that the participation of the atypical silent partner extends to a proportion of the total business assets of the owner, including all silent reserves, at the commencement of the silent partnership. The silent partner's entitlement at the end of the silent partnership should thus be regulated by contract. Where there is no contractual regulation, the capitalized income value of the commercial enterprise would be decisive. However, the parties may agree other standards of valuation.

---

[173] *Ante*, p. 111.
[174] BFH BStBl II 84, 623; 90, 10, with a list of the main elements of the required partnership agreement close to the statutory rules of the Commercial Code. The same applies to family-held companies.
[175] *Ante*, p. 113; BFH BStBl II 80, 477.
[176] §§ 518, 313, 873 BGB, 15 GmbHG, 311 BGB.
[177] BGH NJW 92, 2696.

Rights of jouissance[178]

Rights of jouissance are special dividend rights issued as obligations by the GmbH for financing purposes, which primarily form the basis of rights to a share in the profits and/or in the liquidation proceeds of the company; they do not convey any company law membership rights, but rather merely constitute proprietary interests, and thus exclusively give rise to claims under the law of obligations.

If a special dividend right of the shareholders is to be granted as a founder's advantage or as consideration for a duty to perform additional services, it needs a basis in the articles of association, but otherwise not.

Participating loans[179]

The group of hybrid forms of financing also includes loans on which the interest rate is linked to the profit of the company (the borrower). These so-called participating loans shall be treated as interest-bearing loans, but are subject to special tax regulations.[180] The lender does not participate in the loss.

Reclassification as equity

Although the character of debt capital predominates in the specified forms of participation financing, they can be wholly reclassified as equity under certain preconditions.

With rights of jouissance, this is the case if they are placed at the company's disposal on a permanent basis and ranking after the company's creditors, so that they may not be withdrawn, or may not be withdrawn arbitrarily and without compensation. This precondition is satisfied if the owner of the bonus share is exclusively granted a claim to participation in the profits or the proceeds upon liquidation.

Under certain circumstances, the silent participation shall also be classified as equity. This is the case if the silent partner is placed on an equal footing with a full shareholder as far as proprietary interests are concerned, i.e. participates fully in the profit and loss, or if the silent participation must be placed at the disposal of the company's creditors like liable equity on the basis of a contractual agreement or by statute.[181]

However, these rules only apply to the equity financing by shareholders; where third parties outside the company are concerned, there is no reclassification as equity.

2. Shareholder debt financing

2.1 Equity financing versus shareholder loans

The distinction between debt and equity also has tax consequences. Interest payments on borrowed funds are business expenses and reduce the income of

---

[178] "Genußrechte".
[179] "Partiarische Darlehen".
[180] *Post*, p. 130.
[181] §§ 32a,b.
[182] § 8 para. 3 KStG.

the company, whilst all payments made for the equity provided to a GmbH are classified as the distribution of profits, which does not reduce the company's income and thereby its tax burden.[182]

As it is the shareholders' decision whether they place the capital at the GmbH's disposal in the form of equity or through shareholder loans, they will compare the tax burden of the different forms of financing. Foreign shareholders (so-called persons subject to limited taxation) are excluded from the corporate income tax credit procedure (which avoids double taxation of profits by individual income and corporate income tax). They have the possibility of avoiding the corporate income tax burden on distributed profits of the GmbH by supplying the company with debt instead of equity. The interest on the loans reduces the GmbH's income, and is not burdened with German corporate income tax when received by a shareholder subject to limited taxation, in contrast to distributions of profits by the GmbH.[183]

However, if the shareholder grants the GmbH a loan at an excessive interest rate, then the excessive part of the interest is deemed to be a hidden distribution of profits ("constructive dividend").[184] By contrast, the advantage of an interest-free loan or a loan at a low rate of interest does not give rise to a constructive capital contribution.[185]

For trade tax purposes, half the interest of loans is added in assessing the amount of income for trade tax on income purposes and half the loan is added in assessing the amount of capital for trade tax on capital purposes.[186] Thus the interest on and the principal of the loan only reduce the basis of assessment for trade tax by half.

As far as the shareholders are concerned, the interest on the loan constitutes income from capital investments. The interest income of a foreign shareholder (subject to limited taxation) is only subject to German individual income tax or corporate income tax if the shareholder's loan is secured directly or indirectly by real property in Germany.[187] By contrast, income from profit participating loans and (typical) silent partnerships, received by a shareholder who is subject to limited taxation, is, in principle, taxable in Germany.[188] The German income tax on this is, however, usually settled by the capital yield tax withheld, which may be restricted by tax treaties.[189]

If the shareholder granted the loan within the scope of his business capital, the interest is business income. For a shareholder subject to limited taxation, the interest is only taxable if it is attributable to a permanent establishment in Germany.[190]

---

[183] *Post*, p. 234 on the tax burden on distributions of profits in the case of shareholders who are subject to limited taxation.
[184] "Verdeckte Gewinnausschüttung"; *post*, p. 224.
[185] "Verdeckte Einlage"; however, the economic advantage provided by such loan may trigger gift tax.
[186] *Post*, p. 239.
[187] § 49 para. 1 no. 5c EStG.
[188] § 49 para. 1. no. 5a EStG,
[189] § 43 para. 1 no. 3 in conjunction with § 50 para. 5 EStG.
[190] § 49 para. 1 no. 2a EStG.

2.2 Thin capitalization: restriction on shareholder loans

Principles

The law[191] restricts the substitution of profit distributions burdened with corporate income tax by interest payments, or participations in the profits by silent partners, by means of the so-called thin capitalization rules. In cases of excessive debt financing, interest expenses will not be recognised for tax purposes, in order to ensure that profits of corporations situated within the country remain subject to taxation.

According to the thin capitalization rules, interest payments by a corporation to any shareholder with a substantial participation or to a party related to such shareholder are deemed to be a constructive dividend, if the recipient of the payments is subject to limited taxation and therefore not subject to German income tax, or only to a (final) withholding tax. This treatment of interest payments to the shareholder as constructive dividends results in the same tax burden as if profits had been distributed as a dividend to the shareholder.

The thin capitalization rules are, in effect, only applicable for corporate income tax. The loans continue to be treated as debt; thus, there are no effects on net worth tax and on trade tax on capital. In determining the income of the GmbH, for trade tax on income purposes, interest payments reclassified as a constructive dividend under the thin capitalization rules are to be deducted from the income.[192] As a consequence, the rules also have no effect on trade tax on income.

Substantial participation[193]

The restriction of debt financing by the shareholders as defined in the thin capitalisation rules only applies if a shareholder who is subject to limited taxation holds a substantial participation. This is a direct or indirect participation – including through a partnership – in the share capital of the GmbH by more than 25 per cent.

Profit-based or turnover-based interest

Profit-based or turnover-based interest payments on shareholder loans are treated as constructive dividends as far as the loans of any shareholder exceed a debt/equity ratio with respect to the part of the company's equity attributable to this shareholder of 0.5:1 (safe haven I).

Example:

A shareholder not entitled to a corporate income tax credit participates in a GmbH as a silent partner with an interest amounting to DM 500,000. During the tax year, he receives an (arms's length) remuneration of DM 100,000 for this.

---

[191] § 8a Corporate Income Tax Act (KStG).
[192] § 9 no. 10 Trade Tax Act (GewStG).
[193] "Wesentliche Beteiligung".

The proportional equity attributable to the shareholder as defined in the rules amounts to DM 300,000.

Solution:

Safe haven I:

$0.5 \times 300,000 = 150,000$

Exceeding part of the silent partnership interest:

$500,000 - 150,000 = 350,000$

Constructive dividend:

$$\frac{350,000 \times 100,000}{500,000} = 70,000$$

Interest not based on profits or turnover

As in the case of profit or turnover participating loans, a constructive dividend as defined by the thin capitalization rules may also come into consideration in the case of shareholder loans which bear interest independent of profits or turnover. A constructive dividend must be assumed if, at any time during the business year, the relevant debt exceeds three times the amount of equity attributable to the shareholder at the beginning of the business year, i.e. a debt/equity a ratio of 3:1 (safe haven II).[194]

Example:

By 1 January 1996, a GmbH received a loan of DM 1 million from a shareholder not entitled to a corporate income tax credit, on which (arm's length) interest shall be paid at a rate of 8 per cent per annum. The equity attributable to the shareholder as defined in the rules amounts to DM 300,000 at 31 December 1995.

Solution:

Safe haven II:

$3 \times 300,000 = 900,000$

Exceeding part:

$1 \text{ million} - 900,000 = 100,000$

Constructive dividend on the exceeding part:

8 per cent of 100,000 = 8,000.

The legal consequence provided for in the thin capitalization rules does not take effect if the corporation demonstrates that it also could have obtained the relevant loans under the same circumstances from an unrelated party (arm's length test). The arm's length test must be applied at the time at which the relevant shareholder loan exceeds the debt/equity ratio permissible under the rules. The corporation may produce this evidence by all expedient means of proof (e.g. specified loan offers from banks, results of creditworthiness analyses,

---

[194] § 8a para. 1 no. 2 KStG.

which include at least the amount of the loan, the term, the rate of interest and the securities to be provided, if any).

Concurrence of fixed and variable interest

If shareholders grant profit or turnover participating loans alongside non-participating loans, then the safe havens I and II cannot be used cumulatively. Rather, it must first be examined to which extent safe haven I is exhausted. Any difference which is not exhausted can then be taken into consideration for safe haven II, using a debt/equity ratio of 6:1.

Equity for purposes of the thin capitalization rules

The proportional equity attributable to a shareholder is that part of the equity of the corporation at the end of the preceding business year which corresponds to the proportion of the share capital of the GmbH held by the shareholder.[195] The basis for this determination is the participation in the registered share capital, not the extent of the voting rights. Equity is the share capital less any outstanding capital contributions, plus any capital reserves, retained profits, unappropriated profits brought forward and any annual surplus, less any loss carryforward and any annual deficit as shown on the commercial balance sheet at the close of the preceding business year; half of the special items on the balance sheet which have a reserve proportion[196] must be added.

Holding companies

Special provisions exist for holding companies as defined in the rules.[197] In order to allow for a more flexible financing of their subsidiaries, holding companies are entitled to an extended safe haven II amounting to a debt/equity ratio of 9:1 for loans bearing interest independent of profit or turnover.

Prevention of evasion

The thin capitalization rules apply by analogy if:[198]

- the shareholder is only entitled to a corporate income tax credit because the income from the participation is business income of a permanent establishment within Germany; or
- the participation is held through a partnership and the loan is channelled through the partnership.

This serves to prevent avoidance of the application of the thin capitalization rules by the interposition of permanent establishment and partnerships. However, the application of the thin capitalization rules may still be avoided in individual cases by leasing structures or use of an atypical silent partnership.

---

[195] § 8a para. 2 KStG.
[196] § 247 para 3 HGB.
[197] § 8a para. 4 KStG.
[198] § 8a para. 5 KStG.

3. Debt and equity in bankruptcy

The distinction between equity and debt is also important if the company becomes bankrupt. Even in bankruptcy, the company can call up outstanding capital contributions. Shareholders cannot demand the return of capital contributions which were paid in before bankruptcy proceedings were opened, and they do not found any claims in bankruptcy.[199]

By contrast, in the case of debt, the lender who has not yet paid the loan may be entitled to revoke his promise.[200] Loans already granted form the foundation of claims in bankruptcy.[201] Separate realization can be required for a secured creditor by reason of security rights.[202]

The distinction becomes blurred if borrowed funds are treated like liable equity in a crisis of the company. The most important case in practice of such an equal footing being established is found in the so-called payments of the shareholders which replace equity.[203]

---

[199] BGHZ 69, 274, 280.
[200] § 610 BG The purchaser can depreciate the total acquisition costs which reduces his tax burden.
[201] §§ 12, 61 no. 6, 138 *et seq.* Bankruptcy Act (KO).
[202] §§ 47 *et seq.*, 127 KO:
[203] §§ 32a,b GmbHG, 32 KO; p. 317. Silent capital contributions and bonus share capital may be functionally placed on an equal footing with equity capital; *ante*, p. 129.

Part IV

CORPORATE OFFICERS, MANAGEMENT AND LABOUR LAW

Chapter 10

MANAGING DIRECTORS AND AUTHORIZED REPRESENTATIVES

Dr. Rüdiger Volhard and Dr. Jürgen Taschke

1. Managing directors[1]

1.1 Suitability

Only natural persons can be managing directors. Both nationality and place of residence are unimportant.[2] It must merely be ensured that the managing director can fulfil his statutory obligations from there. This will always be assumed in the case of a place of residence within the EU. If the foreign managing director is resident in Germany, then proof of a residence permit can be required in order to enable him to be registered, and if necessary a confirmation from the foreigners' authority that he is not affected by any prohibition on work.[3]

1.2 Number

The GmbH has one or more managing directors, who are mostly also shareholders in the case of smaller companies.[4] They are the statutory representatives of the company. According to the statutory rules,[5] they can only act jointly. The managing directors may also be granted sole power of representation if the articles of association make provision for this. It is more common for the company to be represented by two managing directors acting jointly, or by one managing director acting together with a procurator (authorized signatory holding full commercial powers of representation). However, according to the relevant statutory provision,[6] as far as the receipt of declarations to be made to the

---

[1] "Geschäftsführer".
[2] The actual place of administration must, however, remain situated in Germany; *ante*, p. 20.
[3] Negative attestation, *post*, p. 283. *Ante*, p. 35 for criminal law convictions and public authority prohibitions which stand in the way of appointment as a managing director.
[4] § 6.
[5] § 35 para. 2.
[6] § 35 para. 2.

company is concerned, a declaration made to one managing director is considered sufficient.

The authorization of one managing director to act for the others is only permissible to a restricted extent for a specific transaction and for specific types of transactions; it may thus not lead to sole representation in practice.[7]

2. Tasks

The managing directors have internal (management) and external (representation) tasks.

2.1 Management[8]

The managing directors are responsible for the management of the business of the company internally, i.e. in relation to the shareholders and the company. This includes all tasks which do not fall within the sphere of competence of the shareholders' meeting by operation of law or by virtue of the articles of association.

Other than is the case with the executive board of the AG,[9] the managing directors do not manage the company on their own authority, but must rather follow the instructions of the shareholders and are bound by the restrictions in the articles of association or in standing rules and regulations, as well as by the individual instructions issued by resolutions of the shareholders.[10]

Whilst the power of representation[11] cannot validly be restricted in relation to third parties,[12] in relation to the company the managing directors are under an obligation to observe restrictions which are imposed on them by the articles of association or by individual instructions.[13]

The typical way of restricting the powers of a managing director is to insert a provision into the articles of association making certain business transactions subject to the prior consent of either the shareholders' meeting or an advisory/supervisory board.[14] This is customary for all transactions which are not considered to be in the ordinary course of business. The effect of such internal restrictions is that a managing director acting in breach of these provisions becomes liable to the company for any damage which occurs in accordance with the strict standard of the "due care of a prudent businessman".[15] In principle, several managing directors are jointly and severally liable (as the case may be restricted to their fault of lack of supervision),[16] without taking into consideration the allocation of tasks.

---

[7] BGH WM 78, 1047.
[8] "Geschäftsführung".
[9] § 76 para. 1 AktG.
[10] § 37 para. 1.
[11] *Post*, p. 139.
[12] § 37 para. 2.
[13] § 37 para. 1.
[14] *Post*, p. chapter 12.
[15] § 43; *post*, p. 152.
[16] *Post*, p. 142.

In addition, criminal liability comes into question in the case of a breach of certain obligations.

2.2 Legal representation[17]

No restrictions
The company is legally represented by the managing directors as its organs. No restrictions can be placed on the scope of the statutory power of representation in relation to third parties.[18] Provisions in the articles according to which the representation is only meant to extend to certain transactions or types of transactions, or the consent of the shareholders or of an organ of the company is required for individual transactions, are void.

Acts for the GmbH are thus in principle valid both for and against the company,[19] even if the managing directors disregard restrictions imposed upon them by the articles of association or restrictions which have been placed upon them by the standing rules and regulations, or by a resolution of the shareholders' meeting. In particular, the power of representation is not restricted by the object of the enterprise, as is the case in the common law jurisdictions.[20] This does not apply if the managing director acts internally, i.e. not in relation to third parties, but rather, for example, in relation to shareholders or members of the advisory board.

Effect of the joint representation
The collective power of representation ordered by statute offers a certain protection. This power means that the managing director is only authorized to represent the company together with the other managing director(s), if there are any.[21] In deviation from this, the articles of association can also lay down a power of sole representation of the managing director or a joint representative power with a procurator.[22]

Legal transactions which are not concluded by all the persons necessary for valid joint representation are provisionally invalid,[23] but they can subsequently be approved by the other joint representative(s). However, for transactions which can be clearly delimited, one representative can be authorized by the other joint representative(s) to conduct the relevant business alone.[24]

Given that modified joint representation (two managing directors or one with a procurator) is usual, it is in most cases sufficient for validity that a written

---

[17] "Gesetzliche Vertretung".
[18] § 37 para. 2.
[19] § 36.
[20] OLG Munich GmbH 92, 533. However, there are transactions which require a shareholders' resolution in order to become effective, e.g. by analogous application of § 179a AktG, the sale of real property which is either all or part of the assets of the company, BGH DB 95, 621.
[21] § 35 para. 2; so-called true joint representation.
[22] BGHZ 119, 379.
[23] § 177 BGB by analogy.
[24] BGH WM 88, 216, 217.

declaration of the GmbH bears two signatures. By contrast to the situation in
the common law jurisdiction, third parties do not require the presentation of a
board resolution or even a resolution of the shareholders, in accordance with
which the signatories are empowered to conclude the transaction. Information
about the authorized representatives and the type of permissible representation
is contained in an excerpt from the commercial register[25] which can be requested by anyone in return for a small fee at the district court of the registered
office of the GmbH.[26]

Abuse of the representative authority
The concept of an abuse of representative authority constitutes the very narrow
exception to this principle. The managing director must not exercise his representative authority to the disadvantage of the company against the presumed
(or even the known) will of the shareholders.[27] In particular, he abuses his
representative authority[28] if he concludes a transaction without asking the
shareholders because he believes that they will not consent to it.[29]

In principle, the company bears the risk of abuse of representative authority.
The contractual party is not under an obligation to find out whether internal barriers to the representative authority exist and whether they have been observed.[30]

Nevertheless, where the principles on the "abuse of representative authority"
apply, the validity of the acts of the managing director for the GmbH can be
denied. Thus, a party is not protected if it co-operated with the representative
to the detriment of the company whilst having positive knowledge of the internal barriers (so-called collusion). Such conduct is contrary to good morals[31]
and the transaction is consequently null and void.[32]

Apart from the case of collusion, the abuse is only relevant under certain narrowly
defined preconditions. Confidence in the representative authority of the managing director is not worthy of protection if he makes use of it in a way which is
obviously suspect, so that the contractual party would necessarily have justified
doubts as to whether the managing director is committing a breach of trust
against the GmbH. The necessity of voicing a query must almost have forced
itself upon the contractual party. There must be objective evidence of abuse
which presupposes massively suspicious circumstances.[33]

---

[25] *Ante*, p. 35.
[26] The purpose of the strict differentiation between the external and the internal relationship is the
protection of legal relations, because there is, in principle, no need to worry about whether the
actions of the managing directors are permissible within the internal relationship or not, BGH NJW
84, 1461, 1462.
[27] OLG Frankfurt GmbHR 89, 254.
[28] *Post*, p. 160.
[29] BGH NJW 84, 1461. This also applies if a duty of consent should exist. In such a case, the managing director must attempt to obtain the resolution and must, if necessary, enforce the company's
claim against the shareholders in court, BGH NJW 84, 489.
[30] BGH NJW 84, 1461 *et seq.*; BGH NJW 94, 2082, 2083.
[31] § 138 BGB.
[32] RGZ 130, 131, 140; according to BGH WM 81, 66 there are at any rate no claims to fulfilment.
[33] BGH GmbHR 91, 264, 268; WM 92, 1362; NJW 94, 2082, 2083.

The legal consequences of the abuse of representative authority for the contractual relationship are not clear. The case-law assumes partial invalidity of the contract, but usually gives the company the defence of fraud[34] which opposes the claims to fulfilment or to compensation out of the (validly concluded) contract.[35] The contract is not null and void, because the GmbH can approve it and can thus bring about its validity.[36]

2.3 Prohibition on self-dealing and exemption therefrom

In order to avoid a conflict of interest, the managing directors are prohibited from appearing on both sides of the legal transaction, i.e. from acting on one side for the company and on the other side in their own name or as representatives of a third party.[37]

There are certain exceptions to the prohibition on self-dealing: thus, transactions which fulfil an obligation which has already been validly created – such as, for example, the payment of a salary or the distribution of dividends on which resolutions have already been passed – or which are purely advantageous to the company, are not subject to the blocking effect.[38]

The managing directors may be granted exemption from the prohibition. The exemption may be declared in the articles of association or by express or implied design of the appointing organ, usually the shareholders' meeting.[39] However, at the least an authorization to grant such exemption must be contained in the articles of association.[40]

According to express direction by statute,[41] the prohibition on self-dealing also applies to the so-called one-man GmbH. Exemption is also possible in this case if the articles of association contain the authorisation for it.[42] The exemption but not the authorization to grant it[43] must be notified to the Commercial Register for registration.[44] It can be restrictively granted and registered for particular types of transactions or for transactions with particular parties.[45]

A transaction which was undertaken in contravention of the prohibition is provisionally invalid.[46] It becomes valid if the company – as the represented

---

[34] § 242 BGB.

[35] "The transaction becomes inoperative", RGZ 134, 67, 72; "invalid", BGH GmbHR 88, 260, 261; "the third party cannot derive any rights against the represented party out of the agreement", BGH WM 80, 953, 954; "no contractual rights or objections" could be derived "from the transaction which is formally covered by the representative authority of the managing director", BGH NJW 84, 1461, 1462.

[36] OLG Hamburg ZIP 92, 1085, 1086.

[37] Prohibition on self-dealing ("Insichgeschäft"), § 181 BGB.

[38] BGHZ 59, 236.

[39] BGH GmbHR 79, 252.

[40] BayOblG DB 84, 1517; OLG Cologne NJW 93, 1018.

[41] § 35 para. 4.

[42] BGHZ 33, 189, 194; 87, 59, 60.

[43] OLG Hamm DB 93, 158; OLG Frankfurt GmbHR 94, 118.

[44] BGHZ 87, 59, 60; BGH WM 91, 891.

[45] OLG Düsseldorf WM 94, 2112.

[46] § 177 BGB.

party – approves it through other managing directors who are not prevented from acting, and it becomes finally invalid if such approval is refused.

The permissible self-dealing must be recognisable as such. It should thus be documented in writing.[47]

2.4 Internal regulations

Standing rules and regulations[48] for the management have the primary purpose of allocating the spheres of responsibility amongst several managing directors in the case where more than one director is appointed. The shareholders are responsible for passing standing rules and regulations. They can regulate the spheres of competence of the managing directors in the articles of association, in the appointment, in the service agreement or in standing rules and regulations. In addition, it is also conceivable that the articles of association may authorize the managing directors to pass standing rules and regulations for themselves, if necessary with the consent of the shareholders or a supervisory board.

The allocation of spheres of competence does not alter the overall responsibility of the managing directors. However, in the case of a breach of duty on the part of another managing director, only those managing directors who themselves were in breach of their duty to monitor will be held liable. Where spheres of responsibility have been allocated, each managing director must keep himself continually informed, must object to individual measures, must intervene if there is the threat of damage to the company and must, if necessary, notify the shareholders.[49]

3. Appointment and removal from office

3.1 Appointment

The managing directors are appointed either in the articles of association or by a resolution of the shareholders, unanimous at the time of formation, later with a resolution passed with a simple majority.[50] A distinction must be made between the appointment as the organ of the company ("appointment" to the office of managing director) and the conclusion of the service agreement with the managing director ("employment" as a managing director).[51]

---

[47] BGHZ 75, 363; BGH NJW 91, 1730. However, the written record thereof is not a precondition of validity, BGH NJW 84, 1461, 1462.
[48] "Geschäftsordnung".
[49] § 46 no. 6, § 49. BGH WM 86, 789.
[50] §§ 6 para. 3, 46 no. 5. A distinction must be made between the appointment made as a legal transaction and the (emergency) appointment by the registry court, for which shareholders and creditors can apply in a case where a managing director is absent or where he is prevented by law from acting (by analogy with § 29 BGB).
[51] *Post*, p. 145; BGHZ 10, 187, 191; 36, 142, 143; 79, 38, 41; BGH WM 92, 691.

Appointment in the articles of association

The inclusion of the managing directors in the articles of association does not make their appointment a material part of the articles, so an alteration of the management does not constitute an alteration of the articles of association.[52] The shareholders thus, in principle, decide on this with a simple majority[53] as long as the articles of association do not stipulate a qualified majority or a unanimous vote.

This is different if the shareholders are granted a special right of management.[54] In such a case, the intervention requires the observance of the provisions governing alterations to the articles of association,[55] together with the consent of each shareholder affected.

The (subsequent) grant of the special right of management thus also requires the majority needed for an alteration to the articles of association,[56] together with notarial recording and the registration of the alteration of the articles in the Commercial Register.

Appointment by shareholders' resolution

The appointment of the managing directors by means of a resolution of the shareholders requiring a simple majority[57] is the usual case. Shareholders can participate in passing the resolution on their own appointment as managing director.[58] If the managing director has not co-operated in his own appointment in the capacity of a shareholder, thereby impliedly accepting the office, then his appointment becomes valid upon the delivery to him of a declaration of appointment and its acceptance by him.[59]

If the appointment is invalid, but the relevant person continues to act unchallenged in the capacity of managing director, then it will be viewed as valid retrospectively for the past, and as valid in the future until such time as the defect is asserted.

Appointment by third parties

The articles of association – and the shareholders too – are at liberty to transfer the appointment to another organ (a supervisory board or an advisory board, a committee of shareholders) or to an individual shareholder, unless the supervisory board which is comprised on the basis of equal representation has exclusive competence.[60]

Apart from this, the appointment of managing directors cannot be trans-

---

[52] BGH GmbHR 82, 129.
[53] § 47.
[54] *Ante*, p. 24.
[55] §§ 53 *et seq.*
[56] § 53 para. 2.
[57] § 6 para. 3 in conjunction with § 46 no. 5.
[58] § 47 para. 4 does not apply for this, BGH GmbHR 86, 156; 90, 452; NJW 91, 172.
[59] BGHZ 52, 316, 321; BGH WM 69, 158, 159.
[60] As is the case where the GmbH has more than 2,000 employees; § 31 MitbestG.

ferred to third parties with no connection with the company, not even by the articles of association (although this view is disputed).

3.2 Removal From office

Managing directors can be removed from office at any time.[61] There is no requirement of conduct constituting a breach of duty or other grounds connected with the person of the managing director. Likewise, no justification is necessary, although no "obviously unobjective grounds" may be relied upon.[62]

Provision may be made in the articles of association that the removal from office shall only be permissible for cause.[63] This is usual for shareholder-directors. Provision is often also made that shareholder-directors can only be removed from office with a qualified majority. Nevertheless, the removal from office for cause is still permissible with a simple majority because it may not be made more difficult.

Cause is considered to be every circumstance which poses a serious threat to the company and makes the managing director's continued occupation of the office unbearable for the company; by way of example, the Limited Liability Companies Act specifies a gross breach of duty and unfitness for proper management.[64] The cause does not have to be connected with the person of the managing director and it must not necessarily at the same time justify a dismissal.[65] It can be connected to the relationship of the managing director with third parties (e.g. loss of confidence by clients or financiers).[66]

The removal from office is free of requirements of form and can take effect at a particular time (e.g. removal from office at the end of the fiscal year), but it may not be made dependent on the occurrence of an uncertain event (condition).

As in the case of appointment, the shareholders' meeting also decides on the removal from office[67] if the articles of association do not stipulate another organ.[68] The supervisory board has exclusive competence in this respect in the case of a company with more than 2,000 employees.[69] Unless otherwise regulated in the articles of association, the shareholders shall decide by a simple majority. The shareholder-director affected can participate in the vote on his own removal from office in the case of normal removal, but not in the case of removal from office for cause.[70]

---

[61] § 38 para. 1.
[62] In the case of smaller companies, the existence of justified doubts as to the propriety of the management may be required, BGH BB 68, 1453; WM 60, 289 for the GmbH with two shareholders.
[63] § 38 para. 2.
[64] § 38 para. 2. In any case, it is necessary to take into consideration the overall circumstances of the individual case, weighing up the interests of both sides, BGH WM 85, 567.
[65] *Post*, p. 148.
[66] BGH WM 60, 289.
[67] § 46 no. 5.
[68] § 45 para. 2.
[69] § 31 MitbestG in conjunction with § 84 para. 3 AktG.
[70] BGH GmbHR 90, 75. If necessary, the shareholder-director must challenge the resolution on removal in the Regional Court (commercial law division) within the time-limit provided for in the articles of association or within a reasonable time-limit. A managing director who is not also a shareholder cannot challenge the resolution, but can pursue a contractual right to management with the action to enforce a right or the action for a declaratory judgment, BGH DB 94, 1761.

The removal from office is considered valid until its invalidity is finally and bindingly decided.[71]

3.3 Resignation from office

The managing director is entitled to resign his office where there is cause. A reason constitutes cause if it makes the managing director's continued occupation of his position unbearable.[72] As is the case with appointment and removal, resignation from office as the act of an entity or organ has no direct influence on the employment relationship. The managing director can restrict himself to the resignation from office[73] or he can also terminate the employment relationship at the same time.[74] It must be determined by interpretation whether the resignation from office also impliedly represents the termination of the contract of employment.[75] The resignation of office by the managing director comes into effect immediately, even if no reasons are given.[76] It must be notified to the Commercial Register for registration by the new or other managing directors.[77]

If the managing director resigns his office without sufficient cause, he may render himself liable to pay compensation by reason of a breach of his duties out of the contract of employment in relation to the company, thereby giving the company the right of extraordinary termination.[78]

4. Employment

4.1 Service agreement

The service agreement between the managing director and the GmbH is a contract for services with the character of agency business.[79] It is not a labour law contract of employment because the managing director – as the representative organ of the company – himself exercises the power of control of an employer in relation to the employees and does not have the same social dependency relationship as the employees.[80] By contrast, within a group of companies[81] the assumption of the position of managing director can be a dependent part of

---

[71] Different for the shareholder-director in the case of the GmbH with two shareholders, BGHZ 86, 177, 181 *et seq.*; OLG Karlsruhe GmbHR 93, 154.
[72] BGH GmbHR 80, 270; WM 78, 319; 61, 241; BFH DB 85, 1326.
[73] BGHZ 78, 82, 84; BGH WM 84, 532.
[74] *Post*, p. 145.
[75] OLG Düsseldorf GmbHR 89, 468, 469 *et seq.* with further references.
[76] BGHZ 121, 257.
[77] If the sole managing director resigns his office, he himself is entitled to notify, OLG Frankfurt WM 94, 2250 with further references.
[78] BGHZ 78, 85; BGH WM 78, 3; BGH ZIP 93, 430.
[79] "Geschäftsbesorgung", §§ 661 *et seq.*, 675 BGB. BGHZ 10, 191; 49, 31; 79, 293; GmbHR 88, 138. In case of an unpaid activity which is mostly in the nature of a secondary office, the provisions governing agency (§§ 662 *et seq.*, BGB) apply as well.
[80] BGHZ 10, 187, 191; BGH GmbHR 88, 138.
[81] *Post*, chapter 15.

the employment contract he has concluded with the controlling enterprise.[82] The same applies in the case of a GmbH & Co. KG to the contract of employment of the managing director of the GmbH acting as personally liable partner within the limited partnership.[83]

4.2 Conclusion

In principle, the managing director concludes the service agreement with the company. However, the contract may be concluded with a third party, such as between the parent company and the managing director of subsidiaries or the limited partnership in the case of service agreements of the GmbH acting as general partner within a GmbH & Co. KG.[84] The third party does not even have to be a shareholder.[85]

If there is no other regulation in the articles of association, the shareholders' meeting is also responsible for concluding the service agreement by reason of its competence to appoint and remove the managing directors.[86] In companies with more than 2,000 employees,[87] the supervisory board is solely responsible for the conclusion of the service agreement.[88]

The conclusion of the agreement is free of requirements as to form, except in cases where the managing director at the same time takes over a share in the company.[89] However, written form is recommended for tax reasons.

4.3 Content

The legally valid appointment of the managing director gives rise to the duty and the entitlement on his part to fulfil his tasks and to exercise the powers conferred on him by statute and by the articles of association. If such regulations are included in the service agreement, they are purely declaratory in nature. The modifying regulations of the powers of management which are usual in practice are in principle permissible (e.g. assurance of certain powers of management, waiver of instructions, etc., but also the narrowing down of competences, reservations of consent to the shareholders' meeting or the supervisory board in the case of certain transactions, prohibitions on competition, etc.).

The central focus amongst the rights of the managing director is usually on the remuneration and, if necessary, the way in which it is to be determined,

---

[82] BAG DB 72, 2358.
[83] BAGE 24, 383; WM 83, 797; for another view OLG Celle GmbHR 80, 32, 35.
[84] BGH WM 64, 13; BAG DB 72, 2358; BGH BB 70, 277; BAGE 24, 383; WM 83, 797.
[85] BGH GmbHR 65, 194.
[86] § 45 no. 6; BGH NJW 58, 945; WM 91, 852; DB 93, 218, 219; OLG Cologne GmbHR 91, 156. For the alteration of the service agreement, see BGH GmbHR 91, 363, abandoning its earlier case-law, in accordance with which the area of tasks of the co-directors is affected.
[87] *Post*, p. 180.
[88] BGHZ 89, 48.
[89] §§ 15, 48 para. 3.

together with any pension entitlements. A basic or fixed salary can be agreed, as can variable pay in the form of commissions for the conclusion of transactions, bonus payments, remuneration in kind, or a hybrid form of these models. The claim to management bonus payments would be structured on the basis of the commercial balance sheet either as participation in the profits (profit-orientated management bonus) or as participation in the turnover (turnover management bonus). The latter is less usual in practice. Often, a minimum management bonus is agreed, which is set off against the profit-orientated management bonus or the turnover management bonus.[90] The amount and the basis of assessment can be freely agreed in the case of a managing director outside the company. In the case of a shareholder-director, the grant of an unreasonably high remuneration[91] can constitute a constructive dividend which – quite apart from the tax consequences – may represent a breach of the prohibition on paying back share capital.[92] If the other shareholders have not given their consent it may also represent a breach of the company law principle of equal treatment.[93]

For the assessment of the remuneration, the type, size and productive efficiency of the business will usually be taken into consideration, along with the training, abilities and professional experience of the managing director and the importance of his activities.

4.4 Expiry

The expiry of the company office of managing director, for example through lapse of a set time-limit or as a result of valid removal from office, does not in itself mean the simultaneous end of the service agreement. If the company wishes to end the agreement, it must thus terminate it. In principle, this also applies if the end of the service agreement is contractually linked to the removal from office.[94]

However, it can be contractually agreed that the removal from office shall always at the same time be a termination of the service agreement without notice.[95] This is particularly advisable – even if only to avoid the risk of failing to observe the brief two-week time-limit – in cases in which the removal from office is only possible for cause.[96] A reason justifying the removal from office does not have to satisfy the requirements regarding "important" cause for an extraordinary termination; but ordinary termination without notice can also be agreed for the service agreement, because it is not a labour law employment contract.

---

[90] If the basis of assessment for the management bonus is not laid down in the contract of employment, then it shall be determined *ex aequo et bono* under the terms of § 315 BGB, BGH BB 94, 96.
[91] Or if it is comprised "in an unusual way": the usual method is viewed as being a fixed remuneration of 75 per cent, and a management bonus of at most 25 per cent, BFH GmbHR 95, 385.
[92] *Ante*, p. 111.
[93] BGH GmbHR 90, 344.
[94] BGH GmbHR 90, 345; WM 89, 1246 in relation to an AG; 84, 151; GmbHR 78, 38, 85; 66, 277.
[95] *Post*, p. 148 on termination.
[96] § 626 para. 2 BGB.

Lapse of time and termination come into consideration as reasons for the expiry, along with contractual cancellation and the death of the managing director (but not the dissolution or the bankruptcy of the company).

Determination by lapse of time

The service agreement can be concluded for a limited time of a certain period.[97] Usually, it is agreed that the employment shall end (without a further declaration being necessary) with the expiry of the month in which the managing director reaches the age of 65.[98]

If the managing director continues to hold office upon attaining the age limit – with the knowledge of the company and without an objection being raised by the company immediately – after the end of the service agreement, then the relationship is considered as having been prolonged for an indefinite period.[99] The continued relationship will be governed by the corresponding regulations which have applied to date, but now by the statutory notice periods.

Termination

The shareholders' meeting is responsible for terminating the service agreement[100] if the termination is connected with the end of the removal from office as managing director.[101] If this connection is missing, such as in the case of the continuation of the agreement after removal from office or resignation from office, the other or new managing directors are responsible.[102] The articles of association may transfer the competence to the supervisory board or to another individual managing director.

If no other agreement has been reached, ordinary termination is possible on the fifteenth day of a month with effect to the end of the month.[103] In addition, termination for cause – even without notice – is always permissible.[104] It presupposes that it would be unreasonable to expect the party terminating the relationship to continue the employment relationship until its ordinary expiry,[105] which does not depend on fault. Termination for cause must have been received by the managing director within two weeks after the time at which the party entitled to terminate received "sure and comprehensive" knowledge of the facts which are decisive for the termination.[106]

---

[97] § 620 para. 1 BGB. If the appointment is for a limited time, e.g. for five years, the contract of employment concluded afterwards – which is not expressly concluded for a limited time – will be viewed as also being for a limited time if it contains regulations which presuppose the activities as a managing director.

[98] BGH NJW 93, 1262; BFH BB 93, 1702.

[99] § 625 BGB.

[100] The supervisory board in the case of a co-determined GmbH.

[101] BGH BB 69, 373; WM 58, 675; 68, 570, 1350; 70, 249; 76, 380; GmbHR 71, 1.

[102] BGH WM 73, 13; WM 84, 533.

[103] § 621 no. 3 BGB.

[104] *Post*, p. 187.

[105] § 626 para. 1 BGB.

[106] § 626 para. 2 BGB; BGH ZIP 96, 636.

Where there are several managing directors, they must all acquire this knowledge.[107]

4.5 Taxation of the income of the (foreign) managing director

Income from employed work

The managing director is taxed on his remuneration package, including fringe benefits, as income from employed work.[108] Remuneration packages include all the payments which the managing director receives from the company. In particular, these may be salary, management bonuses, gratuities or retirement pension, but they may also be so-called payments in kind, such as company cars, loans at favourable rates of interest, cheap residential accommodation and insurance. If the managing director receives payments in kind, these must be brought into the calculation at the usual market price at the place of delivery, less the usual reductions in price.[109] The total remuneration package of the managing director is subject to income tax deduction on wages and salaries (wage tax),[110] for the proper deduction of which the GmbH is liable.[111]

In particular, income from employed work also includes remuneration of the (former) managing director which he receives out of company retirement pension or other forms of deferred compensation after the end of the employment relationship.[112] In principle, this remuneration only has to be taxed at the time of payment (time of influx) to the managing director. By contrast, at the level of the GmbH, of the formation of (pension) reserves already has the effect of reducing profits during the GmbH managing director's active years.[113]

If the managing director receives compensation in connection with his retirement from the GmbH, then this is subject to a reduced rate of half the average tax rate[114] to the extent to which the tax-free allowance of a maximum of DM 36,000 does not apply.[115]

Managing directors subject to limited tax liability

If the (foreign) managing director has neither a place of residence in Germany[116] nor is he ordinarily resident in Germany,[117] then he is only liable for tax within

---

[107] BGH WM 80, 957: If the shareholders' meeting cannot meet and pass a legally valid resolution within this time-limit "for statutory reasons or reasons under the law of the articles of association which are worthy of being recognised", then the time-limit is extended accordingly. See also BGH NJW 93, 46. By contrast, the consent requirement specified in § 103 BetrVG does not prevent the time-limit beginning to run, BAG NJW 78, 661.

[108] § 19 EStG.

[109] § 8 para. 2 EStG.

[110] "Lohnsteuer", § 38 EStG.

[111] § 42d EStG.

[112] §§ 19 para. 1 no. 2, 24 no. 2 EStG.

[113] § 249 HGB, § 6a EStG.

[114] § 34 para. 1, 2 no. 2 EStG.

[115] § 3 no. 9 EStG.

[116] § 8 AO.

[117] § 9 AO.

Germany for certain income generated in Germany itself.[118] His remuneration package as managing director is then subject to income tax within the scope of the so-called limited income tax liability.[119] In accordance with the existing tax treaties, the German tax authorities are usually entitled to the right to tax this remuneration package.[120] This is not dependent on whether the managing director was in Germany for longer than half a year (the so-called 183 days rule) since the remuneration is paid by an employer in Germany (the GmbH).[121] However, usually there is an exception for the remuneration of the (former) managing director out of company retirement pension schemes.[122] They can, in principle, only be taxed in the state of permanent residence;[123] the company retirement pension of the managing director with limited tax liability is thus ultimately tax-free in Germany.

Tax rate

The income of both the managing director with unlimited tax liability and of the managing director with limited tax liability are subject to the progressive income tax rate and can thus be taxed at a rate of up to 53 per cent at the peak level.[124]

A taxable income of DM 100,000 (after all deductions which are permissible for tax purposes), for instance, results in a tax burden at a rate of 30.7 per cent. In the case of a taxable income in excess of DM 120,000, it is calculated in accordance with the following formula:

$$\text{Tax rate} = 0.53 - \frac{22{,}842}{\text{Income}}$$

Thus, the tax rate for a taxable income of DM 200,000 is 41.6 per cent. In the case of the possible joint assessment of the cumulated income of husband and wife, the tax progression can be reduced.

Special features in the case of shareholder-directors

If the managing director is at the same time a shareholder of the GmbH, then as far as the managing director's remuneration is concerned, it must always be examined whether the remuneration constitutes a constructive dividend. If this is answered in the affirmative, the income of the GmbH would be increased by the value of the constructive dividend. If the remuneration of the shareholder-director constitutes a constructive dividend, it will be reclassified as income from capital investments.[125]

In principle, all forms of remuneration are possible and permissible, such as

---

[118] §§ 1 para. 4, 49 EStG.
[119] § 49 para. 1 no. 4 EStG. See § 39d EStG on the implementation of the deduction of employment tax for employees with limited tax liability.
[120] Art. 15 OECD Model Tax Treaty.
[121] Art. 15 para. 2 OECD Model Tax Treaty.
[122] Art. 18 OECD Model Tax Treaty.
[123] Art. 18 OECD Model Tax Treaty.
[124] §§ 32a, 39d, 50 para. 3, 5 no. 2 EStG.
[125] § 20 para. 1 no. 1 EStG; *post*, p. 224 for details of the tax consequences of the constructive dividends.

fixed remuneration, participation in the profits or the turnover, commission, management bonuses and other bonuses. The following applies to the recognition of income from employed work for tax law purposes.

Clear agreement

The deduction by the GmbH of the shareholder-director's remuneration as business expenditure presupposes that there is a service agreement between the GmbH and the shareholder-director.

The agreed remuneration must be clear and explicit from the outset. The agreement must be valid under civil law. Agreements between the managing director and the GmbH he represents can thus be ignored from a tax point of view if they breach the prohibition on self-dealing.[126]

Reasonableness

In order to avoid the legal consequences of a constructive dividend, the total remuneration of the shareholder-director must, in principle, be reasonable. There is no general standard by which to assess the reasonableness of the re-muneration. The following must in particular be taken into consideration for the assessment:

- the type and scope of the activities;
- the future prospective earnings of the business;
- the proportion of the managing director's salary in relation to the overall profit and return on investment;
- the type and the level of the remuneration which businesses of the same type pay their managing directors for corresponding performance.

Management bonuses

Profit-related management bonuses can also be validly agreed under tax law between the GmbH and the shareholder-director. They only constitute con-structive dividends if the reasons for the payments or the levels thereof do not correspond to what an independent third party would receive in return for the management. Generally, the annual overall remuneration package must consist of annual fixed earnings of at least 75 per cent and a performance-related part of at most 25 per cent.

However, the unusual amount of a profit-related management bonus does not justify treating it as a constructive dividend as a whole. Only the proportion of the bonus which is unreasonably high constitutes a constructive dividend.

Turnover-related management bonuses will only be viewed as reasonable if there are special reasons justifying them.

Pension commitments

Reserves for pension commitments shall also, in principle, be recognised for tax purposes, even in the case of controlling shareholder-directors, as long as the

---

[126] § 181 BGB.

preconditions specified in § 6a EStG are fulfilled and the pension commitment can be viewed as having a business motive. A pension commitment is recognised if the promised pension can be earned within a reasonable period. This will not be the case where the period between the promise of the pension and the foreseeable attainment of the start of retirement amounts to less than ten years. In addition, pension commitments will also not be recognised if they are made immediately after the managing director is employed and without the waiting time which usually applies as between third parties.

5. Duties

5.1 General standard of care

Apart from the general tortious liability which exists for all[127] and the special cases which are expressly regulated by statute,[128] the managing director's duties are owed to the company.[129]

The managing director is under an obligation to apply the standard of "the due care of a prudent businessman" in the company's affairs.[130] He is thus subject to the general requirements of the duty of care which a prudent businessman in a responsible management position must observe in the independent management of the assets of third parties.[131] In individual cases, these requirements are dependent on the type and size of the business, its particular area and situation, as well as the importance of the relevant act.[132]

5.2 At the stage of formation

At the time of the formation of the GmbH, the managing directors must apply for registration of the company in the Commercial Register and accept share capital contributions from the shareholders on behalf of the company.

5.3 Commercial Register

The managing director must comply with – and ensure the company's compliance with – all the applicable statutory and other legal obligations and requirements, in particular the filing of the annual statements and of the list of shareholders to the Commercial Register, and the prompt filing of notices of appointment or removal from office of managing directors or procurators.[133]

---

[127] §§ 823, 826, 687 BGB.
[128] § 9a (false information upon formation), § 11 para. 2 (liability of a person acting prior to incorporation), § 31 para. 6 (prohibited repayments), § 43 para. 3 (prohibited acquisition of own shares), § 57 para. 4 (false information upon increases in share capital), § 64 para. 2 (breach of the duty to file a petition for bankruptcy).
[129] § 43; BGH GmbHR 93, 420.
[130] § 43 para. 1.
[131] RGZ 64, 254, 257; OLG Bremen GmbHR 64, 8, 9.
[132] *Post*, Liability p. 161.
[133] *Post*, p. 271.

5.4 Accounting

As a company, the GmbH is under an obligation to keep accounts and to make its commercial transactions and the situation as regards its assets clear in the accounts, in accordance with the principles of proper accounting.[134] These commercial law duties of accounting must also be fulfilled for tax purposes.[135]

The managing directors of the GmbH are under an obligation to ensure the proper accounting for the company.[136] They do not have to do the accounting themselves. Delegation to employees or the commissioning of third parties is permissible. Where there are several managing directors, the accounting can be delegated to one managing director by way of the allocation of duties. This does not exempt the remaining managing directors from their statutory duty,[137] but it reduces it to the participation in an objective selection of the managing director responsible, and the suitable monitoring of him.[138]

5.5 Annual statements

The managing directors are under an obligation to prepare the annual statements.[139]

5.6 Tax

The managing directors are responsible for the fulfilment of the tax duties of the GmbH.[140] These mainly encompass the duty of information,[141] the duty to keep accounts and written records[142] and the duty to submit and rectify tax declarations.[143] If the managing director commits a breach of these duties either deliberately or by gross negligence, and if – as a result – the tax debts of the company are not assessed or fulfilled, or are not assessed or fulfilled in good time, then he is personally liable.[144]

5.7 Staff

The managing directors are responsible for the staff, their selection, familiarization, and supervision.[145] This also includes the prevention or disclosure of

---

[134] § 238 para. 1 HGB.
[135] § 140 AO.
[136] § 41; *post*, chapter 13 on the content of the obligation.
[137] § 41.
[138] BGH NJW 86, 54, 55; BFH BB 84, 1992.
[139] § 264 para. 1 HGB; *post*, p. 211.
[140] § 34 para. 1 AO; *post*, chapter 14.
[141] § 93 AO.
[142] §§ 140 *et seq.* AO.
[143] §§ 149 *et seq.* AO.
[144] § 69 AO. BFH 84, 1992. The managing directors of the GmbH acting as general partner are liable for the tax debts of the limited partnership, BFH GmbHR 79, 44. Particularly stringent requirements apply to the deduction of wage tax, BFH GmbHR 82, 242; GmbHR 87, 444. *Post*, p. 183, and p. 169 on criminal liability.
[145] *Post*, chapter 11.

wrongful conduct by suitable means.[146] The managing director is only liable for his own fault. Wrongful conduct by the staff cannot in principle be attributed to him.[147] However, if the managing director does not fulfil his management responsibility, or does not do so to a sufficient extent, then liability may result from inadequate organisation or insufficient checks and supervision.[148]

5.8 Shareholders' meeting

Every managing director is responsible for calling and preparing the shareholders' meeting.[149] In the GmbH with more than 2,000 employees, the supervisory board is also entitled and obliged to call the shareholders' meeting, as are the managing directors, if the good of the company requires that the meeting be called.[150] Subject to a different regulation in the articles of association, the same applies to the advisory board.[151]

Reasons for calling a shareholders' meeting
Other persons or organs are not entitled to a right to call a shareholders' meeting; however, such a right may be granted in the articles of association.

The meeting shall be called:

- in a case where half the share capital has been lost;[152]
- at the request of shareholders who hold at least 10 per cent of the share capital;[153]
- always in cases where this is necessary in the interests of the company.[154] The calling of a meeting is necessary if the managing directors – according to their best judgment – are of the opinion that the measure to be taken is necessary or at least worth considering, and the shareholders' meeting is competent to deal with the matter.

In certain circumstances, even if only the managing directors' sphere of competence is affected, the interests of the company may require a meeting to be called, such as, for example, in cases of extraordinary transactions and those whose approval by the shareholders is doubtful.[155]

---

[146] BFH BB 74, 1008; BGH GmbHR 90, 207.
[147] Neither by reason of liability for "persons employed in performing an obligation for whom the principal is vicariously liable" (§ 278 BGB) nor of liability for "vicarious agents" (§ 831 BGB).
[148] § 43 para. 2. OLG Bremen GmbHR 64, 8; BGH WM 71, 1548; DB 74, 1619; BB 80, 1344; WM 85, 1293; GmbHR 90, 500, 503. If the managing director makes use of a procurator for the fulfilment of his obligations, e.g. the duty of supervision, then § 278 BGB (liability for persons employed in performing an obligation, for whom the principal is vicariously liable) shall apply, BGHZ 13, 61.
[149] § 49 para. 1. KG GmbHR 66, 36; 68, 118; OLG Frankfurt GmbHR 76, 110.
[150] §§ 25 para. 1 no. 2 MitbestG, 111 para. 3 AktG.
[151] §§ 52 GmbHG, 111 para. 3 AktG.
[152] § 49 para. 3.
[153] § 50 para. 1.
[154] § 49 para. 2.
[155] This duty exists in the case of decisions where a managing director cannot reasonably assume that he was permitted to conclude them exclusively at his own responsibility without the involvement of the general meeting, BGHZ 83, 122.

Instead of calling a meeting, it is often sufficient to inform the shareholders and obtain a written resolution.[156] However, this does not apply in the case where the minority has requested that a meeting be called, the purpose of which is to give the minority a forum for the representation of their interests.[157]

Methods of calling meetings

The notice calling the meeting must state the purpose of the meeting,[158] and must be issued by registered letter with a period of notice of one week[159] between the day of the meeting and the day on which the last shareholder would under normal circumstances have received the letter in the course of due postal delivery.[160] All shareholders who are registered with the company must be invited to attend the shareholders' meeting, including those shareholders who are not entitled to vote.[161]

Defects in calling the meeting (breaches of form or of the period of notice) usually only lead to the voidability of the resolutions adopted.[162] However, certain serious defects in the calling of a shareholders' meeting can also result in such resolutions being null and void.[163] Defects in calling a meeting are only insignificant if all shareholders are present (or represented) and are in agreement that the meeting should be held.[164] A shareholder who objects to this is considered as not being present.[165]

5.9 Maintenance of capital

Managing directors have obligations in respect of the preservation of share capital.[166] If false statements were made for the purpose of forming the company,[167] or increasing its share capital,[168] or if the share capital is improperly repaid, then the managing directors are jointly and severally liable for the reimbursement of the capital. If compensation is required to satisfy the company's creditors, the managing directors' liability is not avoided by their acting in accordance with a shareholders' resolution.

---

[156] *Ante*, p. 46.
[157] It is also usually necessary to call a meeting rather than to obtain a written resolution where half of the share capital has been lost or the meeting is necessary in the interests of the company.
[158] § 51 para. 2.
[159] § 51 para. 1.
[160] BGHZ 100, 264, established case-law. The period of notice is calculated in accordance with the terms of §§ 187 para. 1, 188 para. 2, 193 BGB.
[161] § 16 para. 1.
[162] *Ante*, p. 75.
[163] *Ante*, p. 75; such as, for example, the failure to invite all shareholders, BGHZ 36, 211; OLG Frankfurt DB 83, 2678; the calling of the meeting by persons not competent to do so, BGHZ 11, 235; 87, 1.
[164] § 51 para. 3.
[165] BGHZ 100, 264, 269 *et seq.*
[166] *Ante*, p. 111.
[167] *Ante*, p. 34.
[168] *Ante*, p. 120.

5.10 Information

The managing directors are obliged to furnish each shareholder with information concerning company matters upon request, and to permit them to inspect the company's books.[169] If they consider themselves to be entitled or obliged to refuse to furnish information or permit inspection in order to avoid disadvantages for the company, they must in principle obtain a shareholders' resolution on this.[170]

5.11 Confidentiality

The managing director, as an organ with a trustee function and a special fiduciary position, has an extensive duty of loyalty to the company[171]. This primarily results in duties of protection and of consideration in the form of mandatory requirements to cease and desist from doing something, but also in standards for duties to act, such as, in particular, the duty of management (the so-called "active duties to promote the interests of the company").

The duty of loyalty requires the managing director to maintain secrecy in relation to third parties (business partners, public authorities, the press, etc.) concerning confidential relationships and secrets of the company, namely trade or business secrets. This applies irrespective of whether the managing director obtained the information to be kept secret in the course of his activities as an organ of the company or outside this function.[172]

The duty of confidentiality does not apply in relation to the shareholders and other organs (in particular in relation to the supervisory board); in these instances, the managing director is obliged to furnish comprehensive information. By contrast, employees of the company who do not deal with the matter to be kept confidential by reason of the sphere of activity delegated to them shall also be viewed as unauthorized third parties.

The duty of confidentiality is generally regulated in the service agreement, together with the restraint of competition. The managing director remains under a duty of confidentiality even after the end of the service agreement.[173] The breach of the obligation to protect business and trade secrets which come to the managing director's knowledge in this capacity is placed under threat of criminal sanction.[174]

---

[169] § 51a.
[170] *Ante*, p. 63.
[171] BGHZ 10, 187, 192; 49, 30; BGH GmbHR 68, 114; 77, 43.
[172] Whilst the duty of confidentiality has been regulated by statute in company law in § 93 para. 1 AktG and in the law on co-operative societies in § 34 para. 1 of the Co-Operative Associations Act (GenG), there is no corresponding regulation in the GmbHG.
[173] BGHZ 91, 6; OLG Hamm GmbHR 85, 157.
[174] § 85. BGH WM 75, 678; OLG Koblenz WM 86, 481.

5.12 Restraint of competition[175]

During the term of the service agreement

The duty of loyal conduct towards the GmbH means that the managing director may not compete with it during his term of office either in his own name or in the name of a third party, particularly as he usually owes the company his entire capacity for work. He is prohibited from making use of business opportunities of the company and its group enterprises for his own advantage, particularly opportunities of purchase and sale.[176] The business opportunities will in any case always be due to the company if the company itself has already expressed interest in the transaction and a corresponding resolution has been adopted[177] or if the company has already entered into contractual negotiations or a concrete offer has already been made to it.[178]

A precondition of the restraint of competition is that the GmbH would be in a position to make use of the business opportunity. The company's lack of the necessary funds is not sufficient in itself to exclude this precondition, because the managing director is under an obligation to try to obtain financing. Only once the company has examined all possibilities and has then refused to conduct the transaction, and consents to the managing director making use of the opportunity, can the managing director seize the business opportunity himself.[179] There is no requirement that the restraint of competition must be included in the articles of association or in the service agreement.[180]

Provision may be made in the articles of association for exemption from the restraint of competition in certain individual cases. If such a provision is missing, exemption is possible by means of a shareholders' resolution with the majority required for an alteration of the articles of association.

The scope of the restraint of competition is primarily dictated by the object of the enterprise as specified in the articles of association. In addition, it extends to all areas which fall within the line of development of the company and which offer it business opportunities.[181] If the managing director breaches the restraint of competition, he can be sued to ensure forbearance and for compensation.[182] Furthermore, the prohibited activity can also be liable to criminal prosecution as a criminal breach of trust[183] and can oblige the managing director to pay compensation by reason of tort liability.[184] Alongside this, the company can require that, within the internal relationship, the transaction be considered as if it had

---

[175] "Wettbewerbsverbot".

[176] BGH WM 83, 498; 85, 1443; BB 86, 486: advantage taken by persons close to the managing director; BGH WM 89, 1335: advantage taken by an enterprise which is controlled by the managing director; for the commercial limited partnership BGH ZIP 89, 986.

[177] BGH WM 76, 77.

[178] BGH GmbHR 68, 141.

[179] BGH WM 85, 1444, 1445 (in the case of a shareholder in a commercial general partnership who acts as managing director); BGH GmbHR 86, 42, 43.

[180] BGHZ 49, 30, 31; BGH GmbHR 77, 43.

[181] BGHZ 89, 170.

[182] § 43 para. 2.

[183] § 266 StGB.

[184] §§ 823 para. 2, 826 BGB.

been entered into on the company's account (right to enter into a transaction),
[185] with the consequence that the managing director must hand over to the
company what he received in the transaction.[186]

Post-contract restraint of competition

After the end of the service agreement, the managing director is free[187] unless a
(geographically or materially) restricted restraint of competition was agreed.[188]
It is disputed whether this is only permissible in the case when the managing
director is granted compensation for the duration of non-competition.[189] The
case-law denies this and applies the rules on good morals as a check on unreasonable restrictions.[190] The restraint of competition after the end of the service agreement presupposes that there is an interest of the company worth
protecting (according to place, time and subject-matter of the exercise of a profession) and may not make the commercial activities of the managing director
unreasonably difficult.[191]

According to the case-law, two to three years are usual. The decisive factor is
the continued effect of the business relationships which were established during
the managing director's period of office, which experience has shown usually
disappear within this period, meaning that no significant losses to the company
need be feared any more.[192]

5.13 Shareholders' instructions[193]

Binding character

The shareholders' meeting can issue instructions to the managing directors
in all spheres of the management of the enterprise either generally or in an
individual case;[194] the managing directors are obliged to follow such instructions even if disadvantages for the company could result therefrom.[195]

The right to issue instructions is vested only in the shareholders' meeting,
which shall decide on it with a simple majority, but it is not vested in individual

---

[185] By analogy with §§ 113 para. 1 HGB, 88 para. 2 AktG.
[186] BGHZ 80, 69, 70; 89, 162, 171.
[187] But he may not "take with him" a business opportunity which he ought to have used for the company, BGH ZIP 85, 1984.
[188] OLG Cologne BB 91, 859 (for the shareholder who is not at the same time a managing director); OLG Karlsruhe GmbHR 87, 309 (for the shareholder who is procurator); OLG Hamm
GmbHR 88, 344; LG Bochum GmbHR 92, 670 (for the shareholder-director).
[189] By analogy with §§ 74 *et seq.* HGB.
[190] § 138 BGB; BGHZ 91, 1; OLG Karlsruhe GmbHR 87, 309; OLG Hamm GmbHR 88, 344. BGH
DB 91, 1508 on the set-off of unemployment benefit against the compensation for the duration of
non-competition (if the GmbH has to pay it to the Federal Labour Office under the terms of § 128a
Employment Promotion Act – AFG).
[191] BGHZ 91, 1; BGH WM 86, 1282; GmbHR 90, 77; OLG Hamm GmbHR 88, 344: a subsequent
restraint of competition is null and void, even if it only prohibits subordinate activities in a competing business; the same applies to a restraint of competition beyond the end of the contract over a
period of five years without compensation, OLG Hamm GmbHR 89, 259.
[192] BGH WM 74, 74; NJW 79, 1605, 1606; DB 84, 1717, 1718; NJW 64, 2203.
[193] "Gesellschafterweisungen".
[194] § 37 para. 1.
[195] BGHZ 31, 278; OLG Düsseldorf ZIP 84, 1476, 1478.

shareholders, even if they hold a majority of the votes.[196] However, the right to issue instructions can be transferred to individual shareholders or to another organ (supervisory board, advisory board) in the articles of association.

Limits on the authority to issue instructions

The authority of the shareholders to issue instructions is restricted by public law duties[197] and the generally compulsory statutory rules of civil law.[198] In particular, instructions may not conflict with compulsory statutory rules of company law[199] or with the duty of loyalty under company law.[200] In addition, they also must not contradict the articles of association. The managing directors may not follow instructions which are clearly null and void; compliance with such instructions does not release them from their liability.[201]

Exemption from liability

If the company suffers loss as a result of compliance with a permissible and binding instruction, the managing directors are not bound to pay compensation if there has been no breach of their duties.[202] At most, they are liable to third parties or for faults in the implementation of the instructions. By contrast, a managing director may not follow an impermissible instruction. Otherwise he acts in breach of his duty.[203]

5.14 Announcement of a loss and insolvency petition

If the assets of the GmbH have been reduced to at least half the share capital, the managing directors must notify the loss of assets to all shareholders; failure to make such notification renders the managing director liable to prosecution.[204] The duty of notification arises upon the occurrence of the loss and must be fulfilled without delay as soon as such knowledge is obtained. A balance sheet does not have to be submitted.

The notification can be made by calling the shareholders' meeting,[205] but also by (registered) letter to all shareholders, by notification in the newspapers authorized to publish company announcements or in another form. The announcement must also be made by a managing director who, according to the distribution of spheres of business competence, is not responsible for financial matters.[206] All this likewise applies to the duty to petition for the opening of bankruptcy or composition proceedings in the case of illiquidity or overindebtedness.[207]

---

[196] Only in a one-shareholder GmbH is no shareholders' resolution required, BGHZ 31, 278.
[197] *Ante*, p. 152.
[198] E.g. good morals, § 138 BGB.
[199] E.g. § 30; *ante*, p. 138, or § 64; *post*, p. 204.
[200] BGHZ 31, 258, 278; 76, 159.
[201] BGH WM 80, 30.
[202] § 43 para. 2; BGHZ 31, 278.
[203] BGH WM 80, 30, On liability, *post*, p. 161.
[204] § 84 para. 1 no. 1.
[205] The usual case, § 49 para. 3.
[206] BGH WM 94, 1030; *ante*, p. 142.
[207] §§ 64 para. 1, 84 para. 1 no. 2; *post*, p. 331.

6. Abuse of representative authority

The acts of the managing directors are usually also valid for the GmbH,[208] even if they exceed the limitations of their representative authority which exist within the internal relationship, and which they must observe.[209] A limitation on the managing director's authority to represent the company has no effect on third parties.[210]

Within the internal relationship with the company, the managing director can be liable to pay compensation if he exceeds the power to conduct the business conferred on him.[211] At the same time, the breach of duty can constitute cause for his removal from office.[212]

Liability of the managing director (or of the company) in relation to the contractual party[213] fails in cases of abuse where the contractual party does not merit protection.[214]

7. Civil law responsibility

Managing directors are liable to the company for damage resulting from any breach of their duties. Such a breach may justify the removal from office of the managing director for cause. Furthermore, relevant laws may provide for additional sanctions, e.g. fines or criminal penalties,[215] in order to enforce compliance with the law.

As is shown by a description of the individual duties,[216] numerous direct risks of being personally called to account arise from the activities of a managing director; they already start at the formation stage of the GmbH with the liability for false information in the application for registration in the Commercial Register[217] and can extend to the liquidation stage.[218]

The liability is primarily to the company, the sole party in relation to whom the managing director is under an obligation to manage the enterprise properly. However, liability is also conceivable in relation to individual shareholders[219] and third parties[220] under narrow preconditions.

---

[208] § 36.
[209] § 37 para. 1; *ante*, p. 140.
[210] § 37 para. 2.
[211] § 43.
[212] *Ante*, p. 144.
[213] § 179 BGB in conjunction with § 31 BGB by analogy.
[214] § 179 para. 3 BGB.
[215] *Post*, p. 166.
[216] *Ante*, p. 152.
[217] § 9a; *ante*, p. 152.
[218] *Post*, chapter 21; § 71 para. 4 in conjunction with § 43.
[219] *Post*, p. 161.
[220] *Post*, p. 162.

7.1 In relation to the company/shareholders

Statutory liability

Liability under general provisions

The central statutory provision for civil law claims of the company to compensation stipulates the strict standard of fault of "the duty of care of a prudent businessman".[221] If the GmbH has suffered damage as a result of the managing director's conduct, and if the company can prove that the conduct in question constituted a breach of the managing director's duties, then the managing director must prove that he took the necessary care or that he did not realise that he was committing a breach of duty, or that the damage would have occurred in any case even had he taken the necessary care.[222]

The same applies to the special offences of founders' liability,[223] the liability for incorrect or incomplete notification of an increase in share capital[224] and the claim to compensation for delay in filing bankruptcy petitions,[225] which all refer back to the standard of care.

If the damage is culpably caused by several managing directors or by managing directors and members of the supervisory board, then they are jointly and severally liable, i.e. each of them must take responsibility for the entire damage.[226] This also applies in the case of internal allocation of spheres of competence.[227] The contributory negligence of the other managing directors does not relieve the managing director in relation to third parties. At most, different burdens may be borne within the internal relationship by reason of the joint and several debtors' adjustment.[228]

There is no liability for acts which were undertaken on the basis of binding instructions issued by the shareholders' meeting, but also – in so far as provision is made for this – by other organs, such as the supervisory board or the advisory board.[229]

The culpable breach of duties of an organ in principle does not give rise to liability in relation to the shareholders, even if the managing director culpably believes that an instruction is binding.[230]

---

[221] § 43 para. 1; *ante*, p. 152. The principles of the mitigation of liability which apply to employees in the case of so-called "work which is dangerous *per se*" do not apply to managing directors, BGH WM 75, 467, 469.

[222] BGH BB 74, 994; WM 85, 1293; ZIP 91, 159; GmbHR 92, 303. There is a further-reaching alleviation of the burden of proof in the case of shortfalls in the cash balance or similar circumstances which cannot be explained, BGH BB 1985, 1754.

[223] § 9a.

[224] § 57 para. 4.

[225] § 64 para. 2.

[226] § 43 para. 2 GmbHG in conjunction with §§ 421 *et seq.* BGB.

[227] BGH W; 86, 789; *ante*, p. 142.

[228] § 426 BGB.

[229] *Ante*, p. 158.

[230] The only exception regulated by statute is the special case mentioned in § 31 para. 6; in accordance therewith, the managing director is liable for compensation to the shareholders in the case of a payment made by a culpable breach of § 30 (maintenance of share capital) if they would have had to make the payment themselves by reason of the impossibility of collection of the claim to repayment against the recipient (§ 31 para. 3; *ante*, p. 155 on the duty of the managing directors to maintain the share capital).

Tort liability

The culpable breach of the duties of an organ does not automatically give rise to tort liability to the shareholders.[231] Tort liability is, however, conceivable in the case of breaches of individual rights of the shareholders by the managing directors.[232]

Liability on the basis of the service agreement

The managing director may also be liable to the company by reason of a breach of duties out of the service agreement.[233] However, the service agreement is only significant in so far as the content of the managing directors' duties is specified precisely therein, or additional duties are stipulated. It does not give rise to liability in relation to the individual shareholders, because they are not contractual parties and are thus not included in the protective sphere of the service agreement.

Assertion of liability

The assertion of claims to compensation by the company against a managing director of a GmbH requires a resolution of the shareholders' meeting, irrespective of the basis of the claim.[234] This applies to any form of assertion, even to the oral or written assertion of the claim or the demand, not only for the legal action.[235]

7.2 Liability in relation to third parties

Contractual Liability

Generally, breaches of contractual duty committed by the managing director in relation to business partners do not give rise to liability on the part of the managing director but rather only on the part of the company.

By way of exception, personal liability of the managing director comes into consideration if he does not act for the GmbH in relation to third parties, or signs as a personal business name or an objective firm name without the addition of "GmbH", so that the business partner assumes that he is contracting with a sole trader with unlimited liability or with the personally liable partner of a partnership (OHG or KG),[236] or for breach of pre-contractual duties of conduct.[237] This, in particular, involves two groups of cases.

---

[231] § 43 is not a protective legislative provision as defined by tort liability under the terms of § 823 para. 2 BGB.

[232] Although the membership right of the shareholder is a right protected by § 823 para. 1; RGZ 100, 274, 278 (GmbH); 158, 248, 255 (AG); it is not sufficient for liability of the managing director for wrongful acts that the value of the membership is reduced by a reduction of the assets of the company; RGZ 158, 248, 255 (AG).

[233] BGHZ 75, 321; 76, 326; GmbHR 80, 272.

[234] § 46 no. 8.

[235] *Ante*, p. 64 on the assertion of compensation claims of the company on its behalf by individual shareholders (*actio pro socio*).

[236] Liability out of giving rise to the appearance of a legal position, BGH NJW 81, 1569.

[237] "*Culpa in contrahendo*".

In the one instance, the managing director – by reason of special expert competence – creates an increased trust in his abilities on the part of the business partner, going above and beyond the usual confidence in contractual negotiations, which he then culpably disappoints.[238]

In the other instance, he acts in his own interests. This will only be assumed if there are circumstances going beyond the participation in the GmbH which justify the assumption that he is acting on his own behalf. Yet this must be handled restrictively in order to avoid a contradiction of the principle of limited liability.[239] The fact that the managing director has furnished security for obligations of the company is not sufficient to give rise to such an interest of his own.[240]

Tort liability
Managing directors only have restricted liability for tortious acts in relation to third parties.[241] Primarily, claims to compensation for fraud,[242] criminal breach of trust[243] and delay in filing a bankruptcy petition[244] come into consideration.[245] The managing director is, in principle, not liable in tort for damage caused by other persons belonging to the company, primarily subordinate employees,[246] if he himself does not fulfil the objective and subjective preconditions for a wrongful act.[247]

Apart from directly caused damage to certain legally protected goods – such as traffic accidents on business trips – this can be the case where there is a breach of certain duties in relation to third parties. Such liability is founded by the managing director's position of having management control over the fulfilment of his tasks. Case-law views him as a guarantor or guardian in respect of certain dangers to the public,[248] not only in relation to the company but rather also in relation to third parties.[249]

For the important sphere of product liability, this, for example, means that under the law of torts, the managing director can be held liable alongside the company as the manufacturer of a defective product if the defectiveness

---

[238] Such as, for example, by assuming an additional guarantee (which is not legally binding) for the proper fulfilment of the legal transaction in view; BGH GmbHR 91, 409, 410, with a synopsis of the case-law.

[239] BGH NJW 95, 1544.

[240] BGH ZIP 94, 2203, 2205 *et seq.*

[241] § 823 BGB para. 1, or § 826 BGB, in case of the breach of protective statutory provisions under § 823 para. 2 BGB.

[242] § 263 StGB.

[243] § 266 StGB.

[244] § 64.

[245] It has not been clarified whether § 130 para. 1 OWiG (breach of the duty of supervision) and § 41 (duty to keep proper accounts) and the accompanying criminal provisions in §§ 238, 238b para. 1 no. 1, 3 para. 2 StGB are protective statutory provisions, see BGH ZIP 94, 867; *post,* p. 335 on the liability under § 823 para. 2 BGB in conjunction with § 64 para. 1.

[246] *Ante,* p. 154.

[247] BGHZ 109, 297, 302; LG Lübeck WM 94, 458.

[248] "Verkehrssicherungspflichten".

[249] BGHZ 109, 297, 304; BGH NJW 75, 1827.

resulted from insufficient supervision, but in addition also in the case of insufficient monitoring after the goods were released into circulation. If, after the
commencement of distribution, dangers become evident in the course of practical use which could not have been foreseen up until then, the managing director must take all possible and reasonable steps to ward off the damage, such as
notification or general warning to all consumers, but also the recall of the faulty
product series in the case where there is a threat to health. There is thus an
obligation to monitor the products to detect unknown damaging characteristics
and also to inform oneself of the other dangerous consequences of use by keeping abreast of scientific developments.[250]

7.3 Formal approval of management activities ("discharge")[251]

Discharge is the approval of the management and – at the same time – it also
expresses the shareholders' confidence in the management for the future.

Granting of discharge

In general, the discharge is granted at the end of the financial year. However, it
is also possible to discharge the management within a certain accounting
period, after a specific business transaction, or after a managing director
resigns.

The discharge can cover all managing directors or exclude one or more managing directors. The shareholders are responsible for the discharge,[252] unless
this competence has been delegated to another (executive) body of the company by the articles of association. The shareholders decide by resolution. The
discharge is granted if a corresponding motion receives a simple majority of the
votes cast, unless otherwise provided in the articles of association. A shareholder-director who shall be discharged has no right to vote.[253] This also applies
if someone else's discharge affects his own interests.

It is not necessary to pass a resolution expressly as a resolution of discharge;
however, the adoption of the annual accounts, which are prepared by the managing directors, does not automatically discharge the management from its
responsibilities.

Effect

The discharge precludes the company from asserting any claims against the discharged managing director for misconduct in the past if the facts and circumstances which give rise to such claims were known to the shareholders, or could

---

[250] BGH NJW 81, 1606, 1607 *et seq.* with further references; 90, 2560, *post*, p. 171 on criminal liability
for lack of product safety.
[251] "Entlastung".
[252] § 46 no. 5.
[253] § 47 para. 3.

have been ascertained by them if they had exercised reasonable care, at the time they passed the discharge resolution. Nevertheless, the management remains liable for violating the principles of the preservation of the company's share capital,[254] because this affects the interests of creditors. A discharge which has been wrongfully obtained by false representations is void.

Refusal

No managing director has an enforceable right to be discharged.[255] If the shareholders deny the discharge, each managing director has the right to resign from office and to terminate his service agreement by extraordinary termination. In addition, he might even have a claim to compensation. If the company maintains that it has any claims against the managing director, the managing director has the right to file an action for declaration that the company does not have such claims. However, no further judicial protection exists, particularly against express disapproval of the managing director's management.

7.4 Indemnification of the managing directors and insurance

Claims of the company or the shareholders

It has not yet been decided in the case-law whether it is permissible to indemnify the managing director by agreement (in the articles of association or in the service agreement) from liability in relation to the company from the outset. The main view in the literature is that it is permissible, but not for breaches against the principles of the maintenance of capital, owing to the express statutory regulation.[256] In addition, indemnification from liability for deliberate breaches of duty is impermissible. The same applies for breaches of duty where even an instruction of the shareholders would not justify the managing director's conduct, i.e. breaches of good morals or of provisions whose observance is in the public interest.[257]

Claims of third parties

If a managing director is called to account by third parties, he may under certain circumstances have a statutory claim to indemnity.[258] This is the case where he takes over the office within the framework of an employment relationship with the parent company, provided that he did not act in breach of his duties to the parent company.

---

[254] Capitalization and maintenance of capital; *ante*, p. 111 and p. 155.
[255] BGH GmbHR 85, 356.
[256] § 43 para. 3 in connection with §§ 9a para. 2, 57 para. 4, 43 para. 3 and §§ 30, 33 and 64 para. 2; *ante*, p. 111 and p. 155.
[257] *Ante*, p. 159.
[258] § 670 BGB.

The managing director may also have himself indemnified by the company from liability to third parties either through the articles of association or in an individual contract. However, indemnification in the articles of association or a contractual indemnification from the outset is only valid if a waiver by the company of compensation claims or a settlement concerning such claims would be valid, namely in the case where no creditors' interests are affected. Here, too, the measure may not have any effect on the share capital.

Directors' and officers' liability insurance
Insurance against directors' liability as recognised in the common law jurisdictions is hardly known in Germany. This insurance covers claims of shareholders and third parties against the director and not claims of the company itself. However, the managing director owes his duties to the GmbH. Liability towards shareholders or third parties is the rare exception. It is often connected with blatant wrongdoings which an insurance would not cover anyway. The high risk of liability for negligence towards the company could thus not be insured with the usual directors' liability insurance. While such insurance has been offered for a few years now, it can hardly be marketed due to these reasons.

8. Criminal law responsibility and responsibility under regulatory offences law

8.1 General

According to German law, legal persons cannot commit criminal offences. The criminal law responsibility for the conduct of a GmbH affects the persons acting for the business. The conduct can consist of an action or a breach of duty through failure to act (omission). The managing director of a GmbH can thus render himself liable to criminal prosecution or commit a regulatory offence not only by acts in his own interests but also by such acts as he performs solely in his function as managing director and/or only in the interests of the GmbH.

The jurisdictional basis of the responsibility of the managing director can be both intentional conduct[259] and possibly also negligent conduct[260] (simple negligence). In so far as the criminal offences or regulatory offences require conduct based on wrongful intent, contingent intent[261] is sufficient (also known as "indirect intent"). This is given where the offender recognised the consequences of his actions as possible and acquiesced in their possible occurrence.

The distinction between regulatory offences[262] and criminal offences[263] is a

---

[259] "Vorsatz".
[260] "Fahrlässigkeit".
[261] "Bedingter Vorsatz".
[262] "Ordnungswidrigkeiten".
[263] "Straftaten".

formal one. If a statute provides that the sanction for a particular course of conduct is a sentence (imprisonment or a judicial fine), then a criminal offence has been committed, whereas where provision is made for an administrative fine, then a regulatory offence has been committed. The legal consequences of a judicial fine and an administrative fine are comparable in their financial effects on the parties affected, but they embody different types of value decisions: whilst the imposition of a criminal penalty is intended as an expression of sanctioning the breach of the legal system, the administrative fine constitutes an emphatic reminder of a duty, which is imposed by reason of a breach of the so-called administrative rules.

The administrative fines to be imposed in regulatory offences procedures (and the order for the forfeiture of the advantage gained by committing the regulatory offence) can, however, be very high; the other consequences for the offender and the business (e.g. the revocation of public authority permits) can be drastic and can in extreme cases constitute a threat to continued existence. Thus, the labyrinth of sanctions contained in the regulatory offences provisions should not be underestimated.

Along with the failure to observe statutory provisions or duties of conduct, the breach of general duties or duties developed in the case-law can also lead to criminal liability or to the breach of administrative rules bearing sanctions.

Together with criminal law responsibility (of the managing director and other persons acting for the GmbH), conduct of the persons acting for the GmbH which is liable to criminal prosecution or which is contrary to administrative regulations can lead to the imposition of an administrative fine against the GmbH.[264] In addition, the profit can be siphoned off.[265] Furthermore, items which were used in the commission of the offence or assets acquired through the offence can be confiscated or their forfeiture can be ordered.[266] It should also be mentioned that breaches of duty in the exercise of a trade can be registered in the Central Register of Trade and Industrial Offences.[267] The content thereof is the basis for the admission of the managing director to certain branches of the economy requiring a licence.[268]

8.2 Areas of emphasis in prosecution

Various breaches of duty by the managing director of a GmbH can result in criminal law consequences for him. However there are particular areas of emphasis in the prosecution of managing directors. These are criminal offences in connection with

---

[264] § 30 OWiG.
[265] § 29a OWiG.
[266] § 73 *et seq.* StGB.
[267] "Gewerbezentralregister".
[268] §§ 149 *et seq.* GewO.

- the protection of the assets of the GmbH;
- balance sheets;
- taxes and social insurance contributions;
- product safety and environmental protection;
- corporate corruption, competition and the economy;
- insolvency.

8.3 Offences in relation to the corporate assets

Bogus formation of a company

If the managing director gives false information about particular facts within the framework of the registration of the company or of an increase in share capital, then this will be punished as the bogus formation of the company.[269]

General property offences

In particular, the general criminal offences for the protection of assets, namely fraud,[270] obtaining credit by false pretences[271] and criminal breach of trust[272] protect the GmbH, its shareholders and creditors from damage by the managing director.

The managing director can be accused of fraudulent conduct if he gives false information about the economic situation of the company upon the conclusion of a loan agreement. It can already constitute fraud if the GmbH has taken on a loan in economically healthy times and the managing director fails to point out to the bank the threatening financial collapse of the GmbH in a crisis situation upon the (automatic) prolongation of a loan.

There must have been financial loss, but this may already be given in the case of a concrete threat to the assets, such as for example if the GmbH is granted a loan, the return of which is – contrary to the information provided by the managing directors – totally uncertain. Even if there is no financial loss, incorrect information supplied within the framework of the grant of a credit facility can be liable to prosecution.[273]

The offence of a criminal breach of trust[274] threatens the managing director with a penalty if he deliberately causes a detriment to the assets of the GmbH. In contrast to fraud, it is not necessary that the managing director intended to enrich himself or a third party. Acts of the managing director constituting a criminal breach of trust against the assets of the company can, for example, be:

- collusive behaviour in the conclusion of contracts of the company with third parties to the detriment of the company;

---

[269] "Gründungsschwindel"; § 82 GmbHG.
[270] "Betrug"; § 263 StGB.
[271] "Kreditbetrug"; § 265b StGB.
[272] "Untreue"; § 266 StGB.
[273] § 265b StGB.
[274] § 266 StGB.

- risk transactions with third parties, the grant of loans to or performance by the GmbH in relation to third parties, without corresponding security and without commercial justification;
- the withdrawal of assets of the GmbH for his own purposes or for share-holders, if there is no special authority to do so: if a shareholder-director is affected by an administrative fine, then it is only permissible for the com-pany to reimburse the administrative fine to him out of the assets of the company if a corresponding resolution of the shareholders is adopted. In addition, care must be taken that the tax treatment is correct.

Law on balance sheet crime
The duty of preparing the balance sheet is also included in the protection of the assets of the GmbH. The managing director can, amongst other things, be punished[275] if he deliberately:

- incorrectly states or conceals the GmbH's circumstances in the opening balance, in the annual statements or in the situation report of the GmbH;
- incorrectly states or conceals the group's circumstances in the annual group statements or in the group situation report;
- supplies false information, clarifications or proof to an auditor of the com-pany, an associated enterprise or the group, or incorrectly states or con-ceals the circumstances of the company, of a subsidiary enterprise or of the group, as the case may be.[276]

The managing director's conduct can be punished by an administrative fine if he has failed to observe particular statutory provisions in the preparation and adoption of the annual statements, the group annual statements, the situation report or the group situation report, or acts in contravention of particular provisions relating to disclosure or publication.[277]

8.4 Law on tax crime, social insurance contributions

The managing director of a GmbH can commit criminal tax offences[278] and regula-tory tax offences.[279]

Tax crime
The central criminal offence of criminal law in relation to tax offences is fraud-ulent tax evasion.[280] It is committed where the managing director gives false or incomplete information to the tax authorities or other public authorities con-cerning facts which are relevant for tax purposes, or leaves the tax authorities in

---

[275] § 331 HGB.
[276] § 331 no. 4 HGB.
[277] § 334 HGB.
[278] § 370 *et seq.* AO and the taxation procedure statutes of the Federal States.
[279] §§ 377 *et seq.* AO.
[280] "Steuerhinterziehung".

ignorance of such facts (thereby committing a breach of his duty), and thus reduces taxes or obtains unjustified tax privileges for himself or for another.[281]

Taxes are reduced if the tax creditor (Federation, Federal States and Communities) is not paid or awarded the taxes due to it upon the day they fall due, or is not paid or awarded them in full on that day; this is, in particular, the case if the taxes are not assessed, are not assessed to the full extent or are not assessed in good time.[282] Thus, in the case of value added tax, wage tax and capital yield tax, fraudulent tax evasion has already been committed if the managing director does not submit the preliminary tax return or the tax declaration prescribed by statute in good time by the prescribed day, in the case of annual taxes, or if the amount of tax assessed is too low due to an incorrect declaration, or if tax privileges are granted to which the company has no claim (e.g. lower assessment of advance payments). Fraudulent tax evasion, like the other tax offences,[283] is only punishable if it was committed deliberately.

One of the most common criminal business offences is the failure to deduct wage tax, which the employer must deduct from the wage or salary on a monthly basis and must pay to the tax authorities, or the failure to do so in good time.

Breach of tax regulations

In contrast to the criminal tax offences, regulatory tax offences can also be committed by recklessness. Recklessness[284] constitutes an intensified degree of fault in comparison with negligence: the offender leaves out of count what should be obvious to everyone. The general statutory definition of the crime is the reckless unlawful reduction of tax assessment[285] which – apart from the wrongful intent – corresponds to fraudulent tax evasion.

Self-accusation of tax evasion

Immunity from criminal prosecution can be obtained by a formless voluntary self-accusation of tax evasion to the tax authorities.[286] The precondition therefor is that the managing director at the same time either corrects the incorrect or incomplete information, supplements it or supplies the missing information. If unlawful reductions of the tax assessment have already occurred or unjustified tax privileges have been obtained, then immunity from criminal prosecution can only be gained if the taxes which have been evaded are subsequently paid within a reasonable time-limit to be set by the tax authorities.

However, the effect of immunity from criminal prosecution can no longer be obtained in the case of fraudulent tax evasion if:

- prior to the correction, supplementation or the supply of missing information, an official of the tax authorities has appeared to conduct a tax

---

[281] § 370 para. 1 AO.
[282] § 370 para. 4 AO.
[283] § 369 para. 1 AO.
[284] "Leichtfertigkeit".
[285] "Steuerverkürzung"; § 378 AO.
[286] §§ 371 para. 1, 378 para. 3 AO.

investigation or to investigate a criminal tax offence or a regulatory tax offence, or the initiation of corresponding proceedings has been announced to the managing director; or

• the offence had already been discovered at the time of self-accusation and the managing director already knew this or ought to have anticipated it.[287]

By contrast, in the case of a reckless unlawful reduction of the tax assessment, immunity from prosecution requires no more than a self-accusation prior to the announcement of the initiation of criminal proceedings or administrative fine proceedings.

Withholding of social insurance contributions
The managing director of a GmbH is responsible for ensuring that the contributions to the statutory social insurance scheme are paid to the collecting agency in good time and in full.[288] If a managing director deliberately fails to fulfil the duty to deduct the social insurance contributions, e.g. to spare the company's liquidity, then he may render himself liable to prosecution by reason of withholding, and embezzlement of, employment remuneration.[289] If the managing director can only pay the employees a part of the remuneration due, he must withhold and pay over a corresponding proportion of the amounts to be paid over into the social insurance system.

If "freelance contributors" or "sub-contractors" work for the GmbH's business, and they either wholly or partly follow instructions from management, then in each case it will be examined whether, by reason of the nature of their activities, they shall be treated as "employees". By virtue of a legal fiction, they are then considered as employees in relation to whom the employer has to fulfil all the duties of an employer. Alongside the breaches for failure to deduct and pay social insurance contributions, in the case of deliberate or negligent evasion of compulsory labour law provisions, further criminal offences and regulatory offences under the Employment Promotion Act, the Staff Secondment Act and under tax provisions come into consideration.

8.5 Criminal provisions relating to manufacturing industry

Product safety
The managing director of a GmbH can render himself liable to criminal prosecution if damage is caused by products which are manufactured or marketed by the GmbH.

Crime under the general provisions of the Criminal Code (bodily harm, manslaughter) comes into consideration if products which pose a threat to health are knowingly or negligently introduced into circulation or passed on, but also if the management does not immediately take steps to prevent immi-

---

[287] § 371 para. 2 AO.
[288] *Post*, p. 183.
[289] § 266a StGB.

nent danger once cases of damage have occurred or suspicious circumstances have arisen. If, in spite of the products posing a threat to health, no cases of death or bodily harm occur, the management can be guilty of a criminal attempt if wilful intent was involved.

Where there is more than one managing director, each individual managing director is criminally liable as a result of the comprehensive responsibility of the management, even if the relevant product damage does not fall within his sphere of authority, if he acquired knowledge of the suspicious circumstances or the cases of damage.

The requirements on the guarantee of product safety imposed on businesses by the case-law are very strict. If a managing director has an (unsubstantiated) doubt that damage could be caused by a product, he must take steps to investigate.

Environmental law offences

The scope of the criminal law provisions for the protection of the environment to be observed by the management of a GmbH mainly depends on the GmbH's sphere of activity. Alongside the criminal law provisions in the Criminal Code,[290] there is also a series of environmental criminal provisions in administrative statutes.

8.6 Corporate corruption, offences against competition and the economy

Betrayal of secrets

A managing director who makes unauthorized disclosure of a business secret of the company renders himself liable to criminal prosecution.[291]

Competition

The managing director must likewise observe a series of criminal provisions in the competition sphere, e.g.:

- false statements in advertising;[292]
- (passive and active) bribery of employees;[293]
- business slander;[294]
- unauthorized use of models and patterns;[295]
- illegal use of samples and models of third parties;[296]

---

[290] Pollution of bodies of water, contamination of the soil, air pollution, creation of noise, vibrations and non-ionising radiation, waste disposal posing a threat to the environment, illegal operation of installations, illegal handling of radioactive substances and other hazardous substances and goods, threats to areas worthy of protection, serious threats through the release of toxins, §§ 324 *et seq.* StGB.
[291] §§ 85 GmbHG, 17 UWG.
[292] § 4 Unfair Competition Act (UWG).
[293] § 12 UWG.
[294] § 15 UWG.
[295] § 18 UWG.
[296] § 14 Registered Designs Act.

- illegal exploitation of trade marks, identification marks, types of display and packaging;[297]
- illegal exploitation of geographical information as to origin;[298]
- breaches of copyright law.[299]

Cartel law contains a series of regulatory offences for breaches of market regulation, in particular in the case of the prohibited formation of cartels, price-fixing and breaches of the merger control regulations.

Foreign trade and exports
Certain provisions of criminal law relate to the protection of the rules of foreign trade and exports:

- the export of goods without a permit in cases where the export of such goods is prohibited;[300]
- breaches of the provisions of an embargo;[301]
- breaches of the Military Weapons Control Act.[302]

8.7 Insolvency offences

The detection of numerous criminal offences in connection with insolvency can be traced back to the receiver in bankruptcy. In the case of bankruptcy of the GmbH, the receiver in bankruptcy may discover numerous processes prior to the opening of bankruptcy proceedings within the course of the liquidation of the company. Receivers often make contributions to the investigation of facts and circumstances. Prosecuting witnesses are often the creditors who have suffered a loss, namely the tax and social security authorities. If a demand for prosecution is not necessary, investigations are commenced on an *ex officio* basis.

Failure to file an insolvency petition
A managing director will be liable to prosecution if he fails to file an insolvency petition within three weeks after the onset of illiquidity or the determination of overindebtedness.[303] The duty to file a petition is imposed on each managing director and the duty does not cease upon the resignation from office. This provision is one of the most important statutory provisions relating to business crime.[304]

---

[297] § 143 Trade Marks Act.
[298] § 144 Trade Marks Act.
[299] § 106 *et seq.* Copyrights Act (UrhG).
[300] § 34 Foreign Trade and Payments Act (AWG).
[301] § 34 para. 4 AWG.
[302] §§ 19 *et seq.* KWKG.
[303] §§ 64 para. 1, 84 para. 1 GmbHG.
[304] A managing director already renders himself liable if he fails to notify the shareholders of a loss amounting to half the share capital (§ 84 para. 1 no. 1 GmbHG).

Insolvency offences

Furthermore, illegal conduct in the case of insolvency is punishable as fraudulent insolvency.[305] Where the enterprise is in crisis, i.e. in the case of imminent or actual insolvency, the managing director renders himself liable to prosecution if he:

- deprives the company of items of property, thereby damaging the interests of the creditors;[306]

- enters into risky transactions with an especially high risk of loss or makes uneconomic expenditure;

- dissipates assets;

- feigns the rights of others or recognises fabricated rights;

- fails to keep books of account or keeps them inadequately;[307]

- secretly removes books of account or other documents prior to the expiry of the record retention periods;

- fails to prepare the necessary balance sheets, or fails to do so in good time, or does so incorrectly;

- conceals economic circumstances.

9. Power of procuration[308]

The power of procuration is a representative authority which is granted contractually, in contrast to the statutory representative authority of the managing director. It confers the authority to conduct every kind of business and legal transaction related to the operation of a commercial business,[309] except the sale of the business itself and – unless the procurator has received special permission – the disposal and encumbrance of real property.[310] The courts have added limited exceptional cases to these restrictions when the procurator acts in bad faith in order to cause damage to the company and when the third party has knowledge of the limitation of authority or there are substantial indications of an abuse of the power or procuration.[311] Otherwise, any limitation of the scope of the procurator's authority is invalid with respect to third parties.[312] However, it can be restricted to the operation of a branch if the branch is operated under a different business name.[313]

---

[305] "Bankrott"; §§ 283 *et seq.* StGB.
[306] E.g. fictitious assignment, transfer from the business account to a private account; denial of elements of capital, withholding information where there is a duty to supply it.
[307] In 90 per cent of all petitions for bankruptcy, the books of account were not adequately kept.
[308] "Prokura".
[309] § 49 para. 1 HGB.
[310] § 49 para. 2 HGB.
[311] *Ante*, p. 139.
[312] § 50 HGB.
[313] It is sufficient if there is an addition „branch of . . . GmbH"; § 50 para. 3 HGB.

The power of procuration can be conferred so that a procurator can represent the company alone[314] or jointly with another procurator[315] or a managing director. It is therefore possible to control the wide powers of a procurator by allowing him only to act jointly with a second person.

Although restrictions may be invalid with respect to third parties, the representative is bound internally. He will be liable to the company for any damage if he exceeds his authority, and his employment contract may be terminated under certain circumstances.

The conferral of a power of procuration is not subject to formal requirements, except that it has to be conferred "expressly"[316] by the managing directors upon a shareholders' resolution.[317] It must be registered in the Commercial Register.

The power of procuration is revocable at any time and for any reason. Although this revocation – at least theoretically – has immediate effect, the procurator is able to act for the company in relation to third parties as long as the revocation has not been registered in the Commercial Register or the third party has not otherwise been informed of the revocation.

The purpose of granting the power of procuration is not merely to enable the company to act through this representative. This would also be possible by granting a simple power of attorney to an employee, as is the case with sales staff. The fact that the procurator is registered with the Commercial Register indicates to the public that they can rely on this person as being a fully authorized signatory entitled to act for a company, without having to require any written proof of authorization, or of the scope of the authority. Thus, it is typically only conferred on persons who have extended responsibilities within the company. The holding of a power of procuration substantially increases the social standing and acceptance of the employee in the business community, even if he may only act together with the managing director or another procurator.

10. Commercial agency

The commercial power of agency is also a contractually conferred power of representation. It authorises all acts which the operation of such a commercial business brings with it,[318] but only authorises the sale and encumbrance of real property, the entering into commitments arising from bills of exchange, the taking up of loans and the conduct of court proceedings if these powers are expressly conferred.

Other than is the case with the power of procuration, the commercial power of agency can be restricted as to content, but restrictions are only effective in

---

[314] Individual power of procuration, "Einzelprokura".
[315] Joint power of procuration, "Gesamtprokura".
[316] § 48 HGB.
[317] § 46 no. 7.
[318] § 54 para. 1 HGB.

the external relationship with third parties if they knew or ought to have known of them, and thus did not know of them as a result of negligence.[319]

The commercial power of agency is granted (without requirements as to the form, sometimes impliedly) by the parties entitled to represent the company. It is not entered in the Commercial Register.

11. General power of attorney

The grant of a general power of attorney in practice not only involves a comprehensive power of representation (in relation to third parties), but also a general or far-reaching power to make decisions within the internal relationship. However, as the statutory power of representation is not transferable,[320] a general power of attorney is only valid if it does not replace the representative authority of the managing directors as organs of the company,[321] but rather leaves up to them the sphere of tasks which must be performed at their own responsibility.[322]

Transactions undertaken by a representative on the basis of an invalid general power of attorney are (provisionally) invalid and become valid with the grant of approval, but finally invalid if such approval is refused.

12. Apparent authority, power of representation by estoppel

Acts of a person not in possession of representative authority can also be binding for the company. This is the case if organs of the company (management or shareholders' meeting) should have recognised and prevented the act if they had taken due care, and if the other party to the transaction was entitled to believe in good faith that the company permitted, and approved of, the conduct of its "representative".[323] The conduct of an unauthorized person binds the company if it knowingly does not intervene against his acting in the capacity of a representative and the other party to the transaction could – in good faith – construe this acquiescence as the grant of authorization.[324]

---

[319] § 54 para. 3 HGB.
[320] It also cannot be transferred on a revocable basis or for a limited period of time, BGHZ 34, 27, 31; nor with the consent of all shareholders, BGH WM 76, 1246.
[321] BGHZ 27, 30; NJW 77, 199; WM 78, 1047.
[322] OLG Naumberg GmbHR 94, 556.
[323] Apparent authority ("Anscheinsvollmacht"), BGH NJW 81, 1728.
[324] Power of representation by estoppel ("Duldungsvollmacht"), BGH NJW 56, 460.

Chapter 11

LABOUR LAW OF THE GMBH

Bernt Gach

Once the GmbH is established and has hired employees, the directors will have to deal with labour law.

1. Applicability of German law

The employment relationships of a German GmbH are subject to German law. However, it is also possible to include a choice-of-law clause in a labour agreement making the relationship subject to a foreign legal system (e.g. to the law of the foreign parent company of the GmbH) instead. Even where another legal regime is chosen, the mandatory provisions of German law (e.g. on working hours, protection against dismissal, and continuation of wage payments) remain applicable as long as they are more advantageous to the employee than the corresponding provisions of the legal regime selected.[325]

2. Institutions and sources of German labour law

2.1 Statutory provisions

Labour law is not treated uniformly at the statutory level. In addition to the provisions of the Civil Code (BGB), in particular those regarding service agreements, special labour law statutes (e.g. Unfair Dismissal Act, Working Time Act, Federal Holiday Entitlement Act, Collective Bargaining Agreements Act, etc.), as well as individual labour law provisions contained in other statutes, apply.[326]

---

[325] Art. 30 Introductory Act to the Civil Code (Einführungsgesetz zum Bürgerlichen Gesetzbuch, "EGBGB").
[326] E.g. protection against levy of execution on wages in the Code of Civil Procedure (ZPO).

Despite the multitude of special statutory provisions, many areas – above all, the field of labour disputes law – are not regulated by statute. Consequently, German labour law is predominantly case-law.

2.2 Collective bargaining agreements[327]

In addition to the statutory provisions, collective bargaining agreements govern the employment relationship. In so far as these statutes do not expressly allow for deviations from their provisions, the parties to the collective bargaining agreement may not conclude any agreements to the contrary which disadvantage the employees. A collective bargaining agreement is concluded between two associations (trade union and employers' association) or between a trade union and an individual employer.[328]

Parties to the collective bargaining agreement
In Germany, there are fewer trade unions than in other countries. The German Trade Union Federation (DGB),[329] as the head collective bargaining group, consists of 16 individual trade unions which are responsible for various sectors of the economy respectively. In addition, there are a few smaller unions – among them the German Trade Union for Salaried Employees,[330] which only deals with white-collar employees[331] in all areas of the economy. According to the so-called industrial union principle,[332] based on the organizational form of the trade unions which comprise the DGB, a company's workers are generally members of one and the same union, namely the union responsible for that sector of the economy. The employers' associations have come together in regional associations which can be distinguished from one another by their respective responsibilities for different sectors of the economy.

To become a member in a trade union or employers' association, the employee or employer voluntarily joins the organization. There are no closed shop arrangements.

Substance and effect of the collective bargaining agreement
The collective bargaining agreement contains rules pertaining to the conclusion, substance and termination of the employment relationships governed by it.[333] These have to be applied to all employment relationships between the members of the associations which concluded the collective bargaining agreement, provided that the employment contract falls within the scope of the collective bargaining agreement.[334] Consequently, it is important for a new company

---

[327] "Tarifverträge".
[328] § 2 para. 1 Collective Bargaining Agreement Act (TVG).
[329] "Deutscher Gewerkschaftsbund".
[330] "Deutsche Angestellten-Gewerkschaft".
[331] "Angestellte".
[332] "Industrieverbandprinzip".
[333] § 1 para. 1 TVG.
[334] § 4 para. 1 TVG.

to decide whether it will join an employers' association or not, since it automatically becomes a party to the association's collective bargaining agreement when joining.

By means of a governmental declaration on the universal validity and binding character of collective bargaining agreements,[335] the field of application of collective bargaining agreements can even be extended to employees and employers who do not belong to the associations concluding the agreement.[336] Such a declaration may be issued by the Federal Minister of Labour and Social Affairs upon application by one of the parties to the collective bargaining agreement, if a committee consisting of three members each of the leading collective bargaining groups of the employers and employees approves the declaration. Such a declaration, which is a serious encroachment on the private autonomy of employees and employers has to be justified by the public interest. Such declarations are commonplace in the retail trade.

All employment relationships which are embraced by the collective bargaining agreement are subject to its direct and mandatory provisions. These provisions automatically become part of the employment relationship (no act of transformation is necessary), and the parties to the employment agreement may not deviate from these provisions to the disadvantage of the employee.[337] Collective bargaining agreements affect approximately 90 per cent of employment relationships in Germany; in some cases, the effect is only indirect in that the corresponding provisions of the collective bargaining agreements become the basis of employment contracts concluded between parties who are not members of an association.

2.3 Shop agreements[338]

In addition to statutes and collective bargaining agreements, shop agreements also shape employment relationships. Shop agreements are made between the employer and the works council.

Works council[339]
The works council is an entity (theoretically independent of the labour unions) which represents the interests of a company's employees. A works council may be established in all companies which employ at least five employees (three of whom must have been employed for at least six months) on a regular basis.[340] It is up to the employees of the company to decide whether or not a works council should be established. If the employees choose not to create a works council, they voluntarily abandon all rights granted to works councils by law. According

---

[335] "Allgemeinverbindlichkeitserklärung".
[336] § 5 TVG.
[337] § 4 para. 3 TVG.
[338] "Betriebsvereinbarungen".
[339] "Betriebsrat".
[340] § 1 Employees' Representation Act (BetrVG).

to most estimates, no more than 20 per cent of all enterprises, including small and medium-sized firms, have established a works council.

The works council has the right to co-determine, participate, consult, and be informed in social, personnel, and economic matters. The right of co-determination is the most significant form of participation. The employer may not undertake an action without the works council's approval or participation or, at least, not without any inquiry. Furthermore, it is also incumbent upon the works council to monitor and promote the employment relationship as well as to fulfil its duties regarding the design of the workplace and complaints from employees.

Substance and effect of the shop agreement
Shop agreements can specify the works council's co-determination rights. Other issues not subject to these rights (e.g. establishment of social services) may also be addressed. In so far as shop agreements contain rules for employment relationships, these provisions, like the rules contained in collective bargaining agreements, are mandatory for the employer and employee even without inclusion in a contract.[341]

2.4 Representative committee of executive employees

Executives,[342] i.e. employees who perform supervisory functions in some key position, are not represented by the works council but by a representative committee.[343] These committees are established in businesses with at least 10 executive employees. They do not have any rights of co-determination, but rather have only minimal rights of participation.

2.5 Co-determination at the company level

Apart from participation by labour at the management level, German law contains several statutory provisions relating to co-determination[344] and the representation of employees on the supervisory board.[345]

The mandatory supervisory board of a GmbH has two basic functions: to elect the management and to supervise its activities. In order to fulfil its tasks, the supervisory board has access to extensive information.

The labour representatives on the supervisory board are directly elected by the employees through a complex process. In principle, blue-collar and white-collar employees elect their representatives separately. Under certain conditions, trade union representatives must be elected.[346]

---

[341] § 77 para. 1 BetrVG.
[342] "Leitende Angestellte".
[343] "Sprecherausschuß".
[344] "Mitbestimmung".
[345] "Aufsichtsrat".
[346] *Post*, p. 197.

3. Types of employees

German law differentiates between salaried employees or white-collar workers,[347] who are generally paid by the month, and so-called wage earners or blue-collar workers,[348] whose wages are usually computed by the hour or week. This distinction affects representation in the works council,[349] the social security system, and collective bargaining agreements.

A separate group of salaried employees are the executives. Some employee protection provisions do not apply to executives. Case-law is not yet clear as to which individuals belong to this group. However, there is no question that the managing directors[350] of a GmbH generally do not enjoy employee protection because they are not deemed to be employees under German labour law.

In the case of a GmbH, shareholders often act as managing directors, but also as salaried employees. There are usually no special features which apply to shareholder-employees, but it can be validly agreed in a contract of employment that the dismissal of an employee who is a shareholder requires the prior consent of the shareholders' meeting. Under normal circumstances, consent requirements do not constitute a restriction of the power of respresentation in relation to third parties,[351] but this does not apply if express reference is made in the shareholder's contract of employment to the consent requirement in the articles of association.[352]

4. Search for employees

In the search for a qualified employee, the services of the labour office[353] or private employment agencies can be of assistance. If job announcements are published, the employer may not indicate that he prefers a male or female applicant for the position in question.[354]

Irrespective of whether the employment relationship is ultimately established, employer and employee have certain obligations when conducting job interviews. The employer is obliged to inform the applicant of the job requirements, not to give the applicant any false impressions that he or she might be offered the job, treat the application documents carefully, store and, on request, return them and reimburse the costs incurred by the employee for the job interview. The applicant has an obligation to disclose certain information; in particular, he or she must disclose facts that may render performance in the planned position impossible or considerably difficult.

---

[347] "Angestellte".
[348] "Arbeiter".
[349] "Betriebsrat".
[350] "Geschäftsführer".
[351] *Ante*, p. 139.
[352] BAG ZIP 94, 1290.
[353] "Arbeitsamt"; *post*, p. 286.
[354] §§ 611a, 612b BGB.

However, only permissible questions must be answered truthfully by the employee. Permissible questions are questions concerning the employee's qualifications, health, previous wage or salary and prior criminal records, provided that there is a recognisable connection between these questions and the prospective employment. Questions are impermissible if they concern membership of trade unions, political parties and churches, as well as inquiries as to whether the employee is pregnant.

The employer may list the questions that he may permissibly ask the applicant in personnel questionnaires. If there is a works council, these questionnaires are subject to the works council's prior consent.

5. Conclusion of an employment contract

5.1 Form

Employment contracts (except those for apprentices) do not have to be made in writing. In general, however, written employment agreements are concluded, and a written contract is advisable, particularly when it is not a standard contract. Furthermore, under the Proof of Employment Relationships Act[355] the employer must provide written particulars of the employment including, inter alia, the names and addresses of the parties, the date of the commencement of the employment, a specification or description of the employee's position or tasks, working hours and working place, wage and salary and other payments (e.g. vacation pay, Christmas bonus), entitlement to vacation, notice periods, and reference to applicable collective bargaining and shop agreements. However, employment contracts often cover many other terms, such as confidentiality and restraint of competition.

5.2 Limited employment relationships

As a general rule, employment agreements run for an indefinite period, whereas fixed-term contracts are permitted in limited cases only.[356]

To reduce unemployment by making it easier to create new jobs, the conclusion of limited employment relationships has been legally facilitated until 31 December 2000. Under these regulations, new employment relationships may be limited to a maximum period of 24 months.

5.3 Participation by the works council

The works council must be comprehensively informed of projected personnel measures in good time. In companies with more than 20 employees with voting

---

[355] "Nachweisgesetz".
[356] E.g. for probation periods (a six month maximum) or for certain special assignments.

rights, the works council has the right of co-determination in the hiring of personnel.[357] The works council may only refuse its consent to new hirings for specific reasons. If the consent is refused, the employer may try to obtain it through a labour court ruling.

If the works council is not given the opportunity to participate in the hiring of an employee, the relevant individual cannot be employed. However, the employment contract remains effective, i.e. the employer has to pay the wage or salary agreed upon, but may not make use of the employee's working capacities.

5.4 Registration with the collecting agencies

At the beginning of the employment relationship, the employer is obliged to register the employee who is liable to contribute to social security (i.e. who is not self-employed), to the health insurance institutions.

6. Implementation of the employment relationship

6.1 Remuneration

There are no statutory minimum wages in Germany. Therefore, the parties to an employment contract may freely negotiate the amount of the wage to be paid. However, if a collective bargaining agreement is applicable to an employment relationship, the wages agreed upon collectively have to be observed as a minimum.

Remuneration is generally paid at the end of the month and includes premiums, vacation pay, Christmas bonus, use of company cars, etc. A claim for bonuses or vacation pay only exists if this was contractually agreed, but such a claim may be automatic in some cases (e.g. under collective bargaining agreements or if a custom has been established by an employer).

6.2 Deductions

The employer is legally bound to withhold the required amounts of wage and church taxes as well as the amount for the employee's social insurance contribution. Social security insurance includes:

- health;
- pension;
- unemployment;
- accident insurance;
- nursing cost insurance.

Employer and employee each pay one half of the social security insurance contribution, but the accident insurance contribution must be paid exclusively by
the employer.

The employer has to transfer the amounts retained for wage and church
taxes to the tax authorities and the amounts for the social security insurance
contributions to the health insurer (as the collecting agent for the social insurance institution). Up to a monthly income of DM 8,000, the social pension contribution currently amounts to 19.2 per cent of the salary; 6.5 per cent of the
salary must be paid as the unemployment insurance contribution. With a
monthly salary of up to DM 6,000, the health insurance contribution ranges
between 10 and 14 per cent (depending on the insurer). The accident insurance contributions range between 0.5 and 1 per cent of the salary. The nursing
cost insurance contribution amounts to 1.7 per cent. Thus, the employer has to
pay ancillary wage costs of approximately 20 per cent of the employee's gross
wages by reason of the statutory social security insurance system.

6.3 Occupational pensions

The occupational pension represents a special form of remuneration. This pension is often paid by larger enterprises and represents a voluntary addition to
the social security insurance. The employer may be obliged to pay these benefits if corresponding stipulations are made in the individual employment contracts, the collective bargaining and/or shop agreements, or if he has
unconditionally paid these benefits for the retiring employee over a considerable period of time (internal company practice). The occupational pension
may be paid in the form of a so-called employer's direct insurance[358] entitling
the employee to a claim that can be asserted against the employer directly. As
an alternative, the employer may also take out an insurance contract for the
benefit of the employee, or the enterprise – in its capacity as a legally independent entity – can establish a pension and support fund against which the
employee's claims can be asserted.

6.4 Working time

Generally, the weekly working time ranges between 35 and 40 hours and is spread
over six working days. The duration of the working time is either governed by
the collective bargaining agreement or by an individual employment contract.
Both the collective bargaining agreement and the individual employment contract may not exceed the legally prescribed working time. Labour law stipulates
a 48-hour week with a maximum daily working time of 8 hours.[359] The daily

---

[357] § 99 BetrVG.
[358] "Direktversicherung".
[359] § 3 Working Time Act (Arbeitszeitgesetz – ArbZG).

working time may be increased to 10 hours if the average working time does not exceed 8 hours a day over a period of six months. Further exceptions may be made in collective bargaining or shop agreements.

Overtime work is remunerated by overtime payment or additional time off. Hours worked in addition to the working time prescribed in the collective bargaining agreements or individual employment contracts (overtime) are generally remunerated by overtime payments or in the form of additional time off. However, there is no statutory claim to this remuneration. The legal basis for overtime can be found in the collective bargaining agreements or individual employment contracts.

With regard to the allocation of working time, a few legal regulations have to be observed: in principle, work on Sundays or statutory holidays is impermissible. The new working time regulation provides for a number of exceptions. In particular, the uninterrupted operation of data networks and computer systems is allowed by law, together with a continuous production process, if an interruption of the production process would lead to loss of five per cent or more of the overall production. Moreover, the supervisory authority has to approve work on Sunday and statutory holidays if the competitiveness of the company concerned is endangered.

Employees working between six to nine hours have to be granted breaks of 30 minutes, whereas working times of more than nine hours require break periods of 45 minutes.[360] A work day must be followed by a recreational period of at least 11 hours.[361]

The allocation of working time is mostly settled at the plant level. In this respect, the works council has a peremptory right of co-determination,[362] i.e. the employer cannot make any decisions regarding the working time without the works council's consent. Today, many enterprises agree upon flexible working time (flextime, part-time). In this respect, the relevant legal provisions, collective bargaining agreements and shop agreements provide considerable scope for discretion.

6.5 Vacation

The statutory minimum vacation period amounts to 24 working days[363] per calendar year (working days are defined as the weekdays Monday through Saturday). However, the provisions of the collective bargaining agreements or individual employment contracts mostly exceed this minimum number of vacation days. A vacation period of five to six weeks can be considered normal. During leave, the employee continues to receive his or her regular remuneration[364] and normally receives additional vacation pay. In principle, payments by

---

[360] § 4 ArbZG.
[361] § 5 para. 1 ArbZG.
[362] § 87 para. 1 no. 2, 3 BetrVG.
[363] § 3 Federal Holiday Entitlement Act (BUrlG).
[364] § 11 BUrlG.

way of settlement of vacation time are impermissible even if a corresponding agreement has been made by mutual agreement.

The periods in which leave may be taken are left to the reasonable discretion of the employer.[365] However, he is obliged to consider the employees' wishes and shall grant vacation as requested unless these wishes conflict with competing business requirements or conflict with requests by other employees which have to be given priority for social reasons (e.g. children of school age). The employer may even grant uniform vacation periods (so-called "business vacation"). However, the employer has to give sufficient consideration to the interests of the employees. This renders a postponement of the business vacation to the winter months impermissible.

The works council has a right of co-determination in cases where general principles regarding the yearly distribution of vacation time are established.[366] In case of disputes regarding the periods in which leave may be taken, the works council also has a right of co-determination.

6.6 Paid leave

If employees are incapable of providing their services for medical reasons, they are generally entitled to sick pay at a rate equivalent to 80 per cent their normal remuneration for a maximum of six weeks, unless payment of the full remuneration and/or a longer period is provided for in the individual employment contracts or the collective bargaining agreements. After this six-week period, most employees are eligible to receive benefits from the state health insurance scheme.

In certain special cases, such as marriage, the birth of a child, the death of a close relative, or care for a sick child in certain limited cases, an employee may be entitled to paid leave (even in cases of relatively short absence from work).

The duties of a works council may be performed during normal working hours. In businesses of 300 or more employees, a certain number of members of the works council have to be released completely from their duties under the employment contract while continuing to receive their normal wage or salary.[367] The employer is obliged to provide facilities and financial support for the activities of the works council.[368]

6.7 Unpaid childcare leave

If both parents are gainfully employed, one of them is entitled to childcare leave for the time until the child has completed his or her third year of life, i.e. for a maximum period of 36 months. The parent assuming the care of the child has a claim to a childcare allowance which is granted for the period up to the

---

[365] § 7 para. 1 BUrlG.
[366] § 87 para. 1 no. 5 BetrVG.
[367] §§ 37 para. 2, 38 BetrVG.
[368] § 40 BetrVG.

completion of the child's 24th month of life. During the time childcare leave is granted, the main obligations resulting from the employment relationship are suspended. The employer is released from the obligation to pay the wage or salary.

7. Termination

It is usually difficult for an employer to terminate an employment agreement unilaterally. The termination of an employment relationship may be "extra-ordinary", i.e. for cause and without notice, or "ordinary", i.e. based on contractual or other legal grounds.

7.1 Extraordinary termination

Both parties to an employment relationship may terminate such a relationship without observing any contractual or statutory period of notice or expiry date, provided that there is a valid "cause" justifying such "extraordinary" termina-tion.[369] However, the requirements defined by the courts with respect to the "cause" justifying such a termination are relatively high: the general circum-stances must be such that the party terminating the agreement "for cause" can-not be reasonably expected to continue the contractual relationship even until the end of the regular period of notice, or until the agreed expiry date, whereby all circumstances of the individual case and the interests of both parties must be duly considered when making such a determination.

Cause justifying the "extraordinary" termination of an employment relation-ship is considered as given if the employee:

- submitted false references when hired;
- refuses to work (except if lawfully on strike);
- abuses any powers under the employment contract; or
- commits an offence such as theft, damage to property, or fraud.

7.2 Ordinary termination – Unfair Dismissal Act

Otherwise, the termination must be "ordinary", i.e. in compliance with the pre-scribed period of notice. The minimum notice period is four weeks, with the termination taking effect as of the 15th or the last day of a calendar month.[370] The period of notice is extended by one month if the employment has lasted at least two years, and if the employment relationship lasted five, eight, 10, 12, 15 or 20 years, the period of notice will be two, three, four, five, six or seven months respectively, whereby any notice of termination given will take effect to the end of a calendar month. For the purpose of calculating the duration of

---

[369] § 626 Civil Code.
[370] § 622 para 1 Civil Code.

employment, any periods prior to the time the employee reached the age of 26 shall not be considered. If the parties agree on a probation period, which may not be longer than six months, the period of notice will be two weeks during that probation period.

Where a notice period longer than that provided by statute is agreed upon in an individual employment agreement or collective bargaining agreement, the period which has been agreed on shall apply.

In principle, "ordinary" notice of termination may be given without any particular "cause". However, this does not apply to agreements falling under the Unfair Dismissal Act. This Act concerns all employment relationships which have existed for six months or more, provided that the enterprise normally employs at least six employees.[371] Whenever the Unfair Dismissal Act applies, notice of termination may only be given if this is "socially justified".[372]

"Social justification" requires the balancing of the interests of the employer and the employee. "Business reasons", or reasons relating to the behaviour, conduct or performance of an employee or his personality, may constitute a sufficient cause making the termination of his employment "justified in social terms". However, the employer bears a strong burden of proof to show the presence of compelling reasons which "socially" justify the termination. The employer must provide evidence showing that there is no reasonable possibility of continuing the employment of the employee to be dismissed, e.g. by transferring him to another position or location, assigning other reasonable duties to him, or even training him for another job. Where employees are dismissed for "business reasons" (redundancy, lay-off), the employer must first dismiss those persons having the lowest seniority in terms of age, duration of employment and obligations as to child care and alimony. These are the so-called "social selection" criteria, under which a young, skilled employee without a family to support and with good chances of finding a new job must be dismissed rather than an older employee who has a family to support and would have poor chances of finding a new job.

7.3 Involvement of the works council

Furthermore, dismissal by unilateral notice of the employer requires the involvement of the works council where there is one. Before the notice of termination is served to an employee, the works council must be notified in writing of such intention, including the reasons justifying the termination.[373] If the works council does not respond within one week, it is presumed to approve of the proposed dismissal.[374] The works council may oppose the dismissal of an employee only for certain reasons (usually social reasons) defined by law. Even though the works council cannot actually prevent the dismissal of any

---

[371] §§ 1 para. 1, 23 para. 1 Unfair Dismissal Act (KSchG).
[372] § 1 para. 2 KSchG.
[373] § 182 para. 1 BetrVG.
[374] § 182 para. 2 BetrVG.

employee, any failure to notify the works council renders the dismissal invalid. If the works council opposes the termination, the employer may be obliged to continue the employment and to continue the salary payments beyond the notice period until a final ruling is issued in unfair dismissal proceedings instituted by the employee concerned.

7.4 Action against unfair dismissal

Employees who were given notice of the termination of their employment often challenge their dismissal in the labour courts. Court actions must be filed within three weeks after receipt of the notice of termination.[375] Such court proceedings may cost the employer a considerable amount of time and effort. The employee will seek a declaratory judgment stating that his dismissal is void and that his employment will thus have to be continued. Therefore, before giving notice of termination, the employer should carefully consider whether he can prevail in court by presenting valid, socially justified reasons for terminating the employment relationship.

7.5 Special protection against termination

Certain additional notification requirements may have to be met if the relevant firm or business has more than 20 employees. In particular, a so-called "social plan" may have to be adopted if a certain number of employees are to be dismissed.[376]

Additional restrictions apply with respect to the dismissal, *inter alia*, of disabled persons, pregnant women or women who have recently given birth, members of the works council, or apprentices.

7.6 Termination agreement

Any dismissal by unilateral notice by the employer is subject to numerous restrictions, requirements of form and deadlines. These problems can be avoided in part by entering into a "termination agreement" with the employee. In general, the principal content of such agreements is that the employment shall end by mutual consent and that the employee shall be paid compensation for the loss of his job.

Termination agreements may appear to involve considerable costs for the employer. However, they serve the purposes of avoiding a dispute, achieving a speedy settlement of the matter, and attaining the company's business goals, which may well outweigh the cost factor. There is no clear-cut formula to determine the amount of severance pay under a termination agreement. Under German labour law (unlike some other jurisdictions), an employee is not required to accept a settlement proposal merely because the amount offered by

---

[375] § 4 KSchG.
[376] *Post*, p. 192.

the employer is reasonable. On the contrary, the employee is free to reject a proposal and may challenge any termination unilaterally declared by the employer. However, an attractive severance pay offer is likely to be accepted in most cases.

The amount of such severance pay is generally calculated on the basis of several factors, including the length of employment, the employer's financial situation, the age of the employee, the number of family members he has to support, his prospective ability to find a new job, etc. Furthermore, the employee's chances of successfully challenging his dismissal in labour court proceedings must also be considered.

As a general rule, the employer will have to pay the employee between 0.5 and one month's salary for each year of service, depending on the factors mentioned above.

Before the actual end of his employment, the employee will have to take any remaining vacation to which he is entitled, or will be paid compensation in lieu of such vacation entitlement (including contractually agreed vacation bonus payments, if any). However, compensation payments in lieu of vacation not taken are only permissible in a limited number of cases.

Severance payments are treated favourably for tax purposes. Depending on the age of the individual concerned, a certain sum (DM 24,000) will be tax-free, while the balance will be taxed at a reduced rate. The employer can refer to these tax advantages as an argument to persuade the employee to accept the compensation offered, given that the employee may well be interested in receiving such compensation (rather than salary taxable at the normal rate) as soon as possible.

7.7 Mass dismissals (collective redundancies)

General
Corporate restructuring or reorganization or operational changes may require the closing of an establishment or a considerable reduction of the work force and, thus, constitute a mass dismissal (collective redundancy). "Mass dismissal"[377] means dismissals effected by an employer where, over a period of 30 days, the number of redundancies is:

Total number of employees	Number of employees to be dismissed
21–59	At least 6
60–499	26 or at least 10 per cent
500 or more	At least 30

Dismissals comprise any other termination of employment by the employer except a termination for serious cause (summary dismissal). The regulations

---

[377] Within the meaning of § 17 KSchG, as amended to implement Council Directive 75/129/EEC.

shall also apply where the decision regarding the dismissals is taken by a parent company controlling the employer.

Balance of interests[378]

In an establishment with more than 20 regular employees, the employer shall inform the works council in detail and in good time about operational changes which may result in significant detriment to the staff or to large segments thereof, and shall confer with the works council about the planned operational changes.[379] In particular, this refers to fundamental changes in the organization, relocation of the entire business or a significant part thereof, the amalgamation with other businesses or significant parts thereof, or the division of the business.

The Federal Labour Court held that a mass dismissal is deemed to be an operational change, provided that at least five per cent of the workforce will be made redundant. Thus, the employer shall confer with the works council to conclude a balancing of interests agreement as regards whether or not operational changes will be made and how those changes will be implemented. In particular, the employer and the works council shall cover ways and means of avoiding dismissals or reducing the number of employees affected, and of mitigating the consequences of dismissals.

The employer is obliged to negotiate in good faith to reach such a settlement. However, this obligation does not compel the employer to reach an agreement. The works council has no legal right to force the conclusion of a settlement.

Where a balancing of interest agreement regarding the proposed organisational changes cannot be concluded, the employer shall appeal to the conciliation board.[380] The arbitration board is composed of an equal number of arbitrators appointed by each party and of a neutral chairman chosen by agreement between the parties or by the appropriate labour court if the parties cannot reach an agreement.[381] The conciliation board shall attempt to conclude a voluntary settlement between the parties.[382] This does not compel either party to agree to a proposal or require concessions to be made. If an agreement cannot be reached, the employer has fulfilled his duty to bargain in good faith and may carry out the planned operational changes. However, as the appointment of the conciliation board is time-consuming (between 2 and 12 months) and the costs of the conciliation board have to be borne by the employer,[383] it is generally advisable to conclude a voluntary settlement.

If an employer does not confer in good faith with the works council or if he violates the agreement concluded with the works council, the employees who

---

[378] "Interessenausgleich".
[379] § 111 BetrVG.
[380] "Einigungsstelle".
[381] § 77 para. 2 BetrVG.
[382] § 112 para. 3 BetrVG.
[383] § 76a BetrVG.

are dismissed or suffer other economic disadvantages (e.g. reduction of salary) due to the conduct of the employer, may claim compensation.[384] An amount of up to 12 months' remuneration may be determined as compensation.

Social plan[385]
Notwithstanding his obligation to confer in good faith as regards a balancing of interests agreement, the employer shall negotiate with a works council to conclude a social plan which shall compensate financial disadvantages of the employees arising from the planned organizational change.[386] The social plan has the effect of a shop agreement. This means that the social plan may be enforced by the individual employee.

Where the employer and the works council are not able to agree on a social plan, the conciliation board shall be appointed and shall conclude a compulsory settlement on behalf of both parties. [387]However, the arbitration board shall only set up a social plan, if the number of employees to be dismissed equals or exceeds the number specified below:

Total number of employees	Number of employees to be dismissed
21–59	20 per cent but at least 6
60–249	20 per cent or at least 37
250–499	15 per cent or at least 60
500 or more	10 per cent or at least 60

As regards the content of the social plan, the core regulation is the formula to calculate redundancy payments of the individual employee. In general, the calculation is based on the following criteria:

- the age of the employee;
- years of service of the employee in the establishment;
- monthly remuneration of the employee.

Furthermore, a basic award or additional payments are customary for dependents, disabled persons, etc. As a rule, the amount of compensation is between a half and a full monthly salary for each year of employment, but less than the annual remuneration of the employee.

Notification to the works council
When planning a mass dismissal, the employer shall furthermore supply the works council with all relevant information in good time and notify the works council in writing of:

---

[384] § 113 BetrVG.
[385] "Sozialplan".
[386] § 112 para. 1 BetrVG.
[387] §§ 112 para. 4, 112a para. 1 BetrVG.

- the reasons for the projected redundancies;
- the number and categories of employees to be made redundant;
- the number and categories of employees regularly employed;
- the period over which the projected redundancies are to be effected;
- the criteria proposed for the selection of the employees to be made redundant;
- the criteria proposed for calculating any severance payments.[388]

The employer shall notify the works council at least two weeks before he notifies the local labour office as regards the mass dismissal.[389]

Finally, the employer shall disclose the relevant information which enable the works council to make comments on the projected mass dismissal to the president of the labour office.[390]

Economics committee[391]

An economics committee shall be established if more than 100 employees are usually employed.[392] The employer shall inform the economics committee in good time about the economic aspects of the enterprise, disclose supporting documents, and explain the resulting effects for the staff. Economic matters include in particular:

- the economic and financial situation of the business;
- the production and sales situation;
- the production and investments programme;
- projected rationalization measures;
- production methods and their alteration;
- the curtailment or closing of the establishment or parts thereof;
- the geographical transfer of the business or parts thereof;
- the merger or division of businesses;
- any change as regards the organization or the purpose of the production;
- any other plans which will be of concern for the interest of the employees of the business.[393]

Notification to the president of the state labour office

The employer must inform the president of the state labour office[394] about projected changes in the business operations which are likely to lead to a mass

---

[388] § 17 para. 2 KSchG.
[389] § 17 para. 3 KSchG.
[390] § 8 Employment Promotion Act (AFG).
[391] "Wirtschaftsausschuß".
[392] § 106 para. 1 BetrVG.
[393] § 106 para. 3 BetrVG.
[394] "Landesarbeitsamt".

dismissal within the next 12 months.[395] The notification must be in writing and include comments of the works council.

Notification to the local labour office

The employer shall furthermore notify the local labour office[396] in writing before he dismisses a number of employees within a period of 30 calendar days which constitutes a mass dismissal.[397] Prior to this notification, the employer must notify the works council in good time of the details of the projected mass dismissal. The notification shall contain all relevant information concerning the projected mass dismissal.

Blocking period

Dismissals which have to be notified shall only take effect before the expiry of one month ("blocking period") of the receipt of the notification by the local labour office with the consent of the state labour office; the consent may also be given retroactively to the date of the filing of the notification.[398] The state labour office may determine in an individual case that dismissals will not become effective before the expiry of a maximum of two months after receipt of the notification by the local labour office.[399] An extension of the blocking period is highly likely where the employer has failed to notify the president of the state labour office in good time as required by law.

After the expiry of the blocking period, the dismissals shall be carried out within one month ("dismissal period"). This means that all dismissals of which the labour offices have been notified must take effect within this dismissal period. Where the dismissals do not take effect within one month after the time at which they are permissible after the expiry of the blocking period, a new notification might have to be filed.[400] In this context, the effectiveness of a dismissal refers to the actual termination of the employment relationship.

The combination of the "blocking period" and the "dismissal period" makes the timing of dismissals crucial. The notices must be served in such a way that all the (different) notice periods end during the dismissal period.

8. Restraint of competition

While the employment agreement is in force, the employee may not engage in any form of competition with his employer or the latter's business activities. This also applies even in cases where no express agreement is reached on this in the contract of employment.[401] In general, this ban on competition ends upon

---

[395] § 8 AFG, § 17 KSchG.
[396] "Arbeitsamt".
[397] § 17 KSchG.
[398] § 18 para. 1 KSchG.
[399] § 18 para. 2 KSchG.
[400] § 18 para. 4 KSchG.
[401] By analogy with § 60 para. 1 HGB.

the termination of the employment relationship. Any arrangements deviating from this rule must be specifically agreed upon. However, the maximum permissible duration of any contractual ban on competition is two years after the end of the employment relationship.[402]

In addition, any ban on competition extending beyond the end of the employment relationship is only legally valid if the employer has agreed to make monthly compensation payments to the employee equivalent at least 50 per cent of the employee's last salary,[403] although this compensation claim of the employee is reduced by any sum the employee may earn elsewhere (even on a self-employed basis), or deliberately fails to earn elsewhere. However, this only applies if the compensation payments and the new salary or other income of the employee add up to more than 110 per cent of the last salary the employee received from his old employer.[404]

9. Transfer of enterprises, businesses or parts of businesses

If the proprietor of an undertaking, business or part of a business changes and the new proprietor continues the business operations, the employment relationship of all employees will be transferred to the new owner.[405] Irrespective of how he acquired the business (purchase, leasehold, donation or other form of legal transaction), the new proprietor is the new employer and assumes the rights, obligations and liabilities of the former employer under all employment agreements (e.g. arrears of wages, holiday entitlements, claims under company pension schemes). This means that the acquired rights of the employees are safeguarded in the event of transfers of undertakings, businesses or parts of businesses.

Where these rights and duties are subject to the provisions of a collective bargaining agreement or a shop agreement, these agreements shall govern the employment relationship and may not be altered to the detriment of the employees prior to the expiry of one year after the transfer has taken effect.[406]

Different rules may apply in instances where the new owner is bound by a different collective bargaining agreement or shop agreement.[407] If it is not taken over by the new employer, i.e. it does not become part of the contractual relations with the new proprietor of the business enterprise, these rights and obligations will remain in effect for a period of no less than one year if they are to the employee's advantage.

In the event of the transfer of an undertaking, a business or a part thereof,

---

[402] § 74a para. 1 HGB.
[403] § 74 para. 2 HGB.
[404] § 74c para. 1 HGB.
[405] § 613a para. 1 BGB.
[406] § 613a para. 1 BGB.
[407] § 613a para. 1 BGB.

the employee has the right to object to the transfer of her/his employment relationship to the new proprietor. Given that after the transfer of a business establishment the old employer will in most cases have no further employment for the relevant employees, the old employer will be able to terminate the employment agreement for "business reasons" if an employee objects to the transfer of his employment agreement to the new proprietor. This is the only possible justification for terminating an employment agreement on grounds of transfer of a business.[408]

10. Labour court proceedings

Labour courts form an independent section of the German court system.[409] In addition to the (local) labour courts (of first instance), there are two stages of appeal, i.e. the regional labour courts and the Federal Labour Court. The labour courts have jurisdiction for any disputes

- between the parties to collective bargaining agreements;
- between these parties and a third party arising out of a collective bargaining agreement;
- between employees;
- between an employer and his employees (concerning the employment relationship, whereby such proceedings will lead to a judgment);
- relating to the Employees' Representation Act, the Representative Committee of Executive Employees Act or the Co-Determination Act (decision by order or judgment).

As in civil and most other proceedings, the party that lost its case will have to bear all costs, including the legal costs of the other side. However, in order to enable employees to take their cases to court without this involving an unreasonable financial risk, the court fees of labour courts are below those of other courts. In addition, there is a special rule for labour proceedings stipulating that the party which lost its case before the court of the first instance will not have to bear the fees of the other party's legal counsel.[410]

---

[408] § 613a para. 4 BGB.
[409] § 1 of the Labour Court Act (ArbGG).
[410] § 12a para. 1 ArbGG.

Chapter 12

SUPERVISORY BOARD AND ADVISORY BOARD

Dr. Arndt Stengel

1. Necessity for the formation of a supervisory board

The shareholders may make provision in the articles of association for the formation of a supervisory board,[411] which is mostly referred to as the "advisory board"[412] (the term used for it in this chapter). The composition and the powers of this voluntary body can in principle be regulated at will in the articles of association.[413]

It typically acts as a link between the shareholders and the management. In cases where the shareholders have no desire for involvement in the day-to-day business of the GmbH, or where the number or the type of shareholders make their supervision of the management impractical or ineffective, the creation of an advisory board may be recommended. However, a supervisory board must be formed if this is prescribed by statute for the purpose of co-determination by the employees.

Where a GmbH has more than 500 employees, a supervisory board must be formed, one third of which shall comprise representatives of the employees.[414]

If more than 2,000 employees are employed, half the members of the supervisory board shall be representatives of the employees and the other half shall be representatives of the shareholders.[415] The chairman selected by the shareholders' representatives has the right to a second vote.

---

[411] "Aufsichtsrat"; § 52 GmbHG.

[412] "Beirat".

[413] A distinction must be made between the advisory board formed on a voluntary basis and other bodies, whose primary function is not so much to supervise the management, but rather to advise it. If such bodies are to be formed under the terms of the articles of association, they can then only be abolished with the majority required for the alteration to the articles of association. However, if such a body is formed without provision having been made therefor in the articles of association, then this is not an organ of the company but rather only a discussion group which is not vested with any particular company law competences.

[414] §§ 76, 77 Employees' Representation Act 1952 (BetrVG).

[415] § 77 Co-Determination Act (MitbestG).

Corporate Hierarchy in a GmbH with Non-compulsory
Advisory Board and up to 500 Employees

Shareholders' Meeting
• Amendments of the Articles, Fundamental Decisions
• Important Decisions, Business in Relation to the Managing Directors Delegated to an Advisory Board
• Elects the Members of the Advisory Board

Advisory Board
• Important Decisions
• Business of the Company in Relation to the Managing Directors (Appointment, Service Agreements, Supervision, etc.)
• Right of Direction

Managing Directors
• Legal Representation of the Company
• Day-to-day Management

In a group of companies,[416] the employees of the group companies are in principle attributed to the controlling company.[417] The GmbH which is closest to a foreign parent company is considered as a controlling entity for co-determination purposes.[418]

2. Appointment and dismissal of the members

2.1 In the advisory board

The members of the advisory board are in principle elected by the shareholders' meeting.[419] A simple majority of the votes cast is sufficient,[420] unless a larger majority is necessary in accordance with the articles of association.

The articles of association can make provision for individual shareholders or for all shareholders to send members, so that one or more shareholders are entitled to decide on whom they delegate to the advisory board. However, even delegated members of the advisory board are not bound by instructions and are only under an obligation to protect and promote the best interests of the

---

[416] *Post*, p. chapter 15.
[417] §§ 77a BetrVG, 5 MitbestG.
[418] OLG Stuttgart WM 1995, 928.
[419] §§ 52 para. 1 GmbHG, 101 para. 1 AktG.
[420] § 47 para. 1 GmbHG.

company.[421] Thus, they may not follow the instructions of the delegating share-holder, and must – in the case of a conflict between the interests of the share-holders and those of the company – give priority to the company's interests.

Only natural persons can be members. Any person who is a managing director, a procurist or an authorised agent of the company cannot at the same time be a member of the advisory board.[422] The same applies to the statutory representative of a company which is dependent on the GmbH.[423]

The articles of association specify the number of members of the advisory board.[424] Substitute members may only be appointed if provision is made for this in the articles of association.[425]

Members of the advisory board cannot have their tasks carried out by others. The appointment of deputies is thus, in principle, impermissible, unless this is expressly permitted by the articles of association.[426]

The term of office of members of the advisory board is indefinite, unless the articles of association provide for a limited term. Removal from office is possible at any time. The shareholders' meeting can remove elected members of the advisory board with a simple majority, unless the articles of association prescribe a larger majority. Delegated members of the advisory board can be removed from office by the parties entitled to delegate them or by the shareholders' meeting with the majority required for an alteration to the articles of association.

2.2 In the co-determined supervisory board

In the case of a mandatory supervisory board, the shareholders' meeting or the shareholders can only select a proportion of the members of the supervisory board. Depending on the number of employees in the GmbH, either one third or one half of the supervisory board members will be elected by the employees.

In a company with 501 up to 2,000 employees, the mandatory supervisory board must have a minimum of three but a maximum of 21 members, depend-ing on the regulation in the articles of association and the amount of the share capital; the number of members must be divisible by three.[427] In the GmbH with more than 2,000 employees, the mandatory supervisory board must have a mini-mum of 12 and a maximum of 20 supervisory board members.[428]

A substitute member can be appointed for every supervisory board member who is elected or delegated. Substitute members are not deputies of the super-visory board members who take the place of the latter if they are prevented from carrying out their tasks. Rather, substitute members are only to be

---

[421] BGHZ 36, 306; 90, 381 *et seq.*
[422] §§ 52 para. 1 GmbHG, 105 para. 1 AktG.
[423] §§ 52 para. 1 GmbHG, 100 para. 2 no. 2 AktG.
[424] §§ 52 para. 1 GmbHG, 95 sentence 1 AktG.
[425] Because § 52 para. 1 GmbHG, in contrast to §§ 77 para. 1 BetrVG, 6 para. 2 MitbestG, does not refer to § 101 para. 3 AktG.
[426] §§ 52 para. 1 GmbHG, 111 para. 5 AktG.
[427] §§ 77 para. 1 BetrVG, 95 AktG.
[428] § 7 para. 1 MitbestG.

appointed in case the office of the relevant supervisory board member is vacated (e.g. as a result of death or resignation from office). The appointment of deputies is not permitted.[429]

The term of office for members of the supervisory board (including the substitute members) is usually restricted to five years.[430] In the case of a mandatory supervisory board, the removal from office by the shareholders' meeting requires a majority of three quarters of the votes cast, unless the articles of association specify another majority.[431]

3. Tasks and rights

3.1 In the advisory board

The primary task of the advisory board is to monitor the management. The advisory board must not involve itself in the management. However, in accordance with the articles of association, the consent of the advisory board can be required for certain acts of management. In addition, it falls within the advisory board's sphere of tasks to examine the company's accounting. The advisory board has wide-ranging rights to information and of inspection to assist it in the fulfilment of its tasks.[432]

By contrast to a supervisory board in an AG, the appointment of the statutory representative organ of the company (i.e. the appointment of the managing director) is in principle not a matter for the advisory board of a GmbH. Rather, the appointment of the managing director falls within the sphere of responsibility of the shareholders' meeting;[433] this also encompasses the conclusion of the contract of employment with the managing director. However, the articles of association can transfer the competence to make the appointment to the advisory board, although it should be clarified whether this is intended to create an additional competence (alongside that of the shareholders' meeting) or an exclusive competence for such appointments.

In many cases, the articles of association transfer to the advisory board the right to issue instructions,[434] which would otherwise be due to the shareholders' meeting in relation to the managing directors.

The articles of association usually grant the advisory board the right to decide on certain important business decisions which, according to the articles of

---

[429] §§ 77 para. 1 BetrVG, 25 para. 1 no. 2 MitbestG, 111 para. 5 AktG. The impermissibility of representation in a co-determined supervisory board does not automatically mean that the supervisory board members must participate in the meetings of the supervisory board in person. Rather, they can cast written votes by having them handed in by voting messengers under the terms of § 108 para. 3 AktG.

[430] Under the terms of §§ 77 para. 1 BetrVG, 6 para. 2 MitbestG, 102 AktG.

[431] §§ 77 para. 1 BetrVG, 6 para. 2 MitbestG, 103 para. 1 AktG.

[432] §§ 52 para. 1 GmbHG, 90 para. 3, 111 para. 2 AktG.

[433] § 46 no. 5 GmbHG.

[434] *Ante*, p. 158.

association, the managing directors are not entitled to decide themselves. What falls within the scope of "important business decisions" is usually determined by a catalogue of competence of the advisory board. This can include a list of types of important transactions or certain quantitative limits for transactions which do or do not require prior consent. In many cases, there is a general clause in accordance with which all transactions not considered as being within the ordinary course of business require approval.

3.2 In the co-determined supervisory board

In companies with 501 to 2,000 employees, the appointment of the managing director does not fall within the tasks of the supervisory board.[435] The tasks and rights of the co-determined supervisory board thus for the most part correspond to those of the optional supervisory board.

By contrast, the rights of a co-determined supervisory board in a GmbH with more than 2,000 employees also include the right to appoint the managing directors of the GmbH.[436] First of all, an attempt is made in the first ballot to appoint the managing director with a majority of two thirds of the supervisory board members. If this is not successful and a solution based on mutual agreement between the employees' representatives and the representatives of the shareholders has not been reached, then a second ballot is held. In this second ballot, the chairman of the supervisory board – who is exclusively appointed by the shareholders – has two votes, so that the shareholders can ultimately enforce their will.[437]

4. Committees

The supervisory board can form one or more committees out of its midst, namely in order to prepare its discussions or resolutions, or to supervise the implementation of its resolutions. Committees with the power to pass resolutions, i.e. those with the power to decide on certain matters in place of the whole supervisory board, require a position in the articles of association in the case of the advisory board.[438] In co-determined supervisory boards, certain tasks cannot be transferred to a committee for resolution instead of being submitted to the supervisory board. The conclusion of the contract of employment with the managing director, however, can be transferred to a commissioned member, e.g. the chairman of the supervisory board.

In principle, the members of the supervisory board selected by the shareholders have the possibility of determining the composition of the committees alone, with the help of the second vote to which the chairman of the supervisory

---

[435] § 77 para. 1 BetrVG 1952 does not refer to § 84 AktG.
[436] § 31 MitbestG.
[437] § 31 para. 4 MitbestG.
[438] § 52 para. 1 does not refer to § 107 para. 3 AktG.

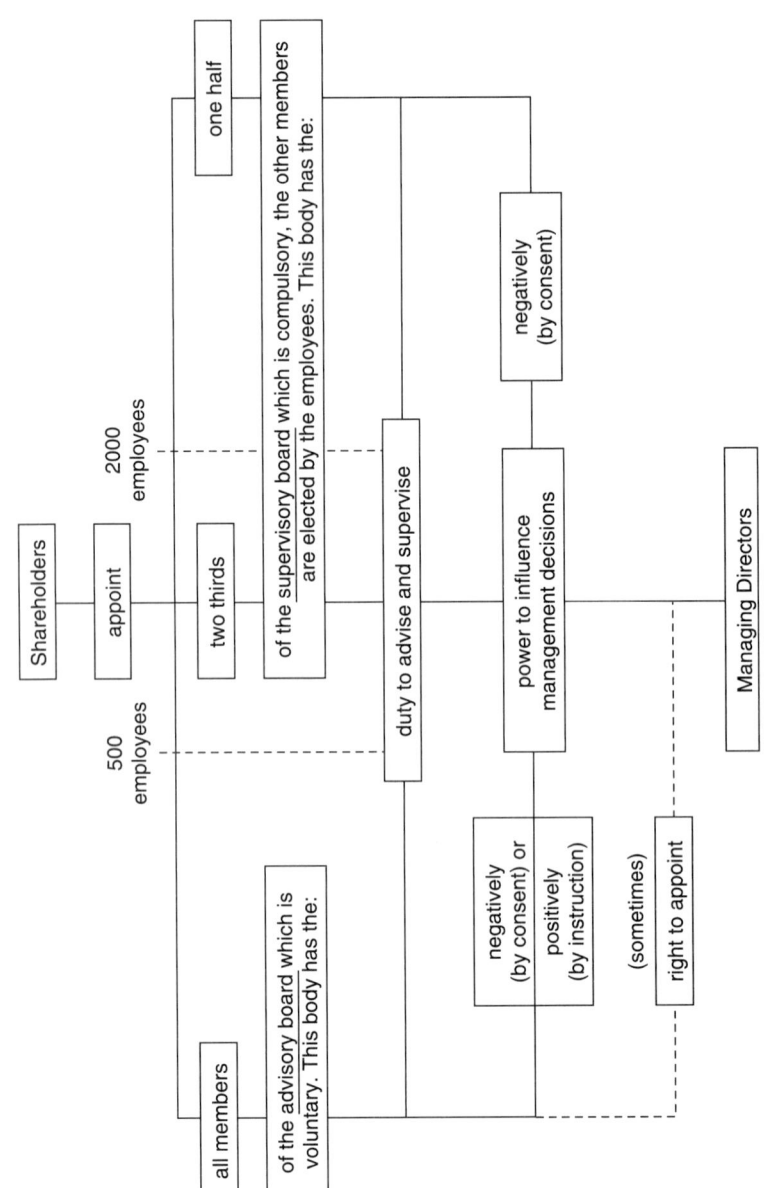

board is entitled. However, case-law views the exclusion of the employees' representatives from all participation in committees on grounds of principle as a wrongful discrimination against the employees' representatives.[439]

Important statutory tasks of the supervisory board in companies with more than 2,000 employees thus cannot be transferred past the employees' representatives to committees constituted exclusively by shareholders, unless there are important objective reasons for doing so. However, case-law recognises the composition of a committee which gives predominance to the shareholders.

5. Standing rules and regulations

The supervisory board can give itself standing rules and regulations in order to regulate its internal order.

5.1 In the advisory board

The advisory board takes its decisions by means of resolutions, for which a simple majority of the votes cast is in principle sufficient. The election of the chairman of the advisory board is regulated in the articles of association; otherwise, it is a matter for the entire advisory board.

In order to avoid chance majorities, the articles of association can provide that the meeting must be adjourned under certain circumstances. Such clauses are permissible if they observe the principles of parity and the equal treatment of the members of the advisory board, and as long as the work of the advisory board is not blocked. The advisory board itself determines the frequency of meetings if the articles of association do not contain more detailed stipulations. Four meetings per year are usual.

5.2 In the co-determined supervisory board

The co-determined supervisory board also decides by a resolution with a simple majority. The mandatory supervisory board must elect a president from amongst its midst.[440] In companies with 501 to 2,000 employees, the chairman of the supervisory board is elected with a simple majority of the votes cast. In companies with more than 2,000 employees, if a two thirds' majority of the supervisory board members is not attained, then only the supervisory board members who represent the shareholders elect the chairman of the supervisory board.[441] The position of chairman is especially important due to the second vote attaching to it.[442]

---

[439] BGH NJW 1993, 2307 *et seq.*
[440] §§ 77 para. 1 BetrVG, 25 para. 1 no. 2 MitbestG, 107 para. 1 AktG.
[441] § 27 MitbestG.
[442] § 31 para. 4 MitbestG.

A meeting of the supervisory board ought usually to be called once every calendar quarter; it must be called once every calendar half year.[443]

6. Relationship of the supervisory board to the shareholders' meeting

The members of the supervisory board are not bound to follow instructions issued by individual shareholders or by the shareholders' meeting, even if they are delegated members of the supervisory board.

By contrast, the shareholders' meeting is authorised to issue instructions to the managing director at any time,[444] even where there is a co-determined supervisory board.[445] This considerably restricts the importance of the employees' co-determination within the GmbH.

---

[443] § 77 para. 1 BetrVG, 25 para. 1 no. 2 MitbestG, 110 para. 3 AktG.
[444] § 37 GmbHG.
[445] BVerfGE 50, 346 *et seq.*; BGHZ 89, 48, 57.

Part V

FINANCIAL

Chapter 13

ACCOUNTING, ANNUAL STATEMENTS AND DISCLOSURE

Dr. Uwe Schimmelschmidt

1. Accounting[1]

The accounting of the GmbH must be prepared in such a way that an expert third party is able to gain an overview of the business transactions and of the situation of the enterprise from them within a reasonable time.[2] The origin and the handling of the business transactions must be clear enough to be followed. In particular, the following requirements must be made of proper accounting.

1.1 Language

The use of a foreign language only comes into consideration if the responsible person does not have a sufficient command of German. If a foreign language is used, the tax authorities can require a translation.[3] If abbreviations, figures, letters or symbols are used, their meaning must be absolutely clear in each individual case.[4]

1.2 Completeness

All business transactions must be fully documented without omissions.

1.3 Correctness

In principle, entries may only be made on the basis of an accounting voucher from which the transaction forming the basis of the record is evident (voucher principle).

---

[1] "Buchführung".
[2] § 238 para. 1 HGB.
[3] § 146 para. 3 AO.
[4] § 146 para. 3 AO.

1.4 Timely registration of entries in the accounts

The entries shall in principle be made in the accounts reasonably soon. Cash receipts and cash disbursements should be documented daily.[5]

1.5 Order

The business transactions must be properly allocated to accounts within a sensible and systematically structured system. The individual transaction must be sufficiently identifiable through the supply of voucher numbers, date or similar information. There are special tax provisions for the recording of receipts of goods and sales.[6] In addition, the value added tax duties to keep records and accounts must be observed,[7] along with the obligation to record certain business expenditure (which is sometimes non-deductible).[8]

1.6 Alterations

Alterations of entries or of other records may not be made in such a way that the original content is no longer determinable. False entries may thus only be corrected in the form of transfer entries or reversing entries. Where a computer-supported accounting system is used, printed records must be kept concerning the alterations which have been made.

1.7 Type of accounting

The accounting of the GmbH must usually be done on a double entry bookkeeping system, in accordance with which the profit or loss is determined both by the comparison of assets (balance sheet) and by the comparison of the expenditure and revenue (profit and loss account). Computer-supported accounting systems are permissible as far as they conform to the principles of proper accounting.

1.8 Safekeeping

Books and records, inventories, annual statements, situation reports, the opening balance and work regulations necessary in order to understand them, and other organisational documents, shall be kept for 10 years, and all other documents shall be kept for six years.[9] The period of safekeeping starts at the end of the calendar year in which the last entry was made in the accounts, in

---

[5] § 146 para. 1 AO.
[6] §§ 143, 144 AO.
[7] § 22 UStG.
[8] § 4 para. 7 EStG.
[9] §§ 257 HGB, 147 para. 1 and 3 AO.

which the inventory, the opening balance, the annual statements or the situation report were prepared, the business letter was received or was sent or the accounting voucher came into being.[10] With the exception of the opening balance, the annual statements and the consolidated group accounts, the accounting documents may also be stored on microfilm recordings or other data carriers, subject to further preconditions.[11]

The period for safekeeping does not expire if, and as long as, the documents are important with regard to tax for which the assessment deadline has not yet expired.[12]

1.9 Beginning and end

The accounting duty begins with the first business transaction after formation which must be entered in the accounts, irrespective of the registration in the Commercial Register. Thus, the accounting duty already affects the Vor-GmbH.

The accounting duty ends after the end of the GmbH, once the last item of property has been sold, the last liability has been settled and any surplus has been paid out to the shareholders.

1.10 Enforcement

The fulfilment of the accounting duties and duties to keep records can be enforced by the assessment of a coercive payment of up to DM 5,000.[13] If accounts or records do not exist or have not properly kept, the tax authority shall estimate the bases of taxation.[14]

If business transactions with regard to which there are accounting duties or duties to keep records are not entered in the accounts or are incorrectly entered from a factual point of view, and if this results in the reduction of tax payments, this constitutes a jeopardy to taxation.[15] As a regulatory offence, it can be punished with an administrative fine of up to DM 10,000. If, in an individual case, a reckless unlawful reduction of tax assessment is given,[16] then the fine can amount to up to DM 100,000.[17] The breach of accounting duties and duties of safekeeping of records is liable to prosecution in the case of the opening of bankruptcy proceedings, the refusal of the bankruptcy petition for lack of assets or the cessation of payments.[18]

---

[10] § 147 para. 4 AO, § 257 para. 5 HGB.
[11] § 257 para. 3 and § 261 HGB, § 147 para. 2 and 5 AO.
[12] § 147 para. 3 AO.
[13] §§ 328, 329 AO.
[14] § 162 AO.
[15] "Steuergefährdung"; § 379 para.1 AO.
[16] § 378 AO.
[17] *Ante*, p. 170.
[18] §§ 283 to 283b StGB, see p. 173. In addition, the breach of accounting duties and duties to keep records can be liable to prosecution if the offence of fraudulent tax evasion is committed (§ 370 AO); *ante* p. 170.

2. Inventory[19]

At the start of its commercial business, and subsequently at the end of each of its business years, the company must list precisely its real property, its claims and liabilities, the amount of its cash funds and its other assets, and must in doing so state the value of the individual assets and liabilities.[20] The statement of inventory shall be prepared within reasonable time.[21]

The stock-taking which is necessary to prepare the inventory shall in principle be carried out in relation to a particular record date or at the intervals associated with the relevant stock-taking procedure used. The stock-taking can consist of a physical stock-taking by counting, measuring and weighing; in an assessment shown in the books by taking over the balances out of accounts and card indices (e.g. in the case of claims and liabilities out of deliveries and services); and in the inclusion of information taken from legal documents (in particular in the case of intangible assets).

2.1 Methods of inventory

In the case of a classical record date inventory, the stock-taking is carried out at the balance sheet record date. However, the stock-taking to the record date can also be carried out near the balance sheet record date, usually within a time-limit of 10 days before and 10 days after the balance sheet record date. If the latter is chosen, it must be ensured with the help of vouchers or records that the changes in the inventory between the balance sheet record date and the day on which the stock-taking was carried out have been accorded due consideration.

The inventory can be prepared on the basis of a permanent stock-taking.[22] In this case, the inventory for the balance sheet record date can be established according to type and quantity with the aid of warehouse books (stock files).

Finally, the annual physical stock-taking can be carried out within the last three months before or the first two months after the balance sheet record date.[23]

---

[19] "Inventar".
[20] § 240 para. 1 HGB.
[21] § 240 para. 2 HGB.
[22] § 241 para. 2 HGB.
[23] § 241 para. 3 HGB.
[24] § 240 para. 4 HGB.
[25] § 240 para. 3 HGB.
[26] "Jahresabschluß".
[27] § 242 HGB.
[28] "Bilanz"; §§ 266-274 HGB.
[29] "Gewinn- und Verlustrechnung";§§ 275-278 HGB.

2.2 Valuation facilitation

The following relief exists for the preparation of the inventory:

- *Group valuation*
  Items of property of the stock-in-trade of the same type and other movable property and liabilities of the same type or of approximately equivalent value can be collected together and entered in the accounts at the weighted average value.[24]

- *Fixed valuation*
  Items of property included in the tangible fixed assets, and raw materials, accessory materials and operating supplies, can – if they are regularly replaced and their overall value is of subordinate importance for the business – be entered in the statements with a constant quantity and a constant value if the stock thereof is only subject to minor fluctuations with regard to its size, its value and its composition. However, a physical stock-taking must usually be carried out every three years.[25]

3. Annual statements[26]

3.1 Components of the annual accounts

At the beginning of its commercial business and for the end of each fiscal year, the GmbH[27] shall prepare a statement reflecting the relationship between its assets and its liabilities (opening balance, balance sheet),[28] along with a comparative analysis of the expenditure and revenues for the fiscal year (profit-and-loss account).[29] The balance sheet and the profit-and-loss account, together with the so-called appendix,[30] form the annual statements of the GmbH.[31]

The appendix shall contain explanations of the balance sheet and the profit-and-loss account to provide an accurate picture of the current situation of the company as regards assets, finances and earnings (the so-called "true and fair view" principle).[32]

In addition to the annual statements, a situation report must be prepared,[33] which contains a description of the course of business, the current economic situation of the company and its foreseeable future development. As with the annual statements, the description must provide an accurate picture of the actual circumstances.

---

[30] "Anhang".
[31] §§ 242 para. 3, 264 para. 1 HGB.
[32] § 264 para. 2 HGB. Details of what information must be supplied are contained in §§ 284 *et seq.* HGB.
[33] "Lagebericht"; §§ 264 para. 1, 289 HGB.

3.2 Size categories

The Commercial Code[34] makes a distinction between three size classes of corporations (small, medium-sized, large). These size categories are important for:

- the preparation and disclosure of the annual statements;
- the structuring of the balance sheet and profit-and-loss account;
- the content of the appendix;
- the obligation to prepare a situation report;
- the requirement to conduct an audit.

The allocation of the GmbH to one of these three size classes is determined by
the balance sheet total, the proceeds from turnover and the average number of
employees. The size characteristics which are in each case relevant to the classi-
fication of the GmbH in one of the three size categories can be seen from the
following overview:

	Balance Sheet Total in DM million	Turnover Proceeds in DM million	Employees
small	≤ 5, 31	≤ 10, 62	≤ 50
medium-sized	≤ 21, 24	≤ 42, 48	≤ 250
large	> 21, 24	> 42, 48	> 250

The allocation of the GmbH to one of the three size categories is made even in
cases where only two of the three characteristics are given on two successive balance
sheet record dates. These must not necessarily be the same two characteristics.
In the cases of new formation or transformation, an allocation to one of the three
size categories is already made if the size characteristics specified above are given
at the first accounting reference date after the new formation or transformation.[35]

3.3 Responsibility for the preparation

The managing directors are responsible for the preparation of the annual statements and the situation report.[36] They can delegate the tasks necessary for the
preparation of the annual statements. However, they always remain responsible
for the annual statements, even in the situation where the responsibility for the
preparation has been transferred to one managing director internally.

The annual statements (but not the situation report) must be dated and
signed by all managing directors.[37]

---

[34] § 267 HGB.
[35] § 267 para. 4 HGB.
[36] § 264 para. 1 HGB.
[37] § 245 HGB.

3.4 Time-limit for preparation

The annual statements and the situation report must, in principle, be prepared within three months after the accounting reference date.[38] In the case of small corporations, it is sufficient if the preparation is done within six months if this corresponds to the ordinary course of business.

3.5 Structure of the balance sheet and profit-and-loss account

The Commercial Code establishes general principles for the structuring of the balance sheet and the profit-and-loss account.[39] In accordance therewith, the form of the presentation – and in particular the structuring of successive balance sheets and the profit-and-loss accounts – shall be retained, unless divergences are necessary in exceptional cases by reason of special (very rare) circumstances. This principle of continuity of presentation is intended to guarantee the comparability of annual statements.

In both the balance sheet and the profit-and-loss account, each item shall be accompanied by the corresponding amount of the previous year.[40] If the amounts are not comparable, then this must be stated and explained in the appendix.

Together with the further general structuring principles[41] there are detailed provisions for the structuring of the balance sheet[42] and the profit-and-loss account,[43] with relief for small and medium-sized corporations.[44]

3.6 Description of the appropriation of profits

The shareholders have a claim to the annual surplus plus any unappropriated profit carried forward and less any loss carryforward, unless the resulting amount is prevented from being distributed to the shareholders by statute, by the articles of association or by a shareholders' resolution. If the balance sheet is prepared in a way which takes into consideration the partial appropriation of profits, or if the reserves are liquidated, then the shareholders have a claim to the balance sheet profit.[45] In this case, the balance sheet profit takes the place of the entries "annual surplus/annual deficit" and "unappropriated profits carried forward/loss carryforward".[46] An existing profit or loss carryforward

---

[38] § 264 para. 1 HGB.
[39] § 265 HGB.
[40] § 265 para. 2 HGB.
[41] § 265 HGB.
[42] § 266 HGB.
[43] § 275 HGB.
[44] §§ 266 para. 1 and 276 HGB.
[45] § 29 para. 1.
[46] § 268 para. 1 HGB.

shall be included in the entry "balance sheet profit/balance sheet loss" and shall be stated separately in the balance sheet or in the appendix.

The balance sheet profit is calculated as follows:

```
        Annual surplus/annual deficit
+/−     unappropriated profits carried forward/loss
        carryforward from previous year
+       withdrawals out of capital reserves
+/−     withdrawals/transfers out of/into the retained profits
−       advance distributions
──────────────────────────────────────────────────────────
=       balance sheet profit/balance sheet loss
```

3.7 Appendix

The annual statements of the GmbH include not only the balance sheet and profit-and-loss account, but also the appendix. It shall contain information which serves the basic explanation of the annual statements of the GmbH. With this information, the appendix is intended – together with the balance sheet and profit-and-loss account – to give an accurate picture of the corporation's situation as regards assets, finances and earnings, in accordance with the principles of proper accounting.[47] In particular, the following are included:

- information about the balance sheet methods and assessment methods used;[48]

- information about the items of the balance sheet;[49]

- information about the items of the profit-and-loss account.[50]

3.8 Situation report

Large and medium-sized GmbHs must prepare a situation report in addition to the annual statements.[51] This has the function of supplementing the annual statements by a description of the overall situation of the business. The situation report is designed to furnish information which is necessary for an overall financial assessment of the business but which cannot be conveyed by the accounting in the annual statements.

The situation report shall at least describe the course of business and the

---

[47] § 264 para. 2 HGB.
[48] § 284 para. 2 HGB.
[49] § 285 no. 1 to 3, 5, 11 and 12 HGB.
[50] § 285 no. 4, 5, 8, 9 and 13. In the preparation of the appendix, there is relief for small and medium-sized corporations (§ 288 HGB). Certain information does not have to be supplied if it is likely to cause a considerable disadvantage to the GmbH, or to a company in which the GmbH owns at least 20 per cent of the shares (§ 286 para. 2 HGB) or which is of subordinate importance for the assets, finances and earnings situation of the GmbH (§ 286 para. 3 HGB). Information on the management remuneration need not be given if the remuneration of an individual member could be determined from this information (§ 286 para. 4 HGB).
[51] § 264 para. 1 HGB.

situation of the GmbH in such a way as to provide an accurate picture of the current position.[52] This can, in particular, include information on:

- substantial alterations within the business, such as, for example, the establishment or abandonment of spheres of business, developments in the shareholdings and changes in the organization;
- developments in the procurement and production sphere;
- financing measures which have been carried out or which are imminent;
- information on personnel (changes in working times, co-determination, employees' participation).

In addition, the situation report shall deal with[53]

- transactions of special importance which arose after the end of the fiscal year;
- the projected development of the GmbH;
- the sphere of research and development;
- permanent establishments of the company.

4. Consolidated group accounting[54]

Consolidated group accounting attempts to depict the group as one single business in the accounting. For this reason, annual consolidated group statements and an annual group situation report shall be prepared alongside the individual balance sheets by the statutory representatives of the parent company, if it is a corporation in Germany.

All subsidiaries which fall under the uniform management of the parent company,[55] and in which the parent company holds a participation or an interest which aims at a permanent inter-company link,[56] shall be included in these group annual statements. Irrespective of a uniform management, the group annual statements shall also include those enterprises in which the parent company has the majority of voting rights or the right to appoint managerial organs, or remove them from office, or in which it exercises a dominant influence[57] on the basis of a controlling agreement.[58]

The group annual statements consist of the group balance sheet, the group profit-and-loss account and the group appendix.[59] The annual statements of the parent company are consolidated together with the annual statements of the

---

[52] § 289 para. 1 HGB.
[53] § 289 para. 2 HGB.
[54] "Konzernrechnungslegung".
[55] *Post*, p. 254.
[56] § 290 para. 1 HGB.
[57] § 290 para. 2 HGB.
[58] *Post*, p. 254.
[59] § 297 para. 1 HGB.

subsidiaries, i.e. the situation as regards assets, finances and earnings is set out in such a way as if these companies together formed one business.[60] The place of the shares held by the parent company in the subsidiaries involved is taken by the balance sheet positions of the subsidiaries.[61]

The group annual statements also include the group appendix, which contains information about the group balance sheet and the group profit-and-loss account, and which provides a breakdown of the shareholdings and important balance sheet items.[62] In addition, the group situation report must give a true account of the course of business and the group's situation.[63]

The consolidated group accounting is subject to compulsory examination by an auditor and to publicity requirements.

5. Audit of the annual statements[64]

In order to guarantee the most accurate possible picture of the financial situation of the business, the annual statements of large and medium-sized GmbHs[65] must be audited by an auditor.[66] If no audit of the annual statements has been carried out, then the annual statements cannot be adopted. If the annual statements are adopted in spite of this, then they are null and void. A resolution on the appropriation of profits which is based on annual statements which are null and void is also null and void itself, with the result that the GmbH has a claim for recovery of distributed profits against the shareholders.

The auditors can be chartered accountants[67] and accounting firms, or sworn auditors[68] or firms of auditors in the case of medium-sized GmbHs.[69] The auditor is selected by the shareholders,[70] unless the responsibility has been transferred to other organs or persons, e.g. a voluntary supervisory board or a group of shareholders, under the terms of the articles of association.[71] Shareholder-directors are entitled to vote.

If no auditor is selected, then an auditor shall be appointed by the district court at the place where the GmbH has its registered office[72] upon the application of the management, the supervisory board or of a shareholder.[73]

Where there are certain conflicts of interest, the position of auditor is

---

[60] § 297 para. 3 HGB.
[61] § 300 para. 1 HGB.
[62] §§ 313 *et seq.* HGB.
[63] § 315 HGB.
[64] "Abschlußprüfung".
[65] *Ante*, p. 212.
[66] § 316 para. 1 HGB.
[67] "Wirtschaftsprüfer".
[68] "Vereidigte Buchprüfer".
[69] § 319 para. 1 HGB.
[70] § 318 para. 1 HGB.
[71] § 318 para. 1 HGB.
[72] § 145 para. 2 Non-Contentious Jurisdiction Act (FGG).
[73] § 318 para. 4 HGB.

excluded,[74] in particular where the auditor himself holds shares in the GmbH to be audited, or is a managing director or a member of the supervisory board of the GmbH or of an associated enterprise[75] or if he advises the company in tax matters or has exercised influence on the preparation of the annual statements.[76]

The managing directors must submit the annual statements and the situation report to the auditor and must, upon request, furnish all clarification and proof which is necessary for a proper audit.[77] The accounting of the GmbH shall be included in the audit of the annual statements.[78]

The auditor shall prepare a written audit report on the results of the audit.[79] The report shall in particular establish whether the accounting, the annual statements, the situation report and – where appropriate – the group annual statements and group situation report correspond to the statutory provisions, and whether the statutory representatives of the GmbH have furnished the necessary clarifications and proof. If, in the course of his activities, the auditor becomes aware of facts which threaten the continued existence of the audited enterprise or which could have significant adverse effects on its development, then he must report on this.[80]

If the objections cannot be taken into account by means of restrictions in the auditor's attestation, then the auditor must refuse the attestation. If no objections are raised with regard to the annual statements, the auditor shall grant an attestation.[81] Occasionally, the attestation is accompanied by supplementary comments or restrictions, in order to avoid a false impression of the audit.[82]

The auditor is subject to strict liability for fault in connection with his activities as auditor, which is restricted to an amount of DM 500,000 in the case of negligent actions.[83] Usually, the auditor is only liable to the company which he audits.

6. Disclosure

The managing directors shall file the attested annual statements with the situation report, and the proposal for and the resolution on the appropriation of profits, together with a statement of the annual surplus or deficit, with the Commercial Register immediately after they have been submitted to the shareholders, at the latest nine months after the balance sheet record date, and shall publish in the *Federal Gazette* the fact that the annual statements have been filed.[84]

---

[74] § 319 para. 2, 3 HGB.
[75] *Post*, p. 253.
[76] OLG Karlsruhe AG 96, 227.
[77] § 320 HGB.
[78] § 317 para. 1 HGB.
[79] § 321 HGB.
[80] § 321 para. 2 HGB.
[81] § 322 HGB.
[82] § 322 para. 2 HGB.
[83] § 323 HGB.
[84] § 325 HGB.

The publicity requirements differ, depending on the size of the company. In the case of "large" GmbHs, the announcement must take place before the filing, and a proof copy of the announcement must be filed with the Commercial Register.[85] The balance sheet and the appendix of "medium-sized" GmbHs need not be as detailed as for "large" GmbHs.[86] In the case of "small" GmbHs, the situation report and the profit-and-loss account can be omitted. The time-limit amounts to twelve months.[87]

If a GmbH fails to fulfil its publicity obligations, then a coercive payment of up to DM 10,000 shall be imposed on the managing directors by the registry court to ensure compliance.[88] However, a coercive payment may only be imposed if a shareholder, a creditor of the company or the works council has applied for the intervention of the registry court.[89]

Currently, only a smallproportion of companies fulfil their publicity obligations.[90] The European Commission has thus commenced an action against theFederal Republic of Germany before the European Court for breach of the EC Treaty, because it has failed to fulfil its obligation to introduce effective sanctions to guarantee the implementation of the obligations of publicity.[91]

---

[85] § 325 para. 2 HGB.
[86] § 327 HGB.
[87] § 326 HGB.
[88] § 335 no. 6 HGB.
[89] § 335 HGB.
[90] Publication of the Federal Attorney General (BMJ) GmbHR 94, 453: at most 10 to 20 per cent.
[91] Art. 5 EC Treaty; Art. 6 First Directive on Company Law. BMJ GmbHR 95, 652; see also OLG Düsseldorf ZIP 1996, 230.

Chapter 14
TAXES OF THE GMBH AND ITS SHAREHOLDERS

Dr. Uwe Schimmelschmidt

1. Types of tax

As a legal person, the GmbH is an independent taxable entity. The taxes of the GmbH can be divided into taxes on income, taxes on property and taxes on transactions.

Taxes on income[92] are taxes whose bases of assessment are linked to the profit of the GmbH. They comprise corporate income tax[93] and trade tax on income.[94] Corporate income tax is the general income tax of the GmbH. The general tax rate is 45 per cent of the taxable income. Corporate income tax is thus the most significant tax on the GmbH in terms of the tax burden it imposes. Trade tax on income is a special tax on profits imposed on the trade income of the GmbH. The communities in which permanent establishments of the GmbH are situated are, in principle, entitled to the tax revenue resulting from the trade tax on income. The rate for trade tax on income usually varies between 10 per cent and 20 per cent, depending on the relevant community entitled to levy the tax, in which the permanent establishment is situated.

Taxes on property are taxes for which parts of the assets of the GmbH form the basis of assessment. These taxes include trade tax on capital[95] (which is likely to be abolished in 1997), real property tax[96] and in special cases inheritance and gift tax.[97] The net worth tax[98] which was levied in Germany in the past at a rate of 0.45 per cent has been abolished as of 1 January 1997.

Taxes on transactions are taxes which are linked to acts of legal transfer or

---

[92] "Ertragsteuern".
[93] "Körperschaftsteuer".
[94] "Gewerbeertragsteuer".
[95] "Gewerbekapitalsteuer".
[96] "Grundsteuer".
[97] "Erbschaft- und Schenkungsteuer".
[98] "Vermögensteuer".

other procedures in trade. These are value added tax[99] on supplies and services at a standard tax rate of 15 per cent and real property transfer tax[100] at a rate of 3.5 per cent of the purchase price agreed upon the purchase of real property.

Alongside these taxes to be paid by the GmbH, the taxation of the shareholders must also be taken into consideration. Thus, the following description also contains an explanation of the fundamental features of the income tax and net worth tax consequences of the participation in a GmbH.

German tax law contains a series of obligations regarding the withholding and remittance of taxes for the account of a third party in the sphere of cross-border payments. Although these taxes do not give rise to an original tax debt of the GmbH, the GmbH can – in the case of a breach of the withholding duties – be liable for the taxes which must be withheld. The withholding duties of the GmbH are thus in each case the subject-matter for separate treatment.[101]

2. Taxation of income

2.1 Corporate income tax

The corporate income tax system

The German corporate income tax system is a tax credit system which aims at avoiding a double taxation of corporations (taxation of the profits at the level of the corporation on the one hand and taxation of the dividends at the level of the shareholders on the other hand). In pursuit of this aim, the basic concept of German corporate income tax law is as follows: ultimately, only the retained profits (and the non-deductible expenditure) are burdened with corporate income tax; the distributed profits are only subject to the individual income tax payable by the shareholders. This aim (at least for the German shareholders) is achieved by a system of full set-off with split rates of taxation. The profits withheld by corporations with unlimited tax liability are taxed at the corporation income tax rate of 45 per cent, whilst the tax is reduced to 30 per cent if these profits are distributed (paid out as dividends). The corporate income tax of 30 per cent levied on the corporation with regard to the dividends is credited to the German shareholder against his individual income tax debt (or corporate income tax debt), or it is reimbursed.

However, the foreign shareholder (who is subject to limited tax liability) is excluded from the system of corporate income tax credits or reimbursements. The double taxation of the profits of German corporations remains, as far as there is no tax treaty applicable which reduces it.

---

[99] "Umsatzsteuer".
[100] "Grunderwerbsteuer".
[101] *Ante*, p. 183 on payroll deduction.

Duty to pay corporate income tax

Unlimited liability for corporate income tax

The GmbH is a legal person under private law, a so-called corporation,[102] and is thus an independent taxable entity.[103] The GmbH formed under German law has its registered office in Germany and is thus subject initially to unlimited tax liability for corporate income tax, with the result that its German and its foreign income are subject to corporate income tax.

Limited liability for corporate income tax

Corporations with neither their management nor their registered office in Germany are subject to limited tax liability.[104] The tax liability is limited to particular German income as defined in the Income Tax Act.[105] The limited tax liability of a GmbH formed under German law can only result from the rare case of the transferral abroad of the registered office and the management to a foreign country. In this case, the unlimited liability of the GmbH for corporate income tax ends, with the result that all the hidden reserves are subject to taxation.[106]

Beginning of the corporate income tax liability

The pre-incorporation association is not liable for corporate income tax. If it is already commercially active, then it is treated as a partnership for tax purposes. Profits and losses are attributed to the partners.[107] Losses of the pre-incorporation association cannot be taken into consideration either by the Vor-GmbH or by the corporation which comes into being at a later stage.

The Vor-GmbH is identical to the later GmbH,[108] so that it is treated in exactly the same way as the GmbH for tax purposes.

Ascertainment of income for corporate income tax purposes

Corporate income tax is measured according to the profits of the GmbH. It is an annual tax. In principle, the calendar year is authoritative,[109] but the GmbH can also ascertain its profits for a fiscal year[110] which differs from the calendar year. The profit is then considered as having been obtained in the calendar year in which the fiscal year ends.[111] The change of the fiscal year to a period other

---

[102] "Kapitalgesellschaft".
[103] § 1 para. 1 no. 1 KStG.
[104] "Beschränkte Steuerpflicht".
[105] § 49 EStG.
[106] § 12 KStG.
[107] § 179 *et seq.* AO.
[108] *Ante*, p. 31.
[109] § 7 para. 3 KStG.
[110] "Geschäftsjahr".
[111] § 7 para. 4 KStG.

than the calendar year is only valid for tax purposes if it is undertaken with the consent of the tax authorities. By reason of the commercial accounting duties of the GmbH, all income is to be treated as income from business operations.[112] Thus, the entire assets of the GmbH are business assets.

Income from business operations is synonymous with profits.[113] Profits are the amount of the difference between the business assets at the end of the current fiscal year and the business assets at the end of the previous fiscal year, increased by the value of the withdrawals and decreased by the value of the capital contributions.[114] For the ascertainment of the profits for tax purposes, the commercial law principles of proper accounting and thus the commercial balance sheet form the basis.

A series of modifications of the commercial balance sheet profit must be made in order to determine the profit for tax purposes.[115] They are mostly of a fiscal nature: whilst the preparation of the commercial balance sheet is dominated by the principle of the cautious ascertainment of profits (principle of conservatism),[116] the full profit for an assessment period should be included for the purposes of taxation. The tax law modifications of the commercial balance sheet profit thus for the most part provide for a fiscally motivated restriction of the deduction of business expenditure. However, despite the tax modifications of the commercial balance sheet profit, there is a very close connection between the tax balance sheet profit and the commercial balance sheet profit. In principle, the commercial balance sheet[117] is regarded as authoritative for the tax balance sheet.[118]

The initial amount for the ascertainment of the taxable income of the GmbH is the commercial balance sheet profit which is then modified in accordance with the special tax law provisions. In contrast to the determination of the taxable income of a partnership, the tax balance sheet profit of the corporation may also be reduced by payments to the shareholders on the basis of contracts. Interest which the corporation pays to the shareholder for the grant of a loan or salaries which are paid to the shareholder on the basis of a service agreement reduce the corporation's balance sheet profit as expenditure. These amounts are, consequently, not included in the initial amount for the ascertainment of the income of the corporation. As a result, they are not subject to either corporate income tax or (in contrast to partnerships) trade tax on income.

Alongside the tax law balance sheet corrections of the commercial balance sheet profit, a series of special characteristics must be observed in the ascertainment of the taxable income of the GmbH. In so far as they appear important, they are examined in the following overview shown opposite.

---

[112] "Einkünfte aus Gewerbetrieb".
[113] § 2 para. 2 no. 1 EStG.
[114] § 4 para. 1 EStG.
[115] § 4 EStG.
[116] "Vorsichtsprinzip".
[117] "Handelsbilanz".
[118] "Steuerbilanz".

	Simplified Plan for the Derivation of the Taxable Income Out of the Commercial Balance Sheet Profit
	Net income/loss according to the commercial balance sheet
+/−	Corrections by reason of special tax law provisions on the ascertainment of profits[119]
=	Net income/loss according to the tax balance sheet
+	Reduction in value resulting from distribution[120]
+/−	Changes in assets which are caused by the relationship with the shareholders
+	Constructive dividends
−	Constructive capital contributions
+/−	Non-deductible expenditure/corresponding earnings
+	Non-deductible business expenditure[121]
+	Allocations to staff pension funds and provident funds[122]
+	Non-deductible German and foreign taxes[123]
+	Non-deductible pecuniary penalties and similar expenditure[124]
+	50 per cent of the supervisory board remuneration and similar payments[125]
+	Donations
+	Other non-deductible amounts
+	Yields out of the reimbursement of non-deductible expenditure
+/−	Tax-free earnings/corresponding expenditure[126]
−	Tax allowances for investments[127]
+	Expenditure in connection with tax-free earnings[128]
+/−	Foreign income/corresponding expenditure
+	Certain negative foreign income[129]
−	Positive income exempted by a tax treaty
=	Sum of the income
−	Deductible donations[130]
+/−	Attribution of earnings of companies integrated in a group[131]
−	Loss carryback/carryforward[132]
=	Taxable income[133]

---

[119] § 4 *et seq.* EStG; § 60 para. 2 EStDV.
[120] § 50c EStG, § 8b para. 6 KStG.
[121] § 4 para. 5 and 6 EStG.
[122] To the extent to which the limits of §§ 4c, 4d EStG are exceeded.
[123] § 10 no. 2 KStG.
[124] § 10 no. 3 KStG.
[125] § 10 no. 4 KStG.
[126] § 3 EStG.
[127] InvZulG 1993.
[128] § 3c EStG.
[129] § 2a para. 1 EStG.
[130] § 9 para. 1 no. 2 KStG.
[131] §§ 14, 17, 18 KStG.
[132] § 8 para. 1, 4 KStG, § 10d EStG, § 2a para. 1 EStG.
[133] § 7 para. 1 KStG.

Corrections of the tax balance sheet profit

Contributions of the shareholders

Contributions[134] of the shareholders do not in principle increase the income which is subject to corporate income tax. In so far as contributions of the shareholders are made in order to raise the share capital, and the shareholders acquire shareholder rights in return, there is no profit for accounting purposes. If payments of the shareholders must be allocated to the capital reserves, they do not affect profits in the commercial balance sheet anyway. But even if this is not the case, increases in the assets of the corporation which arise as a result of the corporate relationship are non-taxable.

If an allocation to the capital reserves does not come into consideration, and an extraordinary revenue is thus entered in the accounts under commercial law, then for the purpose of ascertaining the corporation's income, the balance sheet profit shall be reduced by the shareholders' payments made *causa societatis*. Such payments are called constructive capital contributions, as distinguished from the (open) company law contributions. Examples of such constructive capital contributions include financial assistance, or waivers of debt repayments by the shareholders. In this way, it is also possible to confer advantages on the company in a constructive form without triggering taxation.

However, this does not apply to the grant of advantages of use. Thus, for example, if a shareholder grants the company an interest-free loan or hands over business assets without charge, this benefit acquired below its full price will not be balanced by a correction of the profit. This enables a shift in earnings within the group.

Constructive dividends

Just as contributions of the shareholders to the assets of the company do not form part of the profit which is subject to corporate income tax, reductions in the assets of the corporation in favour of the shareholders which are based on the corporate relationship (so-called constructive dividends) [135] may not reduce the profit which is subject to corporate income tax. As far as the ascertainment of income is concerned, it is unimportant whether the income is distributed or not.[136] As the profit is the result before distribution, constructive dividends must also be taken into consideration in the ascertainment of the profits.[137]

A constructive dividend is a reduction in the assets or a prevention of the increase in assets which is caused by the corporate relationship, which has an effect on the profits of the GmbH and which is not based on a resolution on the distribution of profits (payment of dividends) in accordance with the provisions of company law.[138] Cause on the basis of the corporate relationship is given if a

---

[134] "Einlagen".
[135] "Verdeckte Gewinnausschüttungen".
[136] § 8 para. 3 KStG.
[137] § 8 para. 3 KStG.
[138] § 8 para. 3 KStG.

prudent and conscientious director would not have accepted the reduction in assets or the prevention of the increase in assets in relation to a person who is not a shareholder under circumstances which are otherwise the same.

A constructive dividend thus comes into consideration in the following cases:

- a shareholder receives an unreasonably high salary in return for his activities as managing director (this can, in particular, also be the case if the shareholder manages several companies) or receives special additional remuneration alongside the reasonable salary;
- a shareholder receives a loan from the company either on an interest-free basis or at an unusually low rate of interest;
- a shareholder grants a loan to the company at an unusually high rate of interest;
- a shareholder supplies assets to the company at inflated prices or acquires them below their market price;
- a shareholder leases to the company above price or leases from the company below price.

In practice, the examination of whether prices or salaries are reasonable causes great difficulties, in particular in the sphere of cross-border transfer pricing. The burden of proof for the existence of a constructive dividend or the amount thereof is, in principle, borne by the tax authorities. However, in the case of cross-border relations, increased duties of co-operation are imposed on the GmbH.[139] The GmbH is obliged to ensure that it can show the reasonableness of the consideration paid, with the aid of information from the foreign parent company.

If one shareholder controls the GmbH, additional requirements have to be met in order to avoid a constructive dividend. Payments for services of the shareholder must be based on a clear agreement concluded in advance. If there is no such agreement as to whether – and if so, how much – remuneration shall be paid for the services of a shareholder, or if a clear agreement is not adhered to, for example in cases of co-operation or transfer for use (rental, lease or loan), then the remuneration paid does not reduce the company's profit, because it is viewed as a constructive dividend.

The legal consequence of the constructive dividend is the correction of the income of the company and, consequently, of the basis of assessment for corporate income tax and trade tax,[140] usually by an increase of the profit outside the balance sheet. The outflow of assets from the company triggers dividend taxation within the corporate income tax credit procedure.[141] The constructive dividend and the corporate income tax which is payable on it, and which can be credited, is taxed in the hands of the shareholder as if it were a dividend.[142]

---

[139] § 90 para. 2 AO.
[140] § 8 para. 3 KStG; § 7 GewStG.
[141] *Post*, p. 231.
[142] As far as capital yield tax is concerned, see *post* p. 233, footnote 183.

Reductions of profits which must be treated as constructive dividends consequently do not reduce the basis of assessment for trade tax on income. In the corporate income tax credit procedure, tax consequences which were not planned by the parties usually result from the fictitious constructive dividend attaching to the increase in profits: for example, if a shareholder with unlimited tax liability receives a salary which is excessive by DM 100, then in the credit procedure the assumption of a constructive dividend of DM 100 leads to a total accrual to the shareholder of 142.8 ($100 + 100 \times \frac{3}{7}$) and thus (in so far as the company has no claim for restitution) ultimately to additional enrichment at the expense of the other shareholders. By contrast, for the shareholder with limited tax liability, who is excluded from the corporate income tax credit procedure,[143] an unplanned definitive corporate income tax burden of the profits considered as having been distributed usually results.

According to the present legal situation, once a constructive dividend has been paid out, it cannot be reversed effectively from a tax point of view.

Tax-free income

For the purposes of ascertaining the income, the tax balance sheet profit of the GmbH shall be reduced by all tax-free operating receipts which have increased the profits in the bookkeeping. In particular, the following operating receipts are tax-free:

- all receipts specified in the statutory catalogue,[144–146] in so far as these can arise in the case of a GmbH. In particular, these include the profits from restructuring the GmbH:[147] Profits of the GmbH which arise from liabilities being released for purposes of restructuring are exempted from corporate income tax. A precondition of the exemption from tax is the release from the liability and the necessity of restructuring of the GmbH (i.e. a financial crisis of the GmbH), as well as the intention of restructuring by the creditor and the suitability of the release of the liability to assist the restructuring;

- investment subsidies for investments in the so-called development promotion area (i.e. the new Federal States in the former East Germany). The subsidies are granted for investments in movable business assets of the fixed capital which are subject to wear and tear.[148] At present, it usually amounts to five per cent of the costs of acquisition or manufacture;

---

[143] *Post*, p. 231.
[144–146] § 3 EStG.
[147] § 3 no. 66 EStG.
[148] § 2 InvZulG.

- foreign income which is exempted from German taxation by reason of a tax treaty;

- dividends which accrue to the GmbH and which originate from tax-free foreign earnings of the corporation which distributes them.[149] This ensures that tax-free foreign earnings remain tax-free upon their further distribution from corporation to corporation. Taxation is only imposed once a dividend is paid to a shareholder who is not a corporation with unlimited liability for corporate income tax (in particular natural persons).[150] The same applies under certain preconditions for capital gains from the sale of a share in a foreign company.[151]

In so far as expenditure has a direct connection with tax-free receipts, it cannot be deducted as business expenditure.[152]

Non-deductible expenditure

In the ascertainment of the taxable income of the GmbH, certain business expenditure does not reduce the income, even though it may be connected with the business. To the extent to which such expenditure has reduced the tax balance sheet profit, it must be added once again outside the balance sheet for tax purposes. In particular, the following expenditure is non-deductible:

- expenditure for gifts to persons who are not employees of the company;[153]

- business-linked expenditure for business entertainment of persons on a company occasion, in so far as they exceed 80 per cent of the expenditure which is to be regarded as reasonable by generally accepted standards. By way of proof of the amount of, and the business occasion for, the expenditure, the taxpayer must record the following information in writing: place, date, participants and the occasion of the business entertainment, as well as the amount of the expenditure. If the business entertainment takes place in a restaurant, then it is sufficient if information is provided about the occasion and the participants; the invoice for the entertainment must be attached;

- expenditure for hunting, fishing and yachting;

- corporate income tax, solidarity surcharge,[154] net worth tax, inheritance and gift tax, foreign taxes on income and on net worth;

---

[149] So-called distributions of EK 01. On the structure of EK; *ante*, p. 231.
[150] § 8b para. 1 KStG.
[151] § 8b para. 2 and 3 KStG.
[152] § 3c EStG.
[153] However, this does not apply if the costs of acquiring or manufacturing the items given to the recipient in the course of the fiscal year do not exceed DM 75.
[154] "Solidaritätszuschlag".

- pecuniary penalties;[155]

- half of the remuneration which is paid to members of the supervisory board or other persons commissioned with the supervision of the management.

Donations

The deduction of donations[156] is limited to certain maximum amounts:[157] expenditure may be deducted for the promotion of charitable, church, religious and academic purposes, as well as for certain purposes which are recognised as promoting general welfare and as worthy of promotion (this includes, for example, the promotion of sport and the sponsorship of cultural aims) up to a total amount of five per cent of the income or 2/1000 of the sum of the overall turnover and the wages and salaries paid in the calendar year. The deductible amount of five per cent is increased by a further five per cent for academic and charitable purposes, and for cultural purposes which are recognised as being particularly worthy of promotion. There are additional possibilities for deduction of large donations (individual payments of at least DM 50,000). Donations to political parties are non-deductible.

Deductions of losses

If the non-deductible expenditure and the constructive dividends are added to the tax balance sheet profit, and the tax-exempted earnings and the constructive capital contributions are deducted therefrom, the result is the income from the business operations of the GmbH. The only allowable deduction which can still be made is the deduction of the loss, which is structured as a specially allowed tax deduction.[158]

The GmbH can set off the losses of an assessment period by way of a so-called loss carryback against positive income of the two previous assessment periods. The loss carryback leads to an immediate tax rebate. If losses still remain after a loss carryback, then they can be deducted from the income of the GmbH in the following assessment periods without any restrictions as to time (so-called loss carryforward). There is a right of selection for the loss carryback.[159] In principle, losses should be asserted as far as possible by way of loss carryback, by reason of the immediate tax rebate. However, owing to the special characteristics of the corporate income tax procedure, care should be taken that the loss carryback does not fail by reason of a lack of equity.

---

[155] § 10 no. 3 KStG.
[156] "Spenden".
[157] § 9 para. 1 no. 2 KStG.
[158] § 10d EStG.
[159] § 10d para. 1 EStG.

A precondition for the deduction of a loss[160] is that the GmbH is not only legally but also from a business point of view identical with the entity which has suffered the loss.[161] This provision becomes particularly important in cases of the purchase of so-called shell companies.[162] By purchasing all or nearly all the shares in a corporation which usually has high loss carryforwards, the business of which is no longer operated and which essentially has no assets, the purchaser hopes to obtain future tax advantages by acquiring the loss carryforwards. In the past, such expectations have frequently been disappointed. The utilization of loss carryforwards shall be refused in the case of the acquisition of a GmbH if:[163]

- the GmbH which has been purchased has ceased trading; and
- more than 75 per cent of the shares have been transferred; and
- after the acquisition, predominantly new business assets have been brought in; and
- the company thereafter resumes trading.

In the case of a merger of GmbHs and in the case of the division of the GmbH, the loss deduction is retained.[164]

Attributions of income within integrated inter-company relationships

An integrated inter-company relationship for corporate income tax purposes is given where a legally independent corporation is economically, financially and organisationally integrated into another enterprise. The legally independent corporation is in this case subordinated to the controlling company and is comparable to a mere division or a permanent establishment (integrated corporation). In so far as a profit-and-loss transfer agreement has been concluded between the integrated corporation and the controlling company,[165] the profits of the integrated corporation are attributed to the controlling company for tax purposes.

The main advantage of the integrated inter-company relationship from a corporate income tax point of view is that profits and losses from legally independent group companies which are joined within the integrated inter-company relationship are set off against one another.[166] Each of the following preconditions have to be met for an integrated inter-company relationship:

---

[160] § 10d EStG.
[161] § 8 para. 4 KStG.
[162] *Ante*, p. 38.
[163] § 8 para. 4 KStG.
[164] §§ 12 para. 3 and 15 para. 4 UmwStG; *post*, chapter 18.
[165] *Post*, p. 254.
[166] In addition, tax-free income of the integrated corporation remains tax free when transferred to the controlling company (even beyond the sphere of application of § 8b para. 1 to 3 KStG). Furthermore, if the controlling entity is a partnership, the integrated inter-company relationship also has the effect that the retained profits of the GmbH are only taxed at the rates applicable for the taxation of the owners of the partnership. Without the existence of an integrated inter-company relationship, these amounts would be taxed at the general corporate income tax rate. An integrated inter-company relationship can thus be particularly advantageous by reason of the top tax rate for income tax of 47 per cent for commercial income.

- the conclusion of a profit-and-loss transfer agreement;[167]
- financial integration: the controlling entity must directly hold a majority of the voting rights in the integrated corporation from the beginning of the fiscal year without interruption. An indirect participation is sufficient if each of the holdings on which the indirect participation is based grants the majority of the voting rights;[168]
- organizational integration: the possibility of control which is legally given on the basis of the financial integration must actually take effect in the operating management of the integrated corporation;[169]
- economic integration: the integrated corporation must be integrated into the functions of the controlling entity like a type of division of the business in a way which serves and promotes those functions. Economic integration is usually given if the controlling entity pursues its own commercial activity;
- the controlling entity must in principle be a natural person who has un-limited tax liability or a corporation with unlimited tax liability, or a com-mercial partnership with its management and its registered office in Germany.[170] Exceptionally, the controlling company can also be foreign if it maintains a branch in Germany which is registered in the Commercial Register, and the other preconditions of the integrated inter-company relationship are given in relation to the branch itself.[171]

Tax rates

The usual standard rate of taxation for the taxable income of the GmbH[172] is 45 per cent.[173] If elements of foreign income are contained in the taxable income, then in order to avoid double taxation there is the possibility of credit-ing the foreign corporate income tax attaching to the foreign parts of the income against the German corporate income tax.[174]

Corporate income tax law distinguishes between the corporate income tax burden on the taxable income (standard rate taxation)[175] and the burden on the dividends (tax rate on dividends).[176] The usual tax rate on the taxable

---

[167] § 17 KStG; *post*, p. 254.
[168] § 14 no. 1 KStG.
[169] Upon the conclusion of a controlling agreement as defined in § 291 para. 1 AktG, the fiction of organizational integration is realised (§ 14 no. 2 KStG). In addition, the organizational integration can also be given if there are identical staff in the management organs of the controlling company and the integrated corporation.
[170] § 14 no. 3 KStG.
[171] § 18 KStG.
[172] § 23 para. 1 KStG.
[173] So-called corporate income tax rate. In comparison with this, the maximum tax rate for natural persons who are liable for income tax is 53 per cent or 47 per cent for commercial income.
[174] § 26 KStG.
[175] "Regelbesteuerung".
[176] "Ausschüttungsbelastung".

income is 45 per cent. As far as dividends are distributed to the shareholders, the corporate income tax is reduced to the tax rate on dividends of 30 per cent. The standard rate taxation thus constitutes the corporate income tax burden which results if no dividends are paid. The link between the standard tax rate and the tax rate on dividends is created by the so-called accounting breakdown of the disposable equity. With the aid of this accounting breakdown, it is ensured that the dividends are subject to the 30 per cent rate.

It is thus decisive for the final amount of corporate income tax owed for the relevant assessment period whether the GmbH pays dividends for this period. As far as the 30 per cent tax rate on dividends is applied, the corporate income tax debt for the assessment period is normally reduced but can also be increased if former tax-free parts of the income are distributed.[177]

Corporate income tax credit procedure

The corporate income tax credit procedure[178] serves the purpose of removing the double taxation on dividends. The dividends of the corporation shall only be burdened with the individual income tax of the shareholder. Once the uniform corporate income tax burden of 30 per cent for dividends has been established at the level of the company, the corporate income tax attaching to the dividends is treated as an advance payment of and thus credited against the income tax of the shareholder. This is effected in the following steps.

In the first place, the standard tax rate of 45 per cent for retained profits is applied to the taxable income. In the case of a distribution of profits, the tax rate on dividends of 30 per cent is established at the level of the GmbH for the payment of dividends. Thus, to the extent to which distributed parts of the profits would in the first place have been taxed at 45 per cent, the tax burden is reduced to the 30 per cent tax rate on dividends. On the other hand, the tax burden for parts of the profits of the corporation which were hitherto tax-free or which were only taxed at a reduced rate must be increased to the tax rate on dividends of 30 per cent. Thus, the tax-free parts of the corporation's profits become taxable parts of the profits as a result of the dividend payment.[179]

In the case of a shareholder with unlimited tax liability, the corporate income tax which burdens the dividend payment is credited to the full extent against his personal tax liability. For this purpose, the GmbH paying the dividend must certify the amount of the corporate income tax which can be credited, in accordance with the officially prescribed specimen. The corporate income tax which can be credited has to be added to the income of the shareholders entitled to such credits.[180]

---

[177] The amount of the dividends for an assessment period thus significantly influences the amount of the corporate income tax reserves which must be shown in the commercial balance sheet.

[178] "Körperschaftsteuerliches Anrechnungsverfahren".

[179] This only does not apply if either the capital contributions of the shareholders are paid back or tax-free parts of foreign income are considered as having been used for the distribution.

[180] Income from capital investments, "Einkünfte aus Kapitalvermögen"; § 20 para. 1 no. 3 EStG

Example:

At the Level of the Company	
Profits before deduction of corporate income tax	100
− Corporate income tax 45 per cent	45
= Allocation to the reserves	55
Withdrawal from reserves	55
+ Corporate income tax reduction	15
= Payment of dividend	70
At the Level of the Shareholder	
Payment of dividend	70
+ Claim to corporate income tax credit	30
= Income from capital investments	100
Individual income tax (e.g. 50 per cent)	50
− Corporate income tax which can be credited	30
= Tax burden on the dividend paid	20
Payment of dividend	70
− Tax burden on the dividend paid	20
= Shareholder's profit after tax dividend	50

The main difficulty in the corporate income tax credit procedure is the establishment of the tax rate on dividends of 30 per cent. The necessary calculation of the corporate income tax reduction or increase requires knowledge of the corporate income tax burden on the parts of the equity which are used for distribution. However, as the corporation can generate income which is subject to a tax burden of 45 per cent as well as income which is taxed at a favourable rate or which is tax-free, the various parts of the corporation's income and the corporate income tax burden attaching thereto must each be separately ascertained. The accounting breakdown of the disposable equity[181] serves this purpose. A distinction is made between parts of the equity which arise from:

- Parts of income which remain subject to full corporate income tax. If these parts of the equity capital came into existence after 31 December 1993, they are burdened with corporate income tax at 45 per cent (so-called disposable equity 45);
- Parts of income which are subject to a corporate income tax burden of 30 per cent (disposable equity 30);
- Increases in the assets of the corporation which are not subject to corporate income tax. These are the tax-free foreign parts of the income (disposable

---

[181] "Verwendbares Eigenkapital".

equity 01), other tax free increases in the assets, e.g. tax allowances for investments (disposable equity 02) and capital contributions of the shareholders (disposable equity 04);

The breakdown of the disposable equity to a significant extent determines the possible volume of the dividend and thus the value of the operations of a corporation. Thus, distributions out of disposable equity 45 lead to a tax rebate for the corporation by reason of the corporate income tax reduction calculation to be carried out. By contrast, distributions out of disposable equity 02 lead to additional corporate income tax payments for the corporation since the tax rate on dividends has to be established. Thus, the breakdown of the disposable equity can acquire significant financial importance.

Capital yield tax in the tax credit procedure
Payments of dividends of the corporation are, in principle, subject to capital yield tax.[182] When paying out a dividend, the corporation must withhold capital yield tax from the dividend which usually amounts to 25 per cent of the cash dividend.

Capital yield tax is a special form of collection of income tax on the income from capital investments. It is withheld at source (at the GmbH) and is remitted to the tax authorities for the account of the shareholder.[183]

In the specified example, the following result is obtained, taking into consideration the capital yield tax:

	Cash dividend	70.00
−	Capital yield tax 25 per cent	17.50
=	Amount of the payment out	52.50

The shareholder thus receives the cash dividend from the corporation after the capital yield tax has been deducted. The cash dividend therefore only amounts to 52.5. However, his taxable total dividend remains 100, namely 70 cash dividend plus 30 tax credit. Tax credits of 30 from the corporate income tax paid

---

[182] "Kapitalertragsteuer"; § 43 para. 1 no. 1 EStG.
[183] Capital yield tax arises at the time the capital yields accrue to the shareholder (§ 44 para. 1 EStG). This is the day which is specified in the resolution on the payment of dividends as the day for distribution (§ 44 para. 2 EStG). The company is liable for the capital yield tax which it must withhold and remit (§ 44 para. 5 EStG). In the case of constructive dividends, the obligation to withhold and remit the capital yield tax can fall away if the constructive dividend is encompassed as capital yield at the level of the shareholder within the framework of the assessment procedure. The failure to pass on the burden of the capital yield tax paid by the company to the shareholder is a further constructive dividend. In addition, there is no obligation to withhold and remit the capital yield tax if, at the level of the shareholder with unlimited tax liability, the capital yields are not taxable because of their low levels, and the shareholder submits an exemption certificate or a non-assessment order (§ 44a EStG).

by the corporation and 17.5 capital yield tax withheld on the shareholder's account, meaning a total of 47.5 per cent, must be allowed against the income tax owed by him for 100. Ultimately, therefore, the retention of capital yield tax does not constitute a burden for the shareholder with unlimited tax liability.

Foreign shareholders in the tax credit procedure

In principle, only persons or companies who have unlimited tax liability are entitled to corporate income tax credits. These are persons who either have their place of residence[184] or who are ordinarily resident (presence of more than six months)[185] in Germany or companies whose management or registered office is situated in Germany. By contrast, shareholders with limited tax liability are in principle excluded from the corporate income tax credit system. The individual income tax or corporate income tax payable on their capital yields is paid by the capital yield tax.[186] An exception is only given if the dividend accrues in a German permanent establishment of the shareholder with limited tax liability as operating revenue.[187] However, with the exception of this instance, the corporate income tax of 30 per cent which is paid by the GmbH on the dividends remains. In addition, there is the foreign shareholder's capital yield tax burden. In any assessment of the foreign shareholder for income tax or corporate income tax purposes, the dividends remain out of count by reason of the settlement effect of the capital yield tax.

As far as the amount of the capital yield tax on the dividends is concerned, a distinction must be made:

- for dividends on shares in diversified holdings,[188] the capital yield tax usually reduces to 15 per cent on the basis of the existing tax treaties with most countries;

- for dividends received from affiliated companies,[189] the existing tax treaties often make provision for further-reaching reductions of the capital yield tax to five per cent or 10 per cent;

- for dividends of a German subsidiary company paid to a parent company whose management is located in another member state of the European Union, capital yield tax can be wholly waived under certain circumstances upon application.[190]

---

[184] § 8 AO.

[185] § 9 AO.

[186] § 50 para. 5 EStG; § 51 KStG.

[187] "Betriebseinnahmen".

[188] According to the Model Tax Treaties, these are dividends on equity holdings of less than 25 per cent (OECD Model Tax Treaty) or 10 per cent (UN Model Tax Treaty and US Model Tax Treaty).

[189] These are dividends on equity holdings of usually at least 10 per cent (UN Model Tax Treaty and US Model Tax Treaty) or 25 per cent (OECD Model Tax Treaty)

[190] § 44d EStG.

Irrespective of the reductions specified above, the company paying the dividend must, in principle, withhold and remit the 25 per cent capital yield tax.[191] The reduction of the capital yield tax must then be asserted by the shareholder himself by submitting an application for reimbursement to the Federal Office of Finance.[192] The withholding and remittance of the 25 per cent capital yield tax without taking into consideration the reductions specified above can only be avoided in cases in which the Federal Office of Finance certifies upon application that the preconditions for a reduction of the capital yield tax are fulfilled (so-called exemption procedure).

If the dividends of the GmbH are tax exempt at the level of a foreign shareholder, then the German tax attaching to the distributed profits – after applying the tax rate on dividends of 30 per cent – will amount to the following, depending on the amount of the capital yield tax:

- 40.5 per cent (30 per cent corporate income tax and (15 per cent of 70 =) 10.5 per cent capital yield tax); or

- 37 per cent (30 per cent corporate income tax and (10 per cent of 70 =) 7 per cent capital yield tax); or

- 33.5 per cent (30 per cent corporate income tax and (5 per cent of 70 =) 3.5 per cent capital yield tax).

Tax deduction obligations in the case of foreign relationships

As far as non-residents perform services to the GmbH, an obligation on the GmbH may arise to withhold income tax on behalf of the non-residents subject to limited tax liability by means of a tax deduction from the remunerations paid by the GmbH.[193] This must in particular be taken into consideration in the following sets of circumstances:

- all types of remuneration paid to members of the supervisory board or advisory board of the GmbH who have limited tax liability for the supervision of the management of the GmbH. The supervisory board tax to be withheld and remitted by the GmbH amounts to 30 per cent of the supervisory board remuneration;[194]

- income of non-residents which is generated by performing arts, artistic, sporting or similar performances in Germany or their commercialisation, unless the income is generated through work as an employee, which is subject to tax deduction from wages;[195]

- income of non-residents which stems from remuneration for the use of movable property (e.g. rental payments) or the right to the use of rights, in particular of copyrights and industrial property rights, etc. (royalties).

---

[191] § 50 EStG.
[192] "Bundesamt für Finanzen".
[193] § 50a para. 1 EStG.
[194] § 50a para. 1 İEStG.
[195] § 38 para. 1 no. 1 EStG.

In the latter two cases, the tax amounts to 25 per cent of the gross earnings, including the value added tax attaching to the payments.[196]

Solidarity surcharge

From 1995 onwards, a so-called solidarity surcharge is levied (for an indefinite period) as a special levy on the individual income tax or corporate income tax. The solidarity surcharge amounts to 7.5 per cent of the assessed individual income tax or corporate income tax. The solidarity surcharge is not only levied on the assessed individual or corporate income tax but also on advance payments. In addition, the solidarity surcharge is also payable on the withholding taxes[197] and the capital yield tax to be withheld from the dividends paid by the GmbH.

Tax reductions on the basis of a tax treaty also apply to the solidarity surcharge. If, for example, the capital yield tax is reduced to 15 per cent of the dividends on the basis of a tax treaty, this restriction also applies to the solidarity surcharge.

2.2 Trade tax

General

Every commercial trade[198] operated in Germany[199] is liable for trade tax. The activities of the GmbH are always fully to be viewed as commercial trade.[200] Foreign trade income and foreign trade capital are, in principle, not subject to trade tax on income, in contrast to corporate income tax.[201]

Trade tax is assessed on the basis of a combination of the two bases of tax assessment, namely trade income and trade capital. Trade tax is ascertained by applying a so-called tax factor on a standard basic assessment figure:[202]

---

[196] The withholding tax to be deducted by the GmbH serves to secure the tax claim of the German tax authorities. The GmbH is liable for the withholding and remittance of the tax. In principle, the withholding tax must be withheld by the debtor of the remuneration, the GmbH, irrespective of any exemption of the income in accordance with the provisions of a tax treaty (§ 50d para. 1 EStG). To the extent to which the income is exempted from German tax in accordance with a tax treaty, the reimbursement of the withholding tax must then be asserted by the creditor (recipient) of the remuneration by filing an application for reimbursement to the Federal Office of Finance. However, for remuneration as defined in § 50 para. 4 EStG, the withholding tax can be avoided when the Federal Office of Finance certifies on application that, in accordance with a tax treaty, the preconditions of a tax exemption are met.

[197] § 50a EStG.

[198] *Post*, p. 275.

[199] § 2 para. 1 GewStG.

[200] § 2 para. 2 GewStG.

[201] The duty of the GmbH to pay trade tax begins at the latest with its registration in the Commercial Register. The Vor-GmbH (*ante*, p. 31) is only subject to trade tax if it assumes business activities which are evident to the outside world; the management of the paid-up share capital does not yet trigger liability for trade tax.

[202] § 14 GewStG.

	Trade income × tax index	
+	Trade capital × tax index	
=	Standard basic assessment figure	× tax factor = trade tax debt

Trade tax has for years been the subject of intense discussions on reform. The main points of criticism are the lack of competitive neutrality, discrimination against equity financing, a breach of the ability-to-pay principle and an encroachment on the substance of precisely those enterprises whose earnings are weak. Abolishing the trade tax on capital is being discussed.

Computation basis for trade tax on income

The assessment basis for the trade tax on income is the trade income of the GmbH. These are the profits from the business operations as ascertained in accordance with the provisions of the Corporate Income Tax Act, increased by certain additional amounts[203] and reduced by certain deductions.[204] For the assessment of the trade tax on income, a tax index of five per cent[205] is applied to the trade earnings ascertained in this way, and the basic assessment figure ascertained in this way is then subjected to the municipal tax factor.[206]

Ascertainment of the trade income

Profits from the business operations as the initial amount

In principle, the ascertainment of the trade income is governed by the same provisions on profit ascertainment as apply to the ascertainment of income for corporate income tax purposes.[207] However, not all the provisions which must be applied in the ascertainment of the income for corporate income tax purposes must be observed for the ascertainment of trade income.

For example, there is a special regulation concerning the deduction of losses,[208] in accordance with which only a loss carryforward is possible. There are also significant differences between the ascertainment of the trade income and the income for corporate income tax purposes as far as the tax treatment of the sale of an interest in a partnership is concerned. Whilst the profits (or losses) from the sale of an interest in a partnership are subject to corporate income tax to the full extent, the profits (or losses) from the sale remain out of account in the ascertainment of trade income.

---

[203] § 8 GewStG.
[204] § 9 GewStG.
[205] § 11 para. 2 GewStG.
[206] The additions and deductions predominantly result from the character of the trade tax as a tax on objects. The commercial business as such shall be taxed, and thus the use of the entire capital working in the enterprise. The basis of assessment for trade tax is, in particular, intended to be independent of the type of financing of the business.
[207] § 7 GewStG.
[208] § 10a GewStG.

Simplified plan for the ascertainment of trade income

	Taxable income for corporate income tax purposes
+	corporate income tax loss carryback/carryforward
+/−	Additions to income from integrated corporations[209]
=	Profit from business operations[210]

Additions[211]

+	interest on long-term debt at 50 per cent[212]
+	Pensions and long-term burdens by reason of formation or acquisition[213]
+	Profit shares of typical silent partners[214]
+	Certain rents and leasehold rents at 50 per cent[215]
+	Shares in the loss of partnerships[216]
+	Donations[217]
+	Reductions in the profits by reason of extraordinary depreciations or sales if these reductions in the profits result from dividends which are exempt from trade tax[218]
+	Other additions

Deductions[219–20]

−	1.2 per cent of 140 per cent assessed value of the real property in the business assets[221]
−	Shares in the profits of partnerships[222]
−	Shares in the profits of at least 10 per cent holdings in corporations in Germany and foreign corporations[223]
−	Proportional trade income of foreign permanent establishments[224]
−	Other deductions[225–26]
−	Trade tax loss carryforward[227]
=	Trade income

---

[209] §§ 14, 17, 18 KStG.
[210] § 7 GewStG.
[211] § 8 GewStG.
[212] § 8 no. 1 GewStG.
[213] § 8 no. 2 GewStG, if they are not subject to trade tax at the recipient's level.
[214] § 8 no. 3 GewStG.
[215] § 8 no. 7 GewStG.
[216] § 8 no. 8 GewStG.
[217] § 9 para. 1 no. 2 KStG.
[218] § 8 no. 10 GewStG.
[219–20] § 9 GewStG.
[221] § 9 no. 1 GewStG.
[222] § 9 no. 2 GewStG.
[223] § 9 no. 2a, 7 GewStG; group relief.
[224] § 9 no. 3 GewStG.
[225–26] In particular, donations within the limits of § 9 no. 5 GewStG and certain rents, § 9 no. 4 GewStG.
[227] § 10a GewStG.

Additions

The provisions relating to additions which are important in practice are described here.

Interest on Debt

Half of the interest on debt capital for debts which are connected with the formation, the acquisition, the expansion or the improvement of the business, or which serve the more than merely temporary reinforcement of the business capital (so-called interest for long-term debts), shall be added to the profits from business operations.[228] Thus, half the interest which is connected with debts with a term of more than one year are usually added. By contrast, no duty to add interest exists in the case of debts arising as part of the ordinary course of business, such as in particular trade accounts payable, debts on bills of exchange or promissory notes, and bank debts which were assumed to pay for goods or to pay wages. Similarly, current account debts are generally not long-term debts unless a permanent basic stock of current account debts leads to the assumption of a long-term debt in an individual case.

The addition of half the long-term debt interest can be avoided by leasing financing. As leasing companies can to a significant extent avoid trade tax additions in their own refinancing, in the inter-relationship between the lessor and the lessee there is the possibility of avoiding the burden of additions for trade tax purposes. To this extent, the German tax system systematically favours leasing financing.

Profit shares of the silent partner

If a silent partner participates in the business operations of a GmbH, then shares in the profits which are paid on the capital contribution of the silent partner must once again be added to the trade income if they are not taxable as trade income on the recipient's side.[229]

Rents and leases

In addition, half of the payments for rental, leasing and tenancy of the assets which do not consist of real property, which are owned by another and which would belong to the fixed assets if they were owned by the GmbH, shall also be added to the profits from business operations. To avoid a double trade tax burden, however, this does not apply as far as the rents or lease payments must be added to the trade income of the lessor for trade tax purposes.[230]

The payment of rents to a foreign lessor will thus always trigger additions to the trade tax profit, because the foreign lessor is not liable for trade tax.

---

[228] § 8 no. 1 GewStG.
[229] § 8 no. 3 GewStG.
[230] As is the case with German leasing companies.

Shares in the losses of a partnership

If the trade income is reduced by the loss out of a partnership interest, then in order to avoid the loss being taken into account twice (at the level of the partnership and at the level of the partner), the share of the loss must be added to the profit.[231]

Deductions

The profit increased by the additions[232] is reduced by the deductions.[233] Whilst the majority of the provisions governing additions are based on the object-related character of the trade tax, the provisions concerning deductions aim mainly at the avoidance of a double tax burden on the trade income. The intention is that certain parts of the trade income should not be subject to trade tax or should not be subject to it twice, or should not be subject to both trade tax and real property tax.

Real property

The sum of the profit and the additions is reduced by 1.2 per cent of the assessed value[234] of the real property belonging to the business assets of the enterprise.[235] The aim of this provision is the avoidance of a double taxation on the real property with real property tax and trade tax.

There is a special provision on reduction for companies which exclusively manage their own real property or which also manage their own capital investments alongside their own real property (so-called real property companies). Upon application, such companies can deduct the part of the trade income which accrues from the management and use of their own real estate.[236] Practically, this "extended deduction"[237] provision results in an almost total exemption of real property companies from trade tax.[238]

Profits out of shares in corporations

In the ascertainment of the trade income, dividends from shares in German corporations shall be deducted if the relevant shareholding amounted to at least 10 per cent of the share capital at the beginning of the assessment period.[239]

---

[231] § 8 no. 8 GewStG.

[232] § 8 GewStG.

[233] § 9 GewStG.

[234] "Einheitswert".

[235] § 9 no. 1 GewStG.

[236] § 9 no. 1 GewStG.

[237] "Erweiterte Kürzung".

[238] However, this extended deduction does not come into consideration if the real property – either as a whole or in part – serves the business of a shareholder of the GmbH (§ 9 no. 1 GewStG).

[239] § 9 no. 2a GewStG.

This regulation, also known as the affiliation privilege,[240] is intended to exclude the double taxation of parent and subsidiary companies with trade tax.[241]

Income from foreign permanent establishments
A business is only liable for trade tax if it is operated in Germany.[242] Consequently, the part of the trade income of the GmbH which is not generated in a permanent establishment within Germany shall be deducted.[243]

Income from foreign equity holdings
The provisions for deductions of dividends from foreign shareholdings is similar to that for dividends out of German corporations.[244] If the GmbH has held at least 10 per cent of the shares of a foreign corporation from the beginning of the assessment period, then the dividends are deducted if the income of the subsidiary comes exclusively or almost exclusively from active business or holdings (so-called international affiliation privilege).

Deduction of donations from taxable income
As far as the deduction of donations is concerned, the restrictions in the case of trade tax are similar to those which apply to corporate income tax.[245]

Trade loss
The trade income for the assessment period is reduced by the losses which have resulted in the ascertainment of the trade income for the previous assessment periods.[246] There is no loss carryback.

Owing to the trade tax additions and deductions, the trade loss is usually not identical to the loss which can be deducted for corporate income tax

---

[240] "Schachtelprivileg".
[241] However, the parent company's income is increased by the amount of depreciations to the fair market value resulting from dividends paid by the subsidiary. Reductions in profits through the sale or withdrawal of shares, or through reductions in the share capital, must be added (§ 8 no. 10 GewStG).
[242] § 2 para. 1 GewStG.
[243] § 9 no. 3 GewStG.
[244] § 9 no. 7 GewStG.
[245] §§ 8, 9 GewStG.
[246] Loss carryforward, § 10a GewStG.

purposes.[247] The GmbH can only deduct the trade loss which it has actually suffered. Consequently, the deduction of a loss for trade tax purposes in cases where shell companies are purchased[248] is excluded.[249]

Trade tax on income in an integrated inter-company relationship

If a corporation is financially, organisationally and economically integrated into another German commercial entity,[250] then it is considered as a permanent establishment of the controlling entity.[251] The bases for tax assessment of the integrated corporation (trade income and trade capital) are in this case attributed to the controlling entity.[252]

An integrated inter-company relationship for tax purposes mainly has the consequence that positive and negative trade income and positive and negative trade capital of the integrated corporation and of the controlling company are set off against each other. In the case of trade tax on income, this leads to tax deferrals. In the case of trade tax on capital, the set-off of positive and negative trade capital brings about actual tax relief. In addition, the integrated inter-company relationship becomes important when additions which arise as a result of loan agreement between the companies linked in the inter-company relationship shall be avoided.

Rate of trade tax on income

The part of the trade tax which is attributable to the trade tax on income is calculated by the application of the so-called tax index number[253] of five per cent[254] and the municipal tax factor.[255] The tax factor is laid down by the relevant community in which the business is situated, either for one calendar year or for several calendar years.[256] It is the same for all businesses in the community.[257]

---

[247] § 10d EStG.
[248] *Ante*, p. 38 and p. 228.
[249] § 10a GewStG in conjunction with § 8 para. 4 KStG.
[250] "Organschaft"; § 14 KStG.
[251] § 2 para. 2 GewStG.
[252] However, this does not mean that the integrated corporation and the controlling company would be treated as one entity for trade tax purposes. In principle, the trade income and trade capital are to be ascertained separately and are merely to be attributed to the controlling company for taxation purposes.
[253] "Steuermeßzahl".
[254] § 11 para. 2 no. 2 GewStG.
[255] "Hebesatz".
[256] § 16 para. 2 GewStG.
[257] § 16 para. 4 GewStG.

In the first place, the rate of trade tax on income is calculated by the multiplication of the tax index number and the municipal tax factor. Thus, for example, where there is a municipal tax factor of 400 per cent, the rate of trade tax on income would be 20 per cent. However, trade tax is deductible business expenditure. For trade tax on income, this means that the trade tax on income reduces its own basis of assessment (the trade income) because it is business expenditure.

The formula is as follows:

$$\text{Trade tax on income} = (\text{Trade income} - \text{trade tax on income}) \times \text{Tax factor} \times 5 \text{ per cent}$$

This leads to the formula for the tax burden:

$$\text{Tax rate} = \frac{\text{Tax factor}}{\text{Tax factor} + 20}$$

Given a tax factor of 400 per cent, the actual rate of trade tax on income would thus be 16.67 per cent.

3. Taxes on the substance of property

3.1 Net worth tax

The net worth tax which was levied in Germany in the past at a rate of 0.45 per cent has been abolished as of 1 January 1997.

3.2 Trade tax on capital

Assessment basis for trade tax on capital

The trade capital is the second basis of assessment of trade tax alongside trade income. The trade capital of the GmbH is determined by the value of the business assets, increased by the additions[258-84] and reduced by the

---

258-84 § 12 para. 2 GewStG.

deductions.[285] The trade capital does not include the assets of permanent establishments which the GmbH maintains abroad.[286]

The provisions relating to additions or deductions in the ascertainment of the trade capital correspond to those for the ascertainment of trade tax on income.

There is a tax-free allowance of DM 120,000 for trade capital.[287]

Simplified plan for the ascertainment of the trade capital

Value of the business at the start of the assessment period[288]
Additions[289]   + Long-term debts (50 per cent)[290]   + Pensions and long-term burdens which are economically connected with the formation or the acquisition of an enterprise[291]   + Capital share of the silent partner[292]   + Leased assets which do not consist of real property, unless subject to trade tax on capital at the lessor[293]   Deductions[294]   − Assessed value of the real property in the business assets (140 per cent)[295]   − Interests in partnerships[296]   − Participations in affiliated German corporations[297]   − Participations in affiliated foreign corporations[298]   − Other deductions   + Trade capital of the integrated corporations   = Trade capital   − Tax-free allowance DM 120,000   = Trade capital after tax-free allowance

---

[285] § 12 para. 3 GewStG.
[286] § 12 para. 4 GewStG.
[287] § 13 para. 1 GewStG.
[288] §§ 12 para. 1, 14 para. 2 GewStG.
[289] § 8 GewStG.
[290] § 12 para. 2 no. 1 GewStG.
[291] § 12 para. 2 no. 1 GewStG.
[292] § 12 para. 2 no. 1 GewStG.
[293] § 12 para. 2 no. 2 GewStG.
[294] § 12 para. 3 GewStG.
[295] § 12 para. 3 no. 1 GewStG.
[296] § 12 para. 3 no. 2 GewStG.
[297] § 102 para. 1 BewG; § 12 para. 3 no. 2a GewStG.
[298] § 12 para. 3 no. 4 GewStG.

Rate of trade tax on capital

The trade tax on capital is calculated by the multiplication of the tax index number, i.e. 0.2 per cent of the trade capital,[299] by the municipal tax factor. Thus, if the municipal tax factor is, for example, 400 per cent, the rate of trade tax on capital will be 0.8 per cent.

3.3 Real property tax

The real property of the GmbH is subject to real property tax. The basis of assessment for real property tax is the assessed value of the company property.[300]

As in the case of trade tax, real property tax is calculated by the multiplication of a tax index number[301] by a municipal tax factor on the assessed value of the real property. The tax index number amounts to 0.35 per cent.[302] Thus, if the municipal tax factor for real property tax is 250 per cent, then the rate of real property tax is 0.875 per cent.

4. Taxes on transactions

4.1 Value added tax

The value added tax system

Value added tax is a tax on transactions which is levied on supplies and services of a business in Germany. The German value added tax system pursues the aim of (only) burdening the final end user in each case with a certain percentage of the net final consumption price (currently, the standard rate is 15 per cent, the reduced rate seven per cent).

---

[299] § 13 para. 2 GewStG.
[300] § 13 para. 1 Real Property Tax Act – GrStG.
[301] § 15 para. 1 GrStG.
[302] § 15 para. 1 GrStG.

In order to achieve this, value added tax law provides for the deduction of previously paid value added tax (input tax).[303] In this system, the tax burden of a business generating turnover is reduced by the value added tax which it has been invoiced with by its suppliers (input tax): the value added tax debt resulting from the business's own supplies is set off against the previously paid value added tax out of the supplies received (value added tax invoiced by suppliers), so that only the creation of value generated at the relevant level of turnover is taxed. The end user is not entitled to deduct input tax. The tax burden from the last level of turnover thus remains with the end user.[304]

Tax liability

The GmbH is a business as defined in the Value Added Tax Act.[305] The turnover of the GmbH[306] is thus subject to value added tax at the level of the GmbH. In particular, liability for value added tax attaches to the supplies and services carried out in return for payment within the business of the GmbH. However, German value added tax only burdens the final consumption. A precondition for taxation of the supplies and other services is thus that the place of the supplies or services is in Germany.

Taxable turnover

Supplies

Supplies[307] of the GmbH are transactions by means of which it procures for third parties the power of disposition over an item.[308] Usually, the place of supply is the place at which the item is situated at the time the power of disposition was

---

[303] "Vorsteuer".
[304] *Example*: Business B1 supplies to business B2 at a net price of DM 100 + 15 per cent VAT = DM 15. B2 supplies the same item after processing to the end user (consumer) for DM 150 + 15 per cent VAT = DM 22.50. B2 can deduct the invoiced value added tax of DM 15 as input tax. B2's value added tax debt out of the transaction thus amounts to DM 22.50 - DM 15 = DM 7.50. The consumer, who is not entitled to deduct tax, thus ultimately has to bear the value added tax of DM 22.50 paid by the B1 (DM 15) and B2 (DM 7.50).
[305] § 2 para. 1 Value Added Tax Act (UStG).
[306] As defined in § 1 UStG.
[307] "Lieferungen".
[308] § 3 para. 1 UStG.

procured.[309] Usually, the procurement of the power of disposition is undertaken by the procurement of the ownership in the item supplied. In general, supply is the sale of goods to third parties.

Services

Services[310] are transactions for the benefit of third parties which do not constitute supplies.[311] A service is, in principle, performed at the place at which the GmbH performing the service operates its business.[312] However, there is a series of exceptions to this principle which must be examined in an individual case. For example, an agency service is generally performed at the place at which the turnover resulting from that service is generated.[313] The grant of licences to business entities is performed at the place where the recipient operates his business.[314] Thus, if in the latter case the recipient is a foreign business, then the grant of the licence is not subject to German value added tax, because the place of performance is not in Germany.

Supplies and services to shareholders

If the GmbH supplies, or performs services for, its shareholders for which they pay no consideration, these supplies and services are subject to value added tax.[315–16]

Import and intra-community acquisition

Value added tax is intended to burden the consumer in Germany with German value added tax. In principle, this includes the consumption of imported goods. Consequently, the import of items out of the area outside the European Community is subject to value added tax (so-called import value added tax). Imports of the GmbH out of the area of the European Community are likewise subject to value added tax as so-called intra-Community acquisition, if certain statutory preconditions are fulfilled.[317]

---

[309] § 3 para. 6 UStG.
[310] "Sonstige Leistungen".
[311] § 3 para. 9 UStG.
[312] § 3a para. 1 UStG.
[313] § 3a para. 2 no. 4 UStG.
[314] § 3a para. 3 in conjunction with para. 4 no. 1 UStG.
[315–16] § 1 para. 1 no. 3 UStG.
[317] §§ 1 para. 1 no. 5, 1a UStG.

Tax-free turnover

The Value Added Tax Act recognises a large number of tax exemptions, in particular:

- export supplies;[318]

- intra-Community supplies;[319]

- usually, the turnover in the financial institutions, in particular interest on debt;[320]

- the turnover of the insurance industry;[321]

- the renting and leasing of real property;[322]

- the sale of real property;[323]

- to a large extent the services of doctors.[324]

Basis of assessment for value added tax

Usually, in the case of supplies and services and in other cases of intra-Community acquisition, the value added tax is measured by the consideration paid. Consideration is everything which the recipient of the supply or service pays in order to receive it, but not the value added tax attaching to the supply or service.[325] In the case of supplies or services to shareholders without payment, the value added tax is determined by the costs which have arisen.[326]

Deduction of input tax

As a business, the GmbH is entitled to deduct value added tax invoiced to it by other businesses as input tax.[327] The precondition for the deduction of input tax is an invoice which contains the following information:[328]

[318] § 4 no. 1a in conjunction with § 6 UStG; in particular, supplies in the area outside the European Community.
[319] § 4 no. 1b in conjunction with § 6a UStG; supplies in other countries of the European Community.
[320] § 4 no. 8 UStG.
[321] § 4 no. 10 and 11 UStG.
[322] § 4 no. 12 UStG.
[323] § 4 no. 9a UStG.
[324] § 4 no. 14 UStG.
[325] § 10 para. 1 UStG.
[326] § 10 para. 4 UStG.
[327] § 15 para. 1 UStG.
[328] § 14 UStG.

- the name and address of the performing business;

- the name and address of the recipient of the service;

- the quantity and the name usual in trade for the subject-matter of the supply, or the type and the scope of the service;

- the time of the supply or service;

- the consideration for the supply or service; and

- the amount of value added tax payable on the consideration.

There is relief for invoices whose totals do not exceed DM 200.[329]

The deduction of input tax is excluded in the case of value added tax invoiced by suppliers for supplies or services which the GmbH uses for the generation of tax-free turnover, with the exception of tax-free exports. If the GmbH uses an item supplied for its business or a service only in part for the generation of taxable turnover, then the part of the relevant input tax payments which is attributable to the turnover leading to the exclusion of the deduction of input tax is not deductible. The business can determine the non-deductible partial amounts by way of an objective estimate.

Value added tax option

Value added tax exemptions ultimately do not always have a favourable effect by reason of the associated exclusion from the deduction of input tax for supplies or services received. Thus, under certain preconditions, the GmbH can waive the tax exemption of the turnover (so-called value added tax option). The consequence of opting for value added tax is the possibility of deducting input tax.

A precondition for the waiver of tax exemption is that the GmbH generates the tax-exempted turnover for the business of another business entity.[330] The waiver of tax exemption has practical significance in the leasing of real property.[331] The value added tax option is always favourable if the lessee is entitled to deduct input tax. Yet even in the cases in which the recipient of the service is a business who is not entitled to deduct input tax (such as a doctor), the value added tax option can be advantageous if the input tax which has thereby become deductible is higher than the value added tax payable in the coming years.

---

[329] Invoices for small amounts, § 33 Value Added Tax Regulations (UStDV).
[330] § 9 para. 1 UStG.
[331] § 4 no. 12a UStG.

Tax rates

The standard tax rate is 15 per cent of the basis of assessment for value added tax purposes; this is usually the agreed consideration without value added tax.[332] In certain cases, the rate of value added tax is reduced to seven per cent.[333]

Value added tax in the deductions procedure

If a business located abroad generates taxable turnover for the GmbH in Germany, then the GmbH may be under an obligation to withhold and remit the value added tax due on this turnover in order to secure the tax claim of the German tax authorities.[334] This duty to withhold and remit affects taxable work deliveries[335] and all other services of the business located abroad. Work deliveries are the supply of items which the business produces with the aid of material it has obtained itself. In particular, work deliveries of a foreign business which are taxable in Germany come into consideration in the construction of buildings and in extensive assembly work.[336] The recipient of the service is liable for the tax to be withheld and remitted.[337]

4.2 Real property transfer tax

Subject-matter of real property transfer tax

The subject-matter of real property transfer tax is the purchase or transfer of real property in legal transactions. In particular, the purchase of real property is subject to real property transfer tax. Although ownership is only acquired upon the registration in the Land Register, the tax debt already arises upon the conclusion of the contract of sale.[338]

Along with this, there are a number of substitute instances of transfer of real property which trigger real property transfer tax. These subsidiary or substitute instances are intended to burden procedures in legal transactions with real property transfer tax if they are comparable with the purchase of real property. In particular, real property transfer tax is payable on the transfer of all shares in a corporation, or an essential proportion of the interests in a partnership, in

---

[332] § 12 para. 1 UStG.
[333] For example, on foodstuffs and the supply of works of art and medical equipment; § 12 para. 2 UStG.
[334] § 51 UStDV.
[335] "Werklieferungen".
[336] An exception to the withholding and remittance duty of the recipient of the service for value added tax on contractors' work and materials and other services of a business located abroad exists (§ 52 UStDV) if the foreign business has not issued an invoice with the value added tax stated separately and the GmbH as recipient of the service could take full advantage of the previously paid value added tax if the value added tax were stated separately (so-called "nil rule").
[337] § 55 UStDV.
[338] § 1 para. 1 no. 1 Real Property Transfer Tax Act (GrEStG).

possession of real property. A proportion of more than 95 per cent is assumed to be an essential proportion.[338a] If all shares in a corporation or interests in a partnership which holds real property are brought into single ownership, then this also constitutes the purchase of real property which is subject to real property transfer tax.[339]

Tax rate and basis of assessment

Real property transfer tax amounts to 3.5 per cent of the basis of assessment.[340] The basis of assessment for real property transfer tax is usually the value of the consideration. In the case of the purchase of real property, this is the purchase price.[341]

[338a] § 1 para. 2a GrEStG.

[339] § 1 para. 3 GrEStG.

[340] § 11 GrEStG.

[341] By way of a divergence from this, real property transfer tax is measured in exceptional cases according to the assessed value of the property, which is to be entered at 140 per cent (§ 121a BewG), if there is either no consideration or the consideration cannot be determined; otherwise in the cases of the unification of shares or the transfer of all shares in a company (§ 8 para. 2 GrEStG).

Chapter 15

THE GMBH IN A GROUP

Dr. Rüdiger Volhard

The responsibility of one enterprise for another within the same group of enterprises is regulated by a concept peculiar to German law, namely the law concerning groups. By contrast with stock corporation group law, which has for the most part been codified,[342] the law concerning GmbH groups is not regulated by statute. Case-law and literature have developed independent law for GmbH groups, in particular as a continued development of the law in the interests of the protection of creditors and minorities, in part by the analogous assumption of rules of stock corporation law, and in part through the development of specific rules.

1. Definitions

1.1 Enterprises as addressees

The law concerning groups governs a situation as regards duties between two entities participating in commercial life. They are called "enterprises" in the statute.[343] The duties exist independently of whether a company or a partnership is involved. Other entities too, even individuals, can be regarded as an enterprise, if they have entrepreneurial interests in at least two places.[344] The reason for this lies in the fact that various entrepreneurial interests may conflict

---

[342] §§ 15 *et seq.*, 291 *et seq.* AktG.
[343] "Unternehmen"; §§ 15 *et seq.* AktG. Stock corporation groups law is in part applied to the GmbH by analogy.
[344] E.g. an investor holding a majority shareholding and a 90 per cent partnership interest, or a sole trader holding a majority shareholding and his own business, or a community controlling both its electricity and water utility companies; but not an investor holding a majority shareholding and shares of less than 20 per cent in another company, because the latter holding will not give him significant influence over the company, BGHZ 69, 334 *et seq.*; BGHZ 95, 330, 337.

with one another.[345] The law concerning groups is aimed at dealing with such cases of conflict.

Within the law concerning groups, a distinction is made between enterprises which are dependent on another enterprise, and those which are controlled by another.

1.2 Controlled enterprises

Legally independent companies are controlled if another enterprise has a direct or indirect power of control. The enterprise having such influence is the controlling enterprise.[346] There is a legal presumption that a company is controlled by its majority shareholder.[347]

However, there are cases in which the controlling enterprise (hereinafter nonetheless called the controlling shareholder) is not the shareholder of a controlled company, e.g. in cases of indirect control.

The majority shareholder can refute this presumption only if he can prove that he is unable to significantly influence the management of the majority-owned enterprise.

1.3 Group of companies[348]

If a controlling enterprise and one or more controlled enterprises are combined under the centralised management of the controlling enterprise, they form a group. It is legally presumed that a controlled enterprise and a controlling enterprise form a group.[349]

Such a group can be formed by inter-company agreements, in particular, the so-called control and profit-and-loss transfer agreement. It can also exist on the basis of the factual possibilities of influence of the controlling shareholder over the controlled company.[350]

2. Controlling agreements[351] and profit-and-loss transfer agreements[352]

Under a profit-and-loss transfer agreement, the controlled company is obliged to pay its profits shown in the annual statements to the controlling shareholder,

---

[345] *Simplest case*: a company uses its majority participation in another company in such a way as to ensure that the latter gives up a chance of profit in order that the first company may take advantage of it.

[346] "Herrschendes Unternehmen".

[347] § 17 para. 2 AktG.

[348] "Konzern".

[349] § 18 para. 1 AktG.

[350] *Post*, p. 261.

[351] "Beherrschungsverträge".

[352] "Ergebnisabführungsverträge".

who in turn is obliged to be responsible for possible losses. A control agreement governs the exertion of control of, and the centralisation of, management with the controlling shareholder. Usually, both profit-and-loss transfer, and control, are combined in one agreement.

2.1 Reasons for conclusion

Groups formed on a contractual basis involving the participation of dependent companies with limited liability are usually not founded for reasons of company law. As the shareholders may issue instructions to the managing directors,[353] there is no need for a control agreement. The controlling shareholder has access to the profits in any case. The loss-compensation obligation only places a burden on him.

Primarily, the conclusion of a control and profit-and-loss transfer agreement serves to create an integrated inter-company relationship for tax purposes.[354] It facilitates the direct mutual settlement of the profits and losses generated by the controlled company at the level of the controlling shareholder.[355] The conclusion of a profit-and-loss transfer agreement which is valid under civil law is a precondition thereof.[356]

If the "company integrated in a group" has, moreover, been integrated in the enterprise of the controlling company from a financial, an economic and an organizational point of view uninterruptedly from the start of its business year onwards,[357] then its income for this year will be attributed to the controlling company for the purposes of corporate income tax.[358]

2.2 Controlling agreements and profit transfer agreements between two GmbHs

Content of the agreement

In a controlling agreement and profit transfer agreement, the controlled GmbH submits itself to the management of the controlling GmbH. The latter is authorized to issue instructions directly to the managing directors of the controlled GmbH. It may be advisable to agree that instructions must always be issued in writing and exclusively to the managing directors.

The controlled GmbH must undertake to transfer its entire profits to the

---

[353] *Ante*, p. 158.

[354] "Organschaft"; §§ 14 *et seq.* KStG.

[355] *Ante*, p. 000 for the preconditions and tax consequences of an integrated inter-company relationship.

[356] Such an agreement is not necessary for the integrated inter-company relationship for trade tax on income or turnover tax purposes; here, the financial, economic and organizational integration of the company integrated in a group into the controlling company is sufficient; *ante*, p. 241.

[357] §§ 17, 14 no. 1, 2 KStG.

[358] §§ 17, 14 KStG.

controlling GmbH during the term of the agreement.[359] The controlling GmbH must undertake to settle any annual deficit arising during the term of the agreement.[360] Where the company integrated within the group is a GmbH, this must be expressly agreed in the agreement,[361] preferably by reference to the statutory provision in the text of the agreement.

The controlling agreement cannot be concluded retrospectively to a fixed date in the past.[362] By contrast, the profit transfer obligation can apply retrospectively under civil law[363] and for tax purposes for the start of the business year of the company integrated in the group in which it was agreed, if the agreement becomes valid under civil law at the latest by the end of the following year.[364] However, such retroactive force presupposes that the other preconditions of the integrated inter-company relationship, in particular the economic and organizational integration, were already present at the beginning of the business year.[365]

In order to be valid under tax law, the profit-and-loss transfer agreement must be concluded for at least five years and "implemented during its entire term of validity".[366]

Over and above this minimum content, it is advisable to regulate the preconditions under which the agreement can be terminated or cancelled, or shall end automatically. It is expedient to agree the sale of the controlling GmbH's holding in the controlled GmbH as cause for termination if the controlling GmbH thereby loses the majority of votes in the shareholders' meeting in this way.[367]

Conclusion of the agreement

The agreement shall be concluded by the participating companies. It must be in writing.[368] However, the managing directors' representative authority in relation to the integrated inter-company relationship does not cover the conclusion of the agreement; rather, it requires the consent of the shareholders' meetings of both companies in order to be valid.[369]

---

[359] The right to form other reserves out of profits which are permissible under commercial law, and are reasonable from an economic point of view, can be reserved to it. A transfer of profit may at most encompass the annual net income of the company integrated in the group which would arise if the profit transfer obligation did not exist, less a loss carryforward from the previous year and the amount to be paid into the statutory reserves. Reserves formed out of profits or capital reserves during the term of the agreement may be transferred (§ 301 AktG, which is applicable by analogy to the GmbH as the company integrated within the group under the terms of § 17 KStG).

[360] § 302 para. 1 AktG by analogy.

[361] § 17 no. 2 KStG.

[362] OLG Karlsruhe ZIP 93, 92.

[363] BGHZ 122, 211.

[364] § 14 no. 4 KStG.

[365] § 14 no. 1 and 2 KStG; *ante*, p. 229.

[366] § 14 no. 4 KStG.

[367] *Post*, p. 258.

[368] By analogy with § 293 para. 3 AktG; *ante*, p. 82 for duties of notification or registration under cartel law which may come into question for inter-company agreements under § 23 para. 2 no. 3 *et seq.* GWB.

[369] BGHZ 105, 324; BGH WM 92, 524.

Consent requirement

Subordinate company

The dominant view is that all shareholders of the subordinate company must consent by a notarially recorded resolution;[370] the agreement shall be attached to this as an appendix.[371] The shareholders who do not participate in the voting must give their consent in retrospect. Notarial recording is not necessary for this, but written form is required at least, because the consent has to be proven to the registry court.[372]

Controlling company

A resolution is required for the consent of the shareholders of the controlling GmbH; unless otherwise provided in the articles of association, a three quarters' majority is sufficient for this resolution, and it does not need to be notarially recorded.[373]

Notification/registration

An application must be made for the inter-company agreement and the consent resolution of the shareholders of the controlled enterprise to be registered in its Commercial Register. The application for registration must be accompanied by certified copies of the inter-company agreement and both consent resolutions.[374] The inter-company agreement only becomes valid upon registration in the Commercial Register of the controlled GmbH.

Central group management

On the basis of the controlling agreement, the controlling company is authorised to issue instructions to the subordinate company in the entire management sphere. Fundamental and structural measures which are compulsorily reserved to the shareholders' meeting are the only areas where there is no authority to issue instructions.

The management of the dependent GmbH may also be given disadvantageous instructions as long as they only serve the interests of the principal company or another enterprise associated with the group.[375] The right to issue instructions is restricted by the object of the dependent GmbH as defined in its articles of association. In addition, the right to issue instructions may not place in question its viability and capability of survival.[376]

---

[370] § 53 para. 2 by analogy.

[371] § 293g para. 2 AktG by analogy.

[372] For reasons of caution, the regulations contained in §§ 293a *et seq.* AktG, with effect from 1 January 1995 onwards, should be observed in the preparation and conduct of the shareholders' meeting; in accordance therewith, the management of the participating enterprises must prepare a report on the inter-company agreement, and shall make this available for inspection along with the agreement and the annual statements of the participating companies for the last three business years.

[373] BGHZ 105, 324, 333.

[374] § 294 para. 1 AktG by analogy; BGH WM 92, 524.

[375] § 308 para. 1 AktG by analogy.

[376] OLG Düsseldorf DB 1990, 1394.

Expiry

Revocation

The cancellation of the inter-company agreement by mutual consent must be agreed in writing.[377] It is only expressly permissible to the end of the (current) business year or another contractually agreed accounting period, not retrospectively, and does not require the consent of the shareholders' meetings of the participating companies.[378]

Termination

The inter-company agreement can be terminated by ordinary or extraordinary termination. Ordinary termination is only possible if this has been contractually agreed. The parties may determine at will when the termination shall come into effect; there is no compulsory connection to the business year.[379]

Extraordinary termination for cause is possible. This presupposes that the continuation of the contractual relationship until the end of the term of the agreement cannot reasonably be expected of the contractual party who declares the termination. This will be the case for the controlled GmbH in a situation where the principal company will probably not be in a position to be able to make up for a loss.[380]

Unless agreed in the contract, the sale of shares in the controlled company does not constitute cause for termination.[381]

The contractual exclusion or a restriction of the possibility of termination for cause is impermissible. The declaration of termination must be in writing and becomes valid upon its receipt; registration in the Commercial Register[382] only has declaratory significance.

Other reasons for expiry

Bankruptcy, dissolution or another end to the contractual partner, in particular through a merger transferring the controlled enterprise to the controlling enterprise or to a third enterprise, bring the inter-company agreement to an end.[383]

Consequences of expiry under commercial law

The managing directors of the dependent GmbH shall apply for the registration of the end of the inter-company agreement in the Commercial Register without delay.[384]

---

[377] § 296 AktG.
[378] For the controlled company: OLG Frankfurt ZIP 93, 1790; for the controlling GmbH and the controlled GmbH: OLG Karlsruhe BB 94, 1447.
[379] BGHZ 122, 211.
[380] By analogy with § 297 para. 1 AktG.
[381] OLG Düsseldorf ZIP 94, 1602; *post*, p. 259 for different assessment from a tax law point of view. For the case of the agreed possibility of termination upon the conclusion of a profit transfer agreement with a (new) controlling agreement adjusted in relation to it, see OLG Munich WM 91, 1843; BGHZ 122, 211.
[382] § 298 AktG.
[383] BGHZ 103, 1, 6; LG Mannheim ZIP 94, 1024, 1025.
[384] § 298 AktG.

Within six months of the announcement of the registration, the creditors of the dependent GmbH may require the provision of security for the claims which arose prior to the announcement;[385] if there is no announcement, security can also be requested for claims which arose after the end of the agreement.[386]

Until inter-company agreements are validly brought to an end, the balance sheet consequences associated therewith which arise out of the obligation to transfer profits or bear losses, and possible equalization obligations, remain in existence without restriction.

Tax law consequences of expiry

For the integrated inter-company relationship, tax law requires that the profit-and-loss transfer agreement has been concluded for five years and has also actually been implemented. If the profit-and-loss transfer agreement has been brought to a premature end, the integrated inter-company relationship falls away for the future. If this takes place without there being cause, it even falls away with retrospective effect. The tax authorities recognise the following as constituting cause:

* disposition of shareholdings by the controlling company;

* transformation or merger;

* liquidation of the controlling company or of the company integrated in the group.

If cause is given, the integrated inter-company relationship remains in existence for the past until the start of the business year in which the agreement comes to an end. As the termination agreement and ordinary termination do not presuppose cause, they harbour the risk of a premature end to the profit-and-loss transfer agreement which is disadvantageous from a tax point of view. Only the expiry through lapse of time presents no difficulties, providing that the term of the contract runs for at least five years.[387]

2.3 GmbH as controlling partner, AG as subordinate contractual partner

Whereas all shareholders of a subordinate GmbH must consent to the conclusion of the agreement,[388] and there are thus no minority shareholders in need of protection, the shareholders' resolution merely requires a three quarters' majority in the case of a subordinate stock corporation.[389] For the protection of

---

[385] § 19 para. 2 HGB; by analogy with § 303 AktG.
[386] If the GmbH no longer exists, payment can be claimed instead of security: BGHZ 95, 330, 347; BGH WM 91, 1842 and WM 91, 2137, 2139.
[387] § 14 no. 4 KStG.
[388] *Ante*, p. 257.
[389] § 293 para. 2 AktG.

outside shareholders, the Stock Corporation Act grants them adjustment or settlement claims.

Adjustment and settlement

The outside shareholders of the subordinate stock corporation have a compulsory claim to provision in the profit-and-loss transfer agreement for an annually recurring payment of money related to the nominal amounts of the shares (adjustment payment) as "a reasonable adjustment".[390]

The controlling agreement or the profit-and-loss transfer agreement must provide for the obligation on the part of the dominant GmbH to purchase the shares of the outside shareholders in return for a cash settlement.

The income to be expected in the future is decisive for the determination of the adjustment amount and the settlement rate. The stock exchange price of the shares of the dependent enterprise is not to be taken as a point of reference because of the possible speculative influences on the fixing of prices; rather, the capitalized income value is decisive.[391]

Rescission and court award procedure

The resolution of the shareholders' meeting of the dependent AG, by means of which consent is granted to the conclusion of the inter-company agreement, may be challenged by every outvoted shareholder. In particular, the infringement of the shareholder's rights to information[392] and/or the attempt of the majority shareholder to secure special advantages for himself[393] come into consideration as grounds for rescission, but not the assertion that the settlement was unfair.[394]

The latter can be denounced in special court proceedings, the administrative decision proceedings. The registration (and thus the entry into force) of the inter-company agreement is not prevented by this. The court's specification of the scope of the adjustment and settlement replaces the contractual regulation with retrospective power. Thus, additional contributions may have to be paid for the past. The decision takes effect for and against all outside shareholders.[395]

Subordinate status report

As long as a controlling agreement is not valid, the executive board of the dependent AG must prepare a subordinate status report[396] if there is no profit-and-loss transfer agreement. This report shall list all transactions undertaken by

---

[390] § 304 para. 1. AktG.
[391] *Ante*, p. 98; BGH BB 78, 776; LG Frankfurt WM 87, 559, 560.
[392] § 131 AktG.
[393] § 243 para. 2 AktG.
[394] § 305 para. 5 AktG.
[395] §§ 306 para. 2, 99 para. 5 AktG. If the court changes the adjustment or settlement provided for in the inter-company agreement, the controlling enterprise may then terminate the inter-company agreement without notice with effect for the future (§§ 304 para. 5, 305 para. 5 in conjunction with § 304 para. 5 AktG).
[396] § 312 AktG.

the AG with the controlling GmbH or in its interests in the past business year, or transactions which, at its instigation or in its interests, were not undertaken, with a statement of the performance and the consideration. The executive board must declare that the consideration was always reasonable, and that the AG did not suffer a disadvantage, or that any disadvantage was compensated. The subordinate status report shall be audited and attested by the auditor.[397]

2.4 The faulty inter-company agreement

If the agreement is invalid, but is actually implemented, it will be treated as valid in accordance with the principles concerning the faulty company.[398] It is already considered as having been executed if the controlling company settles the losses of the dependent company. It is not necessary that the power to issue instructions must have been exercised.[399]

3. The GmbH in a non-contractual group

If dependent enterprises are joined together under the uniform management of a controlling enterprise[400] without a profit-and-loss transfer agreement having been concluded, then the resultant group is a non-contractual or "*de facto*" group. The following problem areas are then of immediate importance:

- permissibility of the formation of a group;
- group management and its limits;
- liability.

3.1 Formation of the group

Regulations in the articles of association can make the inclusion of the GmbH in a group more difficult.[401] The cancellation or the introduction of such regulations requires a three quarters' majority in order to alter the articles of association.[402] If the articles of association already provide for the possibility of a dispensation, a simple majority is sufficient.[403]

If there are no clauses in the articles of association to protect the company from inclusion in a group, there is no requirement that the shareholders must consent to the establishment of the dependency. The protection afforded to

[397] § 313 AktG. In addition, the rules developed for the qualified *de facto* group (*ante*, p. 116 and p. 264) may also apply at this time.
[398] *Ante*, p. 41. BGHZ 103,1.
[399] BGH WM 91, 2137.
[400] By analogy with § 18 AktG; *ante*, p. 254.
[401] *Ante*, p. 74.
[402] § 53 para. 2.
[403] BGHZ 80, 69.

minority shareholders is restricted to cases of the use of the possibilities for influence in breach of good faith.[404]

By contrast, the extent to which minority shareholders can prevent a subordinate enterprise from being subjected to the uniform management of the controlling shareholder in a case where no inter-company agreement exists, has not been conclusively clarified. It is predominantly assumed in the literature that the *de facto* inclusion of the GmbH in a group also requires the consent of all shareholders. A dissenting minority shareholder is thus not restricted to attack the consequences of the inclusion in a group; he can also challenge this inclusion in a group itself.

3.2 Group management

If the parent company has a majority holding in the subsidiary, or if it is entitled to the majority of the voting rights, then it is in a position to structure at will all resolutions of the shareholders' meeting which must be passed with a simple majority. For the most part, this affects:

- election and dismissal of managing directors;
- adoption of resolutions on the appropriation of profits;
- composition of a supervisory board;
- issue of instructions in management matters.

The integration of staff between parent and subsidiary enterprises is permissible and widespread. In practice, this leads to ties of loyalty of the subordinate company, even if the management is only under a duty to further the business interests of the subordinate company.

The exercise of influence by the controlling company on the management can be reinforced in the articles of association of the controlled company if certain transactions are only permissible subject to the consent of the shareholders. In addition, the right of the shareholders' meeting to issue instructions may be directly granted to the controlling company as a part of the articles of association of the subordinate company.

Occasionally, the controlling shareholder concludes agreements within or outside the articles of association with the minority shareholders, so-called "group agreements", instead of a controlling agreement with the subordinate company. However, if such agreements have the same content as a controlling agreement and profit-and-loss transfer agreement, the rules relating to the group formed on a contractual basis are applied by analogy.[405]

3.3 Boundaries of the group management

The right of the controlling company to issue instructions is subject to the restrictions specified.[406] Case-law has developed the principle that – by reason of its

---

[404] For the AG: BGHZ 119, 1.
[405] BGH WM 1979, 937.
[406] *Ante*, p. 158.

increased duty of loyalty – the controlling company is prohibited from damaging the subordinate company.[407]

In multi-layered group associations, such a duty of loyalty also exists in relation to sub-subsidiaries.[408] In particular, exploitation of majority power which constitutes a breach of trust is considered as given if exchange relationships within the group are not conducted according to the market conditions as would be the case between third parties (at arm's length),[409] or if contractual relationships or corporate opportunities are diverted to the controlling enterprise itself to the disadvantage of the subordinate company.[410] The assumption of competing activities by the controlling enterprise may also constitute a breach of the duty of loyalty.[411]

Other than is the case in stock corporation law, damaging measures are also prohibited even if the controlling company pays compensation for the detrimental effects.[412] However, detrimental effects are permitted if all shareholders consent to the measure and the share capital is not attacked.[413] Over and above this, the prohibition on causing damage does not apply in the one-man GmbH, because there is no shareholders' duty of loyalty. In this case, the sole shareholder can, in principle, do as he wishes with his company, as long as there are no adverse effects on the share capital or the continued existence of the company.[414]

The exercise of group management is, in principle, incumbent upon the management of the controlling enterprise. However, by way of protection for the minority shareholders in the controlling company, case-law has developed the principle that fundamental decisions in the subsidiary require the consent of the shareholders' meeting of the controlling company.[415] If the breach of the prohibition on causing damage is based on a resolution of the shareholders' meeting, then each shareholder can challenge the resolution.[416] The subordinate company can also require that further damaging measures are avoided. Above all, however, the controlling shareholder is liable.

3.4 Compensation of individual disadvantages (liability in a *de facto* group)

The controlling enterprise is obliged to compensate the dependent company for the damage resulting from the disadvantageous measure. This can be achieved by a reversal of the disadvantageous measure (restitution in kind) or by compensation in money.

---

[407] BGHZ 65, 15; BGHZ 95, 330.
[408] BGHZ 89, 162.
[409] BGHZ 65, 15.
[410] BGH BB 77, 165.
[411] BGHZ 89, 162.
[412] BGHZ 95, 330, 340.
[413] §§ 30, 31.
[414] BGH NJW 93, 193.
[415] For the AG: BGHZ 89, 122, 126 *et seq.*; for the GmbH: OLG Frankfurt GmbHR 89, 254.
[416] By analogy with § 243 para. 2 AktG; *ante*, p. 75; *post*, p. 272.

The GmbH is entitled to the claim for compensation, which shall, in principle, be exercised by the managing directors. The shareholders' meeting decides on the pursuit thereof; the dominant shareholder is not entitled to vote on this.[417] Alternatively, the claim can also be asserted by every shareholder according to the principles of *actio pro socio.*[418] The subordinate company merely has to show[419] that there is a measure which is disadvantageous to it. It is then up to the controlling enterprise to show that it did not cause the measure or that there is no culpable breach of the duty of loyalty.[420]

Creditors of the company can levy execution on the claim to compensation of the subordinate company and have it transferred. A direct right of action of their own comes into consideration if no satisfaction can be obtained from the company.[421]

3.5 Liability for reckless subordination of the subordinate company to the group interests (qualified *de facto* group)

Individual compensation is only possible as long as the disadvantages suffered by the dependent company are identifiable and quantifiable in each individual case. This system of compensation fails if the exertion of influence by the controlling company reaches proportions which make the compensation for damage in an individual case impossible. Then, under certain preconditions, case-law affirms that there is a duty to pay loss compensation. Ultimately, this means the cancellation of the restriction of liability for these cases.[422]

Preconditions

If, when assessed from an objective point of view, the controlling enterprise abuses its position, then the situation is referred to as a qualified *de facto* group. This is the case if it exercises the power of group management in a way which fails to accord due consideration to the interests of the subordinate company, and without the overall disadvantage suffered being capable of compensation by individual compensation measures.[423]

Unreasonable encroachment on own interests

The most frequent case of a breach of the controlled company's own interests is the breach of the arm's length principle. The controlled company may not be induced to perform services for the controlling company which are either not

---

[417] § 47 para. 4.
[418] *Ante,* p. 64; BGHZ 65, 15, 21.
[419] By the analogous application of the principles developed for the liability of the managing director (§ 43).
[420] *Ante,* p. 161.
[421] By analogy with §§ 309 para. 4, 317 paras. 1, 4, 318 para. 4, 323 para. 1 AktG; BGHZ 95, 330, 340.
[422] BGHZ 122, 123.
[423] BGHZ 122, 123, 130; BGH WM 94, 203, 204; BGH ZIP 94, 1690, 1692; BGH NJW 95, 1544.

remunerated at all, or which are only remunerated at internal group transfer prices which are below their actual value.[424]

The inducement of the controlled company to accept joint liability for the claims of third parties, or the provision of security for third party debts, or the mutual set-off of its own claims with the claims of third parties against other enterprises within the group, all constitute encroachments on the controlled company's own interests.[425]

The disadvantageous encroachment may lie in the controlled company being misused as the sole bearer of costs and risks for an activity which, if realised, would above all benefit other companies within the group.[426]

A particularly persistent encroachment on the controlled company's own interests is given if the controlling company induces measures which would lead to the certain destruction of the controlled company's existence, such as, for example, the transfer of funds and business activities to another subsidiary company without proper liquidation.[427] However, the takeover of certain functions of the enterprise by the controlling company is also sufficient, e.g. purchasing and distribution, if the controlled company loses its independent viability as a result.

In the case of a 100 per cent subsidiary, then where there is no duty of loyalty, there will only be an obligation to make individual compensation payments on the part of the controlling enterprise if the share capital is adversely affected,[428] so that the infliction of a disadvantage only constitutes an unreasonable disregard for the subsidiary company's own interests if the subsidiary can no longer fulfil its obligations as a result of the effects exercised in the interests of the group.[429]

No possibility of compensation

In particular, disadvantageous measures cannot be compensated out if the disadvantages inflicted are either not documented at all or are insufficiently documented, and thus can no longer be isolated.[430] A large number of disadvantages inflicted will often lead to confusion, so that they can no longer be ascertained individually. By contrast, where individual disadvantageous measures are concerned, the individual instances of compensation remain.

Causality

The causality of the encroachment for the disadvantages to the controlled company will usually be evident. However, the controlling enterprise can exempt

---

[424] BGH NJW 94, 3288; NJW 95, 1544.
[425] BGHZ 122, 123.
[426] BGH NJW 94, 446, 447; BGH NJW 95, 1544, 1545.
[427] BGHZ 115, 187.
[428] *Ante*, p. 262.
[429] BGHZ 122, 123; BGH ZIP 94, 1690, 1693.
[430] For this to be the case, it would be sufficient for the disadvantages inflicted not to have been entered in the accounts of the dependent enterprise, BGHZ 122, 123.

itself from liability if it demonstrates that the losses incurred have nothing to do with the lasting encroachment on the controlled company's own interests.[431]

Burden of explanation and proof

Anyone asserting the liability of the controlling enterprise must explain, and if necessary prove, the preconditions for the offence. However, it is sufficient, first of all, to set forth the circumstances and if necessary to prove that the controlling enterprise encroached upon the controlled company's own interests in a way going beyond certain individual instances of interference for which concrete compensation can be paid. It is then up to the controlling enterprise to supply further information about the encroachments, because it knows the relevant facts and can reasonably be expected to explain the facts and circumstances. Yet the burden of proof remains with the party who asserts the claim, so that uncertainties must be borne by him.[432]

Legal consequences

The controlling enterprise shall settle the losses of the controlled enterprise incurred during the qualified group control. The compensation for the losses is not restricted to the replenishment of the share capital.[433]

The claim arises upon the expiry of the business year and falls due with the adoption of the annual statement of accounts. It shall be asserted by the managing directors or, in the case of bankruptcy, by the administrator in bankruptcy of the controlled company.

The creditors of the controlled company have a claim against the controlling company to the provision of security. However, if it is certain that they will not obtain satisfaction for their claims, then the claim is transformed into a claim to payment directly against the controlling enterprise.[434] The controlling company can assert objections of the dependent company against the claim.[435]

Avoidance of liability

In order to avoid liability, the controlling enterprise should – if possible – conclude transactions with the controlled enterprise as if with a third party (at arm's length).[436]

Disadvantageous measures should be carefully documented, so that they may be compensated if necessary. The formal independence of the controlled enterprise should always be observed; in particular, the controlled company should be granted sufficient financial margins, e.g. through having sufficient financial

---

[431] BGHZ 107, 7, 19; BGHZ 115, 187, 194. Such external circumstances, for example, also include an unforeseeable recession in an entire branch of business, BGH ZIP 94, 1690, 1693.
[432] BGHZ 122, 123, 133; BGH ZIP 94, 1690, 1693.
[433] § 302 AktG by analogy; BGHZ 107, 7, 16; BGHZ 95, 330; BGHZ 115, 187, 198.
[434] § 302 AktG by analogy; BGHZ 95, 330, 347; BGHZ 115, 187, 200.
[435] § 322 paras. 2, 3 AktG by analogy; BGHZ 95, 330, 348; BGH ZIP 94, 1690, 1693.
[436] If the dependent company is an AG, this is in any case advisable by reason of the subordinate status report; *post*, p. 259.

means available for the day-to-day business, and through the grant of its own line of credit.

Areas of operation which are necessary for the independent existence of the subsidiary should not be transferred to the controlling company or to other enterprises within the group. Subordination at departmental level, in which controlling interference is exercised over the controlled company's relationships by bypassing its managing director, should be avoided.

Part VI

LITIGATION AND REGULATORY MATTERS

Chapter 16

COURTS

Dr. Rüdiger Volhard

1. Registry courts

The Commercial Register serves to disclose the membership of commercial enterprises in a commercial class and their most important relationships which are significant for commercial transactions. It is kept by the courts.[1] The relevant registry court is the district court of the company's registered place of business.[2] Every individual may inspect the Commercial Register and the written documents submitted.[3]

An application for the registration of all important matters is prescribed. This applies to the formation[4] in the same way as for alterations to the articles of association, including changes in capital, inter-company agreements and changes in structure (change of form, division, merger, etc.), which only become valid upon registration in the Commercial Register. It also applies to changes in the representation relationships, where registration merely has a declaratory function.

These relationships are evident from excerpts from the Commercial Register, which every individual may apply for at the district court. Other relationships only need to be notified, but not registered. These include the articles of association and the list of shareholders. They are found in the Commercial Register file, which can be inspected by anyone. Copies of individual documents may be sent on request.

The registry court has a right of examination, the scope of which is not regulated by statute.[5] It can offer the opportunity to rectify ascertained defects in an interim order, and can reject the application if objections are not remedied.

---

[1] § 8 HGB.
[2] § 125 Ex Parte Jurisdiction Act (FGG).
[3] § 9 para. 1 HGB:
[4] *Ante*, p. 33.
[5] *Ante*, p. 33.

Objections may be lodged both against the interim order and the refusal decision (without a time-limit); they shall be decided by the regional court if the registry judge does not already comply with the application for registration under the influence of the argument in support of the appeal.

2. Trial courts

The GmbH, as a legal person, is capable of being a party in a lawsuit and legally capable of conducting proceedings; thus, it can sue and be sued.[6] Statute provides that, in legal proceedings with third parties (including with former managing directors), it is represented by its managing directors.[7] In proceedings with managing directors, it is represented by special counsel to be appointed by the shareholders.[8] In most cases, the regional court at the company's registered place of business is competent for actions against the company (unless agreements as to the place of jurisdiction or arbitration agreements take effect).[9]

3. Disputes concerning resolutions of the shareholders' meeting

If a shareholder or a managing director believes that a resolution of the shareholders' meeting suffers from a defect of form or with regard to its content, he can sue. The legal adoption of resolutions of the shareholders is very often a precondition of validity for internal legal measures (e.g. alterations to the management, instructions, changes in the structure). Therefore, such legal disputes are not infrequent amongst shareholders.

The subject-matter is practically always the accusation of disregard for the rights of the minority:

- abuse of power with a breach of the company law duty of loyalty;
- encroachments on the membership rights of shareholders which have no objective justification (necessity, suitability, proportionality of the encroachment);
- violations of the principle of equal treatment,[10] namely in cases where special advantages are sought; or

---

[6] § 13 para. 1.

[7] § 35.

[8] § 46 no. 8. If the company has a supervisory board, then it is represented by it, compulsorily in the case of co-determined companies (§ 112 AktG), but otherwise only if the articles of association do not regulate the representation in another way or special counsel is appointed.

[9] At second instance, the responsible Higher Regional Court from approximately 25 such courts, at final instance the Federal Supreme Court of Justice. *Ante*, p. 196 with regard to disputes before the labour courts.

[10] §§ 53a, 243 para. 2 AktG.

- where shareholder-directors make prohibited payments to themselves or to third parties close to them.

3.1 Action

Depending on the facts and circumstances of the case, a decision can be reached whether:

- a shareholders' resolution is null and void from the outset or shall be declared null and void on the basis of an action for rescission by the suing shareholder;

- a shareholders' resolution has nevertheless come into being in spite of its rejection having been ascertained according to the minutes, for example, because prohibitions on voting have not been observed; or

- there was a duty to pass a certain resolution.

The first group is the most important. Resolutions may be attacked on formal grounds, e.g. for faults in calling the meeting or in its conduct. Yet a breach of statute or of the articles of association through the content of the resolution can also be attacked.

In addition to shareholders, managing directors and members of the supervisory board also have standing to sue, but only under certain statutory preconditions.[11] The action must be brought against the company.

3.2 Interlocutory injunction

By means of resolutions and/or their implementation, the majority can create a *fait accompli* which cannot be reversed. An interlocutory injunction can be issued where a threat to the rights of a shareholder or the company can be sufficiently substantiated by *prima facie* evidence.[12] It can, for example, prohibit a shareholders' meeting being held (e.g. if it has not been properly called).[13] Under narrow preconditions, the issue of an interlocutory injunction can even come into consideration to prevent a certain resolution.[14]

The company may be prevented from implementing a resolution by a statutory declaration in lieu of an oath, i.e. may abandon it; the dismissed managing director may be allowed to continue his activity for the time being (at most until the decision in the principal claim).[15]

---

[11] § 245 no. 5 AktG.
[12] § 935, 940 ZPO.
[13] OLG Frankfurt WM 82, 282; OLG Koblenz WM 91, 1121.
[14] OLG Frankfurt GmbHR 93, 161. Imminent expulsion as a shareholder can likewise justify an interlocutory injunction: OLG Saarbrücken NJW-RR 89, 1512.
[15] OLG Celle GmbHR 81, 264; in particular in the case of the GmbH with two shareholders, OLG Karlsruhe GmbHR 93, 154. Likewise, an interlocutory injunction is permissible, by means of which the person dismissed is prohibited from further management, BGHZ 86, 177, 183.

3.3 Arbitration tribunal

If the articles of association do not contain an arbitration clause,[16] internal disputes within the company may only be transferred for decision by an arbitration tribunal with the agreement of all parties to the arbitration. Subsequent introduction by an alteration to the articles of association[17] requires the consent of all shareholders.

The submission to an arbitration tribunal and the composition of that tribunal is determined by the content of the arbitration agreement. Normally, each of the parties nominates one arbitrator, and these arbitrators agree on a chairman. All arbitrators conclude an arbitrator's agreement with each of the parties; this agreement also regulates the remuneration to be paid to the arbitrators. Only natural persons may be arbitrators. They may not belong to, or be close to one of, the parties; otherwise, they may be rejected.[18]

The company will be represented in the arbitration proceedings in the same way as in ordinary civil proceedings. As between the parties, the arbitration award has the effects of a legally binding, non-appealable court decision.[19]

Applications for interlocutory injunctions and claims for rescission of a shareholders' resolution may only be submitted to the ordinary courts, not to an arbitration tribunal.[20]

---

[16] *Ante*, p. 25.
[17] § 53.
[18] § 1032 ZPO in conjunction with §§ 41, 42 ZPO.
[19] § 1040 ZPO.
[20] *Post*, p. 340 and p. 345 with regard to bankruptcy and composition courts.

Chapter 17

OFFICIAL AUTHORITIES AND NON-GOVERNMENTAL ORGANIZATIONS

Dr. Arndt Stengel

Free entrepreneurial activity is guaranteed in the Constitution (Grundgesetz) by the general freedom of trade,[21] occupational liberty[22] and the right of ownership.[23] At the same time, the legislator is entitled to a further margin of discretion to create a statutory framework for order – for reasons of the public good – which restricts the exercise of these liberties. The following is intended to provide a brief overview of the tasks and powers of some of the important state agencies for the GmbH and those who work for it,[24] but also the non-governmental organizations important for management.[25]

1. Trade supervision office

1.1 Notification of the business

According to the Industrial Code, every natural or legal person who engages in commercial activity is under an obligation to notify an existing trade[26] to the trade supervision office, a part of the municipal regulatory authorities (community or city administration); the same applies to the transfer elsewhere of the business, or to a change in its object or to the end of the trade.[27]

The concept of trade encompasses all industrial and handicraft production

---

[21] Art. 2 para. 1 Grundgesetz (GG).
[22] Art. 12 GG.
[23] Art. 14 GG
[24] *Post*, p. 275–280, 283.
[25] *Post*, p. 281.
[26] Which means a form of enterprise not being an itinerant enterprise or such as is exercised at fairs or trade exhibitions.
[27] § 14 Industrial Code (GewO).

and processing, wholesale and retail, as well as the commercial services sector. Primary production (e.g. farming and forestry, mining), the so-called "free" professions (doctors, lawyers, architects, etc.), academic and artistic activities and the fulfilment of public tasks (e.g. notaries) are not encompassed by the concept.

The notification is linked to a specific form, and must be made by means of certain pre-printed forms to be requested from the trade supervision office. In so far as provision is made with regard to this, foreign operators of a trade must also submit proof of the residence permit necessary for the trade which is to be notified.[28]

Normally, the certificate is issued after the excerpt from the Commercial Register has been submitted, so that the notification should only be filed after the GmbH has been registered in the Commercial Register. In principle, the trade supervision office confirms the receipt of the notification within three days (certificate of notification of a trade).[29] Failure to make notification constitutes a regulatory offence and can be punished with a fine.[30]

1.2 Licence

Certain commercial activities which harbour risks, or the operation of hazardous installations, require the grant of a licence (permit, concession). At the time the trade is notified, the trade supervision office will provide information about whether a licence is necessary and which public authority is responsible for the issue thereof.

If a reservation on the grant of a licence is provided for by statute, the exercise of the trade is prohibited until the licence is granted (so-called prohibition with reservation on the grant of a licence). Examples of such activities are:

- selling firearms and explosives;
- selling goods by auction;
- retail trade in pharmaceutical products;
- retail trade in food;
- trade in non-precious metals;
- regular passenger and goods transport;
- setting up a labour agency;
- dealing as an estate agent.

Two types of licence must be distinguished: the personal licence and the material licence. They may be necessary in combination.

Personal licence
The grant of the personal licence presupposes relevant specialist knowledge and/ or the reliability of the applicant. If the applicant cannot prove his qualification

---

[28] *Post*, p. 283.
[29] A charge is levied on the certificate (currently approximately DM 35).
[30] § 146 para. 2 no. 1, para. 3 GewO.

(testimonials, etc.) or if he can only do so in an incomplete way, then he can only acquire the licence by sitting an examination at a relevant institution, e.g. the Chamber of Commerce.[31] The question of personal reliability may be decided in the light of past criminal convictions and/or previous bankruptcies of the applicant.

With regard to EC nationals, the requirements specified above have been considerably relaxed in order to facilitate the freedom of establishment as granted in the EC Treaty.[32] A certificate issued by the appropriate authority of the home country, therefore, is sufficient proof of the professional qualification required. Documents relating to the reliability and/or previous bankruptcy of the applicant may be replaced by a declaration made by the applicant under oath or a solemn declaration before a notary.

Material licence

The grant of a material licence is necessary for the operation of certain hazardous installations or installations causing a nuisance. The personal characteristics of the installation's operator are thus irrelevant in this context.

Under the Federal Emission Control Act

The Federal Emission Control Act contains a comprehensive catalogue of measures for the supervision of certain installations which pose a threat to the environment or which pollute it. Thus, the construction and operation of installations which, by reason of their nature, are particularly likely to cause damaging effects on the environment or endanger the general public in another way, requires a licence. An application for such a licence must normally be made to the regional administration presidency, and in certain cases to the emmission control and radiation protection authorities. The application must be made in writing, sometimes involving the use of certain pre-printed forms. Detailed documentation must be included (plans, drawings, descriptions of the installation, etc.), from which the potential effects of the installation can be seen.[33] The statute and an implementation ordinance clarify which installations require a licence.

The competent authority is entitled to issue further orders after the grant of a licence if the operator breaches his duties.[34] If he fails to comply with the orders, operation may be prohibited either completely or in part.[35] For his part, the operator is obliged to apply for the relevant licence if significant alterations to the installation are carried out,[36] and to notify the authority about other alterations in each case after the expiry of two years.[37] Installations which are

---

[31] *Post*, p. 281.
[32] Art. 52 *et seq.*
[33] § 10 paras. 1, 2 Federal Emission Control Act (BImSchG).
[34] § 17 BImSchG.
[35] § 20 para. 1 BImSchG.
[36] § 15 para. 1 BImSchG.
[37] § 16 para. 1 BImSchG.

constructed, operated or significantly altered without the necessary licence will normally be shut down and may, if necessary, also be dismantled and removed.[38]

The statute also places the operation of installations which do not require a licence under strict environmental protection and safety requirements.[39] In order to ensure that this standard is observed, the competent authority may also issue relevant orders up to and including the prohibition of operation.[40]

Under the Equipment Safety Act

Alongside the Federal Emission Control Act, the Equipment Safety Act contains regulations on the supervision of certain installations which serve commercial purposes and which harbour dangers.[41] More detailed provisions are contained in ordinances which provide for obligations of notification, obtaining permission and submission to examinations, as well as general technical requirements.[42]

Retraction of the licence/operation without a licence

The monitoring activities of the state are not concluded with the issue of the licence. Thus, the licence can be retracted under certain preconditions, in particular in the case of:

- issue of a licence as a result of incorrect proofs;
- absence of the necessary qualities, especially unreliability;
- the occurrence of defects in the establishment of the business with regard to spatial or technical requirements;
- failure to observe licence restrictions.

If the operation of a business is commenced without a licence having been obtained, or if it is continued in spite of the retraction of the licence, it may be stopped by the competent authority.[43] The party operating the business also commits a regulatory offence, which may at the same time be a criminal offence.[44]

1.3 Craftsmen

Definition

The commencement of a commercial activity as a craftsman – a "craftsman" being a member of any skilled manual trade or craft – is governed by the Handicrafts Code, a specialist statute under administrative law. In accordance

---

[38] § 20 para. 2 BImSchG.
[39] §§ 22 *et seq.* BImSchG.
[40] §§ 24, 25 BImSchG.
[41] § 2 para. 2a Equipment Safety Act (GSG).
[42] § 11 GSG.
[43] §§ 15 para. 2, 35 GewO.
[44] §§ 144, 148 GewO.

therewith, a craftsmen's business exists if the activity is listed in the Handicrafts Code and is actually operated in accordance with the rules of a craft.[45]

This is the case where the business is managed as an independent organizational unit by a master craftsman with the assistance of qualified craftsmen without specialised division of labour. The concept of craftsmanship thus does not encompass industrial enterprises, which are characterized by a far-reaching division of labour between the management of the enterprise and the technical activities of the skilled workers, large-scale investment of capital, etc. In particular, a situation where the use of machinery leaves no room for the development of manual skills, and where the main task is the operation of the machinery, will weigh against the assumption that a craftsmen's type of business is being conducted.

Master craftsmen's qualification

The qualification as a master craftsman presupposes that the relevant examination for the master craftsman's diploma has been passed, in which the theoretical and practical knowledge of the trade must be proven, along with the specific business management, commercial, legal and professional teaching knowledge. The examination is conducted by state officers at the registered place of business of the relevant Chamber of Handicrafts.[46]

EC foreigners usually do not have to pass the master craftsman's examination if they can produce proof of the relevant evidence of formal qualifications. This may involve the submission of evidence that the person concerned has worked continuously for at least six years in the relevant craft on a self-employed basis after having had a three-year training. To this end, a certificate issued by the appropriate authority of the home country will be required.[47]

Register of craftsmen

The craft may only be exercised after registration in the Register of Craftsmen, a register kept by the relevant Chamber of Handicrafts.[48] Registration is the equivalent of the issue of a commercial licence. Both natural and legal persons have the capacity to be registered. A precondition is that the applicant – or the manager in the case of a legal person – has passed the master craftsman's examination.[49] Exceptionally, the registration may also take place without the master craftsman's examination having been passed, by way of exceptional grant, if the qualification is proven in another way.[50]

Chamber of Handicrafts

Registration in the Register of Craftsmen at the same time establishes the statutory membership of the Chamber of Handicrafts for the relevant district.[51]

---

[45] §§ 1 para. 1, 2 HandwO.
[46] §§ 7, 45, 47 et seq. HandwO.
[47] § 9 HandwO in conjunction with the EEC Regulation on Handicrafts.
[48] §§ 1 para. 1, 6 HandwO.
[49] § 7 para. 1 HandwO.
[50] § 8 HandwO.
[51] § 90 para. 2 HandwO.

The Chambers of Handicrafts are self-governing bodies of the crafts and have the task of safeguarding and promoting the interests of the craft and to participate in the professional training.[52]

1.4 Trade supervision

The person carrying on the trade is under an obligation to protect his employees; for this purpose, he must equip and maintain workrooms, installations, machines, etc. in such a way that there is no threat to life and health.[53] The trade supervision offices are responsible for ensuring that the relevant provisions are observed, e.g. the State Office for Employment Safety and Safety Technology or the regional administration presidencies.

2. Tax office

All tax declarations of the GmbH shall be submitted to the relevant tax office in each case. Usually, the tax office of the district where the GmbH's management is situated is responsible for corporate income tax, trade tax and value added tax.

The management of the GmbH is obliged to notify the relevant tax office of the formation of the GmbH. The tax office will then require the GmbH to submit an opening balance (initial statement of affairs), together with the other information required for the determination of pre-payments of taxes (estimated level of taxable income, amount of the annual aggregate turnover, number of employees, etc.). The GmbH will receive a tax number for the individual types of taxes and is thus covered as a taxable entity.

3. Cartel office

The assessment of facts and circumstances which are relevant as far as cartel law is concerned, and the initiation and implementation of necessary procedures, is the task of the cartel authorities.[54] In accordance therewith, the Federal Cartel Office in Berlin is responsible for all significant decisions or all decisions which affect several Federal States.[55] In exceptional cases, the Federal Minister of Economics takes decisions,[56] and the supreme State authority[57] is responsible for the remainder.

---

[52] § 91 HandwO for details.
[53] §§ 120a *et seq.* GewO.
[54] § 44 GWB; *ante*, p. 82.
[55] See § 44 para. 1 no. 1 GWB for details.
[56] § 44 para. 1 no. 2 GWB.
[57] State Cartel Office, § 44 para. 1 no. 3 GWB.

There are two types of procedure, the administrative procedure[58] and the summary proceedings concerning administrative penalties.[59] The administrative procedure is initiated on an *ex officio* basis or upon application if, on the basis of concrete actual circumstances, there is a suspicion (albeit initial) that a certain offence under cartel law may be established.[60] For this purpose, the cartel authorities have wide-ranging rights to information, rights of examination and of inspection.[61] There is a duty to maintain secrecy with regard to the results of the investigations.[62]

The cartel authorities are entitled to the same rights and duties for the prosecution of regulatory offences in summary proceedings concerning administrative penalties as is the Department of Public Prosecution in the prosecution of criminal offences.[63]

4. Special supervisory offices

Certain spheres of activity which have outstanding importance for the welfare of the overall economy or the general public are placed under the supervision of special state offices with extensive supervisory powers (specialist supervision). Examples of such offices are, amongst others, the credit economy (supervisory authority: Federal Banking Supervisory Board in Berlin), insurance business (Federal Supervisory Office for Insurance Matters in Berlin), aviation (Federal Aviation Authority in Braunschweig), private radio (State Media Authorities).

5. Non-governmental organizations

5.1 Chamber of Commerce

The Chambers of Commerce (Industrie- und Handelskammer – IHK) are regional economic organizations in the form of public law bodies. All natural or legal persons, or commercial companies, must belong to them if they have a commercial place of business, a permanent place of production or a sales office in the relevant area and are liable to pay commercial earnings tax.[64] Craftsmen's businesses which are registered in the Commercial Register and in the Register of Craftsmen can be members of the IHK, but this is not obligatory. The trade supervisory office informs the IHK of every business which is notified to it.

The IHK has the task of promoting the commercial economy, and of support-

---

[58] §§ 51, 80 GWB.
[59] §§ 81-85 GWB:
[60] BGHZ 91, 178; WuW/E 2517, 1961.
[61] § 46 GWB.
[62] § 203 para. 2 StGB.
[63] § 46 para. 2 Regulatory Offences Act (OWiG).
[64] *Ante*, p. 236.

ing and advising the authorities with proposals, expert opinions and reports. The IHK informs and advises the enterprises which belong to it in all questions which are economically relevant. It is also authorized to advise its members on legal and tax matters.[65] The IHK fulfils numerous tasks in the sphere of professional training. In particular, it keeps a register of the vocational training relationships, takes decisions on the reduction or prolongation of training periods, supervises the professional training and conducts examinations. The IHK's expert opinion activity has special importance, particularly when it comes to the possibility of confusing the business names of enterprises or trade names or trade marks.

The registry court usually has to obtain the expert opinion of the IHK upon the registration of new business names and alterations to business names. Thus, for example, the IHK can also be called upon in case of a transfer of the registered place of business of an enterprise if the registry court has doubts about the permissibility of the business name. Alongside this, the IHK supports the registry court in the case of an impermissible use of the business name.[66]

The members are obliged to pay financial contributions to the IHK, which are composed of a standard basic fee graduated according to the income from trade/profits, and a cost-covering contribution on the basis of the commercial earnings tax assessment amounts.[67] The rates of contribution differ from place to place.[68]

5.2 Professional associations

A distinction must be made between the IHKs, as public law chambers with economic self-determination with compulsory membership, and the private associations, which are also termed "trade associations". Their objective is the promotion of the entrepreneurial interests of their members. The so-called specialist associations are particularly important here, through which enterprises from particular economic branches join together at a regional level. They provide their members with information, which would often not be available to them individually, such as specific economic data, new developments in legal policy, etc. The specialist associations are usually subordinate to influential central organisations which represent the overall interests of the economic sphere (e.g. the Federal Association of the Automobile Industry, the Central Association of German Handicrafts, the Federal Association of German Banks).

---

[65] Art. 1 § 3 no. 1 the Legal Advice Act (RBeratG); § 4 no. 3 Tax Advice Act (SteuerberatungsG).

[66] § 126 FGG. As organs with special expert knowledge, the IHKs also support the registry courts as far as all other registrations in the Commercial Register are concerned, in order to prevent incorrect entries and in the correction and completion of the Commercial Register. For this purpose, they are entitled to file applications and to lodge an appeal against orders of the registry courts.

[67] *Ante*, p. 237.

[68] E.g. IHK Frankfurt 1996: Basic fee amounting to between DM 100 to DM 10,000 and cost-covering contribution of 0.42 per cent of the income from trade/profits from the operation of the business.

5.3 Mutual indemnity associations and health insurance schemes

The mutual indemnity associations are the bodies responsible for the statutory accident insurance schemes. They are subdivided according to trade branches. Every businessman whose enterprise has its registered office within the geographical sphere of responsibility of the mutual indemnity association is a member.

Upon entering into an employment relationship, the employee who is subject to compulsory insurance[69] becomes a member of the statutory health insurance scheme, which is subdivided into various types of health insurance scheme tailored to the specific needs of the region, of the type of profession or of the branch.

The payment of contributions for the mutual indemnity associations is borne by the enterprises as members. The contributions for the health insurance schemes are borne in equal shares by the enterprise and the employee who is subject to compulsory insurance.[70]

6. Foreigners' authority and registration office; labour office

If the GmbH has foreign managing directors or if it employs foreign employees, then questions concerning residence permits and work permits are raised. The foreigners' authorities are part of the public order authorities of the communities and administrative districts. They are the competent authorities for all questions concerning foreigners, even if licences and permits are not necessary.

6.1 Entry and residence of EU citizens

Foreign nationals of an EU country who wish to take up employment as employees, wish to take up work as self-employed persons in Germany, or wish to provide or receive services in the German territory are permitted to enter Germany upon presentation of a passport or official identity card.[71] A visa is not necessary for entry.[72] In addition to the person in gainful employment, freedom of movement is also enjoyed by a spouse and children under 21 as well as relatives who are lineal ascendents and descendents, who are supported by the person in gainful employment or his or her spouse.[73]

Upon application, and upon presentation of a declaration of employment by

---

[69] § 5 para. 1 no. 1 Social Security Code (SGB).
[70] § 249 para. 2 SGB V.
[71] § 10 Alien Residence Act-EC (AufG/EWG).
[72] § 2 para. 3 AufG/EWG.
[73] § 1 para. 2 AufG/EWG.

the employer, an employee, self-employed person, provider of services or family relative shall be granted an EC residence permit.[74] The term of validity of the EC residence permit amounts to at least five years for employees and self-employed persons, if it was not requested for a shorter time.[75]

An application need not be filed for an EC residence permit if the forseeable duration of the period of residence does not exceed three months.[76] However, if the forseeable duration of the period of residence exceeds one month, the residence shall be notified to the foreigners' authority without delay.[77]

6.2 Non-EU citizens

Foreigners who enter the German territory and wish to take up residence must be in possession of a valid passport[78] and in principle require a residence permit.[79] Nationals of a number of countries do not require a residence permit if the period of residence does not exceed three months and no gainful occupation is taken up.[80] In such a case, a prolongation of the period of residence for a further three months is possible.

If the assumption of gainful employment is intended, then a residence permit is always necessary. Gainful employment within the territory of the Federal Republic is excluded from this requirement if the operational focus or other focus of the enterprise is located abroad.

The residence permit must usually be obtained in the form of a visa before entering the country.[81]

Nationals of the 15 EU countries and the countries of the European Economic Area (Switzerland, Norway, Liechtenstein and Iceland), and the United States of America, may apply for the residence permit at the foreigners' authority after entering Germany. This also applies to nationals of other countries, amongst other things, if they entered the country legally, and have been legally resident within the Federal Republic for longer than six months.

The visa is issued by the German diplomatic missions.[82] If the foreigner wishes to remain in Germany for longer than three months or if he wishes to take up employment in Germany, then the consent of the competent foreigners' authority at the intended place of residence must be obtained before the issue of the visa.

The visa legalises the entry and – other than is generally the case abroad – also legalises the residence. It is thus already examined abroad as to whether the preconditions for a residence permit are fulfilled.[83]

---

[74] §§ 3 para. 1, 4 para. 1, 5 para. 1, 6 para. 1 AufG/EWG.
[75] §§ 3 para. 2, 4 para. 2 AufG/EWG.
[76] § 8 para. 2 AufG/EWG.
[77] § 9 AufG/EWG.
[78] § 4 para. 1 Aliens Act (AuslG).
[79] § 3 para. 1 AuslG.
[80] § 3 para. 1 AuslG.
[81] § 3 para. 3 AuslG.
[82] § 63 para. 3 AuslG.
[83] §§ 5 *et seq.* AuslG.

In principle, a foreigner who intends to take up residence in Germany for longer than three months will only be issued with a residence permit in order to assume employment as an employee if he or she belongs to a preferred group of professionals or sphere of activity.[84] This includes, on the one hand, academics and university graduates, and, on the other hand, managerial employees and specialists of an enterprise which is present in Germany but which has its registered place of business in the country of origin.[85] This category also includes the managing directors of a GmbH, members of the executive board of an AG, partners of an OHG and managerial employees to whom a general power of attorney or powers of procuration have been granted.[86]

Otherwise, the grant must be in a special public interest, in particular of a regional, economic or employment policy nature.[87]

A residence permit for the purpose of gainful employment may also be granted without these preconditions being fulfilled[88] on the basis of international agreements[89] and in favour of nationals of Australia, Canada, Israel, Japan, New Zealand, the USA and 12 European countries.

The application for the visa should also, amongst other things, be accompanied by information as to the intended employment, the intended place of residence and the employer. If the employment is intended to last longer than three months, then the German diplomatic mission will enquire of the public employment office and the Chamber of Commerce and Industry via the competent local foreigners' authority whether there is a requirement for this activity. If such a requirement exists, then a limited residence permit for three months will be issued first, which can subsequently be extended by the foreigners' authority by one year, and then twice for two years respectively, before an indefinite residence permit is granted.

If a foreigner has a residence permit, then a residence permit may also be issued to foreign relatives of his, provided that there is sufficient accommodation for them and the cost of providing a living for them is secured.[90]

6.3 Registration office

All foreigners who intend to take up permanent residence in Germany or who intend to stay in Germany for longer than two months must register their place of residence (e.g. hotel) with the District Registration Office[91] within one week

---

[84] §§ 1 *et seq.* Work Residence Ordinance (AAV).
[85] § 5 nos. 1-3 AAV.
[86] § 6 AAV in conjunction with § 9 Work Permit Ordinance (AEerlVO), in conjunction with § 5 para. 2 Employee's Representation Act (BetrVG).
[87] § 8 AAV.
[88] § 9 AAV.
[89] § 7 AAV.
[90] § 17 AuslG.
[91] §§ 11 para. 1, 16 para. 1 Residence Registration Framework Act (MRRG).

of entering the country. The registration office forms part of the community administration.

6.4 Work permit

Work permits are issued by the labour offices. They are also responsible for placement and support of the unemployed and for employment promotion. As far as questions relating to work permits are concerned, the foreigners working in Germany can be divided into three groups.

EU citizens
Citizens of member states of the European Community who intend to work in Germany do not require a work permit.

Exempted employment
Under some circumstances, foreigners do not require a work permit if they intend to exercise a dependent type of employment,[92] in particular if they are:

- members of organs of legal persons, partners of an OHG, or managerial or representative members of another aggregate of persons, or persons in similar positions;[93]

- managerial employees as defined in the Employees' Representation Act, who have been given powers of commercial representation or procuration;[94]

- persons who, whilst retaining their ordinary place of residence abroad, are sent to the Federal Republic for not longer than three months to carry out assembly or repair work, give instruction for the operation of installations or for measuring activities;[95]

- foreigners who are employed abroad in the commercial sphere by an employer with its registered place of business in the Federal Republic and who work in the Federal Republic for less than three months whilst retaining their ordinary place of residence abroad.[96]

Licensed employment
Employees who do not belong to one of the groups specified above require a work permit. The decision to grant such a work permit is taken by the labour office. A work permit will only be granted if the foreigner has a residence permit,[97] or is exempted from the requirement of a residence permit.[98]

---

[92] § 6 AAV.
[93] § 9 no. 1 AErlVO.
[94] § 9 no. 1 AErlVO.
[95] § 9 no. 4 AErlVO.
[96] § 9 no. 12 AErlVO.
[97] § 5 AuslG; *ante*, p. 284.
[98] § 5 AErlVO.

The work permit is granted according to the situation and development of the employment market, taking into consideration the situation in the individual case, and can be made dependent upon a waiting period when it is first issued.[99] Furthermore, restrictions to particular businesses, professional groups, branches of the economy and districts are permissible.[100] An unrestricted work permit, which is not dependent on the employment market, is granted for particular privileged groups of persons.[101]

.

[99] § 19 para. 1 Employment Promotion Act (AFG).
[100] § 1 AErlVO.
[101] § 2 AErlVO.

Part VII

TRANSFORMATION, CORPORATE RESCUE, INSOLVENCY AND LIQUIDATION

Chapter 18

CHANGES IN STRUCTURE

Dr. Arndt Stengel

German law provides for great flexibility in changing the structure of one or more companies. The Business Transformation Act covers the following types of transformation:

- mergers;
- divisions with three variants: the split-up, the spin-off, and the drop-down;[1]
- transfer of assets and liabilities;
- changes in legal form.

These different types of transformation are possible for various entities used in a commercial way, including the GmbH and other forms of companies as well as commercial partnerships.

1. Merger[2]

1.1 Introduction

The concept of merger is that of transfer of all assets and liabilities of one legal entity or several legal entities to another existing one (merger by acquisition)[3] or to a newly formed entity (merger by formation of a new entity)[4] by way of universal succession. The transferor entity or entities are dissolved without liquidation, and the members (shareholders, partners, etc.) of the transferor entities are given a participation in the existing or newly formed transferee entity in exchange for their interests in the transferor entity.

---

[1] The EC Division Directive (Sixth EC Company Law Directive of 17 December 1982) does not name these variants, so there is no official English translation.
[2] "Verschmelzung".
[3] §§ 4 to 35 Business Transformation Act (UmwG).
[4] §§ 36 to 38 UmwG.

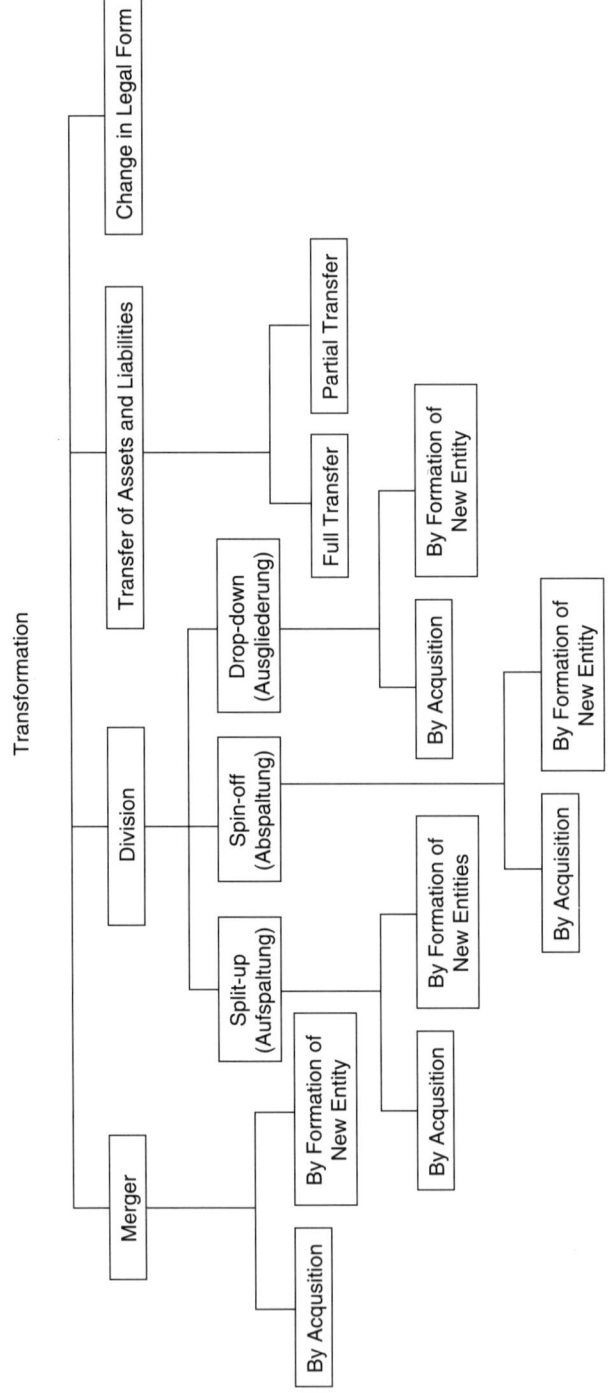

1.2 Merger of two GmbHs

Contract of merger[5]

The legal basis required for a merger is the execution and recording by a notary of a contract of merger. A minimum specific content is prescribed for this contract, which falls within the competence of the managing directors of the GmbH:[6]

- business name and registered office of the participating GmbHs;[7]

- agreement on the transfer of assets of the transferor GmbH as a whole in return for the grant of shares in the transferee GmbH;[8]

- exchange rate of the shares and, if necessary, the amount of the additional payments in cash;[9]

- nominal amount of the relevant share in the business which the transferee GmbH grants to the shareholders of the transferor GmbH;[10]

- the details of the transfer of the shares;[11]

- determination of the time from which the entitlement to profits of the transferee GmbH starts;[12]

- specification of the date of the merger as the day on which the activities of the transferor GmbH are considered as being carried out for the account of the transferee GmbH;[13]

- the rights and advantages which the transferee GmbH grants to individual owners of shares or managing directors or auditors of the participating GmbHs;[14]

- the consequences of the merger for the employees;[15]

- in the case of merger by new formation, the articles of association of the transferee GmbH.[16]

Merger report[17]

The managing directors of the GmbHs concerned have to prepare the merger by a written report on the draft terms.[18] The report is intended to give the

---

[5] "Verschmelzungsvertrag".
[6] §§ 5, 46 UmwG.
[7] § 5 para. 1 UmwG.
[8] § 5 para. 1 no. 2 UmwG.
[9] § 5 para. 1 no. 3 UmwG.
[10] § 46 para. 1 UmwG.
[11] § 5 para. 1 no. 4 UmwG.
[12] § 5 para. 1 no. 5 UmwG.
[13] § 5 para. 1 no. 6 UmwG.
[14] § 5 para. 1 nos. 7, 8 UmwG.
[15] § 5 para. 1 no. 9 UmwG.
[16] § 37 UmwG.
[17] "Verschmelzungsbericht".
[18] § 8 UmwG.

shareholders of the GmbHs concerned a basis for their decision on the pro-posed merger. Therefore, it must describe the details of, and state the reasons for, the merger.

The report can be dispensed with if the shareholders of all GmbHs con-cerned have waived this requirement, and in the case of a merger by acquisition of a wholly owned subsidiary.[19]

Merger audit[20]

To safeguard the interests of the shareholders of the transferor GmbH in par-ticular, the Act gives any shareholder of the GmbHs concerned the right to demand an audit of the draft terms of the merger, and especially of the exchange ratio of the interests and the consideration.[21] The examination must be carried out by independent experts appointed by the managing directors or, at their request, by the competent court.[22] Only qualified public chartered accountants,[23] and sworn public accountants in the case of small or medium-sized GmbHs[24] may act as auditors.

The merger audit can be dispensed with in the case of the merger by acquisition of a wholly owned subsidiary[25] or if all shareholders of the GmbHs involved have waived this requirement.[26]

Resolution by members

Prior to the meeting which is to decide on the merger, the companies have to make available to the shareholders the contract or the draft terms of the merger as well as the merger report.[27] Further documents must be disclosed when the meeting is called.[28]

The resolution on the merger, which is a prerequisite for the validity of the transformation, can only be passed in a meeting of the members.[29] It requires a three quarters' majority of the votes cast, unless the articles of association provide for a larger majority.[30] The resolution must be recorded by a notary.[31]

Registration

The merger becomes valid upon registration in the Commercial Register both

---

[19] § 8 para. 3 UmwG.
[20] "Verschmelzungsprüfung".
[21] §§ 48, 9, 12 UmwG:
[22] § 10 para. 1 UmwG.
[23] "Wirtschaftsprüfer", § 11 UmwG.
[24] *Ante*, p. 211; §§ 11 para. 1 UmwG, 319 HGB.
[25] § 9 para. 2 UmwG.
[26] § 9 para. 3 UmwG.
[27] § 47 UmwG.
[28] § 49 para. 2 UmwG; annual statements and situation reports of the legal bodies participating in the merger, for the last three business years.
[29] § 13 para. 1 UmwG.
[30] § 50 para. 1 UmwG.
[31] § 13 para. 3 UmwG.

at the registered office of the transferor company and that of the transferee company[32] or – in the case of a merger by the formation of a new company – the Register at the registered office of the new GmbH.[33]

Together with the application for registration, all such documents must be filed and all such declarations must be made as will enable the registry court to check the legality of the merger, including official copies of the merger contract, the resolution authorizing the merger and declarations of consent, the merger report and the merger audit report or the declarations of waiver and a new list of shareholders of the transferee company.[34]

The merger may only be registered in the Commercial Register if any increases in capital which may be necessary have been registered.[35] An increase in the share capital is usually necessary in order to grant the shareholders of the transferor company shares in the transferee. However, if the transferee company itself holds shares in the transferor company, an increase in capital is excluded.[36]

Legal effects

The registration last effected in the proper register brings about the validity of the merger. The effects are as follows:[37]

- all assets and liabilities of the transferor company pass to the existing or newly formed transferee company by way of universal succession.[38] The object of the transfer therefore is not an "enterprise", but rather the assets and liabilities of the transferor company;

- the transferor company ceases to exist without liquidation;[39]

- the shareholders of the transferor company become members of the existing or newly formed transferee company.[40] To enable the transferee entity to issue the shares, an increase in capital is necessary except in the case of a merger of a wholly owned subsidiary;[41]

- any defects which may occur in the notarial recording of the contract or the draft terms of the merger or in any required declarations of consent or waiver are cured by registration.[42] Other defects of the merger do not influence the legal effects of registration.[43]

---

[32] § 19 para. 1 UmwG.
[33] § 36 para. 1 UmwG.
[34] §§ 17, 52 UmwG.
[35] § 52 UmwG.
[36] § 54 para. 1 no. 1 UmwG.
[37] § 20 UmwG.
[38] § 20 para. 1 no. 1 UmwG.
[39] § 20 para. 1 no. 2 UmwG.
[40] § 20 para. 1 no. 3 UmwG.
[41] § 54 UmwG.
[42] § 20 para. 1 no. 4 UmwG.
[43] § 20 para. 2 UmwG.

1.3 Merger of a GmbH and an AG

In the case of the merger of a GmbH and an AG, the rules described above apply to the GmbH, whilst several divergences must be observed by the AG.

Contract of merger

The contract of merger must be concluded between the representative organs;[44] as far as the AG is concerned, it must thus be concluded by the executive board.[45]

Along with certain compulsory information,[46] the contract of merger must also contain a cash settlement offer for every shareholder of the transferor company who objects to the merger resolution, if the merger involves legal entities with different legal forms.[47]

Merger audit

The contract of merger must be examined in a merger audit, even without a request from a shareholder to do so.[48] In the case of a wholly owned subsidiary or a waiver by all shareholders, the examination can be dispensed with.[49] The auditors are appointed by the executive board of the AG.[50]

Alongside the points already mentioned above,[51] the auditors shall, in particular, examine the reasonableness of the cash settlement offer.[52]

Resolution of the members

There are some peculiarities which apply to the resolution in the AG. The contract of merger shall be submitted to the Commercial Register even before the shareholders' meeting which is intended to decide on the consent is called. The Commercial Register shall announce the submission.[53] The agenda to be announced together with the calling of the meeting must contain the main content of the contract of merger.[54]

Prior to the shareholders' meeting being called, the contract of merger, the balance sheets (including the annual statements and situation reports of the legal entities participating in the merger for the last three business years), and the merger report and merger audit report, shall be laid open for inspection in the business premises of the company.[55]

The merger resolution requires a three quarters' majority, in so far as the

---

[44] § 4 para. 1 UmwG.
[45] §§ 76, 78 AktG.
[46] *Ante*, p. 293; § 5 UmwG.
[47] Hybrid merger, § 29 para. 1 UmwG. As far as the merger report is concerned; *ante*, p. 293.
[48] § 60 para. 1 UmwG.
[49] § 9 paras. 2, 3 UmwG.
[50] § 10 para. 1 UmwG.
[51] *Ante*, p. 294.
[52] § 30 para. 2 UmwG.
[53] § 61 UmwG.
[54] § 124 para. 2 AktG.
[55] § 63 UmwG.

articles of association do not provide for a larger majority.[56] If there are several classes of shares, then each class of shares must consent with a special resolution.[57]

However, in a case where at least 90 per cent of the shares in the transferor company are already held by the transferee AG, a merger resolution is not necessary.[58] Nevertheless, five per cent of the shareholders of the transferee company can require that a shareholders' meeting be called, in which a resolution on consent shall be passed.[59] The shareholders are informed about the intended merger, because the merger documents must be laid out for inspection one month before the day of the shareholders' meeting of the transferor company, and the executive board shall announce this in the newspaper authorized to publish announcements of the company.[60]

Registration

The merger comes into effect upon registration; the documents specified above must be submitted together with the application for registration.[61]

2. Division[62]

2.1 Introduction

To achieve a division of the business, the company has the choice between an individual transfer of assets, i.e. by way of singular succession,[63] and the concept of division[64] which entails a special succession of the assets.[65] Division can be effected by transfer of assets either to new entities[66] (division by formation of new entities) or to pre-existing entities.[67]

There are three variants of divisions: "split-up", "spin-off" and "drop-down".

Split-up[68]

The split-up is the mirror-image of a merger: the company – on being dissolved without liquidation – splits up its assets and transfers each of the parts as a whole, by way of special succession to these parts, to (at least) two other

---

[56] § 65 para. 1 UmwG.
[57] § 65 para. 2 UmwG.
[58] § 62 para. 1 UmwG.
[59] § 62 para. 2 UmwG.
[60] §§ 62 para. 3, 63 UmwG.
[61] *Ante*, p. 294.
[62] "Spaltung".
[63] "Einzelrechtsnachfolge".
[64] Newly introduced into German law as recently as 1994.
[65] "Sonderrechtsnachfolge".
[66] "Spaltung der Neugründung".
[67] "Spaltung zur Aufnahme", division by acquisition.
[68] "Aufspaltung".

entities.[69] As in a merger, the participations in the transferee entities will be held by the members of the company being divided.

Spin-off[70]

By contrast, in the case of a spin-off,[71] the transferor company being divided remains in existence as a smaller business unit and transfers one part or several parts of its assets as a whole, again by way of special succession, to one or more entities. Here, too, the shareholders of the GmbH being divided receive a participation in the transferee entity.

Drop-down[72]

The drop-down[73] corresponds to the spin-off in that the transferor entity being divided remains in existence as a smaller unit, the difference being that the interests in the transferee company continue to be held by the transferor company.

2.2 Division of GmbH into two GmbHs

Contract or plan of division

The legal basis required for a division is the execution and recording by a notary of a contract of division and acquisition,[74] or of draft terms of division.[75] A specific minimum content is prescribed for this contract which falls within the sphere of competence of the managing directors of the GmbH:[76]

- business name and registered office of the GmbH participating in the division;[77]

- agreement on the transfer of the parts of the assets of the transferor GmbH as a whole in return for the grant of shares in the transferee GmbH;[78]

- in the case of split-up and spin-off, the exchange rate of the shares and, if necessary, the amount of the additional cash payments, the details of the transfer of the shares of the transferee GmbH and the time from which point onwards these shares grant a participation in the balance sheet profit of the transferee GmbH;[79]

- specification of the relevant date for division as the day from which time

---

[69] § 123 para. 1 UmwG.
[70] "Abspaltung".
[71] § 123 para. 2 UmwG.
[72] "Ausgliederung".
[73] § 123 para. 3 UmwG.
[74] In the case of division by acquisition, "Spaltungs- und Übernahmevertrag", § 126 para. 1 UmwG.
[75] In the case of division by formation of a new entity, "Spaltungsplan", § 136 UmwG.
[76] § 126 UmwG.
[77] § 126 para. 1 no. 1 UmwG.
[78] § 126 para. 1 no. 2 UmwG.
[79] § 126 para. 1 nos. 3, 4, 5 UmwG.

onwards the actions of the transferor GmbH are considered as having been carried out for the account of the transferee GmbH;

- as the assets and liabilities to be transferred by division pass to the transferee entity in a single transaction by way of special succession, the usual agreement of transfer of title, delivery of possession and so on are no longer required, but merely an exact identification of the assets and liabilities to be transferred.[80] The requirements follow from the general rules governing transfers of assets by way of singular succession.[81]

Report

Under the rules applying to mergers, the managing directors of the companies participating in the division shall prepare a report on the division,[82] in which the division, the contract or plan of division, the rate of exchange of the shares and the decisive criteria for their allotment must be explained and justified with reasons. In the case of division by the formation of new entities, a report on the formation of a company on the basis of non-cash contributions is also necessary.[83]

Audit

As in the case of merger, an audit of the contract or plan of division, and the report on the division, will be carried out at the request of one of the shareholders of one of the companies involved.

Resolution

The preconditions for the resolution on division correspond to those in the case of a merger.[84] However, if, in the case of a split-up or spin-off, the shareholders of the transferor GmbH do not receive the same participation quota in the transferee or in the newly formed GmbH as they had in the transferor GmbH,[85] the contract or plan of division requires the consent of all shareholders.[86]

Registration

The division becomes effective upon registration in the Commercial Register. Registration must be effected first in the Register at the registered place of business of the transferee and then in the Register at the registered place of business of the transferor.[87]

---

[80] § 126 para. 1 no. 9 UmwG.
[81] § 126 para. 2 UmwG.
[82] § 197 UmwG.
[83] § 138 UmwG in conjunction with § 5 para. 4 GmbHG.
[84] § 125 UmwG.
[85] So-called non-proportional division, "nicht verhältniswahrende Spaltung".
[86] § 128 UmwG.
[87] §§ 130 para. 1, 135, 137 UmwG.

The registration last effected in the proper register has the following effects:

- the assets and liabilities specified in the contract of division or draft terms of division each pass – and are allocated as provided there – to the existing or newly formed transferee company as a whole by way of special succession.[88] For assets "forgotten" or which are insufficiently specified in the contract or draft terms of division, provision is made for a proportionate transfer.[89] In case of a "forgotten liability", all companies involved in the division are jointly and severally liable;[90]

- in the case of a split-up, the transferor ceases to exist without liquidation.[91] In a split-up or spin-off, the shareholders of the transferor company become shareholders of the existing or newly formed transferee companies.[92] In a drop-down, the transferor company becomes a shareholder of the newly formed or existing transferee company.[93]

3. Transfer of assets and liabilities[94]

A transformation by way of an assets and liabilities transfer can take place only from companies to public authorities or among insurance companies.[95] For the GmbH, this form of transformation is largely irrelevant.

4. Change in legal form[96]

4.1 Introduction

The change in legal form leaves the entity's business and legal identity unchanged. The only change is to the legal form and structure of the entity. As a rule, the interests in the transforming entity continue to be held by the same group of persons. The types of transformation of a GmbH into an AG or into a GmbH & Co. KG which are interesting in practice will be discussed below.

4.2 GmbH into AG

Draft resolution on transformation
A GmbH can be transformed into an AG.[97] A draft resolution on the transformation serves as a legal basis.

---

[88] § 131 para. 1 no. 1 UmwG.
[89] § 131 para. 3 UmwG.
[90] § 133 para. 1 UmwG.
[91] § 131 para. 1 no. 1 UmwG.
[92] § 131 para. 1 no. 3 UmwG.
[93] § 131 para. 1 no. 3 UmwG.
[94] "Vermögensübertragung".
[95] § 175 UmwG.
[96] "Formwechsel".
[97] § 226 para. 1 UmwG.

Report

The managing directors of the GmbH must prepare the transformation by a report on the draft terms.[98] The report must describe the details of the transformation. This includes the participation of the shareholders of the GmbH in the newly formed AG. However, the report does not have to contain a list of assets which in other cases has to be added.[99] The report can be dispensed with if the GmbH has only one shareholder or if all shareholders have waived this requirement.[100]

No audit is required for a change in legal form.

Resolution by members

Prior to the meeting which is to decide on the change in legal form, the company must notify the shareholders in writing. The shareholders must be furnished with the transformation report and a so-called settlement offer.[101] This is an offer to leave the company in return for an amount in cash. The resolution on the change in legal form requires a three quarters' majority of the votes cast, unless the articles of association provide for a larger majority.[102] The resolution must be recorded by a notary[103] and must contain the articles of association of the newly formed AG.[104]

Registration

Registration of the new legal form has the effect that the company continues its existence in the new legal form.[105] The identity of the company is not affected by the change in legal form.

4.3 GmbH & Co. KG into GmbH

The transformation of a KG into a GmbH is possible in three ways, either by the limited partner leaving the KG, as a result of which the assets of the KG accrue to the GmbH;[106] or by the limited partners bringing their limited partners' shares into the GmbH in return for the assumption of further GmbH shares out of an increase in capital; or, finally, by a change of legal form.[107]

In the last two cases, the resolution requires notarial recording and the consent of all shareholders.[108] A resolution on the change of legal form with a three

---

[98] § 192 UmwG.
[99] §§ 238, 192 para. 2 UmwG.
[100] § 192 para. 3 UmwG.
[101] §§ 230, 231, 238, 239 UmwG:
[102] § 240 para. 1 UmwG.
[103] § 193 para. 3 UmwG.
[104] § 243 para. 1, 218 UmwG
[105] § 202 para. 1 no. 1 UmwG.
[106] §§ 736, 738 BGB.
[107] §§ 190, 214 UmwG, § 25 Transformation Tax Act (UmwStG).
[108] In the case of shareholders who did not take part in the adoption of the resolution, this consent must be given by a notarially recorded declaration, §§ 217 para. 1, 193 para. 3 UmwG.

Steps of Transformation

Step	Merger	Division	Change of Legal Form
1. Legal basis	Contract of merger, notarially recorded	Contract of division and transfer upon assumption, plan for division in case of new formation, notarially recorded	Draft of the transformation resolution
2. Report	Merger report	Report on division	Transformation report (not in a one-man GmbH)
3. Audit	Merger audit	Division audit (not in the case of drop-down)	Unnecessary as such, but an examination of formation possible under the general rules
4. Consent of the Shareholders	Resolutions on merger, notarially recorded with majority to change articles of association, possibly unanimously in the personal partnership	Resolution on division (like merger)	Transformation resolution (like merger)
5. Application for Registration	First transferor, then transferee	First transferee, then transferor	Notification only to the old register

quarters' majority is only sufficient if the articles of association make provision for this.[109]

In the case of the transformation through change of legal form, the partnership continues to exist upon the registration of the transformation as a GmbH; the transformation takes effect upon registration of the GmbH.[110] The partnership ceases to exist in the event of transformation through accretion.

5. General rules for transformations

5.1 Protection of share capital

In the case of a GmbH, company law protects its share capital as stated in the articles of association from repayment to the shareholders; in the case of an AG, company law protects the entire assets from repayment to the shareholders. This also applies in cases of transformation.

Application of the provisions of formation

The protection is ensured by prescribing, in the cases of formation of new companies by way of merger or division,[111] the applicability of the general rules of law regarding the formation of companies.[112]

Protection in connection with an increase in capital at transferee company

Where a company acquires another entity, or parts of another entity, an increase in capital may become necessary. The increase in capital must have been carried out prior to transformation.[113]

In cases where the liabilities of the transferor company in a merger exceed the assets even after a revaluation in accordance with market values, a capital increase is not possible and the transferee company's financial situation would deteriorate on account of the merger. The transferor company's shareholders then have to pay up the negative value plus the amount of the capital increase prior to the merger. Failing this, they are liable under the rules on insufficient contributions in kind.[114]

---

[109] § 217 para. 1 UmwG. Apart from exceptional cases, all shareholders must participate in the new GmbH (§§ 194 para. 1 nos. 3, 7 et seq. UmwG). The registry courts differ in their assessment of whether this also applies to a personally liable partner who does not participate in the capital of the KG. If necessary, the GmbH acting as personally liable partner would first have to assume a share and then assign it to the limited partners to date, with effect from the registration of the transformation in the Commercial Register.

[110] §§ 2 para. 1 no. 1, 198 para. 2 UmwG.

[111] §§ 36 para. 2, 78, 125, 135 para. 2, 158 UmwG.

[112] On the one hand, the UmwG tightens up the rules of formation (§§ 58 para. 1, 67, 75 para. 1, 78, 138, 159 UmwG), but on the other hand relaxes them (§§ 58 para. 2, 75 para. 2, 78, 125 UmwG).

[113] §§ 53, 66, 78, 125, 176 para. 1, 177 para. 1 UmwG.

[114] § 9 para. 1 GmbHG.

In a division by acquisition, the true value of the capital subscribed in kind must invariably be verified.[115]

Protection in connection with a reduction in capital at transferor company
Where a company engages in a division in the variant of a spin-off, it may become necessary to reduce the share capital because the remaining assets of the transferor company no longer cover the nominal share capital. The reduction in capital must then be completed prior to transformation. The reduction in capital may be effected in a simplified form.[116]

In a simplified reduction in capital made in the course of the transformation, the managing directors of the transferor company must, at the time of filing the application for the spin-off, declare that the share capital will continue to be fully represented by assets after the division has been completed.[117]

5.2 Employment law issues in transformations

Among several provisions of the Transformation Act relating to employment law, three are of particular importance for the GmbH.

Transfer of business
Mergers and divisions involve a transfer of business or of a part of a business from one company to another. Such transformations are treated according to the rules on the transfer of employment relationships.[118]

Notification of works council
Simultaneously with the shareholders, the works councils of the entities involved must be notified of the contract or draft terms of transformation.[119] The period of notice is one month; the provision applies to all types of transformation alike. The aim of this regulation is to make certain that, in particular, the works councils are informed of a planned transformation at an early stage, so that the employees' interests can be properly safeguarded, and the transaction can be implemented without causing unnecessary social hardships.

Compliance with this provision is ensured by the requirement that evidence of timely notification of the works council must be filed together with the application for registration of the transformation. It remains to be seen to what extent the courts will deduce from this notification requirement additional rights of the works councils to interfere with the process of transformation.

Co-determination
Transformation law does not *per se* make any change to co-determination law and can, therefore, operate in a manner either conducive or detrimental to co-

---

[115] § 142 para. 1 UmwG.
[116] §§ 139, 145 UmwG.
[117] §§ 140, 148 para. 1 UmwG.
[118] *Ante*, p. 195; § 324 UmwG.
[119] § 5 para. 3 UmwG.

determination, as the case may be. However, it does provide that co-determination must be maintained for a period limited to five years.[120]

This regulation applies to co-determined enterprises in which, as a result of a spin-off or drop-down, the number of employees falls below that stipulated in the co-determination laws, provided, however, that it does not fall below one fourth of the minimum number required in each case. The aim is to prevent the creation of many-headed supervisory boards in small enterprises.

Any restrictions of the participation rights of the works council resulting, in the course of a division, from failure to meet the statutory requirements can be compensated by shop agreements or collective agreements.[121]

5.3 Taxation of transformations from or into a GmbH

General

Transformations involve the transfer of the assets of a legal entity (the transferor entity) to another legal entity (the transferee entity). This transfer can trigger off tax consequences as follows:

- for the transferor entity;
- for its shareholders;
- for the transferee entity;
- for its shareholders.

A tax neutral transformation is nearly always possible.[122] The transferor entity can record the transferred assets at book value in its closing tax balance sheet. The transferee entity can retain these values in its tax balance sheet. This retention of book values is, however, not compulsory. The transferor entity usually has the possibility of a step-up of the assets transferred to higher values, but at the most at the going-concern values (the so-called fair market value).[123] The transferee entity must obligatorily retain these values in its tax balance sheet.

Where the book values are retained, there is no taxable profit. However, if there is a step-up, then a transfer profit is realised, which is usually taxed.

The general tax regulations are applied on transformations. Thus, real property transfer tax can be triggered by transformation. In addition, the transfer of assets can lead to value added tax unless a business or part of a business is being transferred in the transformation.[124]

Merger of the GmbH into a partnership

Transferor company

The GmbH must prepare a closing balance sheet both under commercial and tax law as of the record date of the transformation. The record date can be any date up to eight months prior to the application for registration of the merger

---

[120] § 325 para. 1 UmwG.
[121] § 325 para. 2 UmwG.
[122] The taxation is regulated in the Transformation Tax Act (UmwStG).
[123] "Teilwert".
[124] § 1 para. 1a Value Added Tax Act (UStG).

to the Commercial Register.[125] Whilst the closing balance sheet under commercial law must be prepared in accordance with the general commercial law provisions for the annual statements, there is a choice as to the type of assessment according to which entries are made in the closing tax balance sheet:[126] the transferor GmbH can either retain the book values or step up on higher values, with the fair market (i.e. going-concern) values being the maximum. If the GmbH retains the book values, there are no special tax consequences. If, by contrast, the GmbH selects to take higher values, then the increase in the book values associated herewith results in a taxable acquisition profit, [127] which is subject to corporate income tax and trade tax to the full extent.

Upon the transfer of assets to the partnership, any trade tax or corporate income tax loss carryforward of the GmbH is lost. However, the conclusion may not be drawn that a step-up should take place in order to take full advantage of the loss carryforwards. A step-up can be advantageous[128] if minority shareholders participate, who:

- hold the GmbH shares in their private assets, and

- have a maximum participation of 25 per cent in the transferor company or are only subject to limited taxation.

Transferee partnership

In its tax balance sheet, the partnership must value the transferred assets according to the closing tax balance sheet of the transferor GmbH.[129] By contrast, there is a freedom of choice for the commercial balance sheet:[130] the book value can be retained or a step-up can take place up to the going-concern value as a maximum. The merger can thus result in divergences between the commercial balance sheet and the tax balance sheet. In this case, the commercial balance sheet is not authoritative for the tax balance sheet, or vice versa.

As a result of the transfer of assets from the GmbH to the partnership, an acquisition profit or loss arises, amounting to the difference between the value at which the transferred assets are taken over and the tax book value of the shares in the transferred company, as at the record date of transfer. In the calculation of the acquisition profit or loss, the value of the transferred assets remains out of account as long as it is allocated to the shares in the transferor company which do not belong to the business assets of the transferee partnership at the record date of transfer. Substantial participations in the transferor GmbH (i.e. participations of more than 25 per cent)[131] and shares which belong to the German business assets of a partner of the transferee partnership are

---

[125] § 2 para. 1 UmwStG; § 17 para. 2 UmwG.
[126] § 3 UmwStG.
[127] "Übertragungsgewinn".
[128] § 4 UmwStG.
[129] § 4 para. 1 UmwStG.
[130] § 24 UmwG.
[131] § 17 EStG.

treated in the calculation of the acquisition profit or loss as if the shares were contributed to the business assets of the partnership on the record date at their acquisition cost or at book value.[132]

The transferee partnership takes the legal place of the transferor company from a tax point of view.[133] Tax privileges of the transferor company (such as, for example, the right to make special depreciations) can thus be retained by the transferee partnership.

Taxation of the partner

The merger procedure can trigger income tax of the partners in the transferee partnership. The following distinction must be made:

Shares held in the business assets

If the shares already formed part of the business assets of the transferee partnership on the record date of transfer, or if they exceeded a proportion of 25 per cent, then an acquisition profit or loss arises out of the difference between the value of the business assets, as recorded in the tax balance sheet of the partnership, and the book value or the acquisition costs of the shares. The acquisition profit is then subject to individual income tax or corporate income tax to the full extent, but not to trade tax.[134]

The acquisition profit is increased and the acquisition loss reduced by corporate income tax credits,[135] if the shares in the transferred entity belong to the business assets of the transferee partnership on the record date of transfer. In addition, the acquisition profit or loss can be increased or reduced by a so-called blocked amount.[136] This is the amount of the difference between the acquisition costs of the shares in the GmbH and the nominal (face) value of the shares.[137] The blocked amount always increases the acquisition profit or reduces the acquisition loss in the cases where:

- the GmbH shares are held by foreign shareholders (with limited tax liability) who are not entitled to corporate income tax credits, since the shares are not held in the German business assets of the shareholder;

- the shareholdings involved exceed 25 per cent; and

- the acquisition profit is not exempted from German taxation by a tax treaty.

If a transfer loss remains after this, then the recorded values of the assets transferred must be stepped up in the balance sheet of the transferee partnership to

---

[132] § 5 paras. 2 and 3 UmwStG.
[133] § 4 para. 2 UmwStG.
[134] § 18 para. 2 UmwStG.
[135] § 10 para. 1 UmwStG.
[136] § 50c EStG.
[137] § 50c para. 4 EStG.

the going-concern values.[138] This creates additional potential for depreciation for the transferee partnership.

It is questionable whether an acquisition profit or loss is taxable in the case of a participation of more than 25 per cent held by a partner with limited tax liability, if the interest is not held in the German business assets. The dominant view, at present, assumes that the acquisition profit is exempted from taxation in Germany in the usual case where a tax treaty applies. It is disputed whether, in such a case, a so-called tax-free acquisition loss must be reduced by a step-up of the transferee partnership, and whether the creation of additional potential for depreciation is also possible in this way in the case of limited tax liability. Nevertheless, it has been established that if the acquisition profit is not subject to German taxation, partners who are subject to limited tax liability are excluded from corporate income tax credit.

Shares held in private assets

If shares in the transferor entity belonged to the private assets of a partner of the transferee partnership at the time the assets are transferred, and if the participation involved does not exceed 25 per cent, then there is a fictional full distribution of the proportion of the reserves of the company which are allocated to this partner.[139] Thus, income from capital investments arises to this extent. If the partner's tax liability is limited, such income is not subject to German taxation. A corporate income tax credit is excluded.[140]

Within the corporate income tax credit procedure, dividends are taxed at a reduced rate of 30 per cent. As the fictional distribution does not provide for a corresponding reduction of corporate income tax, the tax burden of partners with limited tax liability can sometimes be reduced by a distribution of reserves before the merger.

Change of form from a GmbH into a partnership

If a GmbH changes its legal form in accordance with the Business Transformation Act, the tax regulations on the merger with a partnership shall be applied by analogy.[141] Although the change of legal form is regulated as a conversion which preserves the identity of the entity under commercial law, tax law creates the fiction of the transfer of assets from the GmbH to the partnership. For this reason, a transfer balance sheet of the GmbH and an opening balance sheet of the partnership must be prepared for tax law purposes, although the preparation of a transformation balance sheet is dispensed with under commercial law. The balance sheets may also be prepared to a date at the most eight months before the date of the notification of the change of legal form to the Commercial Register.

---

[138] § 4 para. 6 UmwStG.
[139] § 7 UmwStG.
[140] § 10 para. 2 UmwStG.
[141] § 14 UmwStG.

Merger of two corporations

The tax-neutral merger of corporations (GmbHs or stock corporations)[142] is accomplished by transformation tax law as follows:

- the transferor corporation can retain the book values in its closing balance sheet, so that no transfer profit arises;
- acquisition profits or losses are left out of count for tax purposes;
- an exchange of shares – which is neutral from a tax point of view – takes place at the level of the shareholders of the transferor corporation.

Transferor corporation

In the closing tax balance sheet for the last fiscal year of the transferor corporation, the transferred assets as a whole can be recorded at book value.[143] However, the right to retain the book value only applies if the shareholders of the transferor corporation do not receive any other consideration than company rights.

A step-up is permissible, but leads to a taxable acquisition profit. If the transferor corporation had already ceased trading at the time of the entry of the transfer of assets in the Commercial Register, and therefore cannot preserve a loss carryforward,[144] a step-up usually is advantageous.

Transferee corporation

The transferee corporation must take over the transferred assets in its tax balance sheet at the values shown in the closing tax balance sheet of the transferor corporation.[145] By contrast, there is a choice as far as the commercial balance sheet is concerned: the transferred assets can either be recorded at book value, at interim values or at their going-concern value. In this case, the commercial balance sheet is not authoritative for the tax balance sheet or vice versa.

The merger results in an acquisition profit of the transferee corporation if the book values of the assets taken over are higher than the sum out of an increase in the transferee corporation's share capital, ancillary payments,[146] and the book value of the shares of the transferor corporation which are eliminated by the merger. Commercial law requires that the merger profit is allocated to the capital reserves as a premium.[147] For tax purposes, the merger profit remains out of account.[148]

The transferee corporation takes on universal succession under tax law.[149] Tax advantages, such as the right to make special depreciations, are preserved

---

[142] The following applies to a merger of a GmbH and a GmbH and/or GmbH and stock corporation (AG).
[143] § 11 para. 1 UmwStG.
[144] § 12 para. 3 UmwStG; *ante*, p. 304, on the subject of the preparation of commercial and tax transfer balance sheet.
[145] §§ 12 para. 1, 4 para. 1 UmwStG.
[146] E.g. additional cash payments; § 15 UmwG.
[147] § 272 para. 2 no. 1 HGB.
[148] § 12 para. 2 UmwStG.
[149] § 12 para. 3 UmwStG.

for the transferee corporation. Furthermore, a remaining loss carryforward of the transferor corporation passes to the transferee corporation provided that the transferor corporation had not yet ceased trading at the time the transfer of assets was registered in the Commercial Register.[150] If the transferor company had a trade tax loss carryforward, it reduces the trade income of the transferee company.[151]

Shareholders

If the shares in the transferor corporation belong to the business assets, then they are considered as having been sold at book value, and the shares which take their place are considered as having been acquired at this value.[152] If the shares in the transferor corporation do not belong to business assets, and if the participations in question exceed the 25 per cent threshold, then they are considered as having been sold at the cost of their original acquisition, and the shares which take their place are considered as having been acquired at this value.

At the level of the shareholder, therefore, an exchange of shares takes place which is insignificant from a tax point of view. A subsequent sale of the shares, however, has tax consequences.

If shareholders receive additional cash payments in the merger, or receive a cash settlement upon their retirement from the corporation, these lead to a (proportional) capital gain[153] for the shareholders, which is subject to taxation, if the shares are held in business assets or the shareholdings involved exceed 25 per cent.

Transformation of an AG into a GmbH or a GmbH into an AG

The transformation of a GmbH into an AG or an AG into a GmbH is a procedure which is insignificant from a tax point of view. There is no change in the legal entity for tax purposes.

Division of corporations

Division is the mirror image or the reverse of the merger between partnership and corporation or two corporations. It leads to the apportionment of the corporation's assets to at least two legal entities through the distribution of the assets and liabilities by the corporation which is dividing to the recipient legal entities, either as a whole or in part. Tax law, in principle, permits the tax-neutral division of corporations in the same way as mergers.

From the point of view of tax systematics, there are hardly divergences between the division and the merger of corporations with companies or with partnerships.[154]

---

[150] § 12 para. 3 UmwStG.
[151] § 19 para. 2 UmwStG.
[152] § 13 para. 1 UmwStG.
[153] "Veräußerungsgewinn".
[154] §§ 11–13 UmwStG apply by analogy to the transfer of assets by split-up and spin-off into another company (§ 15 UmwStG). §§ 3–8, 10 UmwStG apply by analogy to split-up or spin-off into a partnership (§ 16 UmwStG).

By contrast to the split-up or spin-off, the drop-down, from a tax point of view, is a so-called procedure of capital in kind.[155]

It is always a precondition for the tax-neutral division of a company that a partial business unit[156] is transferred to the acquiring entity. In the case of a spin-off, the assets remaining with the transferor company must likewise belong to a partial business unit. A partial business unit is also considered to include an interest in a commercial partnership or the 100 per cent participation in a company.

Merger of a partnership into a GmbH

The general regulations on contributions of capital in kind to partnerships apply to the merger of commercial partnerships into corporations.[157]

Transferor partnership

The tax consequences of the merger for the partners of the transferor partnership are dependent on the value at which the transferee corporation records the transferred assets in its closing tax balance sheet.[158] The transferee corporation has the right to choose the valuation of the transferred assets by recording them in its balance sheet at book value or at a higher value.[159] The value for the transferred assets which are recorded in the balance sheet of the transferee company applies as the sale price and the acquisition costs of shares in the corporation for the party making the contribution, i.e. the partners of the transferor partnership.[160]

There are usually no income tax consequences at the level of the transferor partnership, because not the partnership itself but rather only its partners are liable for income tax or corporate individual income tax. The transfer profit is not subject to trade tax.

Transferee corporation

The transferee corporation has the right to choose whether to enter the business assets transferred from the partnership in its balance sheet at book values or at higher values, but at the most at going-concern values. If the transferee corporation continues the book values in its transfer balance sheet, then an acquisition profit is avoided for the partnership. Fundamentally, the principle applies that the commercial balance sheet is authoritative for the tax balance sheet. With few exceptions, the transferee corporation has to take over the assets with the same values in both the commercial balance sheet and the tax balance sheet.

---

[155] "Einbringung".
[156] A partial business unit ("Teilbetrieb") is an independent part of the overall business which, when viewed by itself, displays all the characteristics of a business as defined in the Income Tax Act and is viable in itself.
[157] §§ 20–23 UmwStG.
[158] § 20 para. 4 UmwStG.
[159] § 20 para. 2 UmwStG.
[160] § 20 para. 4 UmwStG.

If the corporation records the business assets transferred at book value, then it takes on a partial universal succession to the transferor partnership under tax law;[161] tax advantages, such as the right to make special depreciations, are preserved.

Tax consequences for the partners of the transferor partnership

If the transferred business assets are entered by the transferee corporation in the balance sheet at book value, no transfer profit arises for the transferor partnership. The merger thus does not trigger direct tax consequences for the partners unless an additional cash payment or – in the case of retirement – a settlement is paid. By contrast, where the business assets contributed are entered at going-concern values (above book value), a transfer profit arises, the so-called contribution profit.[162] The contribution profit is taxed at the reduced rate of half the average tax rate.[163]

The value of the transferred assets entered in the transfer balance sheet by the transferee corporation applies to the party making the contribution as the sale price and the acquisition costs of the shares in the company.[164]

If shares in the GmbH are sold which the vendor had acquired in the merger (so-called shares issued upon a contribution of capital in kind)[165] below the going-concern value (contribution at book value or interim value), then the amount by which the sale proceeds – after deduction of the sale costs – exceeds the acquisition costs[166] of the shares is considered as a taxable capital gain. If the vendor is a natural person, then the capital gain is taxed at the reduced rate of half the average tax rate.[167]

The taxation of a capital gain can also arise without a sale of the shares. A capital gain is taxable[168] if:

- the owner of the interest applies for this;
- the German taxation of capital gains is excluded (this legal consequence may, in particular, arise in the case of a change from unlimited tax liability to limited tax liability in the case of removal abroad); or
- the corporation in which the shares are held is liquidated and wound up or the share capital of the corporation is reduced and repaid to the shareholders, as long as the repayment is not classified as a dividend.

Change of form from a partnership to a corporation

If a partnership is transformed into a corporation, the identity of the partnership as such remains unaffected from a civil law point of view. Only the outer

---

[161] § 12 para. 1 UmwStG.
[162] "Einbringungsgewinn."
[163] "Halber durchschnittlicher Steuersatz"; § 20 para. 5 UmwStG, § 34 EStG.
[164] § 20 para. 4 UmwG.
[165] "Einbringungsgeborene Anteile".
[166] § 20 para. 4 UmwStG.
[167] § 21 para. 1 UmwStG, § 34 para. 1 EStG.
[168] § 21 para. 2 UmwStG.

form alters. Nevertheless, there is the fiction of a transfer of assets from a tax point of view. The regulations which apply to the merger of a partnership into a corporation apply here by analogy.[169] The transfer of assets can thus take place at book value, or with a partial or wholescale step-up, with the tax consequences resulting therefrom.[170]

Transformation of a GmbH & Co. KG into the GmbH being its general partner

If the limited partners of a GmbH & Co. KG are at the same time shareholders of the GmbH acting as general partner, then the GmbH & Co. KG can be transformed into the GmbH through the retirement of all limited partners from the KG. The retirement of the limited partners means that the assets of the KG pass to the GmbH by universal succession (so-called accrual);[171] the latter continues the business alone. For the limited partners the dominant view is that the accrual constitutes the closure of the business unit. This triggers privileged taxation of the capital gains from business closure[172] amounting to the silent reserves held in the business assets of the KG.[173]

However, a transformation of the GmbH & Co. KG into the GmbH can be achieved without taxable capital gains by contributing in kind the interests in the KG to the general partner GmbH through an increase in its share capital (the so-called extended accrual model).[174] Tax law deals with this procedure in the way described for the merger of a partnership into a GmbH.[175]

---

[169] § 25 UmwStG.
[170] Tax-privileged profits from sale, increased basis of assessment for depreciation; § 25 in conjunction with § 21 para. 1 UmwStG.
[171] "Anwachsung".
[172] "Betriebsaufgabegewinn".
[173] At a rate of half the average tax rate, § 34 EStG.
[174] "Erweitertes Anwachsungsmodell".
[175] *Ante*, p. 311; § 20 UmwStG

Chapter 19

FINANCIAL CRISIS AND RESTRUCTURING

Dr. Arndt Stengel

1. Corporate rescues in general

German law does not provide particular procedures for corporate rescues other than the last resort of insolvency proceedings. Restructuring[176] is the term commonly used for all rescue activities prior to insolvency. Restructurings fall under the provisions of the legal framework which applies to a company as a going concern. Very few statutes and regulations of German company law are aimed at coping with a financial crisis prior to insolvency. The demand in practice, however, for provisions which deal with companies in financial crisis has led to the development of extensive case-law. The law regarding restructurings is considered to be the most rapidly developing area of German company law.

Sometimes, corporate rescues are package deals made at the very last minute before the company must file for insolvency. Such deals are called a restructuring compromise,[177] which also follow the general rules of company and commercial law.

If the restructuring is not successful, but there is nevertheless a desire to avoid insolvency proceedings, the shareholders will resolve on voluntary liquidation.[178] Insolvency, however, can only be avoided if the shareholders are prepared to pay the creditors to the extent that their debts cannot be satisfied by the company.

Therefore, if efforts to restructure the company fail, insolvency proceedings will almost certainly follow.[179]

---

[176] "Sanierung"; *post*, p. 328.
[177] "Sanierungsvergleich".
[178] "Liquidation"; *post* p. 349.
[179] *Post*, chapter 20.

2. Financial crisis

2.1 Definition

A financial crisis in the legal sense is characterised as a situation in which the company can no longer obtain credit from third parties at market conditions and must thus be liquidated unless payments are made by the shareholders.[180] The concept has particular importance for the treatment of shareholder loans.[181]

The criteria for the determination of a lack of adequate credit standing, or lack of creditworthiness, are assessed on the basis of the information concerning the enterprise which is relevant for the grant of a loan by an external lender – such as, for example, the equity position, the capital quota and reflux of capital quota, the payment behaviour in the past, commitments to provide finance undertaken by the public sector, etc. – which, together with a forecast of the future prospective earnings, facilitate an assessment of the enterprise.[182]

2.2 Duties of the managing directors

The directors have two predominant responsibilities in a crisis and restructuring situation. They have to comply with these duties, which are not as simple as they appear:

- the directors must not pay back the share capital;
- the directors must not delay in filing for insolvency.

At the stage where a lack of adequate credit standing is discovered, the managing director is not yet forced to initiate insolvency proceedings. However, he is affected by the duty to refuse the repayment of shareholder loans and comparable payments, to the extent to which these cover lost share capital (the amount specified in the articles of association and the Commercial Register is decisive) or overindebtedness going above and beyond this loss.[183]

If the situation of a lack of adequate credit standing turns into illiquidity or overindebtedness, this leads to the duty to file for insolvency proceedings.[184] The managing directors are thus obliged to supervise the financial situation of the enterprise with even greater care after it has been established that there is a lack of adequate credit standing.

If half of the share capital has been lost, they must notify this to the share-

---

[180] BGHZ 76, 326, 330; 81, 311, 317 *et seq.*; 90, 370, 380; 105, 168, 184 *et seq.*; BGH WM 90, 182, 183; BGHZ 119, 210 *et seq.*; BGHZ ZIP 92, 1382 *et seq.* cite a list of characteristics of a lack of adequate credit standing. On the concept of illiquidity: BGHZ 57, 67, 68; BayObLG BB 88, 1840. On overindebtedness: BGHZ 119, 210 *et seq.*; OLG Hamm GmbHR 93, 584.
[181] *Post*, p. 318.
[182] BGH ZIP 92, 1382, 1383 *et seq.*
[183] BGHZ 76, 326; *post*, p. 319.
[184] § 64 para. 1; *post* p. 332.

holders and must call a shareholders' meeting.[185] In addition, they must review the financial situation by drawing up a statement of assets and liabilities for the overindebtedness.[186]

2.3 Duties of the shareholders

At no time – not even in case of a crisis – are the shareholders under a legal duty to place capital at the company's disposal above and beyond the original capital contribution.[187] In principle, they are also free in their choice of the type of financing, whether it be financial aid through loans or the contribution of equity capital.[188]

If the company finds itself in crisis, the creditors are in special need of protection. The case-law thus places a special financing responsibility on the shareholders. By reason of the restriction of the liability to the assets of the company,[189] the shareholders are not under an obligation[190] to place at the company's disposal further (equity) capital in order to ward off the overindebtedness. However, if the shareholders give financial aid, they cannot offload the risk associated therewith on to the creditors by giving a loan when the company needs equity capital.[191]

This does not mean that the shareholders only have the choice either to liquidate the company, waiving further financial aid, or to furnish the necessary equity. The shareholders may also make loans. However, such loans will be treated as equity as long as the company is in crisis or if it becomes insolvent.

3. Contributions replacing equity[192]

3.1 General

If debt leads to overindebtedness, the company is insolvent.[193] If the shareholders then grant loans to the company in crisis instead of furnishing it with equity or liquidating the company, then they can only assert their claims out of the loan once the crisis is over.

The case-law has extended the statutory prohibition on paying back the share capital by developing rules for the contributions designed to replace equity,

---

[185] *Ante*, p. 159.
[186] *Post*, p. 325.
[187] § 5.
[188] BGHZ 76, 326, 334 *et seq.*
[189] § 13 para. 2.
[190] Apart from the very rare duty to make additional contributions, § 26.
[191] BGHZ 76, 326, 330; 81, 252, 257.
[192] *Ante*, p. 111.
[193] *Post*, p. 331., on declarations of withdrawal to lower rank; *post*, p. 324.

which were codified in a later amending statute for the case of insolvency.[194] However, the principles of case-law continue to be applicable alongside them.[195]

The preconditions for, and legal consequences of, contributions designed to replace equity are, first of all, explained for loan agreements, and then transferred to other forms of contributions replacing equity.

A further amendment bill is due to be enacted very soon. It will exempt shareholders from the rules on contributions replacing equity if their share-holdings do not exceed 10 per cent of the share capital, and they do not serve as managing directors.

3.2 Shareholder loans replacing equity

Loans

All types of loans of money or in kind can be regarded as contributions re-placing equity. The only exceptions to this are short-term bridging loans if, at the time the loan was granted, it could objectively be expected that the company would be able to redeem the loan.[196]

Loan as a substitute for equity

The loan has a function to replace equity[197] where the shareholders, as responsi-ble businessmen, would have furnished the company with equity instead of the loan. This is the case when the company is in a financial crisis. Then it needs equity, and not debt, to overcome the crisis. In interpreting this concept, the case-law applies the test it has developed, namely that of the lack of adequate credit standing on the part of the company.

A company has a lack of adequate credit standing if it would not have received the capital requirement necessary for continuation through loans from third parties under usual market conditions.[198] In any case, there is a lack of adequate credit standing where insolvency is foreseeable as a result of overindebtedness[199] or the inability to pay due debts.[200] A mere deficit balance[201] is not always sufficient for this, because the creditworthiness also depends on expected profits, the silent reserves, in particular as a result of any special depreciation allowances, and the composition of the liabilities.[202]

If the company has already lost more than half of its share capital, then creditworthiness may only be assumed if considerable silent reserves have been accumulated, which could serve as security for the creditors.[203] By contrast, the

---

[194] §§ 32a, 32b.
[195] BGHZ 90, 370, 376; 90, 381, 388; 95, 188, 192.
[196] BGHZ 31, 258, 268; 75, 334, 337; 90, 381, 394; BGH WM 90, 100; 95, 55.
[197] § 32a para. 1.
[198] BGHZ 76, 326; 81, 366; 90, 390.
[199] BGHZ 69, 274; 75, 334; *post*, p. 332.
[200] BGHZ 31, 258; 67, 171; 105, 168; *post*, p. 332.
[201] Deficit balance, "Unterbilanz", means that the company's equity falls short of the amount of reg-istered share capital; *ante*, p. 111.
[202] BGH ZIP 92, 1381.
[203] BGH WM 96, 256.

full provision of collateral security for credit out of company funds indicates creditworthiness.[204]

The decisive time for the determination whether or not a loan replaces equity is the time of grant. If the company was creditworthy at the time the loan was granted, there will not automatically be a reclassification because the company is no longer creditworthy at the time the loan falls due. A reclassification then presupposes that the loan was continued to be made available during the financial crisis.[205]

Legal consequences

Prohibition on redemption

The shareholder loans replacing equity are treated as equity capital and are subject to the prohibition on the repayment of share capital.[206] They may not be repaid if a deficit balance would be created or increased as a result.[207] Likewise, current interest and arrears of interest may also not be repaid under these preconditions.[208]

The prohibition ends once the crisis has been surmounted. Only then can the main claim and the interest which has accrued up until then be paid out.

Non-assertion in case of insolvency

Shareholder loans which replace equity cannot be asserted if the company becomes insolvent.[209] In each case, the whole loan serves to replace equity. It is not possible to divide such a loan into a part which replaces equity and a part which does not.[210] The unenforceability applies to both the main claim and ancillary claims, as well as to any claims on account of unjust enrichment if the loan agreement was null and void. The set-off against the claim out of a loan replacing equity is also excluded.

The shareholders also do not participate in a composition dividend; thus, following confirmation of the composition, they cannot require proportional satisfaction of their claim which replaces equity.[211]

Duty of reimbursement

A payment made to the shareholder contrary to the prohibition on repayment[212] must be reimbursed to the company.[213] The claim is restricted to the amount

---

[204] BGH WM 87, 1488.
[205] *Post*, p. 321.
[206] § 30.
[207] *Ante*, p. 111.
[208] BFH BB 92, 676; BGH BB 96, 710.
[209] § 32a para. 1.
[210] Other than is the case with the application of the case-law based on §§ 30, 31.
[211] BGH ZIP 95, 816.
[212] § 30.
[213] § 31.

which is necessary to cover the lost share capital or any overindebtedness above and beyond this.[214]

The claim becomes statute-barred in five years,[215] or in 30 years in the case of "malicious actions", i.e. where there was knowledge of the impermissibility of the payment.[216]

If the company becomes bankrupt, the trustee in bankruptcy or any judgment creditor can rescind the satisfaction.[217] The shareholder must then reimburse the payments.[218] This claim for restitution is not restricted to the amount necessary to restore the share capital,[219] but exists for the full amount of the sum paid.

The rescission and the assertion of the claim for compensation must occur within one year after the opening of bankruptcy proceedings.[220] It encompasses only those legal actions which took place within the last year prior to the opening of bankruptcy proceedings or rescission.[221] In addition, there must have been a disadvantage to the creditors, which is only lacking if the creditors could also have obtained full satisfaction out of the assets without the restitution.[222]

If payment has been made to a third party at the instigation of the shareholder, then the third party is liable for repayment alongside the shareholder if he knew of, or ought to have known of, the violation of the precept of capital maintenance.[223]

3.3 Legal acts which are similar in economic terms

The rules for shareholder loans replacing equity are also applied to other legal acts which are equivalent to a loan in economic terms.[224]

Extension, additional time for performance
The extension of a loan which has fallen due or the grant of additional time for payment of a loan claim, or another claim to assets, which has fallen due is treated as equivalent to the grant of a loan if third parties would not have granted such an extension or such additional time. Short additional periods for payment which are usual in the market constitute an exception.[225]

---

[214] BGHZ 76, 326, 335; 90, 188, 193; BGH WM 90, 182, 184; the book values are authoritative for the determination: BGH WM 87, 1040; BGH WM 90, 2112.
[215] § 31 para. 5.
[216] BGH DB 87, 1781, 1782; WM 90, 552.
[217] §§ 32a Bankruptcy Act (KO), 2, 3 Creditors' Avoidance of Transfer Act (AnfG).
[218] §§ 37 KO, 7 AnfG.
[219] Other than is the claim out of § 31.
[220] § 41 para. 1 KO:
[221] §§ 32a KO, 3b AnfG.
[222] BGHZ 105, 168.
[223] BGH NJW 844, 1036.
[224] § 32a para. 3.
[225] BGHZ 76, 329; 81, 253.

Agreements on due dates

An agreement by means of which the date on which a claim to payment falls due is postponed by a length of time which is unusual in the market is considered as equivalent to the grant of a loan.[226]

"Standstill"

The same applies if a shareholder does not allow additional time for payment of a loan claim or other claim for a pecuniary advantage, but also does not assert it in the crisis in spite of its having fallen due.[227] Then the loan is continued to be made available which is basically the same as if the loan was repaid and a new one granted.

If, for example, a shareholder always permits the company to make late settlement of claims from the supplies of goods delivered by him, then this can have the effect of a loan.[228]

A situation where the shareholder does not terminate a loan made before the crisis,[229] although he at least had the possibility of recognising the circumstances which gave rise to the start of the crisis (which is normally usually the case if proper care is taken), is considered equivalent to the "standstill" of a claim which has fallen due.[230]

A further precondition is that the shareholder can withdraw the loan granted or the other credit assistance in the case of crisis.

According to the case-law, a reclassification as equity capital will only be made if the shareholder does not assert the influence to which he is entitled in order to liquidate the company; however, he is permitted a period of two to three weeks for consideration.[231]

Security for shareholder loans

If the company has granted the lender security for the loan, then accessory security (i.e. such security as is dependent on the amount of the secured main claim as far as scope and continued existence are concerned) shall be subject to the same rules as the loan itself, and thus cannot be asserted in case of insolvency.[232]

In the case of security which is not accessory (i.e. such security as is independent of the level of the secured main claim as far as its continued existence is concerned), the receiver in insolvency proceedings may refuse payment on the grounds of the objection of avoidance.[233]

---

[226] OLG Karlsruhe DB 89, 316; LG Hamburg GmbHR 91, 531.
[227] BGHZ 75, 334; 109, 60; 127, 336.
[228] BGH WM 95, 55.
[229] BGHZ 81, 257; 104, 27; 109, 60; 121, 35.
[230] BGH WM 96, 259; WM 95, 55; ZIP 94, 1934 *et seq.*; WM 92, 187, 650, 816.
[231] BGH WM 96, 259; ZIP 93, 189, 191; OLG Munich ZIP 93, 504.
[232] BGHZ 81, 252; 109, 55.
[233] § 32a KO; LG Hamburg ZIP 91, 180.

Transfers for use

According to the case-law, contracts by means of which a shareholder lets or leases (or buys and leases back in a so-called "sale and lease back" arrangement) to the GmbH items of the investment assets are considered as economically comparable to a loan contract, because the transfer for use also facilitates the continuation of an otherwise insolvent company.

The function of replacing equity is given in such cases if the company neither has the means to procure the necessary items nor could raise them on the capital market, and no outside third party would have been prepared to make the item available to the company for use.[234]

If the company was creditworthy at the beginning of the transfer for use, a reclassification will only take place if the shareholder does not terminate the contract in the crisis or does not make use of his possibility of liquidating the company.

The shareholder cannot require the payment of the rent or hire if this would lead to, or increase, a deficit balance.[235] In the case of insolvency, the agreed fee for use cannot be asserted as a debt.[236] The receiver can demand the repayment of a fee for use which was paid in the last year prior to the opening of insolvency proceedings,[237] or which was paid from the share capital in violation of the prohibition on repayment.[238] The shareholder remains the owner of the item which was transferred for use, but cannot demand the handover thereof during the contractually agreed period (or the period which would have been agreed with third parties, if this is longer). The receiver is entitled to utilize the right of use as long as it exists, either by own use or by the transfer to third parties.[239]

Shareholders' security for loans of third parties

Frequently, third party loans are only granted in return for security provided by the shareholders, in particular guarantees. The security has the function of replacing equity if, at the time in question, the company would not have received the loan without the security.[240] However, the conclusion of a lack of adequate credit standing on the part of the company cannot automatically be drawn from a request to the shareholders to provide security, because security in this form is in part customary in some branches of business.[241]

The security is also subject to the rules on contributions replacing equity if the secured loan was granted before the crisis and the shareholder does not withdraw the security in the crisis or – in so far as this is not possible – does not assert his influence in order to liquidate the company.

---

[234] BGHZ 109, 55; 121, 31; 127, 1; 127, 17.
[235] § 30.
[236] § 32a para. 1.
[237] §§ 32a, 37 KO.
[238] § 31.
[239] BGHZ 109, 55; 121, 31; 127, 1; 127, 17.
[240] BGH ZIP 92, 108; ZIP 86, 30.
[241] BGH WM 90, 1292, 1295.

In view of the legal consequences, a distinction must be drawn between the relationship of the company to the outside lender, and to the shareholder.

Outside lenders

Prior to the insolvency of the company, no special characteristics apply to outside lenders. The company cannot refuse the fulfilment of the claim. In the case of insolvency, the lender must first seek satisfaction from the shareholders' security, and only participates in the insolvency proceedings to the extent of the claim for the deficiency.[242]

Shareholders

The shareholder must indemnify the company from the obligation for which he created the security.[243] If he satisfies the creditor, then he has a right of recourse against the company,[244] or acquires the secured claim.[245] However, both constitute a replacement of equity. Thus, the shareholder cannot assert them at all during the insolvency of the company,[246] and can only assert them outside insolvency if this would not lead to, or increase, a deficit balance.[247]

Every payment by the company to the outside lender which releases the shareholder providing security from his liability constitutes a prohibited repayment to the shareholder[248] if a deficit balance is created, or increases, as a result. He must reimburse it up to the amount of the security furnished or to the amount required to restore the share capital.[249]

If the company has paid back the secured loan within the last year prior to the opening of bankruptcy proceedings, it has a claim against the shareholder to reimbursement amounting to the sum of the guarantee or the value of the other security.[250]

Extension of the group of persons

The case-law also applies the principles of contributions replacing equity to a non-shareholder, in so far as he has had powers granted to him which enable him to (co-) determine the company's affairs as if he were a shareholder.[251]

---

[242] § 32a para. 2.
[243] § 32a para. 2.
[244] §§ 670, 812 *et seq.* BGB.
[245] §§ 774, 1143, 1225 BGB.
[246] § 32a para. 1.
[247] § 30.
[248] § 30.
[249] § 31, BGHZ 81, 252, 260; NJW 86, 429, 430; NJW 90, 1730, 1731. The payment as such may neither bring about nor increase a deficit balance, because it only leads to a balance sheet contraction which does not affect the operating result: OLG Düsseldorf WM 94, 1292 with reference to OLG Hamm GmbHR 92, 460; BGH WM 93, 2090. OLG Hamburg WM 86, 130; BGH WM 92, 187 on the duty of reimbursement.
[250] § 32b.
[251] Grantor of a trust: BGH ZIP 90, 1593; NJW 89, 1219; man of straw (e.g. a family member), if he received the funds from the shareholder; BGH ZIP 91, 366; OLG Munich GmbHR 93, 439; associated enterprises: BGHZ 105, 168, 176; ZIP 93, 189; pledgee: BGHZ 119, 191.

3.4 Burden of proof

The preconditions for the character of the loan being considered as replacement of equity must, in principle, be set forth and proven by the party asserting this. However, if a loan was granted before the financial crisis and was continued to be made available to the company, the shareholder must prove that he neither knew nor ought to have known of the occurrence of the financialcrisis.[252]

If the preconditions are not in dispute or have been proven, and if the relevant shareholder asserts that the function as substitute equity has fallen away, then he likewise bears the burden of proof for this.

3.5 Agreement on subordination in rank

By means of a so-called subordination agreement, the shareholder voluntarily places his claim on an equal footing with equity by agreeing that his claim need only be served at the cost of future profits, out of a liquidation surplus or out of the assets which exceed the other liabilities of the company. This removes the duty to enter the obligation on the liabilities side of the balance sheet in the statement of assets and liabilities upon overindebtedness,[253] so that overindebtedness of the company can perhaps be avoided,[254] although the agreement concerning withdrawal to lower rank neither has an effect on the commercial balance sheet or the tax balance sheet, as it does not lead to a removal of the liability.[255]

Given that the shareholder voluntarily accepts equal status with equity, the preconditions for the replacement of capital do not have to be examined. The rules on contributions replacing equity are only to be applied again once the withdrawal to a lower rank has been cancelled.

3.6 Conditional waiver of claims

In this form, the shareholder releases the company from his claim[256] under the condition subsequent[257] that it shall revive in case the situation improves, if an annual surplus or a winding-up profit would otherwise exist. This also dispenses with the duty to enter the claim on the liabilities side of the balance sheet in the pre-insolvency balance-sheet. However, the release, moreover, leads to extraordinary earnings and thus improves the net annual profit shown on the commercial balance sheet.

The treatment of the release is contentious from a corporate income tax point of view and has not yet been conclusively clarified. One view holds that the whole release is considered as a capital contribution of the shareholder at

---

[252] BGH WM 96, 259; WM 95, 2280; BB 92, 799.
[253] *Post*, p. 325.
[254] BGH WM 62, 764; NJW 87, 1697; OLG Hamburg WM 86, 1110, 1112.
[255] BFH NJW 94, 406.
[256] § 397 BGB.
[257] § 158 BGB.

its nominal value[258] with the consequence that the increase in assets in the tax balance sheet would not be taxable. According to another opinion, only the valuable part of the claim constitutes a non-taxable capital contribution, whilst the worthless part will be treated as taxable extraordinary profit.[259]

4. Overindebtedness

4.1 Duty to ascertain overindebtedness

If economic difficulties become apparent, then the managing director shall prepare a pre-insolvency balance sheet[260] and shall update it regularly. The purpose of preparing the balance sheet is to ascertain whether the company's assets are sufficient to satisfy the creditors.[261]

4.2 Overindebtedness and its derivation from the commercial balance sheet

The company is legally overindebted if the pre-insolvency balance sheet shows an excess of liabilities over assets and at the same time the earning capacity, or capacity for survival, of the GmbH is denied.[262] Excess of liabilities over assets is given if, where, based on liquidation values, including the silent reserves, the company's assets fall short of the liabilities. The standards for the preparation of the commercial balance sheet do not apply.[263]

The pre-insolvency balance sheet shall be prepared as an asset and liability statement in such a way that the assets are shown at their realisable current market value[264] and that the actual existing obligations are shown on the liabilities side.[265] The share capital and open reserves shall not be taken into consideration. If sufficient silent reserves (assets side) or inflated provisions (liabilities side) exist, then there is no overindebtedness.

Overindebtedness must be distinguished from the deficit balance and from undercapitalisation. A deficit balance is given if the balance sheet equity capital

---

[258] Which is to be attributed to the tax-exempted equity, §§ 8 para. 1 KStG, 4 para. 1 EStG.
[259] Clarifying decision was initiated by BFH BB 94, 2245 but is still pending. A third view is that the amount is attributed to the tax-exempted equity if the preconditions of the tax-free capital reconstruction (§ 3 no. 66 EStG) are given.
[260] "Überschuldungsstatus".
[261] BGH BB 94, 882, 883.
[262] So-called negative continuation forecast; *post*, p. 333; BGHZ 119, 201, 214; OLG Hamm GmbHR 93, 594.
[263] BGHZ 119, 201, 214. Thus, the appearance of a deficit of equity capital in the trade balance sheet (so-called "balance sheet overindebtedness") does not always lead to an excess of liabilities over assets, not to mention overindebtedness in the legal sense.
[264] BGHZ 119, 201, 214.
[265] On the treatment of loans constituting substitute capital (*ante*, p. 317) in the statement of assets and liabilities for overindebtedness; *post*, p. 332 and OLG Munich NJW 66, 2366.

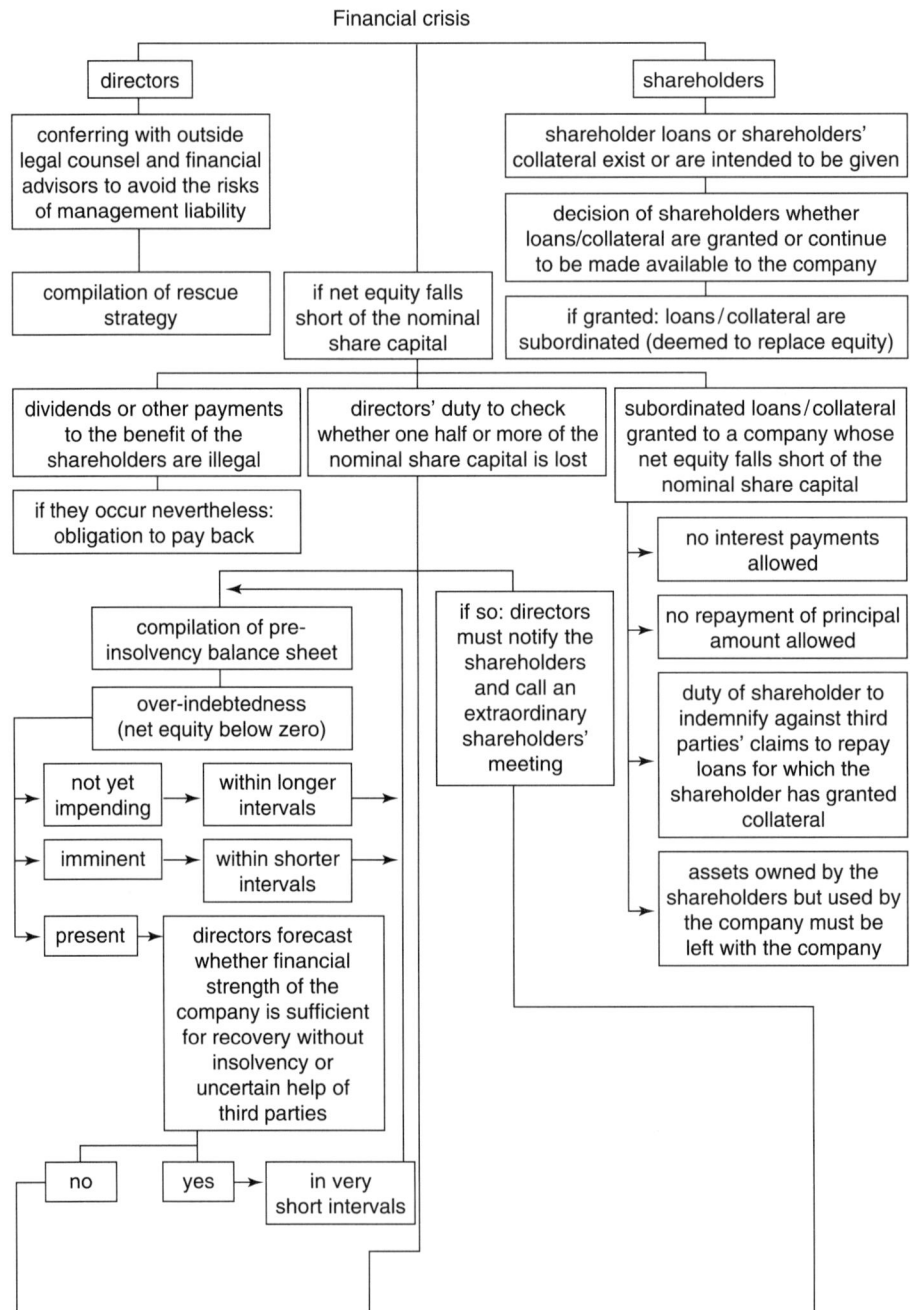

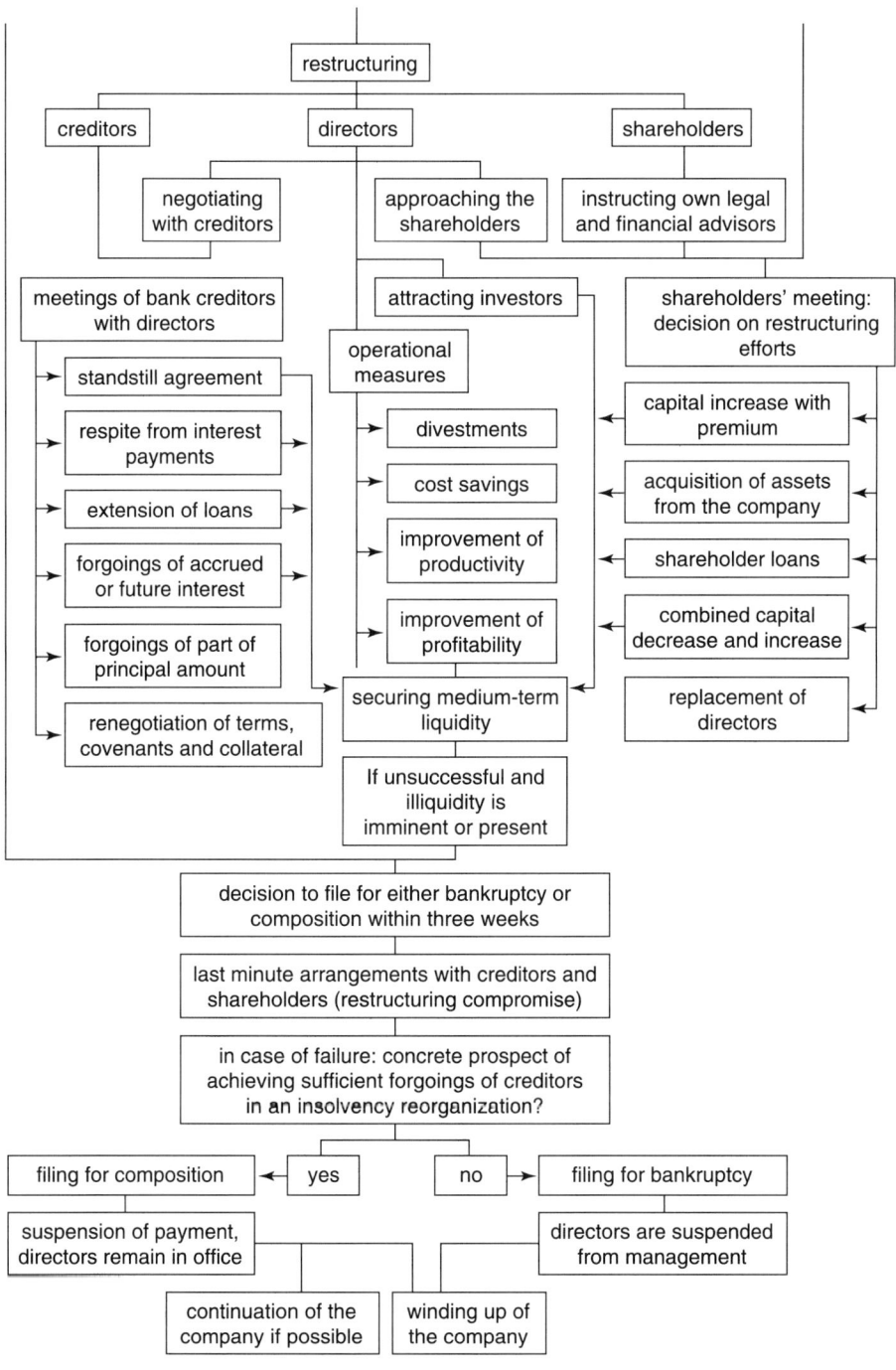

is less than the nominal amount of the registered share capital. The character-istic of undercapitalisation is the lack of a parallel between the equity capital and the financing requirement of the GmbH. This does not lead to a ground for insolvency if the company can retain its solvency, for example through external lenders or shareholder guarantees.

5. Corporate restructuring

The options available to get out of a financial crisis are manifold. The chart indicates the complex considerations in a typical crisis and rescue situation. It shows that, in Germany, the options available stem from the set of legal rules governing the financing of companies which has been described in the previous chapters. A successful corporate rescue requires the co-operation of the manag-ing directors, shareholders and creditors.

5.1 Shareholders' role

Shareholders' options include capital measures, in particular capital increases. This involves a change of the articles of association and thus requires a 75 per cent majority.[266]

The premium for new shares can be more important than their face value. Whilst it is true that a capital increase without premium gives the company liquidity as well, it would leave the balance sheet in disarray: the company's partly or fully depleted share capital would not be restored. Future profits could not be distributed as dividends, a fact which deters investors.

A frequent move which is made to restore the share capital is a combined reduction in capital[267] and increase in capital, according to which the share capital is reduced to the amount close to the net equity in the first step and then restored by a capital increase in the second step.

Theoretically, new equity capital may also be paid in without removing the deficit balance; however, a new investor will hardly be willing to do this, because the future profit would then have to be distributed proportionally amongst the existing shareholders. Thus, the removal of the deficit balance by a reduction of capital is necessary for economic reasons.

The share capital can be reduced in a simplified procedure for the purpose of equalizing reductions in value or to cover other losses, including in the form of retrospective reduction with a simultaneous cash increase in the share capital.[268] However, if the share capital of the overindebted company still has not yet been fully paid up, the simplified capital reduction with capital increase cannot be con-sidered, because it cannot be resolved with the purpose of releasing shareholders

---

[266] § 53 para. 2.
[267] § 58a, *ante*, p. 123.
[268] §§ 58a *et seq.*

from their obligations to make capital contributions. Rather, amounts which have been gained from the reduction in capital may only be used to equalize reductions in value or other losses, or for payment into the capital reserves.

If the preconditions for a simplified reduction of capital are not fulfilled,[269] or if the consequences thereof are not desired[270] then only the ordinary reduction of capital and the ordinary increase in share capital remain. However, this route is problematic if swift action is necessary to avoid insolvency, because the reduction can only be notified and registered if one year has passed since the third announcement thereof.

Further steps the shareholders can take include shareholder loans and the acquisition of assets from the company. In a financial crisis, however, shareholder loans can be subordinated.[271]

5.2 Managing directors' role

When approaching shareholders and creditors, the directors will have to show that the company will be extricated from its dire financial straits if their strategy is pursued. Such strategy always includes operational measures such as cost savings, improvement of productivity, focusing on profitable operational key areas, and enhanced profitability in general. These and other steps to optimise the company's business, however, will not yield liquidity soon enough. Increases in productivity might often require additional investments; other measures will show results only in the future. Therefore, the immediate concerns of the directors are to secure medium-term liquidity and to avoid overindebtedness.[272]

5.3 Creditors' role

Finally, the negotiations with the company's most important creditors, usually banks, are decisive for the success of the restructuring. Standstill agreements or agreements which provide a respite from payment of loans or permit an extension of repayment obligations, are frequently negotiated. They secure the liquid resources of the company.

Although the banks are in many cases reluctant to forego repayments of amounts of loan principal, frequently payments of accrued, and even future, interest are waived. Agreements are often structured in such a way that, conditional on certain key figures of recovery being reached, the bank's claim will be reactivated. This, and the renegotiation of terms and covenants, largely influence future profits and the development of important balance sheet interrelationships.

---

[269] § 58a.
[270] Allocation of any amount of the difference between assumed and actual reductions in value or other losses in the capital reserves, restriction on the distributions of profits; §§ 58c, 58d.
[271] *Ante*, p. 317.
[272] *Ante*, p. 325.

Banks often try to convince management that participation in the rescue requires the banks' uncovered loan positions to be secured by collateral. Many companies make the mistake of providing security too quickly and thus place the banks in such a comfortable position that they refuse to grant any further concessions.

In Germany, banks are usually not prepared to make concessions if they find the shareholders' contribution unsatisfactory. When addressing the creditors, the directors should already know, therefore, what they can expect from the shareholders.

5.4 Rescue company

Additional capital resources can be paid into the GmbH by taking on new shareholders through a rescue company.[273] In the course of this, the claims of important creditors are frequently transformed into equity capital.

The reconstruction company takes over either a participation in the crisis company or its business. In the latter case, it can either take over the existing liabilities of the crisis business or can continue the business without the existing liabilities. This second alternative mostly occurs after the opening of the insolvency proceedings, because the provisions concerning liability upon the takeover of assets[274] and the acquisition of a business with the continuation of the business name[275] are then no longer applicable.

---

[273] Also known as a reconstruction company.
[274] § 419 BGB.
[275] § 25 HGB.

Chapter 20

INSOLVENCY

Dr. Volker Kammel

Once the company is insolvent, i.e. overindebted or unable to meet current liabilities, the directors are obliged to file either for bankruptcy[276] or for judicial composition proceedings.[277] Bankruptcy proceedings as regulated by the Bankruptcy Act aim at the winding-up of the business. Composition proceedings, on the other hand, allow the company to avoid bankruptcy by offering its creditors a specific settlement, the terms of which are laid down in a composition plan. The funds required for the settlement of (residual) debts in accordance with the terms of this plan are either generated by the continued operation or a (partial) winding-up of the business.

The legal situation is different in the territory of the former East Germany. A uniform insolvency procedure[278] as regulated by the Uniform Insolvency Act[279] is applied. This procedure also provides for a reorganization of the business if the majority of the creditors agrees. The most important procedure in Germany providing for reorganization is, however, composition under the terms of the Composition Code.

The GmbH is dissolved by the opening of bankruptcy proceedings,[280] but liabilities generally continue to exist, in particular those arising out of employment relationships, until they are terminated within the framework of the administration of the bankrupt company's estate.

1. Reasons for insolvency

The managing directors have to file for insolvency if the GmbH is unable to pay (illiquidity) or is overindebted.[281]

---

[276] "Konkurs"; *post*, p. 335.
[277] "Gerichtliches Vergleichsverfahren"; *post*, p. 340.
[278] "Gesamtvollstreckungsverfahren".
[279] "Gesamtvollstreckungsordnung".
[280] § 60 para. 1 no. 4; *post*, p. 335.
[281] §§ 63 para. 1, 64 para. 1.

1.1 Illiquidity

The company is insolvent if it is no longer in a position to be able to pay its liabilities which have fallen due out of available funds (which can also be loan funds), probably permanently.

Shareholder loans replacing equity capital[282] shall not be treated as loan obligations which have fallen due, and shall thus be left out of count in the examination of the insolvency. The share capital naturally also does not constitute a "due" liability; rather, it does not constitute a liability at all, in spite of being entered on the liabilities side of the balance sheet.[283]

1.2 Overindebtedness

The company is overindebted if its assets no longer cover its liabilities.[284] "Assets" in this context refers to the assets of the GmbH entered on the assets side of the balance sheet.[285]

The starting point for the determination of overindebtedness is the preparation of a pre-insolvency balance sheet.[286] However, the duty to file for bankruptcy proceedings exists irrespective of whether a balance sheet has been presented; likewise, it may not wait until a balance sheet date. Rather, the situation must be considered in two stages:

- would the creditors probably receive full satisfaction out of the proceeds of liquidation (given the liquidation values, i.e. also taking into consideration silent reserves and liquidation burdens) if the GmbH were wound up at the present time? If this is not the case, there is an excess of liabilities over assets;[287]
- is the financial strength of the company sufficient and is the continued existence of the company to be assumed with overwhelming probability? The GmbH is only legally overindebted if this so-called continuation forecast is negative.[288]

1.3 Contributions replacing equity and overindebtedness

According to a wide-spread view, loans replacing equity must be taken into consideration as liabilities on the liabilities side of the pre-insolvency balance sheet,

[282] *Ante*, p. 318.
[283] *Ante*, p. 22.
[284] § 64 para. 1.
[285] BGHZ 31, 258, 272; BGH NJW 83, 676, 677.
[286] "Überschuldungsstatus"; BGH NJW 92, 2891; BGH NJW 87, 2433; *ante*, p. 325.
[287] "Rechnerische Überschuldung".
[288] "Fortbestehungsprognose"; BGH WM 94, 791; *ante*, p. 325.

because it is difficult to determine whether a loan replaces equity.[289] The other opinion is that they should be treated as equity capital and should therefore not be taken into consideration in the preparation of the pre-insolvency balance sheet.[290]

In the case where there is an agreement on subordination,[291] disclosure as a liability on the balance sheet in the pre-insolvency balance sheet is clearly inappropriate,[292] in particular in the case of waiver of a claim.

1.4 Significance of the continuation forecast

The aim of the continuation forecast is to examine the future prospects of the GmbH, i.e. if it can still be continued, in spite of mathematical overindebtedness, because the future redress of the overindebtedness is to be expected. The continuation forecast is an independent part of the investigation of overindebtedness which may not influence the pre-insolvency balance sheet (concretely, the assessment of the assets).

The managing directors, as the addressees of the duty of investigation, are under an obligation to assess the earning capacity of the enterprise, judged by objective criteria. The forecast decision requires liquidity planning carried out in accordance with business management principles, i.e. a systematic comparison of planned income and expenditure. It is decided positively if, in all probability, the occurrence of insolvency is not to be reckoned with in the foreseeable future.

No particular sequence of examination is prescribed for the preparation of the pre-insolvency balance sheet and the continuation forecast. According to more recent case-law, the duty to prepare a pre-insolvency balance sheet falls away if the positive forecast can be proved and documented.[293] However, if the company is actually mathematically overindebted, then the managing director faces the risk of criminal prosecution for criminal delay in filing a bankruptcy petition.[294] From a civil law point of view, he bears the burden of proof for the correct preparation of the forecast, i.e. he must relieve himself of this by an explanation of the facts forming the basis of the forecast.[295]

---

[289] OLG Hamburg ZIP 86, 1113.
[290] OLG Munich NJW 66, 2966, OLG Munich NJW 94, 3112. As far as the determination of a deficit balance in the formation phase is concerned (*ante*, p. 33), the Federal Supreme Court answers the question of whether loans constituting substitute equity capital are subject to an obligation to be disclosed as a liability in the balance sheet in the affirmative; BGHZ 124, 282.
[291] *Ante*, p. 324.
[292] BGH NJW 87, 1697; OLG Hamburg NJW 86, 1110, 1112. However, they must be disclosed as debt capital in the annual statements, even if there is an agreement on withdrawal to a lower rank; BFH BB 93, 1177; *ante*, p. 324.
[293] BGHZ 119, 201, 215.
[294] § 84 para. 1 no. 2.
[295] BGHZ 126, 181.

2. Insolvency petition

2.1 Notification period

The managing directors are under an obligation to petition for the opening of bankruptcy or judicial composition proceedings in the event of one of the causes of bankruptcy being present, without delay but at the latest within three weeks of the occurrence of the cause of bankruptcy.[296] This time-limit may only be exhausted if there is hope of a capital reconstruction,[297] for example by partial waiver or subordination agreements with creditors.[298] The managing directors must endeavour to effect the capital reconstruction. In extraordinary circumstances, the immediate filing of a petition could lead to liability in relation to the shareholders.[299]

On the other hand, the managing director must file the petition without delay as soon as he realises that a capital reconstruction is not possible; otherwise, he will commit a breach of the duty to petition for insolvency, and can become liable to pay compensation to the creditors. The time-limit may not be exhausted without reasonable cause; the petition must be filed beforehand if it is clear from the outset or becomes evident before the expiry of three weeks that a timely capital reconstruction is not seriously to be expected.[300] The three-week time-limit may not be exceeded.

In accordance with a minority view, an exception would be conceivable if, from the point of view of a prudent and conscientious businessman, an over-stepping of the time-limit appeared necessary for the proper preparation of the composition proceedings, and increased the chances of this significantly.

2.2 Petitioner

Each managing director is obliged to file a petition if the preconditions for this are given. This still applies if he does not have the power of sole representation or is not responsible for finances. The managing director cannot even rely on the fact that his co-directors or the shareholders have forbidden him to file such a petition.

If the other managing directors take the view that the bankruptcy petition was nevertheless filed in an overhasty and unjustified way, they can withdraw the petition. However, they then bear the risk that the petition was justified after all.

2.3 Content of the petition

The petition must be aimed at the opening of bankruptcy or composition proceedings. Often, it will be advisable to petition for composition proceedings in

---

[296] § 64 para. 1.
[297] *Ante*, p. 328.
[298] *Ante*, p. 324.
[299] § 43.
[300] BGHZ 75, 96, 111 on the parallel provision of the AktG.

order to keep open the possibility of the continued existence of the company. This is sufficient to ensure that the managing director fulfils his duty to file an insolvency petition, even where there is no prospect of success for composition proceedings. By contrast, the petition for bankruptcy cannot be turned into a petition for composition proceedings.

If the managing director files a petition for composition proceedings, he shall submit a proposal for the composition proceedings. However, the managing director also fulfils his duty to file an insolvency petition if he does not observe this requirement. The proposal in composition proceedings can be submitted subsequently.

2.4 Consequences of a breach of the duty to file a petition

Under civil law, the managing director is liable to the creditors[301] and the bankrupt's estate[302] to pay compensation if he petitions for insolvency too late.[303] Upon the occurrence of insolvency, the existing creditors (so-called old creditors) can only require reimbursement of the so-called quota damage, i.e. the loss suffered by them as a result of the delayed filing of the petition by the reduction of the bankrupt's assets, and thus their quota upon the winding-up of the insolvency.[304]

The creditors whose claim was only created once the GmbH was already overindebted (new creditors) may, by contrast, require of the managing director that they be placed in a position as if the GmbH had filed for insolvency in good time. Then, the claim would in most cases not have come into being.[305]

The managing directors are also fully liable to the bankrupt's estate. The managing directors are also liable in case of deliberate unconscionable damage of third parties,[306] above all in the case of criminal delay in filing an insolvency petition and undercapitalisation of the GmbH. If the GmbH has not yet been registered in the Commercial Register, they are affected by the liability of persons acting prior to incorporation.[307]

3. Bankruptcy

The company is dissolved by the opening of bankruptcy proceedings.[308] It thereby becomes a liquidating company. The power of administration and of

---

[301] § 823 para. 2 BGB in conjunction with § 64 para. 1.
[302] § 43 para. 2.
[303] *Ante*, p. 173 on criminal law responsibility.
[304] BGHZ 29, 100, 104 *et seq.*
[305] BGHZ 126, 181.
[306] § 826 BGB.
[307] § 11 para. 2, *ante*, p. 32. Finally, it is conceivable in exceptional cases that the shareholder-director could be called to account in the case where the assets of the GmbH are mixed with private assets, which first and foremost is relevant to smaller, medium-sized businesses; *ante*, p. 115.
[308] § 60 para. 1 no. 4.

disposition of the bankrupt's estate passes from the managing directors to the receiver.[309]

3.1 Filing for bankruptcy

The bankruptcy procedure[310] is initiated by an application of either the management or a creditor of the business to the district court[311] in whose district the registered offices of the business are situated. The application can be filed by a creditor if the company meets one of the conditions of insolvency.[312] Unlike the management, a creditor who wishes to file for bankruptcy is required to furnish *prima facie* evidence[313] that the company meets one of these conditions.

3.2 Opening procedure

Once the application has been filed, the court is called on to decide whether bankruptcy proceedings can be opened. It has to ascertain that a condition of insolvency is met and whether the company has sufficient assets to meet the costs of bankruptcy proceedings. To facilitate the latter decision, the directors of the company are obliged to provide a list of assets and liabilities at the request of the court. Lists of debtors, creditors and the company's assets have to be included in the application to the court if the management files for bankruptcy.

During the opening procedure a sequestrator[314] is usually appointed. The sequestrator is obliged to secure the business's assets for the purpose of the bankruptcy procedure. He is required to supervise the management of the company and is frequently called on to furnish the court with a report on whether the company's assets suffice to pay the costs of the bankruptcy procedure. The bankruptcy court can provide him with additional powers, should this be necessary to secure the business's assets. Usually, a general restraining order prohibiting the disposal of the company's assets by the management[315] is passed together with the appointment of a sequestrator.

3.3 Major effects of the opening decision

Once the court is satisfied that the company meets one of the conditions of insolvency and that it has sufficient assets to cover the costs of the bankruptcy proceedings, it opens proceedings. In the opening decision, it appoints a receiver,[316] whose task it is to manage the business and liquidate its assets for the

---

[309] § 6 para. 2 KO.
[310] "Konkursverfahren".
[311] "Amtsgericht".
[312] *Ante*, p. 332.
[313] "Glaubhaftmachung".
[314] "Sequester".
[315] "Allgemeines Veräußerungsverbot".
[316] "Konkursverwalter".

purpose of debt settlement. It sets a deadline for creditors to register claims with the court and determines the dates of the first creditors' meeting and the examinatory court hearing. Debtors of the company are ordered not to settle their debts[317] but to inform the receiver of the debt within a period of time specified in the court order.[318] The opening of the procedure, the name of the receiver and the deadline for the registration of claims are published in the newspaper used for the official publications of the court and the *Federal Gazette.*[319]

Management powers

Once the receiver has been appointed, he replaces the directors as managers of the company. He administers the company and liquidates the available assets. The directors are obliged to assist the receiver but can no longer exercise management powers.

   During the initial stage of the procedure, the receiver tries to obtain a general view of the existing assets and liabilities of the business. The lists of assets and liabilities provided by the directors will assist him. If the sequestrator is appointed receiver, the insight gained prior to the opening of proceedings will obviously facilitate this task.

No debt settlement outside bankruptcy proceedings

Once the bankruptcy proceedings have been opened, creditors are no longer in a position to enforce their debts outside the procedure. By law, execution for the purpose of debt settlement outside bankruptcy proceedings is stayed,[320] and pending litigation is interrupted.[321] Instead, creditors may register their claims with the court and participate in the bankruptcy proceedings. Exceptions apply in the case of creditors who have retained title,[322] those whose claims are secured, e.g. by liens, mortgages,[323] or those who only became creditors after the opening of the proceedings.[324]

Dissolution of the company

The company is dissolved by the opening of bankruptcy proceedings.[325] It then becomes a liquidating company.

Others

The creditor's right of set-off is modified. The receiver can – in principle – decide whether contracts between the company and a third party which provide

---

[317] "Offener Arrest".
[318] § 110 Bankruptcy Act (KO).
[319] "Bundesanzeiger"; §§ 76 para. 1, 81 para. 1, 111 KO.
[320] § 14 KO.
[321] § 240 ZPO.
[322] "Aussonderungsberechtigte Gläubiger".
[323] "Absonderungsberechtigte Gläubiger".
[324] "Massekosten-und Masseschuldgläubiger"; *post,* p. 339.
[325] § 60 para. 1 no. 4.

for reciprocal duties must be fulfilled.[326] Exceptions frequently apply in the case of leasehold and employment agreements.

3.4 The receiver

The receiver is necessarily an individual (not a company) who is experienced in business. Usually a lawyer is appointed, although this is not required by law. It is customary for a lawyer who has been appointed as receiver to rely on the services of other professionals, especially economists, tax advisors and even other lawyers, to ensure a proper management of the company.

The receiver is supervised by the bankruptcy court[327] and – frequently – by a creditors' committee[328] elected by the creditors during the first creditors' meeting after the opening of the bankruptcy proceedings.[329] At this meeting, the receiver reports on the reasons for the company's bankruptcy, the financial situation and the measures he has undertaken.[330] The creditors may also choose another receiver than the one initially appointed by the bankruptcy court. The court may, however, decline to appoint the person chosen by the creditors.[331]

The bankruptcy proceedings aim at sharing the funds obtained from the liquidation of the business assets equally among the participating creditors. To enable him to pay as large a dividend as possible to the creditors, the receiver is obliged to gain possession of all assets of the business.[332] He will seek to void transactions between the directors and third parties reducing assets of the business, especially transactions with third parties who knew of the imminent insolvency,[333] transactions giving away assets for improper consideration[334] or transactions during which the directors had the intention to harm the creditors.[335] The receiver will look closely at transactions between the company and shareholders or former shareholders or relatives to ascertain whether company capital was transferred to them in an illegal manner.[336] If necessary, he will sue defaulting debtors in court.

After the first creditors' meeting, a so-called general examinatory court hearing[337] is conducted, in which the creditors may participate and during which the receiver examines the claims which have been filed by creditors.[338] He then decides whether he recognizes the claims and a possible right to preferential

---

[326] § 17 KO.
[327] "Konkursgericht".
[328] "Gläubigerausschuß".
[329] § 87 para. 2. KO.
[330] § 131 KO.
[331] § 80 KO.
[332] § 117 KO.
[333] § 30 KO.
[334] § 32 KO.
[335] § 31 KO.
[336] *Ante*, p. 113.
[337] "Allgemeiner Prüfungstermin".
[338] § 141 KO.

settlement, and for which debts he declines recognition.[339] The result of his examination is entered into the bankruptcy table.[340] Creditors whose claims or whose right to preferential treatment were not recognised by the receiver may challenge this decision in court.[341]

3.5 Classes of creditors

Not all creditors of the company participate in the bankruptcy proceedings. Creditors who have retained title[342] to the assets they are claiming, may seek settlement in the usual manner.[343] Secured creditors[344] may liquidate collateral outside the proceedings.[345] Funds obtained in excess of the secured creditor's claim are returned to the receiver. If the claim exceeds the amount received during liquidation of the collateral, the creditor participates with the rest of his claim in the bankruptcy proceedings.[346]

Liabilities incurred after the opening of the procedure[347] are settled first.[348] These creditors need not register their claims at the court. Their claims are not entered in the bankruptcy table. The most important creditors who belong to this class are those whose claims result from agreements with, and other actions of, the receiver.[349] The court belongs to this class as far as the costs of the procedure are concerned,[350] as does the receiver with regard to his remuneration.[351] Claims of employees, amongst other things to wages and salaries for the last six months prior to the opening of proceedings, are treated as if they were incurred after the opening of the proceedings.[352]

The creditors participating in the bankruptcy proceedings are divided into different classes, some of which are afforded preferential settlement. The most important of these are: claims of employees regarding wages and salaries for the last year prior to the opening of proceedings, on the one hand;[353] and the state with regard to tax claims for the last year prior to opening,[354] on the other hand. The claims of creditors without a right of preference are settled last.

---

[339] § 144 KO.
[340] "Konkurstabelle"; § 145 KO.
[341] § 146 KO.
[342] "Aussonderungsberechtigte Gläubiger".
[343] §§ 43 *et seq.* KO.
[344] "Absonderungsberechtigte Gläubiger".
[345] §§ 4, 47 *et seq.* KO.
[346] § 64 KO.
[347] "Massekosten und Masseschulden".
[348] § 57 KO.
[349] § 59 para. 1 no. 1 KO.
[350] § 58 no. 1 KO.
[351] § 58 no. 2 KO.
[352] § 59 para. 1 no. 3 KO.
[353] In so far as they are not treated as if they were incurred after the opening of the proceedings: § 61 para. 1 no. 1 KO.
[354] § 61 para. 1 no. 2 KO.

3.6 Debt settlement and termination of proceedings

The receiver will draw up a list of creditors after he has examined the claims filed in one or more examinatory court hearings. As soon as funds are available once assets have been liquidated, the receiver will determine the date and the amount of a first payment on account.[355] Further payments may be made on account if the liquidation of the assets is a lengthy process. Once all the assets have been liquidated, the receiver will determine the date for the final payment.[356] For this purpose, he draws up a final creditors' list.[357] This is discussed with the creditors at a final court hearing.[358] Creditors may object to the list, stating that their claims should – or the claims of other creditors should not – have been included. After the final hearing, the court will terminate the bankruptcy proceedings.[359] The appointment of the receiver ends with the termination of the proceedings.

A supplementary payment after the termination of the proceedings[360] may become necessary[361] if funds kept back by the receiver for pending litigation become available for the settlement of debts because the court ruled in favour of the receiver. For the purpose of the supplementary payment, the office of the receiver is reinstated.

Once the company is without assets, it is deleted from the Commercial Register and ceases to exist.

4. Composition

Composition proceedings aim at allowing the company to avoid bankruptcy[362] by offering its creditors a specific settlement, the terms of which are laid down in a composition plan.[363] Unlike bankruptcy, composition proceedings do not necessarily entail a winding-up of the business, but may allow the business to survive.

4.1 Filing for composition

The proceedings are initiated by an application by the management of the company to the district court of the district in which the enterprise has its registered office.[364] The same court has jurisdiction for both bankruptcy and composition

---

[355] § 149 KO.
[356] "Schlußverteilung"; § 161 KO.
[357] "Schlußverzeichnis".
[358] "Schlußtermin"; § 162 KO.
[359] § 163 KO.
[360] "Nachtragsverteilung".
[361] § 166 KO.
[362] § 1 Composition Code (VglO).
[363] "Vergleich".
[364] § 2 VglO, § 71 KO.

proceedings. Unlike in bankruptcy, a creditor of the company is not entitled to file for composition.[365] The application for composition must, above all, include a composition plan, balance sheets of the last three years and a list of debtors and creditors showing claims and liabilities as well as collateral.[366]

4.2 Opening procedure

The court is required to appoint a preliminary receiver[367] immediately after the application has been filed.[368] It is the duty of the preliminary receiver to analyse the economic situation of the company and to report to the court whether the company will be able to meet its obligations under the composition plan, and whether this plan offers the creditors what they may reasonably expect.[369] The preliminary receiver supervises the management[370] and, in practice, assists the company in completing the application for composition, especially the lists of debtors and creditors and the balance sheets. He usually negotiates with creditors during this early stage of the composition proceedings in order to ensure that the composition plan submitted to the court is acceptable to the creditors, since its validity is subject to their approval. The court and the preliminary receiver will endeavour jointly to secure the company's assets for the purposes of the composition and thus protect the creditors.[371]

During this initial stage of the composition, the court will examine whether the legal requirements for the opening have been met. While it will rely largely on the information provided by the company in its application and the reports of the preliminary receiver, it may also conduct its own investigations, e.g. question the directors of the company or creditors, obtain expert opinions or require the authorities to provide information.

Once it has gathered the necessary information, the court decides on whether to open proceedings or to turn down the application.[372] In the latter case, it will decide simultaneously on whether to open bankruptcy proceedings.[373]

4.3 Effects of the opening decision

In the opening decision, the court appoints the receiver, which is usually the preliminary receiver, and sets a date for the court hearing during which the composition plan is negotiated with the creditors.[374] The decision is published in the newspaper used for the official publications of the court and the *Federal*

---

[365] § 2 VglO.
[366] § 3 *et seq.* VglO.
[367] "Vorläufiger Vergleichsverwalter".
[368] § 11 VglO.
[369] §§ 11 para. 2, 38 *et seq.* VglO.
[370] §§ 11 para. 2, 39 VglO.
[371] § 12 VglO.
[372] § 16 VglO.
[373] "Anschlußkonkurs"; § 19 VglO.
[374] "Vergleichstermin"; § 20 VglO.

Gazette.[375] The company's application to open proceedings and the appointment of the preliminary receiver are published in the same manner. In addition, the opening decision is entered in the Commercial Register of the company.[376] The court may also appoint a creditors' committee,[377] whose duty it is to support and supervise the receiver.[378] Once the composition proceedings have been opened, creditors may file their claims with the court.[379] However, a creditor is only required to register with the court if he was not included in the creditors' list submitted to the court together with the company's application for composition. Unsecured creditors participate in the proceedings. Creditors who retained title, creditors with a right to preferential settlement in bankruptcy and creditors whose claims arose after the opening decision do not participate.[380] Secured creditors only participate with that part of their claim which could not be settled by using collateral.[381] A collective stay of execution applies.[382] Any applications for bankruptcy to which the creditors are generally entitled are suspended for the duration of the composition proceedings.[383]

With the approval of the court, the company may refrain from fulfilling contracts imposing mutual obligations.[384] Exceptions apply in the case of lease and service contracts.[385] If the company refrains from fulfilling contracts imposing mutual obligations, it is liable for damages.[386] Creditors' rights of set-off are modified[387] and the statute of limitations is suspended[388] for the duration of the composition proceedings.

4.4 The receiver

Whilst the receiver is not furnished with management powers by law, in practice he usually determines the future course of the business. The reasons for this are manifold. Frequently, the management of a company in financial difficulties has been discredited, so that shareholders and creditors will look to the preliminary receiver for a way out of the crisis. Furthermore, his legal position can be reinforced by court orders, e.g. a general restraining order prohibiting the disposal of property by the management.[389] Since the court will only appoint persons in whom it has confidence as receiver, it will usually pass such court

---

[375] §§ 22, 119 VglO,
[376] § 23 VglO.
[377] "Gläubigerbeirat".
[378] § 44 VglO.
[379] § 67 VglO.
[380] § 26 VglO.
[381] § 27 VglO.
[382] §§ 47, 48 VglO.
[383] § 46 VglO.
[384] § 50 VglO.
[385] § 51 VglO.
[386] § 52 VglO.
[387] § 54 VglO.
[388] § 55 VglO.
[389] § 59 VglO.

orders as the receiver deems necessary. The receiver is involved in all major management decisions. They are usually only implemented if he approves of them. He supervises the company's business[390] and ensures the safe custody of the company's assets. The receiver is obliged to bring any irregularities in the company's affairs to the attention of the court and to provide the court with information upon request at any time.[391] He has to report to the creditors during the court hearing, especially on the reasons for the failure of the debtor's business, the adequacy of the composition plan and the feasibility of its implementation.[392]

4.5 The court hearing

Simultaneously with the opening of the composition proceedings, the court fixes the date of the court hearing, which must not be later than one month after the opening.[393] The receiver and the company's directors have to attend the hearing.[394] Creditors may question the directors in order to establish if it is likely that the composition plan will succeed.[395]

At the meeting, the contents of the composition plan are described. The composition plan will provide for the company to continue its business, if an extension of the deadlines for payments and a partial discharge of the debt of the company suffice to end its financial difficulties.[396] By law, the plan must offer a settlement of at least 35 per cent of the debts, 40 per cent if the deadlines for payments are extended by more than a year.[397] The company may offer an additional distribution to creditors on the condition that its financial situation improves.[398] If the extension of payment deadlines and a partial discharge of debt do not suffice to end the financial difficulties, the composition plan will provide for the winding-up of the company.[399]

The receiver reports on the adequacy of the composition plan and the feasibility of its implementation. Afterwards, all reported claims are scrutinised and may be contested by the company's directors, the receiver or any participating creditor.[400] Creditors whose claims remain uncontested are entitled to vote on the composition plan.[401] If a creditor's claim is contested, the court will decide on his right to vote. A creditor with several claims only has one vote for the total value of his claims. For the composition plan to be adopted, it must be confirmed by a majority of the creditors present at the meeting, in person or by

---

[390] § 39 VglO.
[391] § 40 VglO.
[392] § 40 para. 3 VglO.
[393] § 20 VglO.
[394] § 68 para. 1 VglO.
[395] § 69 para. 1 VglO.
[396] "Fortführungsvergleich".
[397] § 7 VglO.
[398] "Besserungsschein".
[399] "Liquidationsvergleich"; § 7 para. 4 VglO.
[400] § 71 VglO.
[401] § 71 VglO.

proxy, and a majority representing 75 per cent in value of the total claims entitled to participate in the voting (or 80 per cent of such claims if the settlement offered by the company in the composition plan is less than 50 per cent).[402] If the required majorities are reached, the court in turn will confirm the plan, unless it is of the opinion that the due process of law was not followed in the proceedings.[403] The composition plan is adopted, i.e. becomes valid, with the confirmation by the court.

The court hearing may be adjourned if 75 per cent of the creditors (headcount) apply for such an adjournment, or if only one of the required majorities (headcount or 75 per cent of the claims' value) is reached.[404] If the creditors do not approve the composition plan with the required majorities, either during the original meeting or during the adjournment, or if the court does not confirm, it will terminate the composition proceedings and decide without further delay on whether to open bankruptcy proceedings.[405]

4.6 Effects of the adoption of the composition plan

Once the composition plan has been confirmed by the court, it becomes binding for the company and all participating creditors, including those who were not present at the court hearing and those who voted against the composition plan.[406] The composition plan constitutes a schedule for the settlement of debts, which determines the extent to which, and when, existing debts have to be settled.

If the company defaults on a payment laid down in the composition plan following a written demand made by a participating creditor giving the company a week's extension in which to make the promised payment, the discharge or extension of the deadline for this payment becomes invalid.[407] The composition plan remains unaffected, however, as far as the other creditors are concerned.

The claims of secured and privileged creditors, especially employees, remain unaffected. In view of the financial dimensions of the employees' claims, this is one of the reasons why composition proceedings frequently fail to achieve their actual aim, i.e. to prevent the opening of bankruptcy proceedings.

4.7 Implementation of the composition plan and termination of the composition proceedings

The company must settle its debts to the extent and at the time determined by the composition plan. The implementation of this plan is supervised either by the receiver or by a special trustee,[408] whose duty it is to safeguard the interests

---

[402] § 74 VglO.
[403] §§ 78, 79 VglO.
[404] § 77 VglO.
[405] "Anschlußkonkurs"; § 80 VglO.
[406] § 82 VglO.
[407] § 9 VglO.
[408] "Sachwalter".

of the creditors. A special trustee will only be called upon to supervise the company if its directors agree to this in the composition plan.[409] If this is the case, the court will terminate composition proceedings after the confirmation of the composition plan. If the composition proceedings are continued, the receiver will supervise the implementation and the proceedings will only be terminated once the composition plan has been fulfilled.[410] Restrictions on the powers of the management are maintained until the proceedings are terminated.

If the composition plan provides for the winding-up of the business, the company can be deleted from the Commercial Register once all its assets have been utilised for debt settlement. The company then ceases to exist.

5. Cross-border insolvencies

The effects of insolvency procedures in transnational cases involving Germany are subject to the national laws of the countries concerned, if an insolvency treaty does not apply. In future, cross-border insolvencies (i.e. those in which the company has assets in more than one country) involving Germany and other member states of the European Union will be governed by the new European Insolvency Treaty which is, however, not yet in force. Apart from this (future) treaty, a bilateral treaty between Germany and Austria exists to govern cross-border insolvencies.

Insolvency procedures in cross-border cases can be conducted by a court in Germany if the registered office of the company's business is situated in Germany. Foreign creditors participate in the same way as German creditors. Foreign assets are affected by the proceedings in the same way as domestic assets. Whether the insolvency procedure does in actual fact have the effects on foreign assets attributed to them by German law, depends on the law of the country in which the asset is located. Failure to abide by German law, even as far as foreign assets are concerned, may, however, affect the company's or a creditor's position in Germany.

Foreign insolvency procedures are held to affect assets located in Germany in the way determined by the other country's laws if the following conditions are met:

- foreign law stipulates that foreign procedures affect German assets;
- the foreign court or authority conducting proceedings has international jurisdiction under German law;
- the proceedings were properly instituted under the laws of the country concerned;
- the proceedings conform to the basic principles of German law (public order).

---

[409] §§ 91, 92 VglO.
[410] § 96 VglO.

Chapter 21

DISSOLUTION, LIQUIDATION AND CANCELLATION

Dr. Rüdiger Volhard

1. Dissolution

1.1 Reasons for dissolution

The reasons which lead to the dissolution of the GmbH may have their origins both in statutory law and in the articles of association.[411]

Stipulations as to time

It can be specified in the articles of association that the GmbH shall be dissolved upon the expiry of a certain period,[412] but this is not usual.

Shareholders' resolution

The shareholders may resolve on the dissolution of the company with a three quarters' majority of the votes cast. The articles of association may make provision for a larger or a smaller majority.[413]

In principle, the resolution on dissolution does not require a particular form.[414] In particular, a resolution may also be adopted in a written procedure.[415] However, the resolution then requires notarial recording and a compulsory three quarters' majority if it is a change in the articles of association.[416] This is the case where the articles of association provide for a certain life of the company and the dissolution is intended to take place prior to this time.

---

[411] § 60.
[412] § 60 para. 1 no. 1.
[413] § 60 para. 1 no. 2.
[414] BayObLG WM 95, 714; however, as the registry court can require proof of the dissolution (§ 12 FGG), written form is expedient.
[415] § 48 para. 2.
[416] § 53 para. 2.
[417] § 54 para. 3.

The resolution is valid immediately unless it constitutes a change in the articles of association, which only becomes valid once it is registered in the Commercial Register.[417] In other cases, the registration in the Commercial Register[418] only has declaratory importance.

The resolution does not need any special justification, because there is no right on the part of the minority to the continued existence of the company. Yet it can be voidable if the majority, in adopting the resolution, committed a breach of the company law duty of loyalty.[419] Such a violation of duty will only be considered as given if the majority shareholder attempts to obtain a special advantage by taking over the assets of the GmbH after dissolution, which would for example be the case if, even before the adoption of the resolution, he already prepares the takeover in such a way that other shareholders are – from the outset – denied the legal (not just the actual) possibility of acquiring the company's assets themselves.[420]

Petition for judicial dissolution by a shareholder
If the achievement of the purpose of the company has become impossible, or if there is another important reason in the company's circumstances, share-holders whose shares amount to at least 10 per cent of the share capital can lodge a petition for judicial dissolution against the company.[421] An important reason is given where it is unreasonable to expect the petitioning shareholder to continue the company, which may be the case if there is a fundamental and irreparable rift between the shareholders.[422]

Threat to the general welfare
Theoretically, the supreme state authority – usually the Ministry of Economic Affairs of the relevant Federal State – can dissolve the GmbH by administrative act if the shareholders adopt illegal resolutions or knowingly permit illegal activities of the managing directors.[423] However, this hardly ever happens in practice.

Bankruptcy proceedings
The GmbH is dissolved by the opening of bankruptcy proceedings.[424] The bankruptcy proceedings[425] take the place of liquidation.[426]

Cancellation Act
A further reason for dissolution is the legal force of the court order by which a

---

[418] § 65 para. 1.
[419] BGH ZIP 80, 275 *et seq.*; 88, 301, 303.
[420] BGHZ 76, 352 *et seq.*
[421] §§ 60 para. 1 no. 3, 61.
[422] BGH NJW 85, 1901.
[423] §§ 60 para. 1 no. 3, 62.
[424] §§ 60 para. 1 no. 4, 63.
[425] § 66 para. 1.
[426] *Post,* p. 356.

petition for the opening of bankruptcy proceedings is refused for lack of assets.[427] The dissolution must be entered *ex officio* in the Commercial Register.[428]

Relocation of place of business

The dominant view is that the transfer abroad of the actual main administrative office of the company is also a reason for dissolution.[429]

Transformation

In addition, in the event of a merger or split-up, the company is brought to an end without liquidation.[430] Where there is a change of legal form,[431] the company, by contrast, continues in the legal form determined by the resolution on transformation, even in the case where a GmbH is transformed into a personal partnership (preservation of identity).

1.2 Notification

The dissolution must be notified to the Commercial Register for registration.[432] The liquidators are under a duty of notification in this respect.[433]

1.3 Announcement

The dissolution must be announced three times by the liquidators in the newspapers which the articles of association specify as appropriate for the announcements of the company (mostly only in the *Federal Gazette*), together with a request to the creditors of the company to contact it.[434]

2. Liquidation

The liquidation of the GmbH aims at terminating the business of the company, i.e. the collection of any outstanding claims and the repayment of the liabilities before the remaining assets can be distributed to the shareholders. The company continues to exist until the end of the liquidation but a supplement must be added to the business name (e.g. "i.L." or "i. Abw."), from which it is evident that the company advertising itself has transformed into a liquidation company upon dissolution.[435]

---

[427] § 1 para. 1 Act on the Dissolution and Cancellation of Companies and Co-operatives (LöschG).
[428] § 1 para. 2 LöschG.
[429] *Ante*, p. 21. BGHZ 25, 144 for co-operative; BayObLG BB 92, 1400 for GmbH.
[430] *Ante*, p. 291 and p. 299.
[431] *Ante*, p. 300.
[432] § 65 para. 1.
[433] The managing directors are only under a duty of notification if the dissolution – as a change in the articles of association – only becomes valid upon registration, and both events must be notified at the same time: BayObLG GmbHR 94, 478.
[434] § 65 para. 2.
[435] § 71 para. 5.

The observance of this duty can be enforced with the levy of coercive payments.[436]

As long as the liquidators have not yet commenced the distribution of the company's assets, the shareholders[437] can, in turn, resolve on the continuation of the company with a three quarters' majority.

2.1 Liquidators

The liquidation is carried out by the liquidators. They are either the managing directors as the so-called "born" liquidators[438] or other natural or legal persons to whom this function is transferred by the articles of association or by a resolution of the shareholders as so-called "elected" liquidators. Upon the application of a minority of shareholders with shares amounting to a total of at least 10 per cent of the share capital, the registry court can appoint or dismiss the liquidators for cause.[439]

The liquidators represent the GmbH i.L.[440] on a joint basis according to statute.[441] The power of representation can be differently regulated by the articles of association or by appointment by a resolution of the shareholders. Given that the representative power of the managing directors extinguishes upon the dissolution of the company, the dissolution of the company[442] and the managing directors' appointment and power of representation must be notified by the liquidators to the Commercial Register for registration.[443]

The managing directors are only under a duty of notification if the dissolution, as a change in the articles of association only becomes valid upon registration.[444] This notification at the same time contains the notification that the power of representation of the former managing directors has been cancelled.[445]

2.2 Winding-up procedure

The liquidators must prepare an opening balance sheet and an explanatory report thereof for the start of liquidation.[446] Then, they have the task of terminating the current business transactions, of fulfilling the obligations of the dissolved company, of collecting the claims of the dissolved company and of transforming the assets of the company into money.[447]

---

[436] § 79 para. 1.
[437] By analogy with § 274 para. 1 AktG.
[438] § 66 para. 1.
[439] § 66 para. 2, para. 3.
[440] § 70.
[441] § 68 para. 1.
[442] § 65 para. 1.
[443] Contrary to the – in this context – misleading wording of § 67 para. 1.
[444] BayObLG GmbHR 94, 478.
[445] BayObLG GmbHR 95, 481. The notification must contain the assurance that the liquidators are not prevented: §§ 66 para. 4, 6 para. 2; *ante*, p. 35.
[446] § 71 para. 1.
[447] § 70 para. 1.

2.3 Payment without security for the obligations

The liquidators may only commence the distribution of the assets to the share-holders once the company's debts have been paid or secured, and one year has passed since the third appeal to the creditors in the public newspapers to register their claims.[448] Uncontentious claims which have fallen due must be fulfilled, without it being relevant whether the creditors asserted the claim against the company within the waiting period of one year or not.[449]

For liabilities which are disputed, are not due or cannot be paid for other reasons, security has to be provided in order that the share capital can be paid out to the shareholder. The security can be a mortgage, pledge of a chattel or of certain registered claims, or the deposit of money or documents of title. If none of these alternatives is possible, security can be provided by a guarantee.[450]

If all possible creditors are known, the GmbH can try to reach an agreement with all creditors to try to provide other types of collateral, e.g. deposit in a fiduciary account of notary, lawyer or reputable bank. Alternatively, and per-haps easier to implement, is an agreement with all known creditors that the shareholder of the GmbH assumes such liabilities of its subsidiary.

2.4 Distribution of the remaining assets to the shareholders

The assets of the company remaining after the liabilities have been met shall be distributed to the shareholders in proportion to their participation in the share capital, in so far as the articles of association do not specify anything else.[451]

Before the one year waiting period[452] has expired and the debts of the com-pany are discharged or otherwise secured, no payment may be made to the shareholder, not even a partial payment or down-payment. This provision was established for the benefit of all (even the unknown) creditors, and is therefore compulsory.

2.5 Liquidators' liability

If a distribution of the company's assets was undertaken in breach of the one-year waiting period, or before the repayment or securing of known claims, then the liquidators are personally liable, and jointly and severally liable, for the replacement of the amounts which were distributed.[453] The company is entitled to the claim to compensation, but a creditor of the company can have it pledged to him and transferred to him. In addition, the dominant view is that

---

[448] § 73 para. 1.
[449] For debts which are known but where the creditor does not report, the equivalent amount of money can be deposited with the district court of the place where the obligation is to be performed, according to a special procedure provided in § 73 para. 2 Court Deposit Regulations (HintO).
[450] "Bürgschaft", § 232 BGB.
[451] § 72.
[452] § 73 para. 1.
[453] § 73 para. 3.

the creditors have their own claim to compensation against the liquidators, because the provision is viewed as a protective statute.[454]

However, the risk of liability can be minimized by keeping a sufficient amount of money for the payment of all outstanding debts. If the liquidator decides, in deviation from the statutory procedure, to distribute the share capital to the shareholders before all debts are paid, and maintains a sufficient amount of money for the discharge of all future debts of the GmbH, he will only be liable in relation to the creditors if the latter suffer loss. The creditors may take legal action before any harm occurs, to prevent the liquidator from any act violating the legal rules. However, this risk may not be significant in the case where a sufficient amount of money is kept for the outstanding debts, particularly since most of the creditors may not even know that the liquidator distributes any share capital.

Alongside the claim against the liquidators, the company (not the creditors as well in this instance) is also entitled to a right to recovery against the shareholders in the case of a breach of the statutory liquidation provisions.[455]

2.6 End of liquidation

If the liquidation has ended with the satisfaction of all liabilities and the distribution of the remaining assets amongst the creditors and the "final account" has been drawn up, the liquidators must apply for the end of liquidation to be registered in the Commercial Register.[456] Information must be provided as to who – on the basis of the articles of association or a resolution of the shareholders – will keep the books and documents of the company for the period of 10 years for which they must be kept safe; otherwise, the court will specify the custodian.[457]

3. Cancellation[458]

The GmbH will then be cancelled in the Commercial Register and thus ceases to exist as a legal person. Without liquidation, a GmbH will be cancelled in case of merger, split-up or insolvency.[459]

---

[454] § 823 para. 2 BGB in conjunction with § 73.
[455] RGZ 92, 77; 109, 387 *et seq.*
[456] § 74 para. 1.
[457] § 74 para. 2.
[458] "Löschung".
[459] § 2 para. 1 LöschG.

Part VIII

APPENDIX

Chapter 22

PRECEDENTS AND INDICES

Dr. Rüdiger Volhard and Dr. Arndt Stengel

1. Precedents

1.1 Power of Attorney

<u>Vollmacht</u>

Der Bürovorsteher Horst Lehmann, dienstansässig Niedenau 25, 60325 Frankfurt am Main, ist bevollmächtigt, uns bei der Gründung einer Gesellschaft mit beschränkter Haftung mit Sitz in Frankfurt am Main zu vertreten, für uns Geschäftsanteile zu zeichnen, auch im Rahmen von Kapitalerhöhungen, und sämtliche Gesellschafterrechte auszuüben, einschließlich des Rechts, über die Geschäftsanteile zu verfügen.

Herr Lehmann ist ermächtigt, Untervollmacht zu erteilen; er ist von den Beschränkungen des § 181 BGB befreit.

London, 25. Januar 1996

_____

(Aquarius Computer Ltd.)

<u>Power of Attorney</u>

The senior law clerk, Mr. Horst Lehmann, with his business address at Niedenau 25, 60325 Frankfurt am Main, is authorized to represent us with regard to the establishment of a limited liability company (GmbH) having its registered place of business in Frankfurt am Main, to subscribe to shares, including with respect to capital increases, and to exercise all shareholders' rights, including the right to dispose of the shares.

Mr. Lehmann is authorized to grant a sub-power of attorney to another person; he is exempted from the restrictions of § 181 of the German Civil Code (BGB).

London, 25 January 1996

Aquarius Computer Ltd.
by:

_____

(Notarial verification of signature, board resolution, certificate of secretary, certificate of good standing, apostille)

1.2 Notarial instruction of managing director and confirmation

Robert Jones, Esq.
Aquarius Computer Ltd.
173 Eastcheap
London EC3M
England

Betr.: Aquarius Computer (Deutschland) GmbH

Sehr geehrter Herr Jones,

Hiermit belehre ich Sie formell über Ihre Pflicht, dem Handelsregister gegenüber bestimmte Umstände offenzulegen.

Aufgrund der Bestimmungen des deutschen Gesetzes betreffend die Gesellschaften mit beschränkter Haftung ("GmbH") darf eine Person, die wegen einer Konkursstraftat (Bankrott, Verletzung der Buchführungspflicht, Gläubigerbegünstigung, Schuldnerbegünstigung – §§ 283–283d Strafgesetzbuch) rechtskräftig verurteilt worden ist, auf die Dauer von fünf Jahren seit der Rechtskraft des Urteils nicht Geschäftsführer/Geschäftsführerin ("Geschäftsführer") einer GmbH sein.

Ferner darf eine Person, der die Ausübung eines Berufes, Berufszweiges, Gewerbes oder Gewerbezweiges durch gerichtliches Urteil oder durch vollziehbare Entscheidung einer Verwaltungsbehörde untersagt worden ist, für die Zeit, für welche das Verbot wirksam ist, bei einer GmbH, deren Unternehmensgegenstand ganz oder teilweise mit dem Gegenstand des Verbots übereinstimmt, nicht als Geschäftsführer tätig werden. In die Frist wird die Zeit nicht eingerechnet, in welcher ein Täter auf behördliche Anordnung in einer Anstalt verwahrt worden ist. Der Geschäftsführer einer GmbH ist verpflichtet, dem Gericht (Handelsregister) ohne jede Einschränkung darüber Auskunft zu erteilen, ob Umstände der genannten Art vorliegen, die seiner Bestellung zum Geschäftsführer entgegenstehen.

Der Geschäftsführer einer GmbH hat in der Anmeldung seiner Bestellung zum Handelsregister zu versichern, daß keine Umstände vorliegen, die seiner Bestellung zum Geschäftsführer entgegenstehen und daß er über seine unbeschränkte Auskunftspflicht gegenüber dem Gericht (Handelsregister) belehrt worden ist. Diese Belehrung kann von einem Notar erteilt werden.

_____

(Martin Schön)
– Notar –

Ich bestätige, daß ich o.g. Belehrungen gelesen und verstanden habe.

_____

(Robert Jones)

Robert Jones, Esq.
Aquarius Computer Ltd.
173 Eastcheap
London EC3M
England

Re: Aquarius Computer (Deutschland) GmbH

Dear Mr. Jones,

I hereby formally instruct you of your duty to disclose certain circumstances to the Commercial Register:

On the basis of the provisions of German law with respect to companies with limited liability ("GmbH"), an individual who has been finally adjudged to have committed a bankruptcy offence (bankruptcy, failure to comply with book-keeping requirements, and the fraudulent preference of, or conveyance to a creditor or a debtor under §§ 283–283d of the German Criminal Code (Strafge-setzbuch)) is not permitted to be a managing director of a GmbH for a period of five years from the date on which the judgment becomes legally binding and non-appealable.

Nor, furthermore, may an individual who has been prohibited by the judgment of a court or by an enforceable decision of an administrative authority from practising a profession, branch of a profession, occupation or line of trade, be a managing director of a GmbH the business purpose of which, either wholly or in part, corresponds to such a profession or line of trade, for the duration of such prohibition. The time which an offender is detained in an institution by order of a public authority is not counted as part of the five-year period. The managing director of a GmbH is required by law to fully inform the court (Commercial Register) if circumstances of this nature apply to him which would bar his appointment as managing director.

In the notification of his appointment to the Commercial Register, the manag-ing director of a GmbH must affirm that no circumstances exist that would bar his appointment as managing director, and that he has been instructed with respect to his unconditional duty to inform the court (Commercial Register). Such instruction can be given by a notary.

_____

(Martin Schön)
– Notary Public –

I confirm that I have read and that I understand the above instructions.

_____

(Robert Jones)

1.3 Memorandum of association

<u>UR 80/1996</u>

Verhandelt
zu Frankfurt am Main am 01. Februar 1996

Vor mir, dem unterzeichnenden Notar im Bezirk
des Oberlandesgerichts Frankfurt am Main

Martin Schön

mit dem Amtssitz in Frankfurt am Main,

erschienen heute

1. Herr Kaufmann Konrad Schmitt, Benzstraße 3, 63225 Langen, ausgewiesen durch Personalausweis Nr. 123456, handelnd nicht für sich selbst, sondern als alleinvertretungsberechtigter und von den Beschränkungen des § 181 BGB befreiter Geschäftsführer der Schmitt Bürosysteme GmbH, Frankfurt am Main,

2. Herr Bürovorsteher Horst Lehmann, dienstansässig Niedenau 25, 60325 Frankfurt am Main, von Person bekannt, handelnd nicht im eigenen Namen, sondern als Vertreter der Aquarius Computer Ltd., London, England, aufgrund Vollmacht vom 25.01.1996, die dieser Urkunde in beglaubigter Abschrift beigefügt ist.

Die Erschienenen erklärten:

I.

Wir gründen hiermit eine Gesellschaft mit beschränkter Haftung unter der Firma Aquarius Computer (Deutschland) GmbH, die ihren Sitz in Frankfurt am Main haben soll und schließen den als Anlage beigefügten Gesellschaftsvertrag.

Wir übernehmen folgende Geschäftsanteile:

Aquarius Computer Ltd.	DM 25.000
Schmitt Bürosysteme GmbH	DM 25.000

Das Stammkapital der Gesellschaft beläuft sich auf DM 50.000 und ist damit übernommen.

II.

Zu Geschäftsführern der Gesellschaft bestellen wir Herrn Robert Jones und Herrn Konrad Schmitt. Ein Geschäftsführer vertritt die Gesellschaft allein, solange er einziger Geschäftsführer ist. Werden weitere Geschäftsführer bestellt, so vertreten zwei Geschäftsführer oder ein Geschäftsführer mit einem Prokuristen die Gesellschaft gemeinsam. Die Geschäftsführer sind von den Beschränkungen des § 181 BGB befreit.

III.

Die Kosten der Gründung trägt die Gesellschaft, soweit gesetzlich zulässig.

IV.

Wir bevollmächtigen hiermit die Notariatssachbearbeiterin Regina Schultz, dienstansässig Niedenau 25, 60325 Frankfurt am Main, mit dem Recht zur Erteilung von Untervollmachten, die vorstehenden Erklärungen zu ergänzen und abzuändern. Diese Vollmacht erlischt mit der Eintragung der Gesellschaft in das Handelsregister.

V.

Der Notar wies die Erschienenen darauf hin, daß

– die Gesellschaft als solche erst mit Eintragung in das Handelsregister entsteht und die vor Eintragung für sie Handelnden gesamtschuldnerisch persönlich haften,

– jeder Gesellschafter dafür haftet, daß das Stammkapital voll eingezahlt wird,

– jeder Gesellschafter für den Fehlbetrag haftet, wenn bei Eintragung der Gesellschaft ihr Vermögen geringer ist als das Stammkapital (abzüglich Gründungsaufwand),

– Vermögensanlagen Gebietsfremder vom inländischen Empfänger auf Formular Anlage K 2 zur Außenwirtschaftsverordnung (AWV) zu melden sind, wenn die Leistungen DM 100.000 (i.W.: Deutsche Mark hunderttausend) im Kalenderjahr übersteigen,

– der Allein- oder Mehrheitsgesellschafter einer GmbH, der deren Geschäfte als alleiniger Geschäftsführer führt, persönlich für die Verluste der Gesellschaft haftet, wenn er bei der Verfolgung seiner außerhalb der Gesellschaft bestehenden geschäftlichen Interessen keine angemessene Rücksicht auf die eigenen Belange der von ihm abhängigen Gesellschaft nimmt und insbesondere nicht dafür sorgt, daß diese ihre Schulden bezahlen kann,

– mit Freiheitsstrafe bis zu drei Jahren oder mit Geldstrafe bestraft werden kann, wer zwecks Errichtung der Gesellschaft falsche Angaben macht.

Vorstehende Verhandlung nebst Anlage wurde den Erschienenen vorgelesen, lag ihnen samt Anlage zur Durchsicht vor, wurde von ihnen genehmigt und von ihnen und dem Notar eigenhändig unterschrieben.

UR 80/1996

Recorded
in Frankfurt am Main on 1 February 1996

Before me, the undersigned Notary Public in the district
of the Higher Regional Court, Frankfurt am Main

Martin Schön

practicing in Frankfurt am Main

appeared today:

1. the businessman Mr. Konrad Schmitt, Benzstraße 3, 63225 Langen, who established his identity by submitting his indentity card no. 123456, not acting in his own name but as managing director of Schmitt Bürosysteme GmbH, Frankfurt am Main, with sole power of representation, and exempted from the restrictions of § 181 of the German Civil Code,

2. the senior law clerk Mr. Horst Lehmann, with his business address at Niedenau 25, 60325 Frankfurt am Main, personally known to the Notary, acting not in his own name but on behalf of Aquarius Computer Ltd., London, England, on the basis of a power of attorney dated 25 January 1996, a certified copy of which is annexed to this notarial Deed,

The persons appearing declared:

I.

We hereby establish a limited liability company (Gesellschaft mit beschränkter Haftung) under the business name Aquarius Computer (Deutschland) GmbH, which shall have its registered office in Frankfurt am Main, and adopt the Articles of Association attached to this Deed as an Appendix.

We assume the following shares:

Aquarius Computer Ltd.	DM 25.000
Schmitt Bürosysteme GmbH	DM 25.000

The entire share capital of the company amounts to DM 50.000 and has thus been taken up.

II.

We hereby appoint Mr. Robert Jones and Mr. Konrad Schmitt as managing directors. One managing director may represent the company alone so long as he is the sole managing director. If any further managing directors are appointed, the company shall be represented by a managing director acting jointly with another managing director or with a Procurator (holder of power of procuration). The managing directors are exempted from the restrictions of § 181 BGB (Civil Code).

III.

All costs of formation of the company shall be borne by the company, in so far as is legally permissible.

IV.

We hereby authorize the notarial clerk Ms. Regina Schultz with her business address at Niedenau 25, 60325 Frankfurt am Main, with the right to delegate such authority, to supplement or modify the above mentioned statements. This power of attorney shall expire upon registration of the company in the Commercial Register.

V.

The Notary Public advised the persons appearing that:

- the company as such is only created upon registration in the Commercial Register and that persons acting for the company before its entry in the Commercial Register are jointly and severally liable;

- each shareholder is liable for the share capital being paid up in full;

- each shareholder is liable for the difference, if the company's assets at the time of registration are less than the share capital (less costs of formation);

- capital investments of non-residents must be reported by the domestic recipient to the authorities using the form Appendix K 2 to the Foreign Trade and Payments Ordinance (AWV) if they exceed DM 100,000 (in words: Deutsche Mark one hundred thousand) within a calendar year;

- the sole or majority shareholder of a GmbH, who manages its business as sole managing director, is personally liable for losses of the company, if he does not take proper care of the interests of the company depending on him when following his own business interests outside of the company, in particular if he does not take care that the company can pay its debt;

– incorrect statements for the purpose of the creation of the company are punishable with a term of imprisonment of up to three years or with a fine.

This Deed and the Appendix were read aloud to the persons appearing, submitted to them for inspection, approved by them, and signed in their own hand by them and the Notary.

1.4 Articles of association (short version)

Gesellschaftsvertrag

§ 1 Firma/Sitz

(1) Die Gesellschaft hat die Firma Aquarius Computer (Deutschland) GmbH.

(2) Sitz der Gesellschaft ist Frankfurt am Main.

§ 2 Gegenstand

(1) Gegenstand des Unternehmens ist der Vertrieb von Geräten der elektronischen Datenverarbeitung.

(2) Die Gesellschaft darf alle Geschäfte und Handlungen vornehmen, die dem Gesellschaftszweck unmittelbar oder mittelbar zu dienen geeignet sind. Sie darf sich an anderen Gesellschaften beteiligen.

§ 3 Stammkapital/-einlagen

(1) Das Stammkapital der Gesellschaft beträgt DM 50.000.

(2) Davon übernimmt

Aquarius Computer Ltd., London, England, eine Stammeinlage von DM 25.000, Schmitt Bürosysteme GmbH, Frankfurt am Main, eine Stammeinlage von DM 25.000.

(3) Das Stammkapital ist voll eingezahlt.

§ 4 Verfügungen über Geschäftsanteile

(1) Verfügungen unter Lebenden über Geschäftsanteile oder Teile davon bedürfen zu ihrer Wirksamkeit der Zustimmung der Gesellschafterver-

sammlung. Das gilt auch für die Einräumung von Unterbeteiligungen und die Begründung von Rechtsverhältnissen, aufgrund derer ein Gesellschafter seinen Anteil ganz oder teilweise als Treuhänder eines anderen hält oder die Ausübung seiner Gesellschafterrechte an die Zustimmung eines anderen bindet, falls dieser nicht selbst Gesellschafter ist.

(2) Auf die Zustimmung besteht außer bei Verfügungen zugunsten von Ehegatten oder Abkömmlingen kein Anspruch.

(3) Die Zustimmung bedarf der einfachen Mehrheit der abgegebenen Stimmen.

(4) Stimmt die Gesellschafterversammlung einer Veräußerung zu, hat jeder der übrigen Gesellschafter außer im Falle des Abs (2) ein Vorkaufsrecht, mehrere das Vorkaufsrecht Ausübende im Verhältnis ihrer Kapitalanteile. Ein wegen § 5 GmbHG sich ergebender Spitzenbetrag steht dem zu, der das Vorkaufsrecht als erster ausgeübt hat. Die Ausübungsfrist beträgt einen Monat ab dem letzten Zugang einer beglaubigten Kopie des Vertrags über die Veräußerung. Stimmt die Gesellschafterversammlung der Veräußerung nicht zu, ist der Gesellschafter mit Frist von sechs Monaten zum Jahresende zum Austritt berechtigt.

§ 5 Nachfolge von Todes wegen

(1) Die Geschäftsanteile sind frei vererblich.

(2) Mehrere Nachfolger können die Gesellschafterrechte nur durch einen gemeinsamen Bevollmächtigten ausüben, der entweder Gesellschafter oder Angehöriger der rechts- oder steuerberatenden oder wirtschaftsprüfenden Berufe sein muß. Auch die Vertretung durch einen Testamentsvollstrecker ist zulässig, wenn er Angehöriger der vorgenannten Berufsgruppen ist. Bis zur Bestellung eines Bevollmächtigten ruhen die Gesellschafterrechte mit Ausnahme des Gewinnbezugsrechts.

§ 6 Einziehung/Zwangsübertragung

(1) Die Einziehung ist zulässig.

(2) Die Gesellschafterversammlung kann die Einziehung eines Geschäftsanteils oder seine Übertragung auf die Gesellschaft oder auf die übrigen Gesellschafter im Verhältnis ihrer Kapitalanteile beschließen, wenn ein Gesellschafter aus wichtigem Grund, insbesondere wegen Verletzung von Verpflichtungen aus diesem Gesellschaftsvertrag, aus der Gesellschaft ausgeschlossen werden kann oder seinen Austritt erklärt. Dem Betroffenen steht dabei kein Stimmrecht zu.

(3) Für den Geschäftsanteil ist die in diesem Vertrag bestimmte Abfindung zu zahlen, bei Einziehung von der Gesellschaft, bei Übertragung vom Erwerber.

(4) Einziehung und Übertragung sind nicht von einer Zug um Zug zu erbringenden Gegenleistung abhängig.

§ 7 Geschäftsführung/Vertretung

(1) Die Gesellschaft hat einen oder mehrere Geschäftsführer.

(2) Ein Geschäftsführer vertritt die Gesellschaft allein, solange er einziger Geschäftsführer ist. Hat die Gesellschaft mehr als einen Geschäftsführer, wird sie entweder durch zwei Geschäftsführer oder durch einen Geschäftsführer mit einem Prokuristen vertreten.

(3) Alle oder einzelne Geschäftsführer können zur Alleinvertretung ermächtigt und/oder von den Beschränkungen des § 181 BGB befreit werden, und zwar auch der einzige Geschäftsführer, der allein oder mit der Gesellschaft alle Geschäftsanteile hält.

(4) Die Gesellschafterversammlung kann durch Einzelanweisung oder Geschäftsordnung Geschäfte von ihrer vorherigen Zustimmung abhängig machen.

(5) Die Geschäftsführer sind ermächtigt, für die Gesellschaft bis zu ihrer Eintragung im Handelsregister (Vorgesellschaft) zu handeln, sofern das Vermögen der Gesellschaft dadurch nicht unter den Betrag des Stammkapitals gemindert wird.

(6) Dem Gesellschafter Schmitt Bürosysteme GmbH wird die Tätigkeit im Geschäftszweig der Gesellschaft gestattet.

§ 8 Jahresabschluß/Ergebnisverwendung

(1) Für die Aufstellung und Prüfung des Jahresabschlusses und des Lageberichts gelten die gesetzlichen Vorschriften.

(2) Über die Ergebnisverwendung entscheidet die Gesellschafterversammlung.

§ 9 Verdeckte Gewinnausschüttung

(1) Die Geschäftsführer dürfen außerhalb eines den gesetzlichen Vorschriften entsprechenden Gewinnverteilungsbeschlusses zugunsten von Gesellschaftern oder ihnen nahestehenden Personen oder Gesellschaften vertragsmäßig oder durch einseitige Handlung das Vermögen der Gesellschaft nicht mindern und seine Mehrung nicht verhindern.

(2) Durch Verletzung dieser Bestimmung verursachte Vorteile, einschließlich der anrechenbaren Körperschaftsteuer, hat der Begünstigte der Gesellschaft zu erstatten. Ist er nicht Gesellschafter und kann Erstattung von ihm

nicht beansprucht oder erlangt werden, so ist der ihm nahestehende Gesellschafter zum Wertausgleich verpflichtet. Die Gesellschaft ist insoweit auch zur Aufrechnung gegen künftige Gewinnansprüche berechtigt.

(3) Gesellschafterbeschlüsse über die Verwendung des Gewinns eines Jahrs, in dem verdeckte Gewinnausschüttungen stattgefunden haben, sind nichtig, sofern sie in deren Unkenntnis gefaßt worden sind. Über die Verwendung des Gewinns ist unter Berücksichtigung der verdeckten Gewinnausschüttung erneut Beschluß zu fassen.

§ 10 Dauer/Kündigung

(1) Die Gesellschaft besteht auf unbestimmte Zeit. Sie kann mit einer Frist von einem Jahr zum Ende eines Geschäftsjahrs gekündigt werden, frühestens zum Ende des 5. auf die Gründung folgenden Geschäftsjahrs.

(2) Kündigt ein Gesellschafter, ist sein Anteil gemäß § 6 zu übertragen oder einzuziehen.

§ 11 Abfindung

(1) In allen Fällen des Ausscheidens ist an den Gesellschafter eine Abfindung zu zahlen, die sich aus der Bewertung der Gesellschaft auf den Zeitpunkt des Ausscheidens ergibt. Für diesen Zeitpunkt ist eine Auseinandersetzungsbilanz zu erstellen, für die die ertragsteuerlichen Bewertungsgrundsätze gelten. Bestehende Gewinnrücklagen sowie Gewinn- und Verlustvorträge sind aufzulösen. Ein bis zum Bewertungsstichtag noch entstandener Gewinn oder Verlust ist zu berücksichtigen. Die Bewertungskontinuität zur letzten ordnungsgemäß festgestellten Jahresbilanz ist zu wahren. Ist der Verkehrswert der Gesellschaft niedriger, so gilt dieser. Diese Abfindung bleibt auch dann maßgeblich, wenn die vorausgehende oder folgende Jahresertragsteuerbilanz im Zuge einer Betriebsprüfung geändert wird, so daß später festgestellte Gewinne oder Verluste, Steuernachzahlungen oder Steuererstattungen die Höhe der Abfindung nicht beeinflussen.

(2) Sollte im Einzelfall rechtskräftig festgestellt werden, daß die Abfindung zu niedrig und die Vereinbarung deswegen rechtsunwirksam ist, so ist die niedrigste noch zulässige Abfindung zu gewähren.

(3) Besteht Streit über die Höhe der Abfindung, entscheidet hierüber ein von beiden Parteien benannter Schiedsgutachter, der Wirtschaftsprüfer oder Wirtschaftsprüfungsgesellschaft sein muß. Kommt eine Einigung über dessen Benennung nicht zustande, ist er durch die Wirtschaftsprüferkammer, Düsseldorf, zu bestimmen. Die Kosten für die Ermittlung der Höhe der Abfindung sind von der Gesellschaft und von dem ausscheidenden Gesellschafter jeweils zur Hälfte zu tragen.

(4) Die Abfindung ist in drei gleichen Jahresraten zu bezahlen, die erste Rate drei Monate nach Aufstellung der letzten Bilanz, gegebenenfalls nach Festsetzung der Abfindung gemäß Abs (3), die weiteren Raten jeweils zum Ende des ersten Kalenderquartals der folgenden Jahre. Die Abfindung ist seit dem Tag des Ausscheidens mit 2% über dem jeweiligen Diskontsatz der Deutschen Bundesbank p.a. zu verzinsen. Die Zinsen sind zusammen mit den Hauptraten zu bezahlen. Die Gesellschaft ist berechtigt, die Abfindung ganz oder teilweise früher zu bezahlen. Zur Sicherheitsleistung ist sie nicht verpflichtet.

§ 12 Geschäftsjahr/Bekanntmachungen

(1) Geschäftsjahr ist das Kalenderjahr. Das erste Geschäftsjahr ist ein Rumpfgeschäftsjahr; es endet am 31.12. des Jahrs, in dem die Gesellschaft nach Gründung ihre Geschäftstätigkeit aufgenommen hat.

(2) Bekanntmachungen der Gesellschaft erfolgen im Bundesanzeiger.

§ 13 Gründungskosten

Die Gründungskosten (Notariatsgebühren, Gerichtskosten) von ca. DM 2.000 trägt die Gesellschaft.

Articles of Association

§ 1 Business Name, Registered Office

(1) The business name of the company is Aquarius Computer (Deutschland) GmbH (the "Company").

(2) The Company shall have its registered office (Sitz) in Frankfurt am Main.

§ 2 Object of the Company

(1) The object of the Company shall be the distribution of electronic data processing equipment.

(2) The Company may engage in all such business and perform all such acts as are suited directly or indirectly to further its purpose. The Company can acquire shares in other companies.

§ 3 Share Capital, Share Capital Contributions

(1) The Company's share capital shall amount to DM 50,000.

(2) This share capital shall be assumed in the following way:

Aquarius Computer Ltd., London, England shall contribute a capital share of DM 25,000;
Schmitt Bürosysteme GmbH, Frankfurt am Main, shall contribute a capital share of DM 25,000.

The Company's share capital has been fully paid up.

§ 4 Disposition of Shares

(1) Any disposition inter vivos of shares or parts of shares in the Company require the consent of the shareholders' meeting in order to be valid. The same shall apply to the granting of sub-participations (Unterbeteiligungen) and to the creation of legal relationships by virtue of which a shareholder holds all or part of his share in trust for another person, or a shareholder's exercise of shareholder rights is subject to another person's consent in the case of that person not being a shareholder himself.

(2) Except where dispositions are made for the benefit of shareholders' spouses or descendants, the shareholders shall have no claim to such consent.

(3) A resolution approving the disposition shall require a simple majority of the votes cast.

(4) If the shareholders' meeting gives its consent to a shareholder's transferring his share, each of the other shareholders shall have a right of pre-emption except in the case specified in § 4 para. 2, and in the event that several shareholders exercise their right of pre-emption they shall do so in proportion to their respective shares in the capital. The shareholder who first exercises the right of pre-emption shall be entitled to any residual amount which may arise as a consequence of § 5 Limited Liability Companies Act (GmbHG). The time allowed for exercising the right of pre-emption shall be one month as of the last receipt of a certified copy of the purchase agreement. If the shareholders' meeting declines to consent to the sale, the shareholder in question shall have the right to retire from the Company with a period of notice of six months to the end of the year.

§ 5 Succession Upon Death

(1) The shares shall be freely inheritable.

(2) In the case of there being several successors, they may only exercise their shareholder rights through a joint authorized representative who must be either a shareholder or a member of the legal, tax consulting or auditing professions. Representation by an executor (Testamentsvollstrecker) shall

be permissible, provided that such executor is a member of one of the aforementioned professional groups. Pending the appointment of such a joint representative, the shareholder rights, with the exception of the right to participate in the profits, shall be suspended.

§ 6 Withdrawal, Compulsory Transfer

(1) The withdrawal of shares shall be permissible.

(2) The shareholders' meeting may decide by means of a resolution to withdraw a share or transfer it to the Company or to the other shareholders in proportion to their respective capital shares, if there is cause for the shareholder to be excluded from the Company, in particular by reason of violating obligations imposed by these Articles, or if the shareholder declares his retirement from the Company for cause. The shareholder in question shall have no right to vote on these resolutions.

(3) The share shall be paid for in accordance with the settlement provided for in these Articles; by the Company in the event of a withdrawal, and by the transferee in the event of a transfer.

(4) Neither the withdrawal nor the transfer shall be dependent on any consideration being given simultaneously in return therefor.

§ 7 Management, Representation

(1) The Company shall have one or more managing directors (Geschäftsführer).

(2) One managing director shall represent the Company alone as long as he is the sole managing director. Should the Company have more than one managing director, it shall be represented either by two managing directors acting jointly or by one managing director together with a Procurator (authorised signatory holding full commercial powers of representation).

(3) All or individual managing directors – and this shall include the sole managing director who holds all shares alone or together with the Company – may be given sole power of representation and/or be released from the restrictions imposed by § 181 of the German Civil Code (BGB).

(4) The shareholders' meeting may make transactions subject to its prior consent by specific direction or by its rules of procedure.

(5) The managing directors shall be authorized to act on behalf of the Company until such time as it is entered in the Commercial Register (i.e. while its status is that of a company prior to registration, "Vorgesellschaft"), provided

that the Company's assets will not thereby be reduced to an amount below its share capital.

(6) The shareholder Schmitt Bürosysteme GmbH may engage in the same type of business as the Company.

§ 8 Annual Financial Statements, Appropriation of Profits

(1) The annual financial statements and the situation report shall be prepared and audited in accordance with the relevant statutory provisions.

(2) The shareholders' meeting shall decide on the appropriation of profits.

§ 9 Hidden Distribution of Profits

(1) Unless a resolution approving the distribution of profits has been passed in compliance with the relevant statutory provisions, the managing directors shall neither by contract nor by unilateral act reduce the Company´s assets, or impede an increase thereof, for the benefit of shareholders or persons or companies associated with shareholders.

(2) Any advantage arising from a violation of the preceding provision, including any allowable corporation income tax, shall be reimbursed to the Company by the beneficiary. If the beneficiary is not a shareholder and no reimbursement can be demanded of or obtained from him, then the shareholder closely associated with the beneficiary shall have the obligation to compensate the Company with an amount equal to the value of such advantage. In this respect, the Company shall also have the right to offset its claims against future rights to a share of the profits.

(3) Shareholder resolutions on the appropriation of the profits of a year in which hidden distributions of profits were made shall be null and void if they were adopted without knowledge thereof. A new resolution on the appropriation of profits shall then be adopted, taking into account the hidden distribution.

§ 10 Duration, Termination

(1) The life of the Company shall be indefinite. It may be terminated with a period of notice of twelve (12) months to the end of a business year, however not before the end of the fifth business year following the year in which the Company was formed.

(2) The share of a shareholder who gives notice of his retirement from the Company shall be transferred or withdrawn in accordance with § 6 hereof.

§ 11 Settlement

(1) In all cases of a shareholder's retirement from the Company, the shareholder shall receive a sum determined on the basis of a valuation of the Company as of the date of such retirement by way of settlement. For this purpose, an apportioning balance sheet shall be prepared as at that date, applying income tax principles of assessment. Any existing reserves from profits and any profit or loss brought forward shall be dissolved. Any profit or loss which has arisen up to the valuation date shall be taken into account. The valuation methods applied shall be consistent with those applied in preparing the last duly approved financial statements before that date. If the market value of the Company is lower, then it shall be taken as the basis for determining the settlement amount. This settlement shall remain decisive even if the preceding or following annual tax balance sheet is altered as a result of a tax audit. Accordingly, the amount of the settlement will remain unaffected by any profit or loss or additional tax payments or tax refunds ascertained subsequently.

(2) If, in a given instance, it is established by way of a legally binding, nonappealable judgment that the amount of the settlement is too low and that, consequently, the agreement is invalid, then the lowest permissible settlement amount shall be paid.

(3) Any dispute about the amount of the settlement shall be resolved by an adjudicator appointed by both parties; the adjudicator must be a qualified German public accountant (Wirtschaftsprüfer) or public accounting firm (Wirtschaftsprüfungsgesellschaft). If no agreement can be reached on the appointment of an adjudicator, the appointment shall be made by the Chamber of Public Accountants (Wirtschaftsprüferkammer), Düsseldorf. The costs for determining the amount of the settlement shall be borne in equal shares by the Company and the retiring shareholder.

(4) The settlement shall be paid in three equal annual installments, the first payable three months after the preparation of the most recent balance sheet, or, as the case may be, after determination of the amount of the settlement in accordance with § 11 para. (3), and the further instalments payable by the end of the first calendar quarter of each of the following years. Interest on the settlement amount shall be paid together with the instalments from the date of the retirement at an annual rate of two per cent above the Deutsche Bundesbank's discount rate in effect at the time. The Company shall have the right to pay the settlement or any part thereof prior to the due dates. It shall have no obligation to furnish security.

§ 12 Business Year, Notices

(1) The business year shall be the calendar year. The first business year is a

short business year; it shall end on 31 December of the year in which the Company commences business operations following its formation.

(2) Notices to be announced by the Company shall be published in the *Federal Gazette* ("Bundesanzeiger").

§ 13 Formation Costs

The formation costs (notary's fees, court costs) of approximately DM 2,000 shall be borne by the Company.

1.5 Articles of association (long version)

Gesellschaftsvertrag

§ 1 Firma und Sitz

(1) Die Gesellschaft hat die Firma Aquarius Computer (Deutschland) GmbH.

(2) Sitz der Gesellschaft ist Frankfurt am Main.

§ 2 Gegenstand des Unternehmens

(1) Gegenstand des Unternehmens ist der Vertrieb von Geräten der elektronischen Datenverarbeitung.

(2) Die Gesellschaft darf alle Geschäfte und Handlungen vornehmen, die dem Gesellschaftszweck unmittelbar oder mittelbar zu dienen geeignet sind. Sie darf sich an anderen Gesellschaften beteiligen.

§ 3 Stammkapital/-einlagen

(1) Das Stammkapital der Gesellschaft beträgt DM 50.000.

(2) Davon übernimmt

Aquarius Computer Ltd., London, England, einen Stammanteil von DM 25.000,
Schmitt Bürosysteme GmbH, Frankfurt am Main, einen Stammanteil von DM 25.000.

(3) Das Stammkapital ist voll eingezahlt.

§ 4 Verfügungen über Geschäftsanteile/ Nachfolge von Todes wegen

(1) Verfügungen unter Lebenden über Geschäftsanteile oder Teile davon bedürfen zu ihrer Wirksamkeit der Zustimmung der Gesellschafterversammlung

mit mindestens drei Vierteln der abgegebenen Stimmen. Das gilt auch für die Einräumung von Unterbeteiligungen und die Begründung von Rechtsverhältnissen, aufgrund derer ein Gesellschafter seinen Anteil ganz oder teilweise als Treuhänder eines anderen hält oder die Ausübung seiner Gesellschafterrechte an die Zustimmung eines anderen bindet, falls dieser nicht selbst Gesellschafter ist, nicht jedoch bei Übertragung auf eine Gesellschaft, an der der verfügende Gesellschafter mehrheitlich beteiligt ist.

(2) Ein Gesellschafter, der seinen Geschäftsanteil zu veräußern beabsichtigt, ist verpflichtet, ihn zuvor den anderen Gesellschaftern in notarieller Form zum Erwerb anzubieten. Diese können das Angebot innerhalb eines Monats ab Zugang im Verhältnis ihrer Beteiligung am Stammkapital annehmen. Soweit ein Erwerbsberechtigter von seinem Erwerbsrecht nicht oder nicht fristgerecht Gebrauch macht, steht es den übrigen Gesell-schaftern im Verhältnis ihrer Beteiligung am Stammkapital zu. Die Anteile sind auf volle DM 100 nach unten abzurunden, und kein Anteil darf sich auf weniger als DM 500 belaufen. Dadurch verbleibende Spitzenbeträge ste-hen dem zu, der das Erwerbsrecht als erster ausgeübt hat.

(3) Wird das Erwerbsrecht nicht oder nur zum Teil ausgeübt, ist der Gesell-schafter berechtigt, den Geschäftsanteil abweichend von Abs (1) ohne Zu-timmung der Gesellschafter zu veräußern. Jedoch steht den anderen Gesellschaftern im Verhältnis ihrer Beteiligung am Stammkapital ein Vorkaufsrecht zu, falls der Kaufpreis niedriger ist als der nach Abs (2) geforderte. Abs (2) Satz 3 ff gelten entsprechend.

(4) Der Verkäufer hat unverzüglich sämtlichen Vorkaufsberechtigten eine voll-ständige beglaubigte Abschrift des mit dem Käufer abgeschlossenen Ver-trags zu übersenden. Das Vorkaufsrecht kann nur innerhalb eines Monats seit dessen Zugang und nur durch schriftliche Erklärung gegenüber dem Verkäufer ausgeübt werden.

(5) Die Geschäftsanteile sind frei vererblich.

(6) Mehrere Nachfolger können die Gesellschafterrechte nur durch einen gemeinsamen Bevollmächtigten ausüben, der entweder Gesellschafter oder Angehöriger eines zur Berufsverschwiegenheit verpflichteten rechts-, wirtschafts- oder steuerberatenden Berufs sein muß. Auch die Vertretung durch einen Testamentsvollstrecker ist zulässig, wenn er Angehöriger der vorgenannten Berufsgruppen ist. Bis zur Bestellung eines Bevollmächtigten ruhen die Gesellschafterrechte mit Ausnahme des Gewinnbezugsrechts.

§ 5 Wettbewerbsverbot/Schweigepflicht

(1) Kein Gesellschafter darf während seiner Zugehörigkeit und bis zwei Jahre nach seinem Ausscheiden mit der Gesellschaft unmittelbar oder mittelbar in Wettbewerb treten.

(2) Wettbewerb ist jede selbständige oder unselbständige Tätigkeit im örtlichen und sachlichen Tätigkeitsbereich der Gesellschaft.

(3) Verletzt ein Gesellschafter das Wettbewerbsverbot, so hat er für jeden Fall der Zuwiderhandlung DM 100.000 als Vertragsstrafe an die Gesellschaft zu zahlen. Bei fortgesetzter Zuwiderhandlung gelten je zwei Wochen des Verstoßes gegen das Wettbewerbsverbot als eine Zuwiderhandlung. Das Recht der Gesellschaft, Unterlassung und Schadensersatz zu verlangen, wird hierdurch nicht berührt, doch wird die Vertragsstrafe auf den Schadensersatz angerechnet.

(4) Dem Gesellschafter Schmitt Bürosysteme GmbH wird die Tätigkeit im Geschäftszweig der Gesellschaft gestattet. Als Gegenleistung für den Dispens hat er an die Gesellschaft eine laufende Vergütung in Höhe von 3% des aus seiner Tätigkeit gemäß Satz 1 erzielten Umsatzes zu zahlen. In einem gesonderten Vertrag wird eine klare und eindeutige Aufgabenabgrenzung zwischen der Gesellschaft und dem Gesellschafter Schmitt Bürosysteme GmbH vereinbart.

(5) Jeder Gesellschafter ist verpflichtet, über vertrauliche Angelegenheiten, die ihm in seiner Eigenschaft als Gesellschafter im Rahmen einer Tätigkeit für die Gesellschaft zur Kenntnis gelangen, insbesondere über die Bilanzen sowie die Verhandlungen und Beschlüsse der Gesellschafter Dritten gegenüber Stillschweigen zu bewahren. Diese Verpflichtung besteht auch nach seinem Ausscheiden fort. Die Schweigepflicht gilt nicht für die Vorlage von Bilanzen der Gesellschaft bei Banken. Außerdem darf jeder Gesellschafter vertrauliche Angelegenheiten Angehörigen eines zur Berufsverschwiegenheit verpflichteten rechts-, wirtschafts- oder steuerberatenden Berufs anvertrauen, wenn und soweit dies zur Wahrung seiner eigenen berechtigten Interessen erforderlich ist. Weitere Ausnahmen von der Schweigepflicht können im Einzelfall durch Gesellschafterbeschluß zugelassen werden.

§ 6 Einziehung/Zwangsübertragung

(1) Die Einziehung ist zulässig.

(2) Die Gesellschafterversammlung kann die Einziehung eines Geschäftsanteils oder seine Übertragung auf die Gesellschaft oder, soweit sie zur Übernahme bereit sind, auf die übrigen Gesellschafter im Verhältnis ihrer Kapitalanteile beschliessen, wenn ein Gesellschafter aus wichtigem Grund, insbesondere wegen Verletzung von Verpflichtungen aus diesem Gesellschaftsvertrag, aus der Gesellschaft ausgeschlossen werden kann oder seinen Austritt erklärt. Dem Betroffenen steht dabei kein Stimmrecht zu.

(3) Ein wichtiger Grund liegt insbesondere vor, wenn

(a) in den Geschäftsanteil eines Gesellschafters die Zwangsvollstreckung betrieben und nicht innerhalb eines Monats nach Aufforderung, spätestens bis zur Verwertung des Geschäftsanteils, aufgehoben wird,

(b) über sein Vermögen das Konkurs- oder Vergleichsverfahren eröffnet oder die Eröffnung eines solchen Verfahrens mangels Masse abgelehnt wird,

(c) er die Gesellschaft kündigt oder aus wichtigem Grund seinen Austritt aus der Gesellschaft erklärt,

(d) er seinen Geschäftsanteil ganz oder teilweise unter Verletzung des § 4 Abs (1) ohne die Zustimmung der übrigen Gesellschafter veräußert oder verpfändet,

(e) mindestens 50% der Anteile an einem Gesellschafter direkt oder indirekt in andere Hände gelangen, es sei denn, die neuen Gesellschafter sind Ehegatten oder Abkömmlinge der bisherigen Anteilseigner dieses Gesellschafters, oder der Gesellschafter wird ohne Änderung der wirtschaftlichen Struktur, insbesondere der Beteiligungsverhältnisse, nur rechtlich umgewandelt oder

(f) ein Gesellschafter gegen eine Verpflichtung aus dem Gesellschaftsverhältnis verstößt und den Verstoß trotz Abmahnung nicht unverzüglich abstellt.

(4) Für den Geschäftsanteil ist die in diesem Vertrag bestimmte Abfindung zu zahlen, bei Einziehung von der Gesellschaft, bei Übertragung vom Erwerber. Stichtag für die Auseinandersetzungsbilanz ist in diesem Falle der Tag, an dem die Erklärung über die Einziehung bzw Übertragung seines Anteils dem Gesellschafter zugeht.

(5) Einziehung und Übertragung sind nicht von einer Zug um Zug zu erbringenden Gegenleistung abhängig.

(6) Einziehung und Übertragung werden durch die Geschäftsführung erklärt.

§ 7 Geschäftsführung/Vertretung

(1) Die Gesellschaft hat einen oder mehrere Geschäftsführer.

(2) Eine Geschäftsführerin/ein Geschäftsführer ("Geschäftsführer") vertritt die Gesellschaft alleine, solange er einziger Geschäftsführer ist. Hat die Gesellschaft mehr als einen Geschäftsführer, wird sie entweder durch zwei Geschäftsführer oder durch einen Geschäftsführer mit einem Prokuristen vertreten.

(3) Alle oder einzelne Geschäftsführer können zur Alleinvertretung ermächtigt und/oder von den Beschränkungen des § 181 BGB befreit werden, und zwar auch der einzige Geschäftsführer, der allein oder mit der Gesellschaft alle Geschäftsanteile hält.

(4) Die Geschäftsführer sind ermächtigt, für die Gesellschaft bis zu ihrer Eintragung im Handelsregister (Vorgesellschaft) zu handeln, sofern das Vermögen der Gesellschaft dadurch nicht unter den Betrag des Stammkapitals gemindert wird.

(5) Der Zustimmung der Gesellschafterversammlung bedürfen

    (a) Erwerb von Grundstücken und Grundstücksrechten und Verfügungen darüber sowie entsprechende Verpflichtungsgeschäfte,

    (b) Errichtung und Aufhebung von Zweigniederlassungen,

    (c) Erwerb und Veräußerung von Beteiligungen,

    (d) Abschluß von Anstellungsverträgen, in denen eine Gewinnbeteiligung oder Altersversorgung zugesagt werden soll,

    (e) Übernahme von Bürgschaften oder ähnlichen Haftungen für Dritte,

    (f) Kreditaufnahme und -gewährung von mehr als DM 10.000 im Einzelfall außerhalb des Kunden- bzw Lieferantenkontokorrents,

    (g) alle Geschäfte und Handlungen, die der Betrieb der Gesellschaft nicht gewöhnlich mit sich bringt.

Die Gesellschafterversammlung kann durch Einzelanweisung oder Geschäftsordnung weitere Geschäfte von ihrer vorherigen Zustimmung abhängig machen.

(6) § 5 gilt für den Geschäftsführer sinngemäß.

§ 8 Jahresabschluß/Ergebnisverwendung

(1) Der Jahresabschluß ist von den Geschäftsführern nach den handelsrechtlichen Vorschriften und innerhalb der Fristen, die nach dem HGB für große Kapitalgesellschaften gelten, aufzustellen. Bei der Aufstellung des Jahresabschlusses sind die steuerrechtlichen Vorschriften zu beachten, soweit dies handelsrechtlich zulässig ist.

(2) Der Jahresabschluß ist durch den gewählten Abschlußprüfer nach den Grundsätzen des HGB für große Kapitalgesellschaften zu prüfen.

(3) Unverzüglich nach Eingang des Prüfungsberichtes hat die Geschäftsführung den Jahresabschluß und den Prüfungsbericht sowie den der

Gesellschafterversammlung zu unterbreitenden Vorschlag über die Verwendung des Jahresergebnisses dem Aufsichtsrat und sodann mit dessen Stellungnahme der Gesellschafterversammlung zur Beschlußfassung vorzulegen.

(4) Mit der Einladung zur Gesellschafterversammlung, die über die Feststellung des Jahresabschlusses beschließt, sind jedem Gesellschafter Abschriften der in Abs (3) genannten Unterlagen zu übersenden.

(5) Für die Ergebnisverwendung gilt § 29 GmbHG.

§ 9 Verdeckte Gewinnausschüttung

(1) Die Geschäftsführer dürfen außerhalb eines den gesetzlichen Vorschriften entsprechenden Gewinnverteilungsbeschlusses zugunsten von Gesellschaftern oder ihnen nahestehenden Personen oder Gesellschaften vertragsmäßig oder durch einseitige Handlung das Vermögen der Gesellschaft nicht mindern und seine Mehrung nicht verhindern.

(2) Durch Verletzung dieser Bestimmung verursachte Vorteile, einschließlich der anrechenbaren Körperschaftsteuer, hat der Begünstigte der Gesellschaft zu erstatten. Ist er nicht Gesellschafter und kann Erstattung von ihm nicht beansprucht oder erlangt werden, so ist der ihm nahestehende Gesellschafter zum Wertausgleich verpflichtet. Die Gesellschaft ist insoweit auch zur Aufrechnung gegen künftige Gewinnansprüche berechtigt.

(3) Gesellschafterbeschlüsse über die Verwendung des Gewinnes eines Jahrs, in dem verdeckte Gewinnausschüttungen stattgefunden haben, sind nichtig, sofern sie in deren Unkenntnis gefaßt worden sind. Über die Verwendung des Gewinns ist unter Berücksichtigung der verdeckten Gewinnausschüttung erneut Beschluß zu fassen.

§ 10 Gesellschafterversammlungen

(1) Der Gesellschafterversammlung obliegt insbesondere die Beschlußfassung über die

(a) Feststellung des geprüften und testierten Jahresabschlusses und die Verwendung des Jahresergebnisses,

(b) Entlastung der Geschäftsführer und der Mitglieder des Aufsichtsrats,

(c) Wahl des Abschlußprüfers, der Wirtschaftsprüfer oder eine Wirtschaftsprüfungsgesellschaft sein soll,

(d) Änderung des Gesellschaftsvertrags,

(e) Zustimmung zur Verfügung über Gesellschaftsanteile,

(f) Einziehung und

(g) Zwangsübertragung von Geschäftsanteilen,

(h) Auflösung der Gesellschaft und

(i) Maßnahmen, die über den gewöhnlichen Geschäftsbetrieb hinausgehen oder bei denen Rechte der Gesellschaft gegenüber den Geschäftsführern geltend zu machen sind.

(2) In jedem Geschäftsjahr findet spätestens zwei Monate nach Prüfung des Jahresabschlusses für das vorangegangene Geschäftsjahr eine ordentliche Gesellschafterversammlung statt, deren Tagesordnung mindestens die in Abs (1) a), b) und c) genannten Punkte umfaßt. Die Gesellschafterversammlung tritt außerdem zusammen, wenn nach diesem Vertrag oder nach den gesetzlichen Bestimmungen eine Beschlußfassung erforderlich wird oder auf Verlangen der Geschäftsführer oder von Gesellschaftern, die allein oder zusammen mindestens ein Zehntel des Stammkapitals vertreten.

(3) Die Gesellschafterversammlungen finden am Sitz der Gesellschaft oder an einem anderen Ort statt, dem alle Gesellschafter zustimmen.

(4) Der Abhaltung einer Gesellschafterversammlung bedarf es nicht, wenn sich sämtliche Gesellschafter mit schriftlicher, fernschriftlicher, telegrafischer oder Beschlußfassung durch Telefax einverstanden erklären oder sich an ihr beteiligen.

(5) Die Gesellschafterversammlung wird durch die Geschäftsführer durch eingeschriebenen Brief mit Rückschein an alle Gesellschafter unter Mitteilung der Tagesordnung einberufen, der mindestens zwei Wochen vor dem Tag der Gesellschafterversammlung zugegangen sein muß. Mit Zustimmung aller Gesellschafter kann auf die Einhaltung von Form und Frist der Einberufung verzichtet werden.

(6) Den Vorsitz in der Gesellschafterversammlung führt der vor Eintritt in die Tagesordnung unter der Leitung des ältesten Gesellschafters/ Gesellschaftervertreters gewählte Versammlungsleiter. Hat die Gesellschaft einen Aufsichtsrat, obliegt dessen Vorsitzendem die Versammlungsleitung. Der Versammlungsleiter stellt die Beschlußfähigkeit der Gesellschafterversammlung fest und entscheidet über die Art der Abstimmung, sofern die Gesellschafterversammlung nicht etwas anderes beschließt.

(7) Jeder Gesellschafter kann sich in der Gesellschafterversammlung durch einen schriftlich bevollmächtigten Mitgesellschafter, leitenden Mitarbeiter seines Unternehmens oder Angehörigen eines gesetzlich zur Berufsverschwiegenheit verpflichteten rechts-, wirtschafts- oder steuerberatenden Berufs vertreten oder begleiten lassen.

§ 11 Gesellschafterbeschlüsse

(1) Über die von den Gesellschaftern zu treffenden Bestimmungen werden Beschlüsse gefaßt. Je DM 100 eines Geschäftsanteils gewähren eine Stimme. Für Geschäftsanteile, die der Gesellschaft gehören, ruht das Stimmrecht.

(2) Beschlüsse kommen mit einfacher Mehrheit der abgegebenen Stimmen zustande, falls nicht das Gesetz oder die Satzung eine höhere Mehrheit vorschreibt. Beschlüsse gemäß §§ 4, 5 und 6 bedürfen einer Mehrheit von drei Vierteln der abgegebenen Stimmen. Die einmalige Wiederholung der Abstimmung in derselben Gesellschafterversammlung ist zulässig.

(3) Die Gesellschafterversammlung ist beschlußfähig, wenn mindestens drei Viertel des stimmberechtigten Kapitals anwesend oder vertreten sind. Andernfalls ist, wiederum mit einer Frist von zwei Wochen, eine neue Gesellschafterversammlung einzuberufen, die für die Gegenstände der Tagesordnung der Gesellschafterversammlung, in der sich die Beschlußunfähigkeit ergeben hat, ohne Rücksicht auf die vertretenen Stimmen beschlußfähig ist; hierauf ist bei der Einberufung hinzuweisen.

(4) Soweit rechtlich zulässig und nicht in diesem Vertrag anders bestimmt, ist ein Gesellschafter auch dann stimmberechtigt, wenn die Beschlußfassung die Vornahme eines Rechtsgeschäfts oder die Einleitung oder Erledigung eines Rechtsstreits mit ihm oder mit einem ihm im Sinne des § 17 AktG verbundenen Unternehmen betrifft.

(5) Über die Beschlüsse der Gesellschafterversammlung ist eine Niederschrift anzufertigen, von dem Vorsitzenden der Gesellschafterversammlung zu unterzeichnen und allen Gesellschaftern eine Abschrift zu übersenden. Die Belege über die rechtzeitige Einladung sind aufzubewahren. Bei anderen Beschlüssen ist über den Inhalt, das Abstimmungsverfahren und das Abstimmungsergebnis ein Vermerk anzufertigen, von allen Geschäftsführern zu unterschreiben und allen Gesellschaftern durch eingeschriebenen Brief in Abschrift zu übersenden.

(6) Bei Kapitalerhöhungen sind zur Übernahme des neuen Kapitals zunächst die Gesellschafter im Verhältnis ihrer bisherigen Geschäftsanteile zuzulassen.

§ 12 Anfechtung

Versammlungsbeschlüsse können nur innerhalb von drei Monaten seit der Beschlußfassung und nur unter den Voraussetzungen des § 245 Nr. 1, 2 AktG durch Klage angefochten werden, andere Beschlüsse innerhalb derselben Frist ab der Absendung des Vermerks gem § 11 Abs (5). Das gleiche gilt für die Geltendmachung der Unwirksamkeit von Gesellschafterbeschlüssen.

<u>§ 13 Aufsichtsrat</u>

(1) Die Gesellschaft hat vorbehaltlich Absatz (11) einen Aufsichtsrat. Er besteht aus drei bis neun Mitgliedern, die von der Gesellschafterversammlung bestellt und abberufen werden und aus ihrer Mitte den Vorsitzenden und einen Stellvertreter wählen. Der Vorsitzende, bei Verhinderung der Stellvertreter, vertreten den Aufsichtsrat nach außen und sind ermächtigt, die zur Durchführung der Beschlüsse des Aufsichtsrats erforderlichen Willenserklärungen abzugeben.

(2) Mitglied des Aufsichtsrats kann auch sein, wer an der Gesellschaft nicht beteiligt ist, jedoch nicht, wer

    (a) Geschäftsführer oder Arbeitnehmer der Gesellschaft ist oder

    (b) Organ oder Arbeitnehmer eines Unternehmens, an dessen Kapital die Gesellschaft zu mehr als einem Viertel unmittelbar oder mittelbar beteiligt oder deren Komplementärin sie ist.

(3) Gesellschafter oder Gruppen von Gesellschaftern, die am Stammkapital mit mindestens 20% beteiligt sind, haben das Recht auf Entsendung eines Vertreters in den Aufsichtsrat. Ist ein Entsendungsrecht nicht eine Woche vor einer anstehenden Wahl ausgeübt, entscheiden die Gesellschafter durch Wahl.

(4) Die Aufsichtsratsmitglieder werden jeweils für die Zeit bis zur Beendigung der ordentlichen Gesellschafterversammlung bestellt, die über ihre Entlastung für das vierte volle Geschäftsjahr seit ihrer Bestellung beschließt. Wiederbestellung ist zulässig. Die Amtszeit endet nicht vor der Neu-oder Wiederbestellung. Stellt ein entsandtes Aufsichtsratsmitglied sein Amt zur Verfügung oder scheidet es aus einem anderen Grund aus, so hat der zur Entsendung Berechtigte unverzüglich ein neues Aufsichtsratsmitglied zu entsenden.

(5) Der Aufsichtsrat wird durch seinen Vorsitzenden oder zwei seiner Mitglieder einberufen. Für den Aufsichtsrat gelten im übrigen die Bestimmungen über Gesellschafterversammlungen entsprechend.

(6) Jedes Aufsichtsratsmitglied kann sich in einer Aufsichtsratssitzung, an der teilzunehmen es verhindert ist, durch ein anderes Aufsichtsratsmitglied vertreten lassen. Der Vertreter muß spätestens zwei Tage vor der betreffenden Aufsichtsratssitzung eine schriftliche Vollmacht vorlegen, die zu den Akten zu nehmen ist. Das verhinderte Aufsichtsratsmitglied kann auch in diesem Fall seinen Berater gem § 10 Abs (7) an der Sitzung teilnehmen lassen. Ist dasselbe Aufsichtsratsmitglied dreimal hintereinander verhindert, müssen der/die entsendenden Gesellschafter innerhalb eines Monats

eine andere Person in den Aufsichtsrat entsenden. Anderenfalls entscheiden die übrigen Aufsichtsratsmitglieder allein. Sofern in diesem Falle nur zwei Aufsichtsratsmitglieder vorhanden sind, kann der Aufsichtsrat nur einstimmig entscheiden.

(7) Der Aufsichtsrat vertritt die Gesellschaft gegenüber den Geschäftsführern. Er berät und überwacht die Geschäftsführung und berät die Gesellschafterversammlung, die ihm die Wahrung von Rechten der Gesellschafterversammlung übertragen kann. Er hat das Recht auf Einberufung der Gesellschafterversammlung.

(8) Der Aufsichtsrat gibt sich eine Geschäftsordnung. Er kann aus seiner Mitte Ausschüsse bilden, deren Aufgaben und Befugnisse festsetzen und ihnen Entscheidungsbefugnisse übertragen.

(9) Die baren Auslagen der Mitglieder des Aufsichtsrats werden ersetzt. Über eine Vergütung beschließt die Gesellschafterversammlung.

(10) Die Mitglieder des Aufsichtsrats sind nach Maßgabe des § 93 AktG zur Verschwiegenheit verpflichtet. Im übrigen ist § 52 GmbHG, soweit zulässig, ausgeschlossen.

(11) Die Gesellschafterversammlung kann die vorstehenden Bestimmungen zeitweise außer Kraft setzen und von der Bestellung eines Aufsichtsrats absehen, indem sie keinen Aufsichtsrat wählt. Die in dieser Satzung geregelten Befugnisse des Aufsichtsrats stehen dann der Gesellschafterversammlung zu.

§ 14 Dauer/Kündigung

(1) Die Gesellschaft besteht auf unbestimmte Zeit. Jeder Gesellschafter kann sie unter Einhaltung einer Frist von 12 Monaten zum Ende eines Geschäftsjahrs kündigen, erstmals jedoch zum 31.12.2000. Die Kündigung ist durch eingeschriebenen Brief mit Rückschein gegenüber der Gesellschaft zu erklären, die jeden Gesellschafter unverzüglich unterrichten soll.

(2) Jeder Gesellschafter kann die Gesellschaft aus wichtigem Grund ohne Einhaltung einer Frist kündigen. Abs (1) Satz 3 gilt entsprechend. Ein wichtiger Grund ist insbesondere gegeben, wenn die Gesellschaft die Zahlungen einstellt oder gegen die Gesellschaft Antrag auf Eröffnung des Konkurs-oder gerichtlichen Vergleichsverfahrens gestellt wird.

(3) Die Gesellschaft wird, außer in den Fällen des Abs (2) Satz 3, durch eine Kündigung nicht aufgelöst, sondern von den übrigen Gesellschaftern fortgesetzt.

(4) Jeder Gesellschafter hat das Recht, sich jeder Kündigung innerhalb 12 Wochen mit Wirkung auf denselben Stichtag anzuschließen.

§ 15 Abfindung

(1) In allen Fällen des Ausscheidens ist an den Gesellschafter eine Abfindung zu zahlen, die sich aus der Bewertung der Gesellschaft auf den Zeitpunkt des Ausscheidens ergibt. Für diesen Zeitpunkt ist eine Auseinandersetzungsbilanz zu erstellen, für die die ertragsteuerlichen Bewertungsgrundsätze gelten. Bestehende Gewinnrücklagen sowie Gewinn- und Verlustvorträge sind aufzulösen. Ein bis zum Bewertungsstichtag noch entstandener Gewinn oder Verlust ist zu berücksichtigen. Die Bewertungskontinuität zur letzten ordnungsgemäß festgestellten Jahresbilanz ist zu wahren. Ist der Verkehrswert der Gesellschaft niedriger, so gilt dieser. Diese Abfindung bleibt auch dann maßgeblich, wenn die vorausgehende oder folgende Jahresertragsteuerbilanz im Zuge einer Betriebsprüfung geändert wird, so daß später festgestellte Gewinne oder Verluste, Steuernachzahlungen oder Steuererstattungen die Höhe der Abfindung nicht beeinflussen.

(2) Sollte im Einzelfall rechtskräftig festgestellt werden, daß diese Abfindung zu niedrig und die Vereinbarung deswegen rechtsunwirksam ist, so ist die niedrigste noch zulässige Abfindung zu gewähren.

(3) Besteht Streit über die Höhe der Abfindung, entscheidet hierüber ein von beiden Parteien benannter Schiedsgutachter, der Wirtschaftsprüfer oder Wirtschaftsprüfungsgesellschaft sein muß. Kommt eine Einigung über dessen Benennung nicht zustande, ist er durch die Wirtschaftsprüferkammer, Düsseldorf, zu bestimmen.

(4) Die Abfindung ist in drei gleichen Jahresraten zu bezahlen, die erste Rate drei Monate nach Aufstellung der letzten Bilanz, gegebenenfalls nach Festsetzung der Abfindung gemäß Abs (3), die weiteren Raten jeweils zum Ende des ersten Kalenderquartals der folgenden Jahre. Die Abfindung ist seit dem Tag des Ausscheidens mit 2% über dem jeweiligen Diskontsatz der Deutschen Bundesbank p.a. zu verzinsen. Die Zinsen sind zusammen mit den Hauptraten zu bezahlen. Die Gesellschaft ist berechtigt, die Abfindung ganz oder teilweise früher zu bezahlen. Zur Sicherheitsleistung ist sie nicht verpflichtet.

§ 16 Geschäftsjahr/Bekanntmachungen

(1) Geschäftsjahr ist das Kalenderjahr. Das erste Geschäftsjahr ist ein Rumpfgeschäftsjahr; es endet am 31.12. des Jahrs, in dem die Gesellschaft nach Gründung ihre Geschäftätigkeit aufgenommen hat.

(2) Bekanntmachungen der Gesellschaft erfolgen im Bundesanzeiger.

§ 17 Teilunwirksamkeit/Vertragsänderungen

(1) Sollte eine Bestimmung dieses Vertrags oder eine künftig in ihn aufgenommene Bestimmung ganz oder teilweise unwirksam oder undurchführbar sein oder die Wirksamkeit oder Durchführbarkeit später verlieren oder sich eine Lücke herausstellen, soll hierdurch die Gültigkeit der übrigen Bestimmungen nicht berührt werden. Anstelle der unwirksamen oder undurchführbaren Bestimmung oder zur Ausfüllung der Lücke gilt eine angemessene Regelung, die, soweit rechtlich zulässig, dem am nächsten kommt, was die Vertragsschließenden gewollt haben oder nach dem Sinn und Zweck des Vertrags gewollt hätten, falls sie den Punkt bedacht hätten. Betrifft der Mangel notwendige Satzungsbestandteile, ist eine solche Regelung nach Maßgabe des § 53 Abs (2) GmbHG zu vereinbaren.

(2) Beruht die Unwirksamkeit oder Undurchführbarkeit einer Bestimmung auf einem darin festgelegten Maß der Leistung oder der Zeit (Frist oder Termin), so ist mit einfacher Mehrheit der abgegebenen Stimmen das der Bestimmung am nächsten kommende rechtlich zulässige Maß zu vereinbaren.

(3) Alle das Gesellschaftsverhältnis betreffenden Vereinbarungen zwischen Gesellschaftern oder zwischen Gesellschaft und Gesellschaftern bedürfen zu ihrer Wirksamkeit der Schriftform, soweit sie nicht eines Gesellschafterbeschlusses oder notarieller Beurkundung bedürfen. Das gilt auch für einen etwaigen Verzicht auf das Erfordernis der Schriftform.

§ 18 Gründungskosten

Die Gründungskosten (Notariatsgebühren, Gerichtskosten) von ca. DM 2.000 trägt die Gesellschaft.

§ 19 Gerichtsstand

Gerichtsstand für alle Auseinandersetzungen der Gesellschafter miteinander und mit der Gesellschaft ist der Sitz der Gesellschaft.

Articles of Association

§ 1 Business Name; Registered Office

(1) The business name of the company is Aquarius Computer (Deutschland) GmbH (the "Company").

(2) The Company shall have its registered office (Sitz) in Frankfurt am Main.

§ 2 Object of the Company

(1) The object of the Company shall be the distribution of electronic data processing equipment.

(2) The Company may engage in all such business and do all such acts as are suited directly or indirectly to further its purpose. The Company may acquire shares in other companies.

§ 3 Share Capital; Share Capital Contributions

(1) The Company's share capital shall amount to DM 50,000.

(2) This share capital shall be assumed in the following way:

- Aquarius Computer Ltd., London, England, shall contribute a capital share of DM 25,000;
- Schmitt Bürosysteme GmbH, Frankfurt am Main, shall contribute a capital share of DM 25,000.

(3) The Company's share capital has been fully paid up.

§ 4 Disposition of Shares; Succession Upon Death

(1) Any disposition inter vivos of shares or parts of shares shall for its validity require the consent of the shareholders' meeting by at least a three quarters' majority of the votes cast. The same shall apply to the granting of sub-participations (Unterbeteiligungen) and to the creation of legal relationships by virtue of which a shareholder holds all or part of his share in trust for another person, or binds the exercise of his shareholder rights to another person's consent in the case of that person who is not a shareholder himself; it shall not apply, however, to the transfer to a company in which the disposing shareholder holds a majority interest.

(2) A shareholder who intends to sell his share shall be required first to offer it in notarial form to the other shareholders for sale. These shareholders may accept this offer within one month of receipt thereof, each in proportion to his participation in the share capital. If this right to purchase is not exercised, or not exercised in good time, by a party entitled to acquire the share, it shall pass to the other shareholders in proportion to their respective interests in the share capital. The shares shall be rounded off to full amounts of DM 100, and no share may amount to less than DM 500. The shareholder who first exercises the option to purchase shall be entitled to any residual amounts that arise as a result.

(3) If the right to purchase is not exercised, or is exercised only in part, the shareholder shall have the right – notwithstanding § 4 para. 1 – to sell the

share without the consent of the shareholders. However, the other shareholders are entitled to a right of pre-emption in proportion to their respective interest in the share capital if the purchase price is lower than the price asked under the terms of § 4 para. 2. Sentences 3 et seq. of § 4 para. 2 shall apply by analogy.

(4) The vendor shall send a complete and certified copy of the contract concluded with the buyer to all parties that have a right of pre-emption without undue delay. The rights of pre-emption may only be exercised within one month of receipt of the said copy of the contract and in the form of a written statement to the vendor.

(5) The shares shall be freely inheritable.

(6) In the case of there being several successors, these may only exercise the shareholder rights through a joint authorized representative who must be either a shareholder or a member of the legal, tax consulting or auditing professions. Representation by an executor (Testamentsvollstrecker) shall also be permissible, provided that such executor is a member of one of the aforementioned professional groups. Pending the appointment of such a joint representative, the shareholder rights, with the exception of the right to participate in the profits, shall be suspended.

§ 5 Restraint of Competition; Duty of Confidentiality

(1) No shareholder may, during the time of his membership of the Company and for a period of two years thereafter, directly or indirectly enter into competition with the Company.

(2) "Competition" shall be defined as engaging in any activity, whether self-employed or employed, in the geographical area and the field of activity of the Company.

(3) If a shareholder violates this restraint of competition, he shall in each instance pay a contractual penalty of DM 100,000 to the Company. In the event of continued contravention, every two-week period of an ongoing contravention shall count as a single instance of contravention. This provision shall not affect the Company's right to demand that the shareholder refrain from such conduct and pay damages, but the contractual penalty shall be set off against the compensation.

(4) The shareholder Schmitt Bürosysteme GmbH may engage in the same type of business as the Company. By way of consideration of this dispensation, he shall pay the Company a continuous compensation amounting to three per cent of the turnover generated by his activities referred to in sentence

1. The scope of activity shall be clearly defined and delimited in a separate contract between the Company and Schmitt Bürosysteme GmbH.

(5) Each shareholder shall have the duty not to disclose to any third party any confidential information of which he, in his capacity as shareholder, may obtain knowledge in the course of any activity on behalf of the Company, in particular relating to information concerning the balance sheets as well as the proceedings and resolutions of the shareholders. This duty shall continue in effect after his retirement from the Company. The duty of confidentiality shall not apply to the presentation of the Company's balance sheets to banks. Moreover, the shareholders may, if and to the extent to which this is necessary in order to safeguard their own legitimate interests, disclose confidential information to members of the legal, tax consulting or auditing professions, who are subject to a professional duty of secrecy. In individual cases, the shareholders' meeting may resolve to grant further exemptions from the duty of confidentiality.

§ 6 Withdrawal; Compulsory Transfer

(1) The withdrawal of shares shall be permissible.

(2) The shareholders' meeting may decide by means of a resolution to withdraw a share or transfer it to the Company or – to the extent that they agree – to the other shareholders in proportion to their respective capital shares, if there is cause for a shareholder to be excluded from the Company, in particular by violating obligations imposed by these Articles, or if the shareholder declares his retirement from the Company for cause. The shareholder in question shall have no right to vote on these resolutions.

(3) Cause exists, in particular, in any of the following events:

    (a) If execution is levied upon a shareholder's share and such execution is not cancelled within one month of a demand to this effect or, at the latest, by the time the share is realized;

    (b) if bankruptcy or composition proceedings are instituted against a shareholder's assets, or if the institution of such proceedings is denied for lack of assets;

    (c) if a shareholder gives notice to terminate, or declares his retirement from the Company for cause;

    (d) if a shareholder, in violation of § 4 para. 1, sells or pledges all or part of his share in the Company without the other shareholders' consent;

    (e) if at least fifty per cent of the shares in a shareholder directly or indirectly changes hands, except in the case where either the new holders of such interests are spouses or descendants of the previous holders of such shares in that shareholder, or where that shareholder is transformed merely in terms of its legal form and without changing its economic structure, in particular without changing the proportion of the shareholdings therein; or

(f) if a shareholder breaches any obligation arising from the Company relationship and, despite having been warned, fails to discontinue such a breach without undue delay.

(4) The share shall be paid for in accordance with the settlement provided for in these Articles; by the Company in the event of a withdrawal, and by the transferee in the event of a transfer. The relevant date for the apportioning balance sheet shall in this case be the date on which the shareholder receives the notice of withdrawal or transfer, as the case may be, of his share.

(5) Neither the withdrawal nor the transfer shall be dependent on any consideration being given simultaneously in return therefor.

(6) Both withdrawal and transfer shall be declared by the management.

§ 7 Management; Representation

(1) The Company shall have one or more managing directors (Geschäftsführer).

(2) A managing director shall represent the Company alone as long as he is the sole managing director. Should the Company have more than one managing director, it shall be represented either by two managing directors acting jointly or by one managing director together with a Procurator (authorized signatory holding full commercial powers of representation).

(3) All or individual managing directors – and this shall include the sole managing director who holds all shares alone or together with the Company – may be given sole power of representation and/or be released from the restrictions imposed by § 181 of the German Civil Code (BGB).

(4) The managing directors shall be authorized to act on behalf of the Company until such time as it is entered in the commercial register (i.e. while its status is that of a company prior to registration, "Vorgesellschaft"), provided that the Company's assets will not thereby be reduced to an amount below its share capital.

(5) The following shall require the consent of the shareholders' meeting:

(a) The purchase of real property or of interests in real property, the disposition thereof, as well as any corresponding transactions constituting executory agreements.

(b) The establishment and closure of branch offices.

(c) The acquisition and sale of interests in other companies.

(d) The conclusion of employment contracts that are intended to contain a promise regarding profit participation or pension payments.

(e) The assumption of guarantees or similar liabilities for third parties.

(f) The taking up or grant of loans in excess of DM 10,000 in any one case, except on current accounts of customers or suppliers.

(g) All such transactions and acts as are not ordinarily brought about by the operation of the Company.

The shareholders' meeting may make other transactions contingent upon its prior consent by specific instruction or by its rules of procedure.

(6) The provisions of § 5 shall apply to the managing director by analogy.

<u>§ 8 Annual Financial Statements;</u>
<u>Appropriation of Profits</u>

(1) The annual financial statements shall be prepared by the managing directors in accordance with the provisions of commercial law and within the time limits applicable to large corporations under the Commercial Code (HGB). In the preparation the annual financial statements, the provisions of tax law shall be observed to the extent permissible under commercial law.

(2) The annual financial statements shall be audited by the appointed auditor (Abschlußprüfer) in accordance with the principles set out in the Commercial Code for large corporations.

(3) After receiving the auditor's report, the managing directors shall without undue delay present the Supervisory Board with the annual financial statements and the auditor's report as well as the proposal for the appropriation of the profits that is to be submitted to the shareholders' meeting, and then together with the comments of the supervisory board, submit these to the shareholders' meeting for adoption of a resolution thereon.

(4) Copies of the documents referred to in § 8 para. 3 shall be sent to the shareholders together with the invitation to the shareholders' meeting which decides on the adoption of the annual financial statements.

(5) The provisions of § 29 Limited Liability Companies Act (GmbHG) shall apply to the appropriation of profits.

§ 9 Hidden Distribution of Profits

(1) Unless a resolution approving the distribution of profits has been adopted in compliance with the relevant statutory provisions, the managing directors may neither by contract nor unilateral act reduce the Company's assets, or impede an increase thereof, for the benefit of shareholders or persons or companies associated with shareholders.

(2) Any advantage arising from a violation of the foregoing provision, including any allowable corporation tax, shall be reimbursed to the Company by the beneficiary. If the beneficiary is not a shareholder and no reimbursement can be demanded of or obtained from him, then the shareholder associated with the beneficiary shall have the obligation to compensate the Company with an amount equal to the value of such advantage. In this respect, the Company shall also have the right to offset its claims against future rights to a share of the profits.

(3) Shareholder resolutions on the appropriation of the profits of a year in which hidden distributions of profit were made shall be null and void if they were adopted without knowledge thereof. A new resolution shall then be adopted on the appropriation of profits, taking into account the hidden distribution.

§ 10 Shareholders' Meetings

(1) It is incumbent on the shareholders' meeting to adopt resolutions in particular on the following:

(a) Adoption of the audited and attested annual financial statements, and the appropriation of the net annual profits;

(b) Discharge of the managing directors and the members of the supervisory board;

(c) Appointment of the auditor (Abschlußprüfer), who shall be a qualified public accountant (Wirtschaftsprüfer) or public accounting firm (Wirtschaftsprüfungsgesellschaft);

(d) Any amendment of the Articles of Association;

(e) Consent to any disposition of shares;

(f) Withdrawal and

(g) Compulsory transfer of shares;

(h) Dissolution of the Company; and

(i) Any measure that exceeds the ordinary course of business or involves the assertion of rights of the Company vis-à-vis the managing directors.

(2) An ordinary shareholders' meeting shall be held every business year within two months of the audit of the annual financial statements for the preceding business year. The agenda shall include at least the items mentioned in § 10 para. 1 (a), (b), and (c). A shareholders' meeting shall also be convened if a resolution is required under these Articles or by law, or if requested by the managing directors or by shareholders who either alone or together represent one tenth (1/10) or more of the share capital.

(3) The shareholders' meetings shall be held at the registered office of the Company or at such other place as all the shareholders may agree upon.

(4) A shareholders' meeting need not be held if all the shareholders agree to, or take part in, the adoption of resolutions by letter, telex, cable or fax.

(5) Shareholders' meetings shall be called by the managing directors by a letter to all shareholders, sent by registered mail, requiring confirmation of receipt. The invitation to the meeting shall set forth the agenda and must have been received by the shareholders at least two weeks before the date of the shareholders' meeting. If all shareholders agree, compliance with the form and time requirements for the calling of a meeting may be waived.

(6) The shareholders' meetings shall be chaired by the chairman elected under the direction of the most senior shareholder/shareholder representative prior to proceeding to the business of the meeting. If the Company has a supervisory board, the chairman of the supervisory board shall preside over the meeting. The chairman of the shareholders' meeting shall establish whether there is a quorum, and shall decide on the form of voting, unless the shareholders' meeting resolves otherwise.

(7) Every shareholder may be represented at a shareholders' meeting or accompanied by another shareholder, a senior officer of his enterprise, or a member of the legal, tax consulting or auditing professions by law bound to secrecy by law, provided that they are authorized with a written power of attorney.

§ 11 Shareholder Resolutions

(1) Resolutions shall be adopted on all matters to be decided by the shareholders. Each DM 100 of a share shall grant one vote. The right to vote is suspended for shares which belong to the Company.

(2) Resolutions shall be adopted by simple majority of the votes cast, unless a larger majority is required by law or by these Articles. Resolutions pursuant to §§ 4,5 and 6 shall require a three quarters' majority of the votes cast. Voting may be repeated once at a shareholders' meeting.

(3) The shareholders' meeting shall have a quorum if at least three quarters of the voting capital is present or represented. Failing this, a new shareholders' meeting shall be called, again with two weeks' notice. Such a second shareholders' meeting shall, without regard to the number of votes present or represented, be quorate to pass resolutions on the items that were on the agenda of the shareholders' meeting at which there was a lack of quorum; the shareholders shall be advised thereof in the notice calling the meeting.

(4) To the extent legally permissible, and unless otherwise provided in these Articles, a shareholder shall be entitled to vote even if the resolution to be adopted relates to a legal transaction, or the commencement or discharge of a lawsuit, with him or with an affiliated enterprise as defined in § 17 Stock Corporation Act (AktG).

(5) Minutes of the resolutions adopted by the shareholders' meeting shall be prepared and signed by the chairman of the shareholders' meeting, and a copy thereof shall be sent to each shareholder. Proof that the invitation to the shareholders' meeting was sent off in good time shall be kept on file. On resolutions other than those adopted at a shareholders' meeting, a memorandum shall be drawn up stating the contents of the resolution, the voting procedure, and the outcome of the vote; the memorandum shall be signed by all managing directors, and a copy thereof shall be sent by registered mail to each shareholder.

(6) In the event of increases in share capital, the shareholders shall have subscription rights to the new capital which they may exercise in proportion to the shares they have hitherto held.

§ 12 Rescission

Resolutions adopted by the shareholders' meetings may be challenged by legal action only within three months from their adoption and only if the requirements of § 245 nos. 1 and 2 AktG are fulfilled, and other resolutions only within three months from the date of mailing of the memorandum pursuant to § 11 para. 5 hereof. The same shall apply to any action asserting the invalidity of shareholders' resolutions.

§ 13 Supervisory Board

(1) Subject to § 13 para. 11, the Company shall have a Supervisory Board. It shall consist of three to nine members whose appointment and removal shall be incumbent on the shareholders' meeting, and it shall elect its chairman and a deputy chairman from among its members. The chairman or, in his absence, the deputy chairman shall represent the supervisory board vis-à-vis third parties and be authorized to give the declarations of intent requisite for implementing the resolutions of the supervisory board.

(2) Persons who do not hold shares in the Company can be members of the supervisory board, but not such persons as are

    (a) managing directors or employees of the Company, or

    (b) members of an executive body, or employees, of an enterprise in which the Company directly or indirectly holds an interest of twenty-five per cent or more, or of which the Company is a personally liable partner.

(3) Shareholders, or groups of shareholders, holding twenty per cent or more of the share capital shall have the right to delegate a representative to the Supervisory Board. If no representative has been delegated prior to one week before an election, then these shareholders or groups of shareholders shall decide by vote.

(4) The members of the supervisory board shall be appointed in each case for a period ending at the end of the ordinary shareholders' meeting at which a resolution is adopted concerning their discharge during the fourth full business year since their appointment. They may be appointed for further terms of office. No term of office shall end prior to the appointment of a new member or appointment for a further term. If a delegated member of the supervisory board hands in his resignation, or for some other reason retires from office, a new member shall be delegated to the supervisory board by the person or persons entitled to do so, without undue delay.

(5) Meetings of the supervisory board shall be called by its chairman or two of its members. As for the rest, the provisions relating to shareholders' meetings shall apply by analogy.

(6) Each member of the supervisory board may authorize another member to represent him at any meeting of the supervisory board that he is unable to attend. The representative shall present a written proxy two days before the supervisory board meeting in question. It shall be kept on file. In this case, too, the supervisory board member unable to attend the meeting may have his adviser take part therein in accordance with § 10 para. 7. In the event that one and the same member of the supervisory board is unable to attend three consecutive meetings, the shareholders who delegated that member shall delegate a different person to the supervisory board within one month. Failing this, the other supervisory board members shall decide by themselves. If, in such a case, there are only two supervisory board members present, that decision must be unanimous.

(7) The supervisory board shall represent the Company vis-à-vis the managing directors. It shall advise and supervise management and advise the shareholders' meeting; the latter may entrust the supervisory board with safeguarding rights of the shareholders' meeting. The supervisory board shall have the right to call shareholders' meetings.

(8) The supervisory board shall give itself rules of procedure. It may form committees with members chosen from among those of the supervisory board, lay down the duties and powers of such committees, and confer upon them the power to take decisions.

(9) The Members of the supervisory board shall be reimbursed for any out-of-pocket expenses. The shareholders' meeting shall decide on their remuneration by means of resolution.

(10) As under § 93 AktG, the members of the supervisory board shall be bound to secrecy. To the extent permitted, § 52 GmbHG shall not apply in other respects.

(11) The shareholders' meeting may temporarily suspend the foregoing provisions, and dispense with appointing a supervisory board by not electing a supervisory board. Then the powers of the supervisory board as provided for in these Articles shall be exercised by the shareholders' meeting.

§ 14 Duration; Termination

(1) The life of the Company shall be indefinite. It may be terminated by any shareholder with a period of notice of twelve months to the end of any business year, provided that no such termination shall take effect prior to 31 December 2000. Such termination shall be declared by registered letter to the Company, with confirmation of receipt requested, and the Company shall inform each of the shareholders thereof without undue delay.

(2) Every shareholder may serve notice to the Company for cause without observing a period of notice. § 14 para. 1 sentence 3 shall apply by analogy. Cause exists, in particular, if the Company suspends payments, or if a petition for institution of composition or bankruptcy proceedings has been filed against the Company.

(3) Save in the cases set out in § 14 para. 2 sentence 2, a notice of termination will not result in the dissolution of the Company; rather, the Company shall be continued by the remaining shareholders.

(4) Every shareholder shall have the right to join in any termination within twelve weeks from the date thereof and effective to the same relevant date.

§ 15 Settlement

(1) In all cases of a shareholder's retirement from the Company, the shareholder shall receive a sum determined on the basis of a valuation of the Company at the time of such retirement by way of settlement. For this purpose, an apportioning balance sheet shall be prepared as at that date, applying valuation principles applicable to income tax. Any existing reserves from profits and any profit or loss brought forward shall be

dissolved. Any profit or loss which has arisen up to the valuation date shall be taken into account. The valuation methods applied shall be consistent with those applied in preparing the financial statements last duly approved before that date. If the market value of the Company is lower, then it shall be taken as the basis for determining the settlement amount. The settlement amount thus determined shall remain unchanged even if the preceding or following annual tax balance sheet is altered as a result of a tax audit. Accordingly, the amount of the settlement will remain unaffected by any profit or loss or additional tax payments or tax refunds ascertained subsequently.

(2) If, in a given instance, it is established by way of a legally binding, non-appealable judgment that the amount of the settlement is too low and that, consequently, the agreement is invalid, then the lowest permissible settlement amount shall be paid.

(3) Any dispute about the amount of the settlement shall be resolved by an adjudicator appointed by both parties; the adjudicator must be a qualified German public accountant (Wirtschaftsprüfer) or public accounting firm (Wirtschaftsprüfungsgesellschaft). If no agreement can be reached on the appointment of an adjudicator, the appointment shall be made by the Chamber of Public Accountants (Wirtschaftsprüferkammer), Düsseldorf.

(4) The settlement shall be paid in three equal annual instalments, the first payable three months after the preparation of the most recent balance sheet, or, as the case may be, after determination of the amount of the settlement in accordance with § 15 para. 3, and the further instalments payable by the end of the first calendar quarter of each of the following years. Interest on the settlement amount shall be paid together with the instalments, from the date of the shareholder's retirement at an annual rate of two per cent above the Deutsche Bundesbank's discount rate in effect at the time. The Company shall have the right to pay the settlement, or any portion thereof, prior to the due dates. It shall have no obligation to furnish security.

§ 16 Business Year; Notices

(1) The business year shall be the calendar year. The first business year is a short business year; it shall end on 31 December of the year in which the Company commences business operations following its formation.

(2) Notices to be announced by the Company shall be published in the *Federal Gazette* (Bundesanzeiger).

§ 17 Severance Clause; Alterations to the Articles

(1) Should any provision of this Agreement, or any provision subsequently incorporated herein, be or become invalid or unenforceable as a whole or

in part, or should this Agreement be found to be incomplete due to a gap, this shall not affect the validity of the remaining provisions. In place of the invalid or unenforceable provision, or in order to fill in a gap, a reasonable replacement provision shall be agreed upon which comes closest to what the parties concluding the agreement wanted or would have wanted in view of the sense and purpose of the Agreement, had they considered the particular point. If the invalid, unenforceable or omitted provision concerns an essential part of these Articles, the replacement provision shall be agreed upon in accordance with § 53 para. 2 GmbHG.

(2) If the invalidity or unenforceability of a provision is owing to the measure of performance or time (period or deadline) laid down therein, then such other measure shall be agreed, by a majority of the votes cast, as corresponds to the greatest degree possible to the original provision and permitted by law.

(3) All understandings and agreements concerning the relationship among the shareholders, or that between the Company and the shareholders, must be in writing in order to be valid or, where required by law, by resolution of the shareholders or recorded in a notarial instrument. The same shall apply to any provision waiving the written form requirement.

§ 18 Cost of Formation

The formation costs (notary's fees, court costs) of approximately DM 2,000 shall be borne by the Company.

§ 19 Place of Jurisdiction

The place of jurisdiction for all disputes arising among the shareholders, or between the shareholders and the Company, is the registered office of the Company.

1.6 List of shareholders

Liste der Gesellschafter
Aquarius Computer (Deutschland) GmbH

Gesellschafter	Anteil
1. Aquarius Computer Ltd., London, England	DM 25.000
2. Schmitt Bürosysteme GmbH, Frankfurt am Main	DM 25.000

Frankfurt am Main, den 01. Februar 1996

_____   _____
(Robert Jones)   (Konrad Schmitt)

List of Shareholders
Aquarius Computer (Deutschland) GmbH

Shareholder	Share
1. Aquarius Computer Ltd., London, England	DM 25,000
2. Schmitt Bürosysteme GmbH, Frankfurt am Main	DM 25,000

Frankfurt am Main, 1 February 1996

(Robert Jones)   (Konrad Schmitt)

1.7 Application for registration

An das
Amtsgericht
– Handelsregister B –

60528 Frankfurt am Main

<u>Betrifft</u>: Neu gegründete Aquarius Computer (Deutschland) GmbH

Als Geschäftsführer überreichen wir

1.   Ausfertigung des notariellen Protokolls UR 80/1996 des Notars Martin
     Schön vom 01.02.1996,

2.   Liste der Gesellschafter,

3.   Stellungnahme der Industrie- und Handelskammer

und melden die Gesellschaft und unsere Bestellung zu Geschäftsführern zur
Eintragung an.

Ein Geschäftsführer vertritt die Gesellschaft allein, solange er einziger Geschäftsführer ist. Werden weitere Geschäftsführer bestellt, so vertreten zwei Geschäftsführer gemeinschaftlich oder ein Geschäftsführer in Gemeinschaft mit einem Prokuristen die Gesellschaft. Die Gesellschafterversammlung kann alle oder einzelne Geschäftsführer zur Alleinvertretung ermächtigen und/oder von § 181 BGB befreien.

Wir vertreten die Gesellschaft gemeinsam mit einem weiteren Geschäftsführer oder einem Prokuristen. Ist nur ein Geschäftsführer bestellt, vertritt er die Gesellschaft allein. Wir sind von den Beschränkungen des § 181 BGB befreit.

Wir zeichnen, wie wir diese Anmeldung unterzeichnen.

Wir versichern, daß

- folgende Einzahlungen auf die Stammeinlagen erfolgt sind: je DM 25.000 auf die beiden Geschäftsanteile von DM 25.000 und damit die Anforderungen des § 7 Abs (2) GmbHG erfüllt sind, daß nämlich auf jede Stammeinlage mindestens ein Viertel eingezahlt ist, und daß auf das Stammkapital insgesamt mindestens DM 25.000 eingezahlt sind;

- sich die eingezahlten Beträge endgültig in unserer freien Verfügung befinden;

- außer den im Gesellschaftsvertrag bezifferten durch die Gründung entstandenen Kosten, die die Gesellschaft von Gesetzes wegen zu tragen hat, keine Belastungen des Stammkapitals aus der Zeit vor der Unterzeichnung dieser Anmeldung vorliegen, sondern eine entsprechende Zuzahlung erfolgt ist;

- wir in den letzten fünf Jahren nicht rechtskräftig wegen einer Konkursstraftat nach den §§ 283-283 d StGB (Bankrott, Verletzung der Buchführungspflicht, Schuldner- oder Gläubigerbegünstigung) verurteilt worden sind und uns weder durch gerichtliches Urteil noch durch vollziehbare Entscheidung einer Verwaltungsbehörde die Ausübung eines Berufs, eines Berufszweigs, Gewerbes oder Gewerbezweigs untersagt worden ist. Uns ist bekannt, daß in die Frist die Zeit nicht eingerechnet wird, in der ein Täter auf behördliche Anordnung in einer Anstalt verwahrt worden ist. Wir sind vom Notar darüber belehrt worden, daß wir zur unbeschränkten Auskunft hierüber verpflichtet sind und daß falsche Angaben nach § 82 Abs (1) Nr 4 GmbHG strafbar sind.

Die Geschäftsräume der Gesellschaft befinden sich in Frankfurt am Main, Eschersheimer Landstraße 150.

Die Notariatssachbearbeiterin Regina Schultz, dienstansässig Niedenau 25, 60325 Frankfurt am Main, wird hiermit mit dem Recht zur Erteilung von Untervollmachten bevollmächtigt, diese Handelsregisteranmeldung zu ergänzen und abzuändern. Diese Vollmacht erlischt mit der Eintragung der Gesellschaft in das Handelsregister.

Frankfurt am Main, den 01. Februar 1996

_____   _____

(Robert Jones)   (Konrad Schmitt)

District Court
– Commercial Registry B –

60528 Frankfurt am Main

Re: The newly established Aquarius Computer (Deutschland) GmbH

In our capacity as managing directors, we submit the following documents for registration in the Commercial Register B

1. An official copy of the notarial record no. 80/1996 of the Notary Public Martin Schön dated 1 February 1996,

2. List of the shareholders,

3. Comments of the Chamber of Commerce.

We hereby apply for registration of the Company and of our appointment as its managing directors.

The Company shall be represented by one managing director alone as long as he is the Company's only managing director. If additional managing directors are appointed, the Company shall be represented by two managing directors jointly or by one managing director jointly with a Procurator (holder of a power of procuration). The shareholders' meeting may authorize individual or all managing directors to represent the Company alone and/or exempt them from the restrictions of § 181 BGB (Civil Code).

In our capacity as managing directors, we are entitled to represent the Company with another managing director or a Procurator (holder of power of procuration). If one of us is the sole managing director, he represents the company alone. We are exempted from the restrictions of § 181 BGB.

We sign our names as we sign this application.

We give the assurance that:

– the following payments in of the original capital contributions have been effected: DM 25,000 on each of both shares in the amount of DM 25,000. We furthermore affirm that the requirements of § 7 para. 2 Limited Liability Companies Act (GmbHG) are thus met, that no less than one quarter of the nominal amount of each share has been paid up and that no less than DM 25,000 of the share capital has been paid;

– the funds are paid in at our free and unrestricted disposal;

– except for the incorporation costs, to be paid by the Company by operation of law and which have been stipulated in the Articles of Association, the Company's share capital is not subject to any liabilities incurred before the time the present application for registration in the Commercial Register was signed; any such liabilities have been paid separately;

– we have not been sentenced for any bankruptcy offence under §§ 283-283 d StGB (Criminal Code) (bankruptcy, breach of the book-keeping duty, fraudulent preference of or conveyance to a debtor or creditor) in the last five years and that no court judgment and no enforceable order of an administrative authority exists under which we are prohibited from engaging in any particular profession, professional branch, trade, or branch of trade. We are aware of the fact that the time during which an offender is detained by order of any public authority is not counted as part of the five-year period. We have been cautioned by the Notary that we are obliged to disclose all information in this respect and that any incorrect statements in this connection are punishable as a criminal offence under § 82 para. 1 no. 4 GmbHG (Limited Liability Companies Act).

The Company's business premises shall be located at Eschersheimer Landstraße 150, Frankfurt am Main.

The law clerk Ms. Regina Schultz, business address Niedenau 25, 60325 Frankfurt am Main, is authorized and with the right to delegate such authority, to supplement or modify this application. This power of attorney shall expire upon registration of the Company in the Commercial Register.

Frankfurt am Main, 1 February 1996

_____   _____
(Robert Jones)   (Konrad Schmitt)

1.8 Managing director's service agreement

<u>Anstellungsvertrag</u>

zwischen

Aquarius Computer (Deutschland) GmbH, Eschersheimer Landstraße 150, 60325 Frankfurt am Main,

– nachfolgend "Gesellschaft" genannt –

und

Robert Jones, 70 Randolph Avenue, London W9, England,

– nachfolgend "Geschäftsführer" genannt –

<u>§ 1 Geschäftsführungs- und Vertretungsbefugnis</u>

(1) Der Geschäftsführer vertritt die Gesellschaft gemeinsam mit einem weiteren Geschäftsführer oder Prokuristen gerichtlich und außergerichtlich.

(2) Der Geschäftsführer führt gemeinsam mit weiteren Geschäftsführern die Geschäfte der Gesellschaft nach Maßgabe der Gesetze, der Satzung und dieses Anstellungsvertrags. Er hat Weisungen der Gesellschafterversammlung Folge zu leisten.

<u>§ 2 Zustimmungsplichtige Geschäfte</u>

(1) Die Befugnis zur Geschäftsführung umfaßt die Vornahme aller Maßnahmen im Rahmen des gewöhnlichen Geschäftsbetriebes der Gesellschaft.

(2) Zur Vornahme von Rechtsgeschäften, welche über den gewöhnlichen Geschäftsbetrieb der Gesellschaft hinausgehen, muß die vorherige Zustimmung der Gesellschafterversammlung eingeholt werden. Dies gilt insbesondere für folgende Rechtsgeschäfte:

(a) Veräußerung und Stillegung des Betriebs oder wesentlicher Betriebsteile sowie die Aufgabe wesentlicher Tätigkeitsbereiche.

(b) Errichtung von Zweigniederlassungen.

(c) Gründung, Erwerb oder Veräußerung von anderen Unternehmen oder Beteiligungen der Gesellschaft an anderen Unternehmen.

(d) Erwerb, Veräußerung und Belastung von Grundstücken und grundstücksgleichen Rechten sowie die Verpflichtung zur Vornahme solcher Rechtsgeschäfte.

(e) Bauliche Maßnahmen und Anschaffung von Sachmitteln aller Art, soweit die hierfür erforderlichen Aufwendungen einen Betrag von DM 10.000 übersteigen.

(f) Abschluß, Änderung oder Aufhebung von Miet-, Pacht- oder Leasing-Verträgen mit einer Vertragsdauer von mehr als 12 Monaten oder einer jährlichen Verpflichtung von mehr als DM 10.000.

(g) Inanspruchnahme oder Gewährung von Krediten oder Sicherheitsleistungen jeglicher Art, welche DM 10.000 übersteigen. Hiervon ausgenommen sind die laufenden Warenkredite im gewöhnlichen Geschäftsverkehr mit Kunden und Lieferanten der Gesellschaft.

(h) Übernahmen von Bürgschaften jeder Art.

(i) Einstellung und Entlassung von Arbeitnehmern, deren Jahresverdienst DM 50.000 übersteigt. Bewilligung von Gehaltserhöhungen und zusätzlichen Vergütungen, welche zu einem Übersteigen der Verdienstgrenze gemäß S. 1 führen. Hiervon ausgenommen sind Anpassungen der Gehälter entsprechend den Tariferhöhungen.

(j) Erteilung von Versorgungszusagen aller Art, durch welche zusätzliche Verpflichtungen der Gesellschaft über die Leistungen der gesetzlichen Sozialversicherung begründet werden.

(k) Erteilung und Widerruf von Prokuren und Handlungsvollmachten.

§ 3 Selbstkontrahieren

Der Geschäftsführer ist von den Beschränkungen des § 181 BGB befreit.

§ 4 Pflichten und Verantwortlichkeit

(1) Der Geschäftsführer hat die Geschäfte der Gesellschaft mit der Sorgfalt eines ordentlichen Kaufmannes zu führen und die ihm nach Gesetz, Satzung sowie diesem Vertrag obliegenden Pflichten gewissenhaft zu erfüllen.

(2) Der Geschäftsführer nimmt die Rechte und Pflichten des Arbeitgebers im Sinne der arbeits- und sozialrechtlichen Vorschriften wahr.

(3) Der Geschäftsführer hat innerhalb von 3 Monaten nach Abschluß des Geschäftsjahrs die Bilanz und Gewinn- und Verlustrechnung für das abgelaufene Geschäftsjahr aufzustellen und diese mit einem von ihm zu erstattenden Geschäftsbericht jedem Gesellschafter zu übersenden.

§ 5 Arbeitszeit und Nebentätigkeit

(1) Der Geschäftsführer hat seine volle Arbeitskraft sowie sein ganzes Wissen und Können in die Dienste der Gesellschaft zu stellen. Er ist in der Bestimmung seiner Arbeitszeit frei, hat jedoch jederzeit, soweit dies das Wohl der Gesellschaft erfordert, zu ihrer Verfügung zu stehen und ihre Interessen wahrzunehmen.

(2) Dem Geschäftsführer ist während der Dauer dieses Vertrags jede entgeltliche oder unentgeltliche Nebentätigkeit für sich oder Dritte untersagt. Veröffentlichungen und Vorträge, welche den Tätigkeitsbereich der Gesellschaft betreffen, sowie die Übernahme vom Ämtern in Aufsichtsgremien anderer Unternehmen und Ehrenämtern in Organisationen bedürfen der vorherigen schriftlichen Zustimmung durch die Gesellschaft. Die zur Übernahme eines Amtes erteilte Zustimmung ist jederzeit widerruflich, wobei im Falle eines Widerrufs etwaige Fristvorschriften für die Beendigung des übernommenen Amtes berücksichtigt werden.

§ 6 Wettbewerbsverbot

(1) Dem Geschäftsführer ist untersagt, während der Dauer dieses Vertrags in selbständiger, unselbständiger oder sonstiger Weise für ein Unternehmen tätig zu werden, welches mit der Gesellschaft in direktem oder indirektem Wettbewerb steht. In gleicher Weise ist es dem Geschäftsführer untersagt, während der Dauer dieses Vertrags ein solches Unternehmen zu errichten, zu erwerben oder sich hieran unmittelbar oder mittelbar zu beteiligen.

(2) Der Geschäftsführer ist verpflichtet, über alle betrieblichen und geschäftlichen Angelegenheiten der Gesellschaft gegenüber unbefugten Dritten striktes Stillschweigen zu wahren. Diese Verpflichtung gilt auch nach Beendigung des Anstellungsvertrags.

§ 7 Vergütung

(1) Der Geschäftsführer erhält ein festes Jahresgehalt in Höhe von DM 100.000 brutto, welches in 12 gleichen Raten zum Ende eines jeden Monats gezahlt wird.

(2) Darüber hinaus erhält der Geschäftsführer eine Tantieme als freiwillige Leistung, deren Festsetzung in freiem Ermessen der Gesellschafter liegt.

§ 8 Vergütung bei Dienstverhinderung und Tod

(1) Im Fall der Erkrankung oder sonstigen unverschuldeten Dienstverhinderung werden dem Geschäftführer seine vertragsgemäßen Bezüge für die Dauer von 3 Monaten fortgezahlt.

(2) Verstirbt der Geschäftsführer während der Dauer dieses Anstellungsvertrags, so werden an seine Ehefrau die vertragsgemäßen Bezüge für die auf den Sterbemonat folgenden 3 Monate fortgezahlt. Ist die Ehefrau zu diesem Zeitpunkt bereits verstorben, so steht der Anspruch den unterhaltsberechtigten Kindern des Geschäftsführers zu.

§ 9 Sonstige Leistungen

(1) Die Gesellschaft schließt für die Dauer dieses Anstellungsvertrags auf ihre Kosten eine Unfallversicherung ab, welche den Geschäftsführer mit DM 500.000 bei Invalidität und DM 300.000 bei Unfalltod versichert. Bezugsberechtigt aus der Versicherung sind im Invaliditätsfall der Geschäftsführer, im Todesfall die von ihm benannten Personen, bei Fehlen einer solchen Bestimmung seine Erben.

(2) Die Gesellschaft gewährt dem Geschäftsführer für die Dauer dieses Anstellungsvertrags einen Zuschuß zur Krankenversicherung in Höhe des Arbeitgeberanteils, wie er bei Krankenversicherungspflicht des Geschäftsführers bestünde, höchstens jedoch in Höhe der Hälfte des Betrags, welchen der Geschäftsführer für seine Krankenversicherung aufzuwenden hat.

(3) Die Gesellschaft stellt dem Geschäftsführer für seine Tätigkeit im Rahmen dieses Vertrags einen Dienstwagen der Marke Volkswagen, Typ Passat oder ein vergleichbares Fahrzeug zur Verfügung. Hierüber wird ein gesonderter Dienstwagenvertrag abgeschlossen. Die für die Fahrzeug-Haltung und -Nutzung anfallenden Kosten werden durch die Gesellschaft getragen. Der Dienstwagen darf durch den Geschäftsführer auch zu privaten Zwecken genutzt werden. Für den in der Privatnutzung liegenden geldwerten Vorteil wird ein monatlicher Pauschalbetrag in der steuerlich jeweils geltenden Höhe zugrundegelegt. Dieser geldwerte Vorteil steht dem Geschäftsführer neben seiner Vergütung gemäß § 7 dieses Vertrags zu; die hierauf entfallende Lohnsteuer trägt der Geschäftsführer. Für den Fall einer Freistellung des Geschäftsführers von seinen Dienstpflichten ist der Dienstwagen an die Gesellschaft herauszugeben, ohne daß insoweit ein Anspruch auf finanziellen Ausgleich des in der Privatnutzung liegenden geldwerten Vorteils besteht. In gleicher Weise ist der Geschäftsführer bei Beendigung des Anstellungsvertrags zur Herausgabe des Dienstwagens verpflichtet.

(4) Für Geschäftsreisen, welche im Interesse der Gesellschaft erforderlich sind, hat der Geschäftsführer Anspruch auf Erstattung seiner Spesen. Übersteigen die aufgewendeten Spesen die steuerlich zulässigen Pauschalbeträge, so sind sie durch Belege nachzuweisen.

§ 10 Urlaub

Dem Geschäftsführer steht jährlich ein Erholungsurlaub von 30 Arbeitstagen zu. Die zeitliche Lage des Urlaubs ist unter Berücksichtigung der geschäftlichen Belange der Gesellschaft festzulegen.

§ 11 Vertragsdauer und Kündigung

(1) Dieser Vertrag tritt mit Wirkung zum 01.02.1996 in Kraft und ist auf unbestimmte Dauer geschlossen.

(2) Beide Parteien können diesen Vertrag mit einer Frist von 3 Monaten zum Kalenderquartalsende kündigen.

(3) Eine Abberufung des Geschäftsführers, welche jederzeit durch Beschluß der Gesellschafterversammlung erfolgen kann, gilt zugleich als Kündigung durch die Gesellschaft zu dem gemäß Abs (2) nächst zulässigen Termin und ist dem Geschäftsführer in der Form gemäß Abs (6) mitzuteilen.

(4) Die Gesellschaft ist in jedem Fall der Kündigung berechtigt, den Geschäftsführer unter Anrechnung auf etwaigen noch offenstehenden Urlaub während der Kündigungsfrist von der Verpflichtung zur Dienstleistung freizustellen.

(5) Das Recht zur Kündigung aus wichtigem Grund bleibt unberührt.

(6) Jede Kündigung bedarf der Schriftform. Empfangszuständig für eine Kündigung durch den Geschäftsführer ist jeder weitere Geschäftsführer der Gesellschaft oder für den Fall, daß ein solcher nicht im Amt ist, derjenige Gesellschafter, der über die höchste Kapitalbeteiligung der Gesellschaft verfügt.

(7) Dieser Vertrag endet in jedem Fall mit Ablauf des Monats, in welchem der Geschäftsführer das 65. Lebensjahr vollendet oder eine Berufsunfähigkeit festgestellt wird.

§ 12 Herausgabe von Unterlagen

Bei Beendigung des Anstellungsvertrags oder im Fall einer durch die Gesellschaft erfolgenden Freistellung von der Dienstleistung hat der Geschäftsführer unverzüglich sämtliche die Angelegenheiten der Gesellschaft betreffenden Gegenstände und Unterlagen, insbesondere Schlüssel, Bücher, Modelle, Aufzeichnungen jeder Art einschließlich etwaiger Abschriften oder Kopien, welche sich in seinem Besitz befinden, vollständig an die Gesellschaft herauszugeben. Dem Geschäftsführer steht aus keinem Rechtsgrund ein Zurückbehaltungsrecht gegenüber der Gesellschaft an diesen Gegenständen und Unterlagen zu.

§ 13 Schlußbestimmungen

(1) Sämtliche Änderungen oder Ergänzungen dieses Vertrags – auch dieser Bestimmung – bedürfen zu ihrer Wirksamkeit der Schriftform und der Zustimmung durch Beschluß der Gesellschafterversammlung.

(2) Sollte eine Bestimmung dieses Vertrags rechtsunwirksam sein oder werden, so wird die Geltung der übrigen Bestimmungen dieses Vertrags hierdurch nicht berührt. Die Parteien sind in einem solchen Fall verpflichtet, die rechtsunwirksame Bestimmung durch eine rechtlich zulässige und mit den Bestimmungen dieses Vertrags vereinbare Regelung zu ersetzen, welche dem wirtschaftlich verfolgten Zweck der ungültigen Bestimmung am nächsten kommt.

Frankfurt am Main, den 01. Februar 1996

_____   _____

(Aquarius Computer   (Robert Jones)
(Deutschland) GmbH)

Service Agreement

between

Aquarius Computer (Deutschland) GmbH, Eschersheimer Landstraße 150, 60325 Frankfurt am Main,

– hereinafter called the "Company" –

and

Robert Jones, 70 Randolph Avenue, London W9, England,

– hereinafter called the "Managing Director" –

§ 1 Power of Management and Power of Representation

(1) The Managing Director shall represent the Company in and out of court acting jointly with a further managing director or a Procurator (a holder of powers of procuration).

(2) The Managing Director shall conduct the business of the Company, acting jointly with further managing directors and in accordance with the law, the company's articles of association and this contract. The Managing Director shall comply with the instructions of the shareholders' meeting.

§ 2 Transactions Requiring Consent of Shareholders

(1) The Managing Director's powers of management shall include the right to carry out all measures falling within the normal scope of business of the Company.

(2) The prior consent of the shareholders' meeting shall be obtained before any legal transactions are engaged in which go beyond the normal scope of business of the Company. This shall apply in particular to the following legal transactions:

(a) Sale and closure of the business or considerable parts thereof, and the discontinuation of significant areas of activity;

(b) Establishment of branch offices;

(c) Foundation, acquisition or sale of other enterprises or holdings of the Company in other enterprises;

(d) Acquisition, sale or encumbrance of real property or rights equivalent to real property and the assumption of commitments to engage in such legal transactions;

(e) Building work and the procurement of materials of any kind if the expenses involved exceed the sum of DM 10,000;

(f) Conclusion, modification or cancellation of tenancy, leasehold or leasing agreements with a term of more than 12 months or involving a financial obligation of more than DM 10,000 per year;

(g) Taking advantage of or granting loans or the provision of collateral of any kind exceeding DM 10,000. This shall not include current trade credits with customers and suppliers of the Company in the course of ordinary business dealings;

(h) Assumption of guarantees of any kind;

(i) Appointment and dismissal of employees with an annual earnings exceeding DM 50,000; approval of salary increases and additional remunerations as a result of which the earnings threshold referred to in sentence 1 above is exceeded; this shall not apply with regard to salary increases under collective bargaining agreements;

(j) Assumption of pension commitments of any kind giving rise to obligations on the Company going beyond the benefits provided for under the statutory social insurance scheme;

(k) Grant and revocation of registered powers of procuration and commercial powers of attorney.

§ 3 Self-Dealing

The Managing Director shall be exempted from the restrictions under § 181 of the German Civil Code (BGB).

§ 4 Duties and Responsibilities

(1) The Managing Director shall conduct the business of the Company with the due care and diligence of a prudent businessman and shall comply with all obligations imposed on him by law or under the Company's articles of association or the present contract.

(2) The Managing Director shall assume the rights and obligations of the Company as employer as defined in labour and social security law provisions.

(3) Within three months following the end of each business year, the Managing Director shall draw up the balance sheet and the profit and loss account for the completed business year, and shall send these to each shareholder together with a business report to be prepared by him.

§ 5 Working Hours and Secondary Activities

(1) The Managing Director shall place his entire working capacity as well as all his knowledge and abilities at the disposal of the Company. The Managing Director shall be free to fix his own working hours, but shall make his services available to the Company and safeguard its interests at any time if the well-being of the Company requires this.

(2) The Managing Director shall, for the duration of this Agreement, be forbidden to engage, with or without payment, in any secondary activity for his own account or that of a third party. He shall require the prior written consent of the Company before publishing any material or giving any lectures relating to the Company's area of activity, and before taking up any functions on supervisory bodies of other enterprises or assuming functions in an honorary capacity in any organization. The Company's consent to such functions being assumed may be revoked at any time; in this event, any periods of notice required when giving up such functions shall be taken into account.

§ 6 Restraint of Competition

(1) The Managing Director shall, for the duration of this contract be forbidden to work for any enterprise which is a direct or indirect competitor of the Company, be it as an employee or on a freelance or any other basis. Similarly, the Managing Director shall be forbidden for the term of this Agreement to establish, or directly or indirectly participate in, any such enterprise.

(2) The Managing Director shall maintain strict confidentiality vis-à-vis third parties with respect to all business and commercial matters concerning the Company. This obligation shall continue to apply following termination of this Agreement.

§ 7 Remuneration

(1) The Managing Director shall receive a fixed annual salary of DM 100,000 gross, which shall be paid in twelve equal monthly instalments at the end of each month.

(2) In addition, the Managing Director shall also receive a bonus, the amount of which shall be determined at the Company's discretion.

§ 8 Remuneration in the Event of Inability to Work or Death

(1) If the Managing Director falls ill or is otherwise unable to work through no fault of his own, his contractually agreed renumeration shall continue to be paid for a period of three months.

(2) If the Managing Director dies during the term of this Agreement, his salary shall continue to be paid to his wife for the three months following the month in which his death occurred. If his wife is already deceased at such time, then the Managing Director's dependent children shall be entitled to his salary for this period.

§ 9 Other Benefits

(1) For the duration of this Agreement, the Company shall take out an accident insurance policy for the Managing Director at its own expense, providing for the payment of DM 500,000 in the event of invalidity and DM 300,000 in the event of death by accident. The beneficiary under the policy shall be the Managing Director in the event of invalidity and, in the event of death, the persons specified by the Managing Director; if no such persons are specified, the Managing Director's heirs shall be the beneficiaries under the policy.

(2) The Company shall, for the duration of this Agreement, provide the Managing Director with a contribution towards health insurance cover equivalent to the employer's share which would be payable if the Managing Director were a compulsory member of a social health insurance scheme; the payment made by the Company shall not, however, exceed half the sum which the Managing Director is required to pay for his health insurance cover.

(3) The Company shall provide the Managing Director with a company car (make: Volkswagen, type: Passat) or a comparable vehicle for his activities

provided for under this Agreement. A separate agreement shall be concluded concerning this company car. Any costs arising in connection with the running and use of the car shall be borne by the Company. The company car may also be used by the Managing Director for private purposes. The value of the pecuniary advantage which the private use of the company car represents shall be fixed as a monthly lump sum in accordance with tax regulations. The Managing Director shall be entitled to this pecuniary advantage in addition to his remuneration referred to in § 7, and any income tax payable thereon shall be borne by the Managing Director. If the Managing Director is relieved of his contractual duties, the car shall be returned to the Company without the Managing Director having any claim to a payout of the pecuniary advantage represented by the private use of the car. Similarly, the Managing Director shall be obliged to return the company car upon termination of this Agreement.

(4) The Managing Director shall be entitled to reimbursement of any expenses incurred by him on business trips undertaken in the interests of the Company. If the expenses incurred exceed the standard lump-sum rates permitted under tax regulations, then evidence of each expense items shall be provided.

§ 10 Holiday Entitlement

The Managing Director shall be entitled to 30 working days' holiday per year. The timing of any holiday shall be arranged to take account of the business interests of the Company.

§ 11 Duration and Termination of the Agreement

(1) This Agreement shall enter into effect on 1 February 1996 and is concluded for an indefinite term.

(2) Either party may terminate this contract with three months' notice to the end of a calendar quarter.

(3) The dismissal of the Managing Director, which may be required at any time by means of a shareholders' resolution, shall also constitute termination of this Agreement by the Company with effect to the earliest date possible under para. 2 above; notice of such termination shall be given to the Managing Director in the form stipulated in para. 6 below.

(4) In the event of termination of this Agreement, the Company shall be entitled to relieve the Managing Director of his duties during the period of notice, whereby any holiday to which the Managing Director may still be entitled

shall be taken into account in the period during which he is relieved of such duties.

(5) The right to terminate this Agreement for cause shall remain unaffected.

(6) Notice of termination must always be given in writing. If this Agreement is terminated by the Managing Director, notice thereof shall be given to any other managing director or, in the event that no other managing director has been appointed, to the shareholder with the largest holding in the Company.

(7) This Agreement shall in all events come to an end upon the expiry of the month in which the Managing Director reaches the age of 65, or if he becomes unable to pursue his occupation.

§ 12 Return of Documents

Upon termination of this Agreement or in the event that the Company relieves the Managing Director of his duties, the latter shall return to the Company without delay all objects and documents relating to the affairs of the Company which are in his possession, in particular keys, accounts, models and records of any kind, including any copies or photocopies thereof. Any right of retention of the Managing Director shall be ruled out with respect to these items and documents, irrespective of its legal basis.

§ 13 Final Provisions

(1) In order to be legally valid, any amendments or additions to this contract shall be made in writing, and require approval under a shareholders' resolution.

(2) Should any provision of this Agreement be or become legally invalid, this shall not affect the validity of the remaining provisions. In such an event, the parties shall be obliged to replace the invalid provision with a legally permissible provision which is compatible with the other provisions hereof and which comes as close as possible to the economic intentions of the parties.

Frankfurt am Main, 1 February 1996

————————————   ——————————
(Aquarius Computer   (Robert Jones)
(Deutschland) GmbH)

1.9 Sale and transfer of share (basic version)

<u>UR 215/1996</u>

Verhandelt
zu Frankfurt am Main am 02. August 1996

Vor mir, dem unterzeichnenden Notar im
Bezirk des Oberlandesgerichts Frankfurt am Main

Martin Schön

mit dem Amtssitz in Frankfurt am Main,

erschienen heute:

1. Herr Kaufmann Konrad Schmitt, Benzstraße 3, 63225 Langen, von Person
    bekannt, handelnd nicht im eigenen Namen, sondern als alleinvertretungs-
    berechtigter Geschäftsführer der Schmitt Bürosysteme GmbH mit Sitz in
    Frankfurt am Main,

    – "Verkäuferin" –,

2. Herr Bürovorsteher Horst Lehmann, dienstansässig Niedenau 25, 60325
    Frankfurt am Main, von Person bekannt, handelnd nicht im eigenen
    Namen, sondern als Vertreter der Aquarius Computer Ltd., London, Eng-
    land, aufgrund Vollmacht vom 25.01.1996, die dieser Urkunde in
    beglaubigter Abschrift beigefügt ist,

    – "Käufer" –.

Die Erschienenen baten um die Beurkundung des folgenden

<u>Vertrags über den Verkauf und die Abtretung
eines Geschäftsanteils:</u>

<u>§ 1 Gegenstand des Vertrags</u>

(1) Verkäuferin ist an der Aquarius Computer (Deutschland) GmbH in Frank-
    furt am Main, eingetragen im HRB Nr. 1234 des AG Frankfurt am Main, mit
    einem Geschäftsanteil von DM 25.000 beteiligt. Der Anteil ist voll eingezahlt.

(2) Diesen Geschäftsanteil verkauft Verkäuferin an Käufer zu den nachstehenden
    Bedingungen.

§ 2 Kaufpreis und Gewährleistung

(1) Der Kaufpreis beträgt DM 35.000 (in Worten: Deutsche Mark fünfund-dreißigtausend).

(2) Der Verkauf erfolgt unter Ausschluß jeglicher Gewährleistung, soweit gesetzlich zulässig. Er ist heute fällig.

§ 3 Gewinnbezugsrecht

Mit dem Geschäftsanteil geht das Bezugsrecht für den auf ihn entfallenden, etwa noch nicht verteilten Gewinn auf Käufer über.

§ 4 Abtretung

Verkäuferin tritt den verkauften Geschäftsanteil hiermit unter der aufschiebenden Bedingung der Zahlung des Kaufpreises an Käufer ab, der die Abtretung hiermit annimmt und sich verpflichtet, die Abtretung gemäß § 16 GmbHG bei der Gesellschaft anzumelden.

§ 5 Zustimmung

Die nach dem Gesellschaftsvertrag erforderliche Zustimmung der Gesellschaft zur Abtretung ist als Anlage 1 beigefügt.

§ 6 Kosten/Steuern

Die Kosten trägt der Käufer. Die Gesellschaft hat keinen Grundbesitz.

Der Notar belehrte über die Haftung für rückständige Stammeinlagen, über die Differenzhaftung und darüber, daß geprüft wird, ob Grunderwerbsteuer entsteht.

Vorstehende Verhandlung nebst Anlage wurde den Erschienenen vorgelesen, lag ihnen nebst Anlage zur Durchsicht vor, wurde von ihnen genehmigt und von ihnen und dem Notar eigenhändig unterzeichnet.

UR 215/1996

Recorded
in Frankfurt am Main, on 2 August 1996

Before me, the undersigned Notary Public in the district
of the Higher Regional Court, Frankfurt am Main

Martin Schön,

practising in Frankfurt am Main,

the following persons appeared today:

1. the businessman Mr. Konrad Schmitt, Benzstraße 3, 63225 Langen, personally known to the notary, not acting in his own name but as managing director of Schmitt Bürosysteme GmbH, Frankfurt am Main, with sole power of representation,

– "Vendor" –,

2. the senior law clerk Mr. Horst Lehmann, with his business address Niedenau 25, 60325 Frankfurt/Main, personally known to the Notary, acting not in his own name but on behalf of Aquarius Computer Ltd., London, England, with power of attorney dated 25 January 1996, a certified copy of which is attached to this Deed,

– "Purchaser" –.

The parties appearing requested recording of the following

Agreement on the Sale and Assignment
of a Share

§ 1 Subject of this Agreement

(1) The Vendor holds a capital share of DM 25,000 in Aquarius Computer (Deutschland) GmbH, a limited liability company in Frankfurt am Main, registered in the Commercial Register of the district court ("Amtsgericht") of Frankfurt am Main under no. HRB 1234. The share has been fully paid up.

(2) The Vendor hereby sells this share to the Purchaser subject to the following conditions.

§ 2 Purchase Price and Warranty

(1) The purchase price amounts to DM 35,000 (Deutsche Mark thirty five thousand).

(2) The sale takes place subject to the exclusion of all warranties, in so far as legally possible. It is due today.

§ 3 Right to Participate in the Profits

The share is assigned together with the right to participate in any profits attributable to this share which have not yet been distributed.

§ 4 Assignment

Subject to the condition precedent of receipt of the purchase price, the Vendor hereby assigns to the Purchaser the share which has been sold. The Purchaser hereby accepts this assignment and agrees to notify the Company of the assignment according to § 16 Limited Liability Companies Act ("GmbHG").

§ 5 Consent

The Company's consent to the assignment of the share which is required under the company's articles of association, is attached as Appendix 1.

§ 6 Costs

The costs of this Agreement shall be paid by the Purchaser. The company does not own real property.

The Notary advised the persons appearing of their liability for outstanding capital contributions or capital contributions that have not been fully paid up ("Differenzhaftung"). Moreover, the Notary cautioned the parties that there will be an examination as to whether real property transfer tax will be payable.

This Agreement and its Appendix were read to the persons appearing, submitted to them together with the Appendix for inspection, approved by them, and personally signed by them and the Notary.

2. Foreign authorities issuing an apostille

Argentina	Ministry of Foreign Affairs and Culture.
(Austria)	(No requirements)
(Belgium)	(No requirements)
(Canada)	(Legalisation)
(Czech Republic)	(Legalisation)
(Denmark)	(No requirements)
Finland	Notary Public of the Registry of each Jurisdictional District.
(France)	(no requirements)
(Greece)	(Zwischenbeglaubigung – interim authentication)

Hong Kong	– Registrar, Supreme Court. – Deputy Chief Secretary, Supreme Court. – Deputy Registrar, Supreme Court. – Assistant Registrar, Supreme Court.
Hungary	The Ministry of Foreign Affairs.
(Iceland)	(Legalisation)
Indonesia	(Legalisation)
Israel	Ministry of Foreign Affairs.
(Italy)	(No requirements)
Japan	The Ministry of Foreign Affairs.
Liechtenstein	The Governmental Chancellery.
Luxemburg	The Ministry of Foreign Affairs, Luxemburg.
(Mexico)	(Legalisation)
Netherlands	The Registrars of the regional courts.
Norway	– The Ministry of Foreign Affairs – The department governors.
(Poland)	(Legalisation)
Portugal	– The General Prosecutor. – The Prosecutor at the Court of Appeals.
Russian Federation	Ministry of Foreign Affairs.
(Saudi Arabia)	(Legalisation)
(Singapore)	(Legalisation)
(South Africa)	(Legalisation)
(South Korea)	(Legalisation)
Spain	The chairman of the relevant notary public association.
(Sweden)	(Legalisation)
Switzerland	– Authority of the confederation: The Federal Chancellery. – Authority of the cantons : State Chancellery.
Turkey	– in Provinces: Governor, Deputy-Governor, Director of Juridical Matters, – in towns: Vice-Governor.
UK	Her Majesty's Principal Secretary of State for Foreign and Commonwealth Affairs, Foreign and Commonwealth Office.

USA
- Authentification Officer and Acting Authentification Officer, United States Department of State.
- Clerks and deputy clerks of the following courts: The Supreme Court of the United States, the Courts of Appeals for the First through the Eleventh Circuits and the District of Columbia District, the United States Court of Claims, the United States Court of Customs and Patent Appeals, the United States Court of International Trade, the District Court of Guam, the District Court of the Virgin Islands, and the District Court for the Northern Mariana Islands.
- District of Columbia: Secretary of the District of Columbia.
- The Secretary of State of the individual states except Hawaii and Alaska: Lt. Governor.

Note: Interim authentication (Zwischenbeglaubigung) is an examination of the authenticity of the attestation note. It is undertaken by courts or public authorities of the state in which the attestation note has been granted. The sphere of responsibility for this is regulated by the law of the relevant state. There is no unity of form and procedure as in the case of the Apostille.

3. Terminology

Abberufung	–	removal from office
Abfindung	–	settlement
Abgabenordnung (AO)	–	Code of Taxation Procedure
Abhängigkeitsbericht	–	subordinate status report
Abrechnungszeitraum	–	accounting period
Abschlußprüfer	–	auditor
Abschlußprüfung	–	audit of the annual statements
Abschreibung	–	allowable tax depreciation
absonderungsberechtiger Gläubiger	–	secured creditor
Abspaltung	–	spin–off
Abtretung	–	assignment
Abwicklung	–	liquidation
Abwicklungsgesellschaft	–	liquidating company
Aktie	–	share
Aktiengattung	–	class of shares
Aktiengesellschaft (AG)	–	stock corporation
Aktiengesetz (AktG)	–	Stock Corporation Act
Aktienrecht	–	stock corporation law
Aktionär	–	shareholder of a stock corporation
Aktiva	–	assets

Alleingesellschafter	–	sole shareholder
allgemeiner Prüfungstermin	–	general examinatory court hearing
allgemeines Veräußerungsverbot	–	general prohibition of disposal of company's assets by the management
Amtsgericht (AG)	–	district court
Andienungspflicht	–	duty to tender
Anfechtung	–	avoidance/rescission
Anfechtungsgesetz (AnfG)	–	Creditors' Avoidance of Transfer Act
Anfechtungsklage	–	action for rescission
Angestellter	–	white–collar employee
Anhang	–	appendix
Anlagevermögen	–	fixed assets
Anmeldung	–	application for registration
Anrechnungsmethode	–	credit–method
Anrechnungsverfahren	–	tax credit procedure
Anscheinsvollmacht	–	apparent authority
Anteilseigner	–	owner of share or interest
Anteilsschein	–	share certificate
Anwachsung	–	accrual
Apostille	–	apostille
Arbeiter	–	blue–collar worker
Arbeitnehmerüberlassungs- gesetz (AÜG)	–	Staff Secondment Act
Arbeitsamt	–	labour office
Arbeitsaufenthaltsverordnung (AAV)	–	Work Residence Ordinance
Arbeitserlaubnisverordnung (AErlVO)	–	Work Permit Ordinance
Arbeitsförderungsgesetz (AFG)	–	Employment Promotion Act
Arbeitsgericht	–	labour court
Arbeitsrecht	–	labour law
Arbeitszeitgesetz (ArbZG)	–	Working Time Act
Aufenthaltsgesetz/EWG (AufG/EWG)	–	Alien Residence Act – EC
Auffanggesellschaft	–	rescue company
Aufhebungsvertrag	–	cancellation agreement
Auflösung	–	dissolution
Aufrechnung	–	set–off
Aufsichtsrat	–	supervisory board
Aufspaltung	–	split–up
Aufstockung	–	step–up
Auftrag	–	agency
Auseinandersetzungsbilanz	–	apportioning balance sheet
Auseinandersetzungsguthaben	–	credit balance in case of partition
Ausgliederung	–	drop–down

Auskunftsrecht	–	right to information
Ausländergesetz (AuslG)	–	Aliens Act
Ausscheiden	–	retirement
Ausschließung	–	expulsion
ausschüttungsbedingte Teilwert-	–	extraordinary depreciation to the partial
abschreibung		value by reason of distribution
Ausschüttungsbelastung	–	tax rate on dividends
Außenwirtschaftsgesetz (AWG)	–	Foreign Trade (and Payments) Act
aussonderungsberechtiger Gläubiger	–	creditor who has retained title
Austritt	–	resignation

Bankrott	–	fraudulent insolvency
Bareinlage	–	contribution in cash
Bayerisches Oberstes Landesgericht (BayObLG)	–	State Supreme Court of Bavaria
bedingter Vorsatz	–	contingent intent
Beherrschungsvertrag	–	control agreement
Beirat	–	advisory board
Belehrungspflicht	–	obligation to instruct
Berufsverschwiegenheit	–	professional duty of confidentiality
beschränkte Steuerpflicht	–	limited tax liability
Bestellung	–	appointment
Betrieb	–	business
Betriebsaufgabegewinn	–	capital gains from business closure
Betriebsausgaben	–	operating expenditure
Betriebsrat	–	works council
Betriebsstätte	–	permanent establishment
Betriebsvereinbarung	–	shop agreement
Betriebsverfassungsgesetz (BetrVG)	–	Employees' Representation Act
Betrug	–	fraud
Beurkundungsgesetz (BeurkG)	–	Official Recordings Act
bewegliche Sache	–	movable property
Bewertungsgesetz (BewG)	–	Tax Valuation Act
Bezugsrecht	–	subscription right
BGB–Gesellschaft	–	civil law partnership
Bilanz	–	opening balance, balance sheet
Bilanzgewinn	–	balance sheet profit
Bilanzstichtag	–	balance sheet date
Börsenkurs	–	stock exchange price
bösgläubig	–	in bad faith
Bruchteilsgemeinschaft	–	co–ownership
Buchführung	–	accounting

Buchwertklausel	–	book value clause
Bürgerliches Gesetzbuch (BGB)	–	Civil Code
Bürgschaft	–	guarantee
Bundesamt für Finanzen	–	Federal Office of Finance
Bundesanzeiger	–	*Federal Gazette*
Bundesarbeitsgericht (BAG)	–	Federal Labour Court
Bundesaufsichtsamt für das		
Kreditwesen	–	Federal Banking Supervisory Office
Bundesdatenschutzgesetz	–	Data Protection Act
Bundesfinanzhof (BFH)	–	Federal Fiscal Court
Bundesgerichtshof (BGH)	–	Federal Supreme Court
Bundesgesetzblatt	–	*Federal Law Gazette*
Bundesimmissionschutzgesetz		
(BImSchG)	–	Federal Emission Control Act
Bundeskartellamt	–	Federal Cartel Office
Bundesnotarodnung (BNotO)	–	Federal Rules and Regulations on Notaries
Bundessozialgericht (BSG)	–	Federal Social Insurance Court
Bundessteuerblatt (BStBl)	–	*Federal Department of Revenue Gazette*
Bundesurlaubsgesetz (BUrlG)	–	Federal Holiday Entitlement Act
Bundesverfassungsgericht		
(BVerfG)	–	Federal Constitutional Court
Bundeszentralregistergesetz		
(BZRG)	–	Federal Central Register Act
culpa in contrahendo	–	pre–contractual duties of conduct
Darlehen	–	loan
Darlehensgeber	–	lender
Darlehensnehmer	–	borrower
Depotgeschäft	–	safe–deposit service
Dienstvertrag	–	service agreement
Diskontgeschäft	–	discount business
dispositive Gesetzesrecht	–	optional statutory law
Doppelbesteuerungsabkommen	–	tax treaty
Duldungsvollmacht	–	power of representation by estoppel
Durchgriff	–	piercing the corporate veil
Effektengeschäft	–	securities dealing
eigene Geschäftsanteile	–	own shares
Eigenkapital	–	equity
Einbringung	–	contribution

Einbringungsbilanz	–	contribution balance sheet
einbringungsgeborene Anteile	–	shares issued upon a contribution of capital in kind
Einbringungsgewinn	–	contribution profit
Einforderungsbeschluß	–	resolution to call
Einheitsgesellschaft	–	unitary partnership
Einheitswert	–	assessed value
Einigungsstelle	–	conciliation board
Einkommensteuer	–	(individual) income tax
Einkommensteuergesetz (EStG)	–	Income Tax Act
Einkünfte aus Gewerbebetrieb	–	income from business operations
Einkünfte aus Kapitalvermögen	–	income from capital investments
Einlagengeschäft	–	deposit business
Einlagenrückgewähr	–	return of capital contributions
Einlagepflicht	–	duty of capital contribution
Einleger	–	contributor
Einsichtsrecht	–	right of inspection
Eintragung	–	registration
Einzelprokura	–	sole power of procuration
Einzelrechtsnachfolge	–	singular succession
Einziehung	–	withdrawal
Einziehungsverfahren	–	forfeiture/withdrawal proceedings
Enkelgesellschaften	–	sub–subsidiaries
Entlastung	–	discharge
Entnahme	–	withdrawal
Entziehung	–	disqualification/revocation
Ergebnisabführungsvertrag	–	profit–and–loss transfer agreement
Erbschaft- und Schenkungsteuer	–	inheritance and gift tax
Ergebnisverwendung	–	appropriation of profits
Erlaubnis	–	licence
Eröffnungsbilanz	–	opening balance sheet
Ertragsteuern	–	taxes on income
Ertragswert	–	capitalized income value
Ertragswertklausel	–	capitalized income value clause
erweiterte Kürzung	–	extended deduction
erweitertes Anwachsungsmodell	–	extended accrual model
Erwerb	–	acquisition
Fahrlässigkeit	–	negligent conduct
Fahrnis	–	chattel
faktischer Konzern	–	non–contractual (*de facto*) group of companies
Feststellung des Jahresabschlusses	–	adoption of the annual statements
Feststellungsklage	–	action for a declaratory judgement

Finanzgericht	–	fiscal court
Firma	–	firm name
Formwechsel	–	change in legal form
Fortbestehensprognose	–	continuation forecast
Freibetrag	–	allowance
freie Verfügung	–	disposal at will
Freistellung	–	indemnification/indemnity
Fremdfinanzierung	–	debt financing
Fremdkapital	–	debt
Fremdmittel	–	borrowed funds
Gehalt	–	salary
Genossenschaftsgesetz (GenG)	–	Cooperative Societies Act
Genußrecht	–	right of jouissance
Gerätesicherheitsgesetz (GSG)	–	Equipment Safety Act
gerichtliches Vergleichsverfahren	–	(judicial) composition proceedings
Gerichtsverfassungsgesetz (GVG)	–	Judicature Act
Gesamthandseigentum	–	joint property
Gesamthandsgemeinschaft	–	joint ownership
Gesamthandsvermögen	–	joint assets
Gesamtprokura	–	joint power of procuration
Gesamtrechtsnachfolge	–	universal succession
Gesamtvollstreckungsordnung	–	Uniform Insolvency Act
Gesamtvollstreckungsverfahren	–	uniform insolvency procedure
Geschäftsanteil	–	share
Geschäftsbesorgung	–	agency business
Geschäftsführer	–	managing director
Geschäftsführung	–	management
Geschäftsordnung	–	standing rules and regulations
Geschäftswert	–	goodwill
Gesellschaft	–	company
Gesellschaft bürgerlichen Rechts	–	civil law partnership
Gesellschaft mit beschränkter Haftung (GmbH)	–	limited liability company
Gesellschafter-Geschäftsführer	–	shareholder-director
Gesellschafterbeschluß	–	shareholders' resolution
Gesellschafterdarlehen	–	shareholder loan
Gesellschafterfremdfinanzierung	–	shareholder debt financing
Gesellschafterversammlung	–	shareholders' meeting
Gesellschaftcrwcisung	–	shareholders' instruction
Gesellschaftsvermögen	–	company assets
Gesetz	–	statute
Gesetz gegen den unlauteren Wettbewerb (UWG)	–	Unfair Competition Act

Gesetz gegen Wettbewerbs-beschränkungen (GWB)	–	Restraint of Competition Act
Gesetz über betriebliche Alters-versorgung (BetrAVG)	–	Company Pension Schemes Act
Gesetz über Freiwillige Gerichts-barkeit (FGG)	–	German Ex Parte Jursidiction Act
Gesetz über Gesellschaften mit beschränkter Haftung (GmbHG)	–	Limited Liability Companies Act
Gesetzentwurf	–	bill
Gesetzliche Vertretung	–	legal representation
Gewerbeamt	–	trade supervision office
Gewerbebetrieb	–	business operation
Gewerbeertrag	–	trade income
Gewerbeertragsteuer	–	trade tax on income
Gewerbekapital	–	trade capital
Gewerbekapitalsteuer	–	trade tax on capital
Gewerbeordnung (GewO)	–	Industrial Code
Gewerbesteuer	–	trade tax
Gewerbesteuergesetz (GewStG)	–	Trade Tax Act
Gewerbezentralregister	–	Central Register of Trade and Industrial Offences
Gewinn– und Verlustrechnung	–	profit–and–loss account
Gewinnabführungsvertrag	–	profit transfer agreement
Gewinnrücklagen	–	retained profits
Gewinnverteilung	–	distribution of profits
Gewinnverteilungsbeschluß	–	resolution on the distribution of profits
Gewinnverwendung	–	appropriation of profits
Gewinnverwendungsbeschluß	–	resolution on the appropriation of profits
Gewinnvortrag	–	unappropriated profit carried forward
Girogeschäft	–	credit transfer business
Gläubigerausschuß	–	creditors' committee
Gläubigerbegünstigungen	–	fraudulent preference of a debtor
Gläubigerbeirat	–	creditors' committee
Glaubhaftmachung	–	*prima facie* evidence
GmbH & Co. KG	–	commercial limited partnership whose sole general partner is a GmbH
GmbH–Gesetz	–	Limited Liability Companies Act
Gründer	–	founder
Gründervorteil	–	founder's advantage
Gründung	–	formation
Gründungsaufwand	–	formation expenses

Gründungsprotokoll	–	minutes of the formation meeting
Gründungsschwindel	–	bogus formation of the company
Grundbuch	–	land registry
Grunderwerbsteuer	–	real property transfer tax
Grunderwerbsteuergesetz (GrEStG)	–	Real Property Transfer Tax Act
Grundgesetz (GG)	–	The German Constitution
Grundhandelsgewerbe	–	general commercial business
Grundsteuergesetz (GrStG)	–	Real Property Tax Act
Grundstück	–	real property/real estate
Grundstücksgesellschaft	–	real property company
gutgläubig	–	in good faith
halber durchschnittlicher Steuersatz	–	half-average tax rate
Handelndenhaftung	–	liability of person acting prior to incorporation
Handelsbilanz	–	commercial balance sheet
Handelsgesetzbuch	–	Commercial Code
Handelsgewerbe	–	commercial business
Handlungsbevollmächtigter	–	authorized agent
Handwerksordnung (HandwO)	–	Handicrafts Code
Handwerksrolle	–	Register of Craftsmen
Hauptniederlassung	–	principal place of business
Hebesatz	–	municipal tax factor
herrschendes Unternehmen	–	controlling enterprise
Hinterlegungsordnung (HintO)	–	Court Deposit Regulations
Höchststimmrecht	–	maximum voting right
Inhaberpapiere	–	bearer instruments
Innengesellschaft	–	sub–partnership
Insolvenz	–	insolvency
Instanzgericht	–	court of first or second instance
Interessenausgleich	–	balance of interests
Inventar	–	inventory
Jahresabschluß	–	annual statements
Jahresergebnis	–	annual profit or loss
Jahresgewinn	–	annual profit
Jahresüberschuß	–	annual surplus
juristische Person	–	legal person

Käufer	–	purchaser
Kammergericht (KG)	–	Higher Regional Court of Berlin
Kapitalanlagegesellschaft	–	capital investment company
Kapitalaufbringung	–	raising of capital
Kapitalerhaltung	–	maintenance of share capital
Kapitalerhöhung	–	increase in share capital/capital increase
Kapitalerhöhung aus Gesellschaftsmitteln	–	capital increase out of corporate funds
kapitalersetzend	–	replacing equity
kapitalersetzende Leistung	–	contribution replacing equity
kapitalersetzendes Darlehen	–	loan replacing equity
Kapitalertragsteuer	–	capital yield tax
Kapitalgesellschaft	–	corporation
Kapitalherabsetzung	–	reduction in share capital
Kapitalisierungszinsfuß	–	capitalization interest rate
Kapitalrücklagen	–	capital reserves
Kapitalschnitt	–	capital write down
Kauf	–	purchase
Klage	–	legal action
Körperschaftsteuer	–	corporate income tax
Körperschaftsteuerabzug	–	corporate income tax credit
Körperschaftsteuergesetz (KStG)	–	Corporate Income Tax Act
Kombinationsmodell	–	combination model
Kommanditgesellschaft	–	commercial limited partnership
Kommanditgesellschaft auf Aktien (KGaA)	–	partnership limited by shares
Kommanditist	–	limited partner
Kommanditkapital	–	capital contributed by limited partners
Komplementär	–	personally liable partner
Konkurs	–	bankruptcy
Konkursantragspflicht	–	obligation to file a bankruptcy petition
Konkursforderung	–	debt in bankruptcy
Konkursgericht	–	bankruptcy court
Konkursordnung (KO)	–	Bankruptcy Act
Konkurstabelle	–	bankruptcy table
Konkursverfahren	–	bankruptcy procedure
Konkursverwalter	–	receiver in bankruptcy
Kontrollbefugnisse	–	supervisory powers
Konzern	–	group of companies
Konzernrechnungslegung	–	consolidated group accounting
Konzernrecht	–	law concerning groups of companies
Kostenordnung (KostO)	–	Regulations on Ex Parte Costs

Kredit	–	loan
Kreditbetrug	–	obtaining credit by false pretences
Kreditwesengesetz (KWG)	–	Banking Act
Kündigungsschutzgesetz (KSchG)	–	Unfair Dismissal Act
Kürzung	–	deduction
Kursbildung	–	fixing of prices

Lagebericht	–	situation report
Landesarbeitsamt	–	state labour office
Landesarbeitsgericht (LAG)	–	state labour court
Landgericht (LG)	–	Regional Court
Leichtfertigkeit	–	recklessness
leitender Angestellter	–	executive
Lieferungen	–	supplies
Liquidation	–	voluntary liquidation
Liquidationserlös	–	liquidation proceeds
Löschung	–	cancellation
Lohn	–	wage
Lohnsteuer	–	wage tax

Mantelgesellschaft	–	shelf company
Massekosten- und Masseschulden	–	liabilities incurred after the opening of the procedure
Mehrstimmrechte	–	multiple voting rights
Melderechtsrahmengesetz (MRRG)	–	Residence Registration Framework Act
Mitbestimmung	–	co–determination
Mitbestimmungsgesetz (MitbestG)	–	Co-Determination Act

Nachschüsse	–	additional contributions
Nachweisgesetz	–	Proof of Employment Relationships Act
natürliche Person	–	natural person
Nebenleistungspflichten	–	duties of additional performance
Nichtigkeitsklage	–	proceedings for annulment
Niederlegung	–	resignation
Nießbrauch	–	usufruct
Nießbrauchsberechtigter	–	usufructuary
Notar	–	notary
notarielle Beglaubigung	–	notarial attestation of signature
notarielle Beurkundung	–	notarial recording

Obergesellschaft	–	principal company
Oberlandesgericht (OLG)	–	Higher Regional Court
OECD-Musterabkommen	–	OECD Model Tax Treaty
offene Handelsgesellschaft (OHG)	–	general commercial partnership
Ordnungswidrigkeit	–	regulatory offences
Ordnungswidrigkeitengesetz (OWiG)	–	Regulatory Offences Act
Organgesellschaft	–	company integrated in a group
Organschaft	–	integrated inter-company relationship
Organträger	–	controlling entity
partiarisches Darlehen	–	participating loan
Passiva	–	liabilities
Personengesellschaft	–	partnership
Pfändung	–	levy of execution
Pfandrecht	–	pledge
Pool–Vertrag	–	pooling agreement
Prokura	–	power of procuration
Prokurist	–	procurator
Prozeßvertretung	–	legal representation in court
Publikums-KG	–	publicly held limited partnership
Quellensteuerabzug	–	tax deduction at source
Rangrücktritt	–	subordination
Realteilung	–	split of assets
rechnerische Überschuldung	–	excess of liabilities over assets
Recht	–	law
Rechtsanwalt	–	attorney-at-law
Rechtsberatungsgesetz (RBeratG)	–	Legal Advice Act
Rechtsträger	–	legal entity
Regelbesteuerung	–	standard rate taxation
Regierungspräsidium	–	regional administration presidency
Regreßanspruch	–	right of recourse
Reichsgericht (RG)	–	Supreme Court of the German Reich
Rückgewähranspruch	–	claim for restitution
Rückgriffsforderung	–	claim under a right of recourse
Rücklage	–	reserve
Rückstellung	–	provision

Sacheinlage	–	contribution in kind
Sachgründungsbericht	–	report on formation by contributions in kind
Sachwalter	–	special trustee
Sanierung	–	restructuring
Sanierungsvergleich	–	restructuring compromise
Satzung	–	articles of association
Satzungsdurchbrechung	–	overriding the articles of association
Satzungsverletzung	–	violation of the articles of association
Schachtelprivileg	–	affiliation privilege
Schlußtermin	–	final court hearing
Schlußverteilung	–	date for the final payment
Schlußverzeichnis	–	final creditors' list
Sequester	–	sequestrator
Solidaritätszuschlag	–	solidarity surcharge
Sonderrecht	–	special right
Sonderrechtsnachfolge	–	special succession
Sozialgesetzbuch (SGB)	–	Social Security Code
Sozialplan	–	social plan
Spaltung	–	division
Spaltung zur Aufnahme	–	division by acquisition
Spaltung zur Neugründung	–	division by formation
Spaltungs- und Übernahmevertrag	–	contract of division and acquisition
Spaltungsplan	–	terms of division
Spende	–	donation
Sprecherausschuß	–	representative committee
Spruchstellenverfahren	–	special court proceedings
Spruchverfahren	–	administrative decision procedure
Stammeinlage	–	original capital contribution
Stammkapital	–	share capital
Steuerberater	–	tax advisor
Steuerbilanz	–	tax balance sheet
Steuergefährdung	–	jeopardy to taxation
Steuerhinterziehung	–	fraudulent tax evasion
Steuermeßzahl	–	tax index number
Steuersatz	–	tax rate
Steuerverkürzung	–	reckless unlawful reduction of tax assessment
Stimmbindung	–	voting trust
Stimmbindungsvertrag	–	voting agreement
Stimmkraft	–	voting power
Stimmrecht	–	voting right
Strafgesetzbuch (StGB)	–	Criminal Code
Straftat	–	criminal offence
Substanzwert	–	material value

Tarifvertrag	–	collective bargaining agreement
Tarifvertragsgesetz (TVG)	–	Collective Bargaining Agreement Act
Teilbetrieb	–	partial business unit
Teilung	–	partition
Teilwert	–	fair market value
Thesaurieren von Gewinn	–	retain profits
Treuepflicht	–	duty of loyalty
Treugeber	–	grantor of a trust
Treuhänder	–	trustee
Treuhand	–	trust
Übernahmegewinn	–	acquisition profit
Überschuldung	–	overindebtedness
Überschuldungsstatus	–	pre–insolvency balance sheet
Übertragungsgewinn	–	transfer profit
Umlaufvermögen	–	current assets
Umsatz	–	business generating turnover
Umsatzsteuer	–	value added tax
Umsatzsteuergesetz (UStG)	–	Value Added Tax Act
Umwandlung	–	transformation
Umwandlungsgesetz (UmwG)	–	Business Transformation Act
Umwandlungsmodell	–	transformation model
Umwandlungssteuergesetz (UmwStG)	–	Transformation Tax Act
Unterbeteiligung	–	sub–participation
Unterbilanz	–	deficit balance
Unternehmen	–	enterprise/business
Unternehmensbeteiligungsgesell-schaft	–	risk–capital investment company
Unternehmensverträge	–	inter–company agreements
Untreue	–	criminal breach of trust
Urhebergesetz (UrhG)	–	Copyrights Act
Veräußerungsgewinn	–	capital gain
verdeckte Einlage	–	constructive capital contribution
verdeckte Gewinnausschüttung	–	constructive dividend
verdeckte Sacheinlage	–	undisclosed contribution in kind
verdeckte Vermögensverlagerung	–	undisclosed relocation of assets
vereidigter Buchprüfer	–	sworn auditor
Verfügungsgeschäft	–	executory agreement
Vergleich	–	composition plan
Vergleichsordnung (VglO)	–	Composition Code

Zahlungsunfähigkeit	–	illiquidity
Zeichner	–	subscriber
Zielgesellschaft	–	target company
Zins	–	interest
Zivilprozeßordnung (ZPO)	–	Code of Civil Procedure
Zusammenlegung	–	amalgamation
Zwangsvollstreckung	–	execution
Zweckbestimmung	–	specification of aim
Zweigniederlassung	–	branch
zwingendes Gesetzesrecht	–	mandatory statutory law
Zwischenbilanz	–	interim balance sheet
Zwischenholding	–	intermediate holding company

accounting	–	Buchführung
accounting period	–	Abrechnungszeitraum
accrual	–	Anwachsung
acquisition	–	Erwerb
acquisition profit	–	Übernahmegewinn
action for a declaratory judgement	–	Feststellungsklage
action for rescission	–	Anfechtungsklage
additional contributions	–	Nachschüsse
administrative decision procedure	–	Spruchverfahren
adoption of the annual statements	–	Feststellung des Jahresabschlusses
advisory board	–	Beirat
affiliation privilege	–	Schachtelprivileg
agency	–	Auftrag
agency business	–	Geschäftsbesorgung
Alien Residence Act – EC	–	Aufenthaltsgesetz/EWG (AufG/EWG)
Aliens Act	–	Ausländergesetz (AuslG)
allowable tax depreciation	–	Abschreibung
allowance	–	Freibetrag
amalgamation	–	Zusammenlegung
annual profit	–	Jahresgewinn
annual profit or loss	–	Jahresergebnis
annual statements	–	Jahresabschluß
annual surplus	–	Jahresüberschuß
apostille	–	Apostille
apparent authority	–	Anscheinsvollmacht
appendix	–	Anhang
application for registration	–	Anmeldung
appointment	–	Bestellung
apportioning balance sheet	–	Auseinandersetzungsbilanz

appropriation of profits	–	Ergebnisverwendung/Gewinnverwendung
articles of association	–	Satzung
assessed value	–	Einheitswert
assets	–	Aktiva
assignment	–	Abtretung
attorney-at-law	–	Rechtsanwalt
audit of the annual statements	–	Abschlußprüfung
auditor	–	Abschlußprüfer
authorized agent	–	Handlungsbevollmächtigter
avoidance	–	Anfechtung
balance of interests	–	Interessenausgleich
balance sheet	–	Bilanz
balance sheet date	–	Bilanzstichtag
balance sheet profit	–	Bilanzgewinn
Banking Act	–	Kreditwesengesetz (KWG)
bankruptcy	–	Konkurs
Bankruptcy Act	–	Konkursordnung (KO)
bankruptcy court	–	Konkursgericht
bankruptcy procedure	–	Konkursverfahren
bankruptcy table	–	Konkurstabelle
bearer instruments	–	Inhaberpapiere
bill	–	Gesetzentwurf
blue-collar worker	–	Arbeiter
bogus formation of the company	–	Gründungsschwindel
book value clause	–	Buchwertklausel
borrowed funds	–	Fremdmittel
borrower	–	Darlehensnehmer
branch	–	Zweigniederlassung
business	–	Betrieb/Unternehmen
business generating turnover	–	Umsatz
business operation	–	Gewerbebetrieb
Business Transformation Act	–	Umwandlungsgesetz (UmwG)
cancellation	–	Löschung
cancellation agreement	–	Aufhebungsvertrag
capital contributed by limited partners	–	Kommanditkapital
capital gain	–	Veräußerungsgewinn
capital gains from business closure	–	Betriebsaufgabegewinn
capital increase	–	Kapitalerhöhung

capital increase out of corporate funds	–	Kapitalerhöhung aus Gesellschaftsmitteln
capital investment company	–	Kapitalanlagegesellschaft
capital reserves	–	Kapitalrücklagen
capital write down	–	Kapitalschnitt
capital yield tax	–	Kapitalertragsteuer
capitalization interest rate	–	Kapitalisierungszinsfuß
capitalized income value clause	–	Ertragswertklausel
capitalized income value	–	Ertragswert
carrying values	–	Wertansätze
Central Register of Trade and Industrial Offences	–	Gewerbezentralregister
change in legal form	–	Formwechsel
chartered accountant	–	Wirtschaftsprüfer
chattel	–	Fahrnis
Civil Code	–	Bürgerliches Gesetzbuch (BGB)
civil law partnership	–	BGB-Gesellschaft
civil law partnership	–	Gesellschaft bürgerlichen Rechts
claim for restitution	–	Rückgewähranspruch
claim under a right of recourse	–	Rückgriffsforderung
class of shares	–	Aktiengattung
Code of Civil Procedure	–	Zivilprozeßordnung (ZPO)
Code of Taxation Procedure	–	Abgabenordnung (AO)
Co-Determination Act	–	Mitbestimmungsgesetz (MitbestG)
co-determination	–	Mitbestimmung
collective bargaining agreement	–	Tarifvertrag
Collective Bargaining Agreement Act	–	Tarifvertragsgesetz (TVG)
combination model	–	Kombinationsmodell
commercial balance sheet	–	Handelsbilanz
commercial business	–	Handelsgewerbe
Commercial Code	–	Handelsgesetzbuch
commercial limited partnership	–	Kommanditgesellschaft (KG)
commercial limited partnership whose sole general partner is a GmbH	–	GmbH & Co. KG
company	–	Gesellschaft
company assets	–	Gesellschaftsvermögen
company integrated in a group	–	Organgesellschaft
Company Pension Schemes Act	–	Gesetz über betriebliche Altersversorgung (BetrAVG)
Composition Code	–	Vergleichsordnung (VglO)
composition dividend	–	Vergleichsquote
composition plan	–	Vergleich
composition proceedings	–	gerichtliches Vergleichsverfahren

conciliation board	–	Einigungsstelle
consolidated group accounting	–	Konzernrechnungslegung
constructive capital contribution	–	verdeckte Einlage
constructive dividend	–	verdeckte Gewinnausschüttung
contingent intent	–	bedingter Vorsatz
continuation forecast	–	Fortbestehensprognose
contract of division and acquisition	–	Spaltungs- und Übernahmevertrag
contract of merger	–	Verschmelzungsvertrag
contribution	–	Einbringung
contribution balance sheet	–	Einbringungsbilanz
contribution in cash	–	Bareinlage
contribution in kind	–	Sacheinlage
contribution profit	–	Einbringungsgewinn
contribution replacing equity	–	kapitalersetzende Leistung
contributor	–	Einleger
control agreement	–	Beherrschungsvertrag
controlling enterprise	–	herrschendes Unternehmen
controlling entity	–	Organträger
Cooperative Societies Act	–	Genossenschaftsgesetz (GenG)
co-ownership	–	Bruchteilsgemeinschaft
Copyrights Act	–	Urhebergesetz (UrhG)
Corporate Income Tax Act	–	Körperschaftsteuergesetz (KStG)
corporate income tax credit	–	Körperschaftsteuerabzug
corporate income tax	–	Körperschaftsteuer
corporation	–	Kapitalgesellschaft
Court Deposit Regulations	–	Hinterlegungsordnung (HintO)
court of first or second instance	–	Instanzgericht
credit balance in case of partition	–	Auseinandersetzungsguthaben
credit transfer business	–	Girogeschäft
credit-method	–	Anrechnungsmethode
creditor who has retained title	–	aussonderungsberechtiger Gläubiger
Creditors' Avoidance of Transfer Act	–	Anfechtungsgesetz (AnfG)
creditors' committee	–	Gläubigerausschuß
creditors' committee	–	Gläubigerbeirat
criminal breach of trust	–	Untreue
Criminal Code	–	Strafgesetzbuch (StGB)
criminal offence	–	Straftat
current assets	–	Umlaufvermögen
Data Protection Act	–	Bundesdatenschutzgesetz
date for the final payment	–	Schlußverteilung
debt	–	Fremdkapital
debt financing	–	Fremdfinanzierung
debt in bankruptcy	–	Konkursforderung

deduction	–	Kürzung
deficit balance	–	Unterbilanz
deposit business	–	Einlagengeschäft
discharge	–	Entlastung
discount business	–	Diskontgeschäft
disposable equity	–	verwendbares Eigenkapital
disposal at will	–	freie Verfügung
disqualification	–	Entziehung
dissolution	–	Auflösung
distribution of profits	–	Gewinnverteilung
district court	–	Amtsgericht (AG)
division	–	Spaltung
division by acquisition	–	Spaltung zur Aufnahme
division by formation	–	Spaltung zur Neugründung
donation	–	Spende
drop-down	–	Ausgliederung
duties of additional performance	–	Nebenleistungspflichten
duty of capital contribution	–	Einlagepflicht
duty of confidentiality	–	Verschwiegenheitspflicht
duty of loyalty	–	Treuepflicht
duty to tender	–	Andienungspflicht

economics committee	–	Wirtschaftsausschuß
Employees' Representation Act	–	Betriebsverfassungsgesetz (BetrVG)
Employment Promotion Act	–	Arbeitsförderungsgesetz (AFG)
enterprise	–	Unternehmen
Equipment Safety Act	–	Gerätesicherheitsgesetz (GSG)
equity	–	Eigenkapital
excess of liabilities over assets	–	rechnerische Überschuldung
execution	–	Zwangsvollstreckung
executive	–	leitender Angestellter
executory agreement	–	Verfügungsgeschäft
expulsion	–	Ausschließung
extended accrual model	–	erweitertes Anwachsungsmodell
extended deduction	–	erweiterte Kürzung
extraordinary depreciation to the fair market value by reason of distribution	–	ausschüttungsbedingte Teilwertabschreiung

fair market value	–	Teilwert
Federal Banking Supervisory Office	–	Bundesaufsichtsamt für das Kreditwesen
Federal Cartel Office	–	Bundeskartellamt

group of companies formed on a contractual basis	–	Vertragskonzern
guarantee	–	Bürgschaft
half-average tax rate	–	halber durchschnittlicher Steuersatz
Handicrafts Code	–	Handwerksordnung (HandwO)
Higher Regional Court	–	Oberlandesgericht (OLG)
Higher Regional Court of Berlin	–	Kammergericht (KG)
illiquidity	–	Zahlungsunfähigkeit
in bad faith	–	bösgläubig
in good faith	–	gutgläubig
income from business operations	–	Einkünfte aus Gewerbebetrieb
income from capital investments	–	Einkünfte aus Kapitalvermögen
Income Tax Act	–	Einkommensteuergesetz (EStG)
increase in share capital	–	Kapitalerhöhung
indemnification	–	Freistellung
indemnity	–	Freistellung
(individual) income tax	–	Einkommensteuer
Industrial Code	–	Gewerbeordnung (GewO)
inheritance and gift tax	–	Erbschaft- und Schenkungsteuer
input tax	–	Vorsteuer
insolvency	–	Insolvenz
Insurance Supervision Act	–	Versicherungsaufsichtsgesetz (VAG)
integrated inter-company relationship	–	Organschaft
intentional conduct	–	Vorsatz
inter-company agreements	–	Unternehmensverträge
interest	–	Zins
interest-bearing loan	–	verzinsliches Darlehen
interim balance sheet	–	Zwischenbilanz
intermediate holding company	–	Zwischenholding
inventory	–	Inventar
jeopardy to taxation	–	Steuergefährdung
joint assets	–	Gesamthandsvermögen
joint ownership	–	Gesamthandsgemeinschaft
joint power of procuration	–	Gesamtprokura
joint property	–	Gesamthandseigentum
Judicature Act	–	Gerichtsverfassungsgesetz (GVG)
(judicial) composition proceedings	–	gerichtliches Vergleichsverfahren

labour court	–	Arbeitsgericht
labour law	–	Arbeitsrecht
labour office	–	Arbeitsamt
land registry	–	Grundbuch
law	–	Recht
law concerning groups of companies	–	Konzernrecht
legal action	–	Klage
Legal Advice Act	–	Rechtsberatungsgesetz (RBeratG)
legal entity	–	Rechtsträger
legal person	–	juristische Person
legal representation	–	Gesetzliche Vertretung
legal representation in court	–	Prozeßvertretung
lender	–	Darlehensgeber
levy of execution	–	Pfändung
liabilities	–	Passiva
liabilities incurred after the opening of the procedure	–	Massekosten- und Masseschulden
liability of person acting prior to incorporation	–	Handelndenhaftung
licence	–	Erlaubnis
Limited Liability Companies Act	–	Gesetz über Gesellschaften mit beschränkter Haftung (GmbHG)/GmbH-Gesetz
limited liability company	–	Gesellschaft mit beschränkter Haftung (GmbH)
limited partner	–	Kommanditist
limited tax liability	–	beschränkte Steuerpflicht
liquidating company	–	Abwicklungsgesellschaft
liquidation	–	Abwicklung
liquidation proceeds	–	Liquidationserlös
loan	–	Darlehen/Kredit
loan replacing equity	–	kapitalersetzendes Darlehen
loss carryback	–	Verlustrücktrag
loss carryforward	–	Verlustvortrag
loss compensation	–	Verlustausgleich
maintenance of share capital	–	Kapitalerhaltung
management	–	Geschäftsführung
managing director	–	Geschäftsführer
mandatory statutory law	–	zwingendes Gesetzesrecht
material value	–	Substanzwert
maximum voting right	–	Höchststimmrecht
merger	–	Verschmelzung
merger audit	–	Verschmelzungsprüfung

merger report	–	Verschmelzungsbericht
minutes of the formation meeting	–	Gründungsprotokoll
movable property	–	bewegliche Sache
multiple voting rights	–	Mehrstimmrechte
municipal tax factor	–	Hebesatz
mutual insurance association	–	Versicherungsverein auf Gegenseitigkeit
mutual settlement	–	Verrechnung

natural person	–	natürliche Person
negligent conduct	–	Fahrlässigkeit
Net Worth Tax Act	–	Vermögensteuergesetz (VStG)
non-contractual (*de facto*) group of companies	–	faktischer Konzern
notarial attestation of signature	–	notarielle Beglaubigung
notarial recording	–	notarielle Beurkundung
notary	–	Notar

obligation to file a bankruptcy petition	–	Konkursantragspflicht
obligation to instruct	–	Belehrungspflicht
obligationary agreement	–	Verpflichtungsgeschäft
obtaining credit by false pretences	–	Kreditbetrug
OECD Model Tax Treaty	–	OECD-Musterabkommen
Official Recordings Act	–	Beurkundungsgesetz (BeurkG)
opening balance	–	Bilanz
opening balance sheet	–	Eröffnungsbilanz
operating expenditure	–	Betriebsausgaben
optional statutory law	–	dispositive Gesetzesrecht
original capital contribution	–	Stammeinlage
overindebtedness	–	Überschuldung
overriding the articles of association	–	Satzungsdurchbrechung
own shares	–	eigene Geschäftsanteile
owner of share or interest	–	Anteilseigner

partial business unit	–	Teilbetrieb
participating loan	–	partiarisches Darlehen
partition	–	Teilung
partnership	–	Personengesellschaft
partnership limited by shares	–	Kommanditgesellschaft auf Aktien (KGaA)

Regional Court	–	Landgericht (LG)
Register of Craftsmen	–	Handwerksrolle
registration	–	Eintragung
Regulations on Ex Parte Costs	–	Kostenordnung (KostO)
regulatory offences	–	Ordnungswidrigkeit
Regulatory Offences Act	–	Ordnungswidrigkeitengesetz (OWiG)
removal from office	–	Abberufung
replacing equity	–	kapitalersetzend
report on formation by contributions in kind	–	Sachgründungsbericht
representation	–	Vertretung
representative committee	–	Sprecherausschuß
rescission	–	Anfechtung
rescue company	–	Auffanggesellschaft
reserve	–	Rücklage
Residence Registration Framework Act	–	Melderechtsrahmengesetz (MRRG)
resignation	–	Austritt/Niederlegung
resolution on the appropriation of profits	–	Gewinnverwendungsbeschluß
resolution on the distribution of profits	–	Gewinnverteilungsbeschluß
resolution to call	–	Einforderungsbeschluß
restraint of competition	–	Wettbewerbsverbot
Restraint of Competition Act	–	Gesetz gegen Wettbewerbsbeschränkungen (GWB)
restriction of transferability	–	Vinkulierung
restructuring	–	Sanierung
restructuring compromise	–	Sanierungsvergleich
retain profits	–	Thesaurieren von Gewinn
retained profits	–	Gewinnrücklagen
retirement	–	Ausscheiden
return of capital contributions	–	Einlagenrückgewähr
revocation	–	Entziehung
right of inspection	–	Einsichtsrecht
right of jouissance	–	Genußrecht
right of pre-emption	–	Vorkaufsrecht
right of recourse	–	Regreßanspruch
right to information	–	Auskunftsrecht
risk-capital investment company	–	Unternehmensbeteiligungsgesellschaft
safe-deposit service	–	Depotgeschäft
salary	–	Gehalt
sale	–	Verkauf

statute	–	Gesetz
step-up	–	Aufstockung
stock corporation	–	Aktiengesellschaft (AG)
Stock Corporation Act	–	Aktiengesetz (AktG)
stock corporation law	–	Aktienrecht
stock exchange price	–	Börsenkurs
subordinate status report	–	Abhängigkeitsbericht
subordination	–	Rangrücktritt
sub-participation	–	Unterbeteiligung
sub-partnership	–	Innengesellschaft
subscriber	–	Zeichner
subscription right	–	Bezugsrecht
substantial participation	–	wesentliche Beteiligung
sub-subsidiaries	–	Enkelgesellschaften
supervisory board	–	Aufsichtsrat
supervisory powers	–	Kontrollbefugnisse
supplies	–	Lieferungen
Supreme Court of the German Reich	–	Reichsgericht (RG)
sworn auditor	–	vereidigter Buchprüfer

target company	–	Zielgesellschaft
tax advisor	–	Steuerberater
tax balance sheet	–	Steuerbilanz
tax credit procedure	–	Anrechnungsverfahren
tax deduction at source	–	Quellensteuerabzug
tax index number	–	Steuermeßzahl
tax rate	–	Steuersatz
tax rate on dividends	–	Ausschüttungsbelastung
tax treaty	–	Doppelbesteuerungsabkommen
Tax Valuation Act	–	Bewertungsgesetz (BewG)
taxes on income	–	Ertragsteuern
terms of division	–	Spaltungsplan
The German Constitution	–	Grundgesetz (GG)
trade capital	–	Gewerbekapital
trade income	–	Gewerbeertrag
trade supervision office	–	Gewerbeamt
trade tax	–	Gewerbesteuer
Trade Tax Act	–	Gewerbesteuergesetz (GewStG)
trade tax on capital	–	Gewerbekapitalsteuer
trade tax on income	–	Gewerbeertragsteuer
transfer of assets and liabilities	–	Vermögensübertragung
transfer profit	–	Übertragungsgewinn
transformation	–	Umwandlung

INDEX